The Collected Essays of Asa Briggs

Volume II: Images, Problems, Standpoints, Forecasts

The Collected Essays of Asa Briggs
Volume I: Words, Numbers, Places, People

The Collected Essays of Asa Briggs

Volume II:
Images, Problems, Standpoints, Forecasts

Asa Briggs

Provost, Worcester College, Oxford

THE UNIVERSITY OF ILLINOIS PRESS
URBANA AND CHICAGO

First published in the United States of America by
University of Illinois Press, Urbana and Chicago

Manufactured in Great Britain

Library of Congress Cataloging in Publication Data

Briggs, Asa, 1921-
   The collected essays of Asa Briggs.

   Includes indexes.
   Contents: v. 1. Words, numbers, places, people – v. 2.
Images, problems, standpoints, forecasts.
   1. England – Social conditions – 19th century – Addresses,
essays, lectures.   2. Social history – 19th century – Addresses,
essays, lectures.   3. Great Britain – History – 19th
century – Addresses, essays, lectures. I. Title.
HN385.B7577   1985   306'.0942   84-24484
ISBN 0-252-01217-8 (v. 2)
ISBN 0-252-01228-3 (set)
ISBN 0-7108-0510-1 (UK edition, Harvester)

The attitudes of individuals and groups of individuals to their own situation in society and the conduct these attitudes dictate are determined not so much by actual economic conditions as by the image in the minds of the individual groups.

Georges Duby, <i>Les Sociétés médiévales:
une approche d'ensemble</i> (1971)

But stay – the present and the future – <i>they</i> are another's; but the past – that at least is ours.

W. S. Gilbert, <i>The Gondoliers</i> (1889)

Contents

List of Illustrations   ix

The Originals   xi

Preface   xiii

I POETS AND NOVELISTS

1   Writers and Cities in the Nineteenth Century   3

2   Ebenezer Elliott, The Corn Law Rhymer   36

3   *Middlemarch* and the Doctors   49

4   Private and Social Themes in *Shirley*   68

5   Trollope the Traveller   89

6   The Appeal of William Morris   116

II PROBLEMS AND POLICIES

7   Public Opinion and Public Health in the
      Age of Chadwick   129

8   Cholera and Society in the Nineteenth Century   153

9   The Welfare State in Historical Perspective   177

III LOOKING BACKWARDS

10 Saxons, Normans and Victorians   215

11 G. M. Trevelyan: The Uses of Social History   236

12 G. M. Young: The Age of a Portrait   253

13 Gilberto Freyre and the Study of Social
      History   272

IV LOOKING FORWARDS

14 Towards 1900: The Nineteenth Century
      Faces the Future   291

15 The Historian and the Future   310

Index   318

List of Illustrations

Plate 1: Choleraphoby

Plate 2: Elliott's monument,
Weston Park, Sheffield

Plate 3: Harold, returned from
Normandy: Daniel Maclise
depicts an episode in his
*Story of the Norman
Conquest*

Plate 4: The first *Annales:*
the prospect for 1965 (1919)

The Originals

A version of 'Writers and Cities in the Nineteenth Century' first appeared in D. Daiches and A. Thorlby (eds), *Literature and Western Civilisation, The Modern World*, vol. II, *Realities* (1972). I have added some material from the number of the *History of the Twentieth Century* (ed. A.J.P. Taylor and J.M. Roberts) which I guest-edited (1970). It was called 'The City, Heaven or Hell?'.

'Ebenezer Elliott, The Corn-Law Rhymer' first appeared in different form in the *Cambridge Journal*, vol. IV (1950) and 'Middlemarch and the Doctors', also in different form, in the same journal in vol. I (1948).

'Private and Social Themes in *Shirley*' was in its first unpublished form a lecture delivered to the Brontë Society at Haworth on 17 May 1958. It subsequently appeared in the *Transactions of the Brontë Society*.

'Trollope the Traveller' first appeared in J. Halperin (ed.), *Trollope Centenary Essays* (1982). It has subsequently been revised.

'The Appeal of William Morris' first appeared in shorter form in *William Morris and Kelmscott* (The Design Council, 1981).

'Public Opinion in the Age of Chadwick' was first delivered as a lecture in the New Art Gallery at Leicester in the 37th Annual Lecture Series of the Chadwick Trust on 4 October 1949. It was subsequently published as a pamphlet by the Chadwick Trust. It has been substantially revised, but the shape has not been changed, nor have the main lines of the argument.

'Cholera and Society in the Nineteenth Century' first appeared in *Past and Present*, no. 19 (1961).

'The Welfare State in Historical Perspective' first appeared in the *European Journal of Sociology*, vol. II (1961).

'Saxons, Normans and Victorians' was first delivered as a lecture to the Hastings and Bexhill Branch of the Historical Association and was published by them as a pamphlet in 1966.

'G.M. Trevelyan, the Whig Inheritance' and 'G.M. Young: the Age of a Portrait' are new essays.

'Gilberto Freyre and the Study of Social History' was a paper delivered at Professor Freyre's eightieth-birthday conference in Brasília in October 1980.

'Towards 1900: the Nineteenth Century faces the Future' is based on the last chapter of the Thames & Hudson volume which I edited, *The Nineteenth Century: The Contradictions of Progress* (1970).

'The Historian and the Future' first appeared in *Futures*, December 1978.

Preface

The essays and papers assembled in this volume, most of them substantially revised, were written, like those in the first volume, at various times, sometimes long ago, and were published in various places. Nonetheless, in retrospect at least they have a unity. They are all concerned with social and cultural change and, equally important, with how it was perceived, particularly after the advent of steam-driven industry. The essays and papers in this volume follow the same approach as the essays in the first. The two volumes might well have been printed as one.

Because they were written at various times, the first of them in the late 1940s, they will be of interest, I hope, not only because of their content but because they chart some of the most important changes which have re-shaped the study of social history between the late 1940s and the early 1980s. The only ones which I have not revised, like the essay on the welfare state, are included in their original form because they conveniently capsulate historical scholarship as it stood at a particular moment in time, and they may be valuable precisely for that reason. I am still planning to write a volume in the Longman Social and Economic History series, which I edit, on *The Welfare State*. It will be a different book from that which I would have written in 1961 not just because subsequent research has qualified what would then have been my conclusions but because social attitudes and policies have changed drastically. The recovery of lost attitudes is already important. I have also retained in this volume the shape and style of a number of lectures on less controversial subjects when there was a particularly strong sense of occasion which also should not be lost.

The extent of the transformation in the study of social history in recent years is well known to professional historians but is still not generally appreciated. From being at best one (among many) relatively neglected and often trivialised sub-branches of history, usually bracketed (at its most serious) with economic history, social history has moved more closely towards becoming an integrated history of particular societies and of 'society'; and other 'sub-histories' within social history have boomed, notably urban history and labour history. I have been deeply committed to both. They were seldom studied in depth during the late 1940s and early 1950s. Nor were they institution-alised. I was privileged to take them up at that point. Doubtless my interest in these subjects can be explained in terms of my background and temperament. I was brought up in the North of England in a district where moorland and industry met. The Brontës were not strangers, they were almost neighbours. And I always learnt as much from landscape and townscape as from books. After the sub-histories became institutionalised – and I played an active part at their institu-tional inception – I did not want to become imprisoned in the new institutional frames which I had helped to construct. I still wanted to be a historian *tout court*.

Having once produced a *History of Birmingham* and the bundle of articles which preceded it or accompanied it and which are assembled in the first of these volumes of essays, I have never lost an interest in the city or its historiography and I have reviewed most of the new books about Birmingham when they have appeared. Yet I soon felt that it was not enough to look at Birmingham and other particular cities in order to understand the nineteenth-century environment. It was necessary, too, to consider problems which affected *all* cities – notably public heath – and through such consideration to assess what was the part of public opinion – and expert opinion – in forcing through change. The change, moreover, was often change in the mind, particularly a major change in the attitudes towards 'fate' and 'social control' (the latter a term which has more recently been used or misused in far too many contexts). There were common features in the response everywhere, although the timing was different.

Public health began to interest me during the 1940s – before the social history of medicine became fashionable – and the Chadwick Lecture reprinted here, one of the first public lectures I was invited to deliver, has been 'enriched' by material I collected a little later for two articles I wrote for *The Times* in 1948 for the Centenary of the Public Health Act. It also includes material which I did not then have space to include but which does not change my approach or conclusions. I have kept the form of my lecture, however, and I have not drawn on any subsequent work by other historians, beginning with Professor S. E. Finer's readable and scholarly *Life of Chadwick*, much of it highly relevant. The reason is that I would like to move completely afresh into this field in the future. It was because of my continuing interest in it that I greatly appreciated being asked to serve for a year in 1976 as President of the Society for the Social History of Medicine, the *Bulletin* of which has become essential reading for me.

Through public health I became more interested in people's reactions to their environment – and their often contrasting percep-tions of it – than in physical data concerning it. And with this shift in

my own interests I passed increasingly willingly, even eagerly, from
social history as economic history with the politics put in to social and
cultural history with the technology put in; and rather than generalis-
ing more – on the basis of limited and often over-exploited evidence – I
began to pay particular and close attention to the relationship between
the distinctive views of individual writers and artists and the kind of
culture which they shared. I have drawn heavily in my writing not only
on newspapers and even more 'ephemeral' sources, but on 'literature',
noting both the opportunities and difficulties of doing so. I have
always believed that the historian should be concerned both with the
'social sciences' (not least demography) and with literature, sensing
that the gulf between writing in the 'social sciences' and 'literature' is
as wide as the 'two-cultures' gulf between 'sciences' and 'the arts'.
Several essays in this volume seek, therefore, like my essay on
'*Middlemarch* and the Doctors', to cross what are often thought of as
disciplinary divides.

The essays in this volume which deal with writers should be related
to my first book on the mid-Victorian years, *Victorian People* (1954),
which set out to trace patterns of value through the experience of
individual people. In these essays I was trying to explore a 'whole
culture', while recognising, first, that there was no one single shared
perception of what life was like after the advent of steam-driven
machinery – inevitably, therefore, there were many sub-cultures – and,
second, that ambitious attempts were made in the nineteenth century
and have been made since both to discover one and to impose one. The
reason why the attempts failed was not so much intellectual – a matter
of 'science' – but social – a matter of 'experience'. There were such
sharply contrasting varieties of experience after the advent of the
steam engine – not least within the same factory or the same city – that
neither statistical nor verbal modes of explanation received general
assent. Even pictorial modes failed to do so also.

Of course, there had been sharply contrasting varieties of experience
in pre-industrial societies, but with the rise of industry new forces were
brought into action and old factors given new weighting – individual
and group aspirations, in particular, views of what life might be. These
led both to voluntary initiatives and, through often intricate processes, to the formation of new public policies, local or national.
Shapes of the future flit through the changing past, as my essay on the
'Welfare State' shows.

Shared or contrasting perceptions reflected, of course, shared or
contrasting values, some traditional, although these were often under
threat, some new values in the crucible. Neither the articulated version
of 'individualism' nor that of 'solidarity' in the middle years of the
nineteenth century can be explained without searching back through

the centuries before the rise of steam-driven industry. Nor can the late-nineteenth century 'revolt' be considered simply as a revolt against mid-Victorian values (and institutions); it was a revolt also against far older values (and institutions). An era was under assault, not a generation.

It is impossible to move through the nineteenth century, however, without recognising that this was a period when new 'scientific theories' were advanced (by the end of the century they had often been clustered into 'disciplines' with 'professional' practitioners) and new 'ideologies' generated (including among many *isms* one unique *ism* associated with the name of a monarch, 'Victorianism'). The relationship between 'theories' and 'ideologies' is complex. In particular, there were separated if related versions of 'political economy' which some, at least, of their expositors and adherents considered to be the key to the 'science of society'.

I have never believed that it was or is, or at least that it was or is the only key; and for this reason several essays in this second volume are concerned with the approaches not of contemporaries but of historians. G. M. Young is one historian with whom I have felt a close affinity, although not a political one. I have written introductions, too, to Trevelyan's *History of England* and his *Social History*, and while I know his work well and appreciate it, my own *Social History* (1983) is a different kind of book from his. I used to listen to Trevelyan's lectures as an undergraduate in Cambridge, and I must have been among the first readers – and reviewers – of his *Social History*. Freyre is the kind of historian from outside – in this case from distant Brazil – who writes the kind of cultural history I find most attractive. I was proud to be present at his eightieth-birthday celebrations. It is not a coincidence that all these writers are as much interested in literature as in history.

It is a mistake, in my view – if a favourite one, even among academics – to treat history as 'background' and 'literature' as text. Both history and literature deal with human experience, common or individual, although some 'literature', of course, is 'escapist' and there is an element of fantasy even, perhaps not least, in the work of novelists like Trollope who endear themselves to historians. The word 'common' can relate either to the experience of a whole society or culture, or to social groupings and their 'sub-cultures' within it. Given the many divisions in nineteenth-century English society and culture, divisions determined by 'place' (a concept specifically considered in one of my essays) as well as by class, we have to identify rather than take for granted what was 'common' and to explain in each case how that which was inherited was eroded and how that which was new was secured.

Within this context, there is a need to explore the 'mental maps of

the social scene', a term used, long before it became fashionable, by
F. M. Martin in 1954 in Professor David Glass's important collection
of papers *Social Mobility in Britain*. The statistical mode of perception
was only one – and not the most common. It was through the study of
cities rather than through the study of class that I became as interested
both in 'cityscapes' and people's very varied perceptions of them.
While I was influenced by Patrick Geddes's plea in his remarkable
Columbo Plan of 1921 for the supplementation of 'verbal pre-
sentments by the fullest possible use of accompanying plans and
diagrams', I began to realise that this was not enough. I was ready,
therefore, for Kevin Lynch's *The Image of the City* (1960), for the later
studies in this country of Peter Smith, and for the 'new geography'.

We turn both to 'literature' and to 'art' for common experience,
uncommonly depicted – the images carry meanings which might
otherwise be lost through time – and for distinctive, often highly
distinctive, individual experience communicated through the 'arts' to
numbers of others who did not share it. In the latter case, indeed, we
can tap the diversity of a society and a culture. There is some
'literature' and 'art', of course, which transcends such framework and
bears new 'meanings' in all new times, being both reinterpreted and
reassessed in the process. There is nineteenth-century 'escapist'
literature, too, which illuminates many aspects of the century – not
least 'nonsense' literature, often accompanied by sketches which are as
revealing as the texts. We often seem to be untapping the unconscious
here.

A curious element of fantasy can creep into a volume of twentieth-
century historical essays even like mine when essays written at
different times, in different places and for different readers are put
together. Odd links appear. Mrs Thomas Attwood, for example, was
a surprising ancestor of E. A. Freeman, the historian described at some
length in 'Saxon's, Normans and Victorians'. Cholera did *not* strike in
Lyons, although the Prefect feared that it would. Ebenezer Elliott
extolled the virtues not of poetry but of prose. 'Verse is a trick which
the age has seen through – and despises', Beveridge, a key figure in the
history of the welfare state, was wont to quote from *Middlemarch*.
And George Eliot, the subject of another essay, herself supplied me
with a motto which I might have used as a motto for the whole of my
collection:

> To live over other people's lives is nothing unless we live over their
> perceptions, live over the growth, the varying intensity of the same – since
> it is by these they themselves lived.

Instead, I chose my motto for both volumes from a professional historian, but a historian concerned primarily with the middle ages and not a historian of the nineteenth century. He and Marc Bloch mean much to me, for they pull me back before my 'own period'.

I have owed much in my endeavours to pupils and much to the University of Sussex, where I could encourage others as well as myself to cross the boundaries between disciplines. I had colleagues there with whom I could discuss all the issues raised in these papers while at the same time combining my delights as a historian with the labours of a Vice-Chancellor. And I also look back in time further still to the *Cambridge Journal*, where some of my first pieces appeared under the tender editorial care of Michael Oakeshott. After that, my six years at the University of Leeds were not an interlude. I wrote much then, and it was good to be back in a Victorian city while it still was a Victorian city. It is not only the pursuit of history which has changed during the last thirty years. Most recently, a small group of colleagues in Oxford, meeting informally in each others' homes, has kept alive not only my personal pursuit of history, but theirs.

Asa Briggs

I
POETS AND NOVELISTS

The poetry of the poor was the product of the positivist spirit in England: it borrowed its methods from political economy and presented the material and moral statistics of the lower classes.

Louis Étienne, *Revue des deux mondes*
(1856)

George Eliot ... like the poet, takes a more commanding standpoint. Her eyes are occupied with the high and deep places of the human spirit, and the larger and profounder questions of human destiny.

W. H. Mallock on George Eliot

If we write novels so, how shall we write History?

Henry James on George Eliot's *Middlemarch*

1 Writers and Cities in the Nineteenth Century

Already before the middle years of the nineteenth century a British writer had described the period in which he was living as 'the age of great cities' and Benjamin Disraeli had advised his fellow countrymen to visit Manchester, 'the most wonderful city of modern times', if they wished to understand the world was moving.[1] Fifty years later, across the Atlantic, huge new cities, such as Chicago and Pittsburgh, had sprung into existence, gripping the imagination – and sometimes provoking the alarm – of natives, immigrants and visitors alike. Their boosters called them 'prodigies'; their critics 'cancers on the body politic'. In every country, at every level of response, there was pro-urban and anti-urban criticism. Yet, whatever the value-judgements, in 1899 a commentator of a new generation and outlook was echoing the unanimous view that 'the tendency towards concentration or agglomeration is all but universal in the Western world'.[2]

'Concentration' or 'agglomeration' could be associated with either old or new settlement. While old capital cities, like London and Paris, grew in size – as did old cities, like Milan or Frankfurt – in many parts of Europe, as in the United States, there were much-discussed centres of new 'populous districts' on the map: it was the newer places which represented change as much as growth, places which had been far smaller in 1750, if they were there at all, than they were a hundred years later. Manchester itself was an example, like Gelsenkirchen or Lille. In England in 1800, there was no town, with the exception of London, with a population of more than 100,000: in 1891 there were twenty-three. By contrast, both Germany and Italy had large numbers of old cities with a long history – Nuremberg, Rothenburg, Cologne, Lübeck, for example, or Venice, Padua, Florence and Naples. Yet in Germany there were still only eight cities with more than 100,000 inhabitants in 1871, and the sharp rise came only between 1871 and 1910, when there were forty-eight. The most remarkable expansion was in the United States, where in 1800 there were only six towns with a population of 8000 or more; in 1880 there were 286. And by then there were cities with more than 100,000.

The 'urban fact' was related to the expansion of industrial, market economies, and was often – and in face of strong opposition – identified with the march of progress. Yet it was not just the industrial city which fascinated – or horrified – writers. London or Paris inspired or provoked as much as Manchester or Lille. The movement of the huge metropolitan city – the newness and noise of many of its streets, the brightness of its lights, the 'flow' of its traffic and of its crowds (what Carlyle called a 'living flood'), the quickened sense of time – all broke the continuities of urban history. Cities could have cults in the late nineteenth century, so that while Oscar Wilde could claim that 'a modern city is the exact opposite of what everyone wants', another of the 'decadents' could write of London:

> London, London, our delight,
> Great flower that opens but at night.

The enormous mass of nineteenth-century writing about both particular cities and *the* city has been read and re-read during recent years in the light of changing twentieth-century urban experience, and the volume of new writing, including writing about the relationship between cities and countrysides, sometimes seems to out-bulk contemporary writing.[3] The city remains as much a problem centre of modern civilisation as it was during the nineteenth century, although in the meantime the pressures of industrialisation and economic development have taken new forms and brought in new countries. The scale and speed of urban growth in Brazil or Hong Kong, to quote two conspicuous examples, has greatly outstripped nineteenth-century experience.

Taking nineteenth-century writing on its own terms, it is perhaps distinguished at its best by a strong sense of the particularity of place, a sense that survived not only the building of factories but also the building of railway stations and hotels. This sense, now for various reasons in danger of being lost, emerges – often with direct force, sometimes obliquely – not only in diaries, travel notes, and lectures, but also in the pages of newspapers, rightly thought by the first 'urban sociologists' on both sides of the Atlantic to catch the essence of city patterns of life and thought.[4] The newspapers dealt with both the commonplaces and with the dramas of daily life in particular places, emphasising the sense of local community. At the same time, the anonymity (and so-called rootlessness) of the very big cities, what the Germans called *Grossstädte*, shocked traditionalists who claimed that they were destroying human ties and human concerns and were responsible for loneliness and alienation.

To think of *the* city (or to have it in mind when talking about a particular city) demanded an extension either of immediately topical or of profoundly philosophical preoccupations. It also demanded a framework of reference. Old symbols related nineteenth-century cities to the cities of the past or to the ideal city. Manchester, for example, had to be related across the centuries, as Disraeli related it, to Athens; Birmingham, priding itself on its 'civic gospel', to Florence; Paris, with greater imagination than historical accuracy, to Babylon; the new cities of the century to the New Jerusalem. The new symbols were often made out of iron – the great railway stations; the Eiffel Tower. The sociological generalisations about cities came later, although there was an attempt throughout most of the century to formulate them. By then the iron seemed curiously impermanent.

The relevant nineteenth-century writing, no less alarming in its bulk and complexity than the cities themselves, has been re-examined and reviewed recently in years of boom in urban studies; and the facts of urban growth in different countries – no two countries had the same chronology – have been subjected to increasingly systematic compilation, classification and analysis.[5] They are facts that bear not only on particular cities or the relations between cities, but also on what was happening to human relations inside cities – relations between individuals and between groups. Topographic contrast and segregation have been mapped, thereby bringing together geography and psychology. Attention has been paid also to urban morphology – the forms of city organisation and growth – and, most recently, to the sights, sounds, and (not least) smells that provoked argument both about economics and about aesthetics.[6]

It is plain from the writing that reactions were mixed – even at one moment of time or for one individual – towards both the growth in the size of existing cities, familiar or strange, and the increase in the number of big cities. The same city meant different things to different inhabitants and to the same inhabitant at different stages of his or her life; and travellers' tales were equally variegated. Compare what Carlyle and Disraeli had to say about Manchester, or the differences in mood expressed within Carlyle himself, or even earlier in the poet Wordsworth, who pondered long on the significance of 'the increasing accumulation of men in cities'. Contrast far later in the century the unequivocal comments of Kipling on Chicago:

I have struck a city – a real city – and they call it Chicago .... This place is the first American city I have encountered. It holds rather more than a million people with bodies, and stands on the same sort of soil as Calcutta. Having seen it, I urgently desire never to see it again .... I went out into the streets, which are long and flat and without end. And verily it is not a good thing to live in our East for any length of time. Your ideas begin to clash with those held by every right-thinking white man. I looked down interminable vistas flanked with nine, ten and fifteen storied houses, and crowded with men and women, and the show impressed me with a great horror. Except in London – and I had forgotten what London is like – I had never seen so many white people together, and never such a collection of miserables. There was no colour in the street and no beauty, only a maze of wire-ropes overhead and dirty stone flagging underfoot ... I spent ten hours in that huge wilderness.[7]

It is possible to set alongside Kipling's picture a whole gallery of alternative pictures of Chicago,[8] just as it is possible to anthologise almost indefinitely about London or New York.[9] Manchester and Chicago stand out, however, in that they were the real shock cities first of the 1840s and then of the 1890s, both of them conspicuous for unsolved problems (of class and race respectively) and for bustling vitality, both pointing not to the past but to the future. You had to understand them if you were to understand the world. As the journalist, W.T. Stead, put it in 1894, Chicago was 'not laden down by any *damnosa hereditas* of the blunders and crimes of the past; her citizens are full of faith in the destiny of their city'.[10] For Carlyle, Manchester in the 1840s had been 'every whit as wonderful, as fearful, as unimaginable, as the oldest Salem or prophetic city'.[11]

If the nineteenth-century reactions to the city were mixed, they were no different in this respect from most other nineteenth-century reactions to the phenomena of economic and social change: to steamengines, locomotives and steamboats; to furnaces and to forges; to machines of every kind; to mills and to banks. It remains difficult, indeed, even in retrospect, to separate reactions to what sociologists came to call urbanisation from reactions to industrialisation and progress. Nor does the difficulty disappear when we recall, first, that many of the towns and cities that grew fastest during the nineteenth century were not really industrial cities at all; and second, that most of what we consider to be characteristic nineteenth-century reactions had been preceded by anticipations during the pre-industrial eighteenth century. Rousseau in *Émile* (1762) had warned that 'the breath of man is fatal to his fellows ... Cities are the burial pit of the human species.'[12] He was not speaking simply for himself or even for an *avant-garde* in his own generation, but with the weight of a substantial body of current opinion and a long tradition, back to the classics, behind him. Voltaire, who extolled the benefits of 'civilization', had an equally rich tradition behind what he had to say about the qualities of London as a capital city;[13] so, too, had Dr Johnson.

There are greater complexities than the transmission from generation to generation of urban gossip or of pastoral escape. More than a century before Kipling, a traveller from the world's Far East, where there were already huge cities, looked into the faces of the *misérables* in Chicago. William Blake, the home-based citizen, for whom London was more than a world, spelled out his own experiences:

I wander thro' each charter'd street,
Near where the charter'd Thames does flow,
And mark in every face I meet
Marks of weakness, marks of woe.[14]

When a student of the relationships between civilisation and literature confronts passages of this kind from different historical periods, from different parts of the world and from different literary genres – there are comparable passages about cities in Wordsworth's poetry and Dickens's novels – he is forced to take into account not merely a dialectical theory of nineteenth-century culture ('the long revolution', as Raymond Williams has called it) but different layers of interpretation and criticism[15] – immediate and contemplative, intuitive and ratiocinative, inherited and idiosyncratic, participative and alienated. In turning to the symbols and in trying (to use a phrase of Northrop Frye's) to 'crack symbolic codes', it is necessary to wend a devious critical path not only through the cities but through literature itself, old and new.[16]

I

The literature of the United States provides the most easily accessible set of initial examples. During the nineteenth century the 'virgin continent' was transformed into a modern society, although it was not until the 1880s, fifty years after Britain, that urbanisation, dramatic urbanisation, became a controlling factor in American national life. In one turbulent decade the number of towns of between 12,000 and 20,000 people increased from 76-107, the number of towns of between 20,000 and 40,000 people from 55-91, the number of cities of between 40,000 and 75,000 people from 21-35, and the number of still bigger cities from 23-39.[17] Not surprisingly, popular writers made the most both of the new horizons of individual opportunity and of the new turmoil of social relationships. Yet what Henry Nash Smith has called 'the myth of the garden', Richard Hofstadter 'the agrarian myth', and Leo Marx 'pastoralism' (popular and sentimentalised or private and subtle) survived the great transformation.[18] 'The soft veil of nostalgia that hangs over our urbanized landscape,' Marx writes, 'is largely a vestige of the once dominant image of an undefiled, green republic, a quiet land of forests, villages, and farms dedicated to the pursuit of happiness.'[19] There were many late nineteenth-century echoes of Thomas Jefferson's Notes on Virginia (1785) – 'the mobs of great cities add just so much to the support of pure government, as sores do to the strength of the human body. It is the manners and spirit of a people which preserve a republic in vigour. A degeneracy in these is a canker which soon eats to the heart of its laws and constitution.'[20]

To explain American pastoralism Marx returns via Emerson, Thoreau, Hawthorne, Jefferson, Wordsworth, Goldsmith, Thompson, and Shakespeare's *Tempest* to Virgil's *Eclogues*. Yet he notes a basic nineteenth-century twist. Taking as his starting point Nathaniel Hawthorne's description in 1844 of a neighbourhood known as 'Sleepy Hollow', he points to Hawthorne's intrusion of 'the whistle of the locomotive', 'a startling shriek' that 'brings the noisy world into the midst of our slumbrous peace'. This passage from Hawthorne, far from being unique, may be paralleled without difficulty in Thoreau's *Walden* (1854), Melville's *Moby Dick* (1851), and Mark Twain's *Huckleberry Finn* (1884), three of the classics of American literature.

What distinguished such passages from those in earlier pastoralist literature was the role of the locomotive whistle, 'a little event' in a century of great events. 'In the stock contrast between city and country', a contrast with ancient origins,

each had been assumed to occupy a more or less fixed location in space; the country here, the city there. But in 1844 the sound of a train in the Concord woods implies a radical change in the conventional pattern. Now the great world is invading the land transforming the sensory texture of rural life – the way it looks and sounds – and threatening, in fact, to impose a new and more complete dominion over it.... The distinctive attribute of the new order is its technological power, a power that does not remain confined to the traditional boundaries of the city. It is a centrifugal force that threatens to break down, once and for all, the conventional contrast between these two styles of life.[21]

Marx over-emphasised the role of machines in the new technological order, and ignored bridges. He was more interested in mechanical engineering than in civil. The integrative power of technology is missing from his analysis. Yet he was right to emphasise the sense of threat. Moreover, as the American cities grew during the last decades of the nineteenth century, at a rate that would have surprised Hawthorne, the threat of the city was heightened. The fact that city boosters set out to enhance its lure and to extol its material power merely added to the feeling that within the American city, man had created a 'wilderness' of his own – a term that, as we have seen, was used by Kipling, and was to be used by many writers after him.

Even Walt Whitman, who, on returning to New York in 1870, praised 'the splendour, picturesqueness and oceanic amplitude' of the great American cities, dreamed in his *Passage to India* (1868) – making

Kipling's journey in reverse – of a primal return to the 'gardens of Asia' where history began:

> ... the voyage of his mind's return,
> To reason's earthly paradise,
> Back, back to wisdom's birth, to innocent intuitions,
> Again with fair creation.[22]

Henry James, who also journeyed eastward (although no farther than Europe, which was his 'new world'), found 'a kind of sanctity' in London just because it was not a wilderness. 'It is the single place in which most readers, most possible lovers, are gathered together; it is the most inclusive public and the largest social incarnation of the language, of the tradition.'[23] It might not be a 'pleasant, agreeable, or cheerful place' or 'exempt from reproach': it was 'only magnificent ... the biggest aggregation of human life, the most complete compendium of the world'.[24]

Whitman's capacity to comprehend everything in his own compendium of the United States and the world meant that he could praise Nature's wonders and men's cities with equal enthusiasm. He was comprehensive, too, about the city itself: as he wrote in *Song of Myself*:

> This is the city and I am one of the citizens,
> Whatever interests the rest interests me, politics, wars, markets, newspapers, schools,
> The major and councils, banks, tariffs, steamships, factories, stocks, stores, real estate and personal estate.

It is the kind of catalogue which might have been compiled by an urban historian. As in *Salut au Monde*, also part of *Leaves of Grass*, he had a geographical list:

> I see the cities of the earth and make myself at random a part of them
> I am a real Parisian,
> I am a habiter of Vienna, St Petersburg, Berlin, Constantinople.
> I am of Adelaide, Sydney, Melbourne,
> I am of London, Manchester, Bristol, Edinburgh, Limerick,
> I am of Madrid, Cadiz, Barcelona, Oporto, Lyons, Brussels, Berne, Frankfort, Stuttgart, Turin, Florence,
> I belong to Moscow, Cracow, Warsaw ....
> I descend upon all these cities, and rise from them again.

The comprehensive character of the list prompts a desire to return to particularity, to the rooted knowledge of place which had behind it the longest traditions.[25]

II

There was, however, no single dominant city in America, no city that was both metropolis and capital, like London or Paris or Vienna; and in turning from American to European reactions to the city, London, Paris and Vienna occupy a special place in the literature not only of their own countries but of the countries of visitors, exiles and people who, like Whitman, were writing about what they had not actually seen. Moreover, since no European country could claim the pedigree of a virgin land, and in every case – not least in Papal Rome, 'the oldest city' – there were so many layers of historical experience, reactions were bound to be complex. F.A. Vizetelly, the well-known translator into English of Émile Zola's *Paris* (1898), one of 'a trilogy of the three cities' (along with *Lourdes* and *Rome*), quoted in his introduction some lines written about Paris by a very different writer from Zola, Lord Byron:

> I loved her from my boyhood; she to me
> Was as a fairy city of the heart.

Vizetelly also quoted Victor Hugo:

> Before possessing its nation, Europe possesses its city [Paris]. The nation does not yet exist, but its capital is already here .... It is from three cities, Jerusalem, Athens, Rome, that the modern world has been evolved. They did the work. Of Jerusalem there now remains but a gibbet, Calvary; of Athens, a ruin, the Parthenon; of Rome, a phantom, its empire. Are these cities dead then? No, a broken eggshell does not necessarily imply that the egg has been destroyed; it rather signifies that the bird has come forth from it and lives .... From Rome has come power; from Athens, art; from Jerusalem, freedom; the great, the beautiful, the true .... And they live anew in Paris, which in one way has resuscitated Rome, in another Athens, and in another Jerusalem; for from the cry of Golgotha came the principle of the Rights of Man. And Paris also has its crucified; one that has been crucified for eighteen hundred years – the People .... But the function of Paris is to spread ideas. Its never-ending duty is to scatter truths over the world .... Paris is a sower, sowing the darkness with sparks of light. It is Paris which, without a pause, stirs up the fires of progress .... It is like a ship sailing on through storms and whirlpools to unknown Atlantides, and ever towing the fleet of mankind in its wake.[26]

The most remarkable point about this grandiloquent passage is the total omission of London from Hugo's list. Yet there were many English writers also in the nineteenth century who would have taken issue with James and granted Paris the primacy, at least in the arts, even if, as has been claimed, many of them 'learnt far less about France from all the works of Flaubert and Zola than from George Moore's slender *Confessions of a Young Man* (1888).'[27]

Hugo himself had written of medieval Paris, seeking to establish its identity, in his *Notre-Dame de Paris* (1831), a huge Gothic canvas, inspired by Scott, with rich tableaux, some grotesque, others sublime, very different in purpose and scale from any American writing about cities. The buildings became the heroes of the novel, some of them being compared fancifully with living or mythical animals. The Île de la Cité is a tortoise, the Louvre a hydra, and the Cathedral itself a sphinx, with its rose window resembling the eye of a Cyclops. For contemporary Paris we have to turn to Eugène Sue's best-seller *Les mystères de Paris* (1842-3), which is significant also because it was imitated in many other countries, as well as translated. *The Mysteries of London*, by G.W.M. Reynolds, T. Miller, and E.L. Blanchard, was published between 1846 and 1850; *The Mysteries of Berlin* appeared in 1845; and E.Z.C. Judson's *The Mysteries and Miseries of New York* appeared in 1848.

This was the decade when, as we have seen, there was a new consciousness of living in 'the age of great cities', and Sue, rightly labelled a social romantic, was anxious to reveal to his readers what a socially disturbed place the modern city really was:

> The only thing we can hope to do is to draw the attention of the intelligentsia and the more prosperous classes to the great deprivation and suffering in society, facts that can be deplored but not denied.[28]

Sue could be as theatrical as Hugo, but he interspersed statistics with his melodrama, drawing heavily on new data that were then available for the study of cities. In this connection, as in so many others, Paris was the right place to start, although already by the end of the 1830s the 'statistical method' – arithmetical figures in place of figures of speech – was winning adherents everywhere.[29] The annual *Recherches statistiques sur la ville de Paris* had begun to appear in 1817, and twelve years later Parent-Duchâtelet and Villermé had launched their *Annales d'hygiène publique et de médecine légale*, the first regular journal in the world to concentrate on problems of public health – or what came to be called more comprehensively 'the sanitary idea'.[30] This 'idea', which inspired a battle against fate, was to fascinate many of the greatest writers of the nineteenth century, notably George Eliot in England.[31]

Sue, like many nineteenth-century writers after him – with a very different novelist, Dickens, outstanding amongst them – was con-

cerned with the horrors of poverty and disease and with the correlations between them, which had nothing to do, in his context, with
the industrial revolution or with the advance of steam technology. He
was even more concerned, however, with the activities of the Parisian
underworld and the colourful, often criminal, exploits of what were
called (and not only in Paris) *les classes dangereuses*.[32] He knew that a
large and respectable reading public could be entertained and titillated
with details of the curiosities of city life. A percipient critic noted in
the English liberal newspaper the *Daily News*, which for a brief time
was edited by Dickens:

> The French novelists seem to set about ... pictures [of vice] in a kind of
> jocular, half-credulous vein, which they communicate to their readers, and
> which inspires a feeling of half-reality, very consoling in horrors, and
> leaving full enjoyment of the comic gayer scenes. No Englishman could at
> all attempt that light *charlatanerie* of the French, and for us to rival it by
> taking such stories more *au sérieux* is equally hopeless.[33]

Similar documentation to that consulted by Sue was to be used more
seriously – and more memorably – in French by Hugo in his second
long novel about Paris, *Les Misérables*, not published until 1862, long
after it was written.

There remains a great divide between Hugo, whom Zola attacked
virulently, and Zola himself, although (as we have seen) Vizetelly
cheerfully used the former to introduce the latter. In the meantime,
there had been large-scale political changes influencing life in Paris and
the relationship between the capital and the provinces of France. Paris
remained, as it had been before the Revolution of 1848, a city without
large-scale industry and consequently without a large industrial pro-
letariat, but it never lost its revolutionary propensities or its revolutionary reputation. Above all, it continued to grow, whatever the
regime. It had doubled its size between 1800 and 1850 – at a time when
the population of France as a whole was growing far more slowly than
that of any of its neighbours – and during the hustling Second Empire,
when large parts of it were redeveloped by Haussmann, it continued to
expand, annexing many of its burgeoning suburbs in 1859. By 1881 it
had more than 2 million people, and in 1900 it was still the largest city
in Europe after London. Zola was as much impressed by its immensity
as Henry James was with the 'numerosity' of London; he also made
much of its variety and of its contrasts.

Before the 1848 Revolution the exile Henrich Heine, one of a large
number of German refugees in Paris, had stated that Paris was 'really
France'. 'The latter', he went on, 'is only the countryside round its
capital .... Everything outstanding in the provinces soon makes its

way to the capital, the focus of all light and brilliance.'[34] During the Second Empire, when many Frenchmen, like Hugo, were in exile from their own country, Paris glittered in all its glory as a centre of fashion and display for the whole of Europe. And during the very different regime of the Third Republic, which seemed in domestic terms to be the regime of the provinces,[35] the city continued to attract writers and artists from all countries. 'All good Americans', declared Thomas Appleton, 'when they die, go to Paris.'[36] 'It boasts today', wrote the English essayist Frederic Harrison in 1894, 'that it is the most brilliant, the most ordered, the most artistic city of men, and one of the most sanitary and convenient for civilised life. And no reasonable man can deny that the substantial part of this boast is just.'[37]

For Zola, as for Balzac before him, interesting themes for the novelist could be found in the French provinces as well as in Paris. Yet he was always interested in big cities. In the novel *Paris*, the young Abbé Froment, who has arrived there via Rome and Lourdes, continues his personal quest. As in so many other novels about men in cities, the colour and mood of the place, even its weather, correspond closely to the hero's personal feelings. We begin in the first few pages with 'the Paris of mystery, shrouded by clouds, buried as it were beneath the ashes of some disaster', and we end the novel with Paris bathed in rich evening sunlight.

> This was no longer the city of the sower, a chaos of roofs and edifices suggesting brown land turned up by some huge plough .... Nor was it the city whose divisions had one day seemed so plain to Pierre: eastward, the districts of toil, misty with the grey smoke of factories; southward, the districts of study, serene and quiet; westward, the districts of wealth, bright and open; and in the centre, the districts of trade with dark and busy streets. It now seemed as if one and the same crop had sprung up on every side, imparting harmony to everything, and making the entire expanse one sole, boundless field, rich from the same fruitfulness .... And Paris flared – Paris which the divine sun had sown with light, and where in glory waved the great future harvest of Truth and Justice.

We are not so far from Hugo after all, and it is not surprising that in the light of passages like this, heavy with symbolism, recent writers on Zola have dwelt less on his scientific aims, on his appeal to naturalism, and on his clinical methods, than on the mythic and poetic qualities of his work. Nonetheless, in two of the volumes in the novel cycle *Les Rougon-Macquart* (1871-93), Zola dealt realistically with a market and a department store, two of the great nineteenth-century city institutions. *Le Ventre de Paris* (1873) (The Belly of Paris) explores Les Halles: at the same time, it gives Zola a chance to explore some of the

conflicts of interest that influence the relationships between people in
cities and people outside. The market-gardener, Mme François, has
every reason for distrusting *ce diable de Paris. Au bonheur des dames*
(1883) presents a department store that in the mechanism of its daily
operations harnesses the same kind of ruthless drive as any factory in
an industrial city. Both these novels about urban institutions could
have been written only at that particular period in the evolution of
Paris. They were of their time and for their time, continuing, in Zola's
own estimate, the heritage of Stendhal and Balzac.[38]

There is one very different heritage from nineteenth-century
France, represented in a new and distinctive set of attitudes toward
Paris and the city. It is a heritage associated not with the novel – which,
it has been claimed, is the distinctive literary genre of the city[39] – but
with poetry. The key figure is Baudelaire, a link with the earlier
Romantic poets, to whom later generations of poets turned. Baudelaire was born in Paris, lived there for more than forty years, and died
there. He drew some of his most powerful poetry from the city that he
knew so well, and about which he had no illusions:

> Paris change, mais rien dans ma mélancholie
> N'a bougé! Palais neufs, échafaudages, blocs,
> Vieux faubourgs, tout pour moi devient allégorie,
> Et mes chers souvenirs sont plus lourds que des rocs.

(Paris changes, but nothing in my melancholy has moved! New public
buildings, scaffoldings, blocks, old suburbs, everything becomes an
allegory for me, and my dear memories are heavier than rocks.)

Zola saw the city as a challenge, an intricate institutional complex with
a past and a future, where individuals and groups, even when in
conflict, were held within the city's grip. Baudelaire saw the city as a
place of perpetual change, never still, where individuals pursued inner
adventures of the mind, prompted by the sensations of each fleeting
moment – moments that were linked through memories and pressed
forward through desires:

> Fourmillant cité, cité pleine de rêves,
> Où le spectre, en plein jour, raccroche le passant.

(Swarming city, city full of dreams, where in broad daylight ghosts accost a
man in the street.)

There might be the same 'dirty yellow fog' that we meet in Zola – or in
Dickens – but there were very different shapes in the fog. There might
be the same scorn for bourgeois values, but whereas Zola, like Balzac,
plotted the chart of bourgeois fortunes, Baudelaire affirmed contemptuous counter-values, making a Bohemia out of the whole city. No

writer was more conscious of what Walter Pater called 'the quickened multiple consciousness' that the city made possible.[40] Baudelaire's quickened consciousness encompassed evil and good, 'multitude' and 'solitude' (terms that he wanted to make 'equal and interchangeable'), boredom and the 'drunken spree of vitality'.[41]

When Baudelaire wanted to get out of Paris, the idea of the 'voyage' returned in a different context; it was not of a 'sleepy hollow' that he was dreaming, but of exotic journeys of escape, which he well knew had no real destination, but which lured his imagination into 'the sinuous folds of ancient capitals, where all things, even horrors, turn to magic'. His list was quite different from Whitman's, and he felt that in the last resort the alternative to life in the city was not escape from it, but death.

Baudelaire's romanticism was fundamental. His use of symbols stopped far short of the symbolism in Verlaine, Mallarmé and Rimbaud, all of whom took Baudelaire's city for granted. Yet the fact that they could take it for granted was due in part to the way in which Baudelaire had begun to transform the nature of poetry under the pressure of modern city life. Imagery acquired a new topography.[42] Thereafter, writers of other countries and of many cities persistently reverted to Baudelaire's images. Eliot's 'Unreal City' in *The Waste Land* is London, but the phrase suggests Baudelaire's *cité pleine de rêves*: for Eliot, in the confusion of twentieth-century war, the towers were everywhere falling: Jerusalem, Athens, Alexandria, Vienna, London. James Joyce, who, as Harry Levin has pointed out, lived in as many cities as the author of the *Odyssey*, each more polyglot and more metropolitan than the last, depended for his unique sense of the city not only on his own experience, but on a rich texture of literary and historical association. Feelings of attraction and recoil, absorption and disengagement, are all expressed in his work, which is not only of immense imaginative power but of the most subtle complexity – as complex, indeed, as the nineteenth- and early twentieth-century city itself.[43]

Through this second heritage we move far away from the simplicities of the nineteenth-century American deviation from pastoralism, which was to lead back to the urban picaresque, or from the stylised kind of contrasts between city and countryside that we find in the verse of an English writer such as Matthew Arnold:

> Calm Soul of all things; make it mine
> To feel, amid the city's jar,
> That there abides a Peace of Thine
> Man did not make, and cannot mar.[44]

Not all writers after Baudelaire placed the city beyond Good and Evil.

The Flemish poet, Emile Verhaeren, a socialist as well as a symbolist, thought of cities as scenes of nightmare, and in his *Les villes tentaculaires* (1895) described them as sucking the life-blood out of the countryside. Similarly the German poet Rainer Maria Rilke, who lived until 1926, was oppressed by what he called 'the guilt of cities' and generalised about their destructive power:

> Die Städte aber wollen nur das Ihre
> und reissen alles mit in ihren Lauf.
> Wie hohles Holz zerbrechen sie die Tiere
> und brauchern viele Völker brennend auf.

(But cities will only ends of their own and sweep up everything into their own running. They smash up animals like hollow wood and devour many peoples by burning.) [45]

III

Germany, which was not united until 1871, and which even after that date did not include all German-speaking peoples within its boundaries, was a country of many historic cities that had stood out during the middle ages as oases of freedom. In the eighteenth century some had been associated with court, others with middle-class, rule. In the nineteenth century many of them became centres of 'liberalism' until new forces began to emerge late in the century.[46] Yet there was no German equivalent of Paris, even after 1871. Berlin's population grew from less than 200,000 at the end of Napoleonic Wars to just under 400,000 at the time of the 1848 Revolution, and was approaching 2 million at the end of the century;[47] but with few exceptions, notably the novelist Theodor Fontane, the leading German writers lived in other places. Friedrich Hebbel, distinguished poet and dramatist, who hailed from Schleswig-Holstein, worked in many cities before settling in Vienna, which was the home of Austria's 'national' playwright, Franz Grillparzer, more than twenty years older than he was, and of what was probably the most lively German-speaking theatre anywhere. The Austrian novelist, Adalbert Stifter, on the other hand, spent the last twenty years of his life in Linz, after becoming disillusioned with the character of revolutionary politics in the capital during 1848. Although the Swiss novelist Gottfried Keller left the provincial confines of Zürich to study in Munich and Heidelberg, and then went on to Berlin, he returned to live in his native Switzerland. So too did the Swiss poet Conrad Ferdinand Meyer, after spells in France and Italy. The great philosopher G.W.F. Hegel held a Chair in Berlin until his death in 1831; but J.C. Burckhardt, the great Swiss historian, refused a Chair in Berlin with some virulence after Leopold von Ranke died. Germany meant not only Berlin, but also Munich, Leipzig, Frankfurt, Cologne and Hamburg, not to speak of Zürich, Basel and Vienna. Moreover, on the eve of unification, 63·8 per cent of the inhabitants of the area that was to be unified lived in places with less than 2000 inhabitants. Even as late as 1910 the proportion was 39·9 per cent.[48] There was never any shortage of 'village tales' in nineteenth-century Germany.

Mme de Stäel had noted in *De l'Allemagne* (1810) that no single set of influences radiated outward from one centre throughout Germany; even at the end of the century, in the golden years of the Wilhelmine Empire, the remark would still have been true. There was more fear of the *Grossstadt* in Germany than in any other country as the proportion of Germans living in *Grossstädte* went up four times between 1871 and 1910, from less than 5 per cent to more than 20 per cent, and sociologists such as Ferdinand Tönnies made the most of the differences between the hectic and feverish life of the metropolis and the ordered existence of smaller, more conservative, more homogeneous, and more self-contained urban communities. It was in Germany, indeed, that the now familiar sociological distinction between 'face-to-face' communities and cities with a network of secondary relationships was first established.[49] The *Landstadt* (country town), it was maintained, was genuinely related to the countryside; even though it could not escape the changes of the century, it had more of the characteristics of the *Dorf* (village) than of the *Grossstadt*.[50] Despite the growth of industry, particularly during the last decades of the century, and the emergence of busy new industrial towns in the Ruhr and Silesia, which were almost completely neglected by German writers, most writers – and many of them were Swiss – looked backward rather than forward, and inward, particularly through the *Bildungsroman* and the *Novelle*, rather than outward.[51] They depicted not cosmopolis but man *before* cosmopolis as seen from inside 'the *ancien régime* of mankind'.[52] Certainly, writers who did not conform to these patterns were rebels not only against cities or history – but against everything.

Yet some, at least, of the writers of the *Novellen* had seen enough of the outside world, as Keller had, to be critically aware of the forces of change and the personal dilemmas they posed, while the *Landstadt* itself was changing enough to encourage a different kind of speculation and response from villages that remained settled in ancient ways. Keller's Zürich grew in his lifetime, for example, from a community of less than 30,000 to a city of over 150,000, and there was inevitable uprooting. Moreover, it is impossible to write of Germany at any period of its history – after the first legendary moves from the forests, which so interested nineteenth-century German historians – without taking towns and cities into the reckoning. Attitudes were set long before the nineteenth century began, and they influenced ways of thinking in the more mobile society that developed with industrialisation.[53] A positive attitude toward the cities of the past and the values associated with them is well reflected in the writings of some members of the generation of 'nationalists' during the early years of the century. This positive attitude is at least as clearly defined as the *völkisch*, anti-urban writing of a new generation at the end of the century.[54] According to Fichte, for example, it was in the medieval cities that 'every branch of cultural life' had quickly developed into 'the fairest bloom'. The medieval burghers had transmitted to Germans of a later time qualities that they most needed: 'loyalty, uprightness [*Biederkeit*], honour, and simplicity'. The age of the great medieval cities was 'the nation's youthful dream of its future deeds ... the prophecy of what it would become once it had perfected its strength'.[55]

Obviously such writing was designed to assert a special German identity. The fact that unity, when it eventually came, was achieved not through the political revolutions of 1848 but through Bismarck's long-term policies of 'blood and iron', encouraged writing about the past within an accepted set of traditions, and about the present in terms of the best way in which the individual German, who was often supposed to be essentially not a 'political' creature in the Anglo-French sense of the word, could realise his full stature within a united Germany. Nor did it need Germans of Bismarck's Germany to dwell on the safe keeping of what was best in the German heritage. Adalbert Stifter, after writing a number of early stories about life in Vienna, concentrated on individuals within small groups: nobility of soul was as natural as fresh air. The more people lived in cities, the more necessary it was to return to the country, not only to the domesticated countryside but to the primitive country of mountains and forests. Only there could the 'wretched degeneration' of the times be adequately countered. *Der Nachsommer* (1857) (The Indian Summer), written in the form of a *Bildungsroman*, was, in the words of a contemporary American critic, 'an ideal portrait, just far enough removed from reality to make it idyllic'.[56] Perhaps not surprisingly, Stifter's writing was compared at the time with Hawthorne's, and comparisons were also made with Wordsworth.[57] Yet in Stifter's Arcadia there was no intimation of the kind of intruding 'little event' that we noted in American 'pastoralism'. As Fuerst has pointed out, both the 'elemental' Stifter and the 'sentimental' Eichendorff used railways extensively, but 'shrank from mentioning them in literature'.[58] The first German writer to do so was Gerhardt Hauptmann, in his short story *Bahnwärter Thiel* (1887) (Railwayman Thiel), and it is significant that the story is told from the point of view of a peasant-like railwayman in the country, a 'real' human being unable to comprehend the impersonal, destructive force of the passing trains.

In the writings of Keller there is always a contrast, implicit or explicit, between nature and civilisation. The rural landscape is bathed in golden light, whereas the towns and cities are darkened by intrigue and infamy. Keller was aware also of the dialectic of his times and of the ambivalent influence of 'progress' even on the small town itself – the intrigues and iniquities of bourgeois life in *Martin Salander* (1886) make this abundantly clear, and so, also, do his satirical poems – but by preference he settled for the norms that he believed were everywhere being threatened, and his miniature world in Seldwyla, an imaginary little Swiss town, is a counter-world of the mind and the heart to the metropolis that he feared rather than understood.

Theodor Fontane remains something of an exception within the pattern. Although he was born on the North Sea coast of Prussia, wrote sensitively about the landscape and history of Brandenberg, and described Junker attitudes, past and present, with insight and under-standing, he chose to make Berlin his home. His novels belong to the last years of his life, and the best of them concern Berlin itself and Berlin society. They were not the first nineteenth-century German novels to focus on Berlin or on the bourgeoisie. Wilhelm Raabe's *Die Chronik der Sperlingsgasse* (1857) (The Chronicle of Sparrows Alley) had dealt with a small street in a big city, though in a lyrical, old-world manner, and there had been other writers willing to explore the metropolis.[59] Fontane, however, conceived of his Berlin novels as a cycle that would portray what life in Berlin was really like.[60] The novels were far removed from the *Bildungsroman* and the *Novelle*, for they explored aspects of class, the effects of economic pressures on trad-itional class status and bourgeois pretensions to 'culture'. Fontane did not so much depict as talk about the industrial working class itself, 'the fourth estate', which formed a sizeable proportion of the Berlin population even in 1848. But in his letters and fiction, particularly in his last novel, *Der Stechlin* (1898) there were references to the growth of this new class and of the Social Democrats who represented them.

The question that preoccupied Fontane, as it was to preoccupy his admirer Thomas Mann, was what would happen to the old Prussian values of a military aristocracy and an essentially 'unbourgeois' *Bürgertum* in the very rapid social and economic transformation of Germany that was then taking place. Von Stechlin's old black and white flag badly needed to be patched, but if 'anything red were to be sewn onto it, it will surely tear to bits'. Fontane realised the inevitability of urban change, but was too ironical and too old a writer to be able to champion progressive ideas. He also regretted what was being lost; and he was both exasperated and amused by the pretensions of the new Berlin and of its new middle classes, who had neither genuine aristocratic nor progressive allegiances. As a result, one of his responses to the main challenge of the city was to take refuge in the humorous anecdote. His preference 'for the anecdotal and the mannered ... because if you can see what's behind the incidental details, they always show you the really human quality in events',[61] was the secret both of his strength and his weakness as a writer. He has achieved less fame abroad than any writer of comparable stature, yet no novelist has caught more exactly the very accent and character of a city, a city with a very distinct identity.

While Berlin was growing, Vienna – a more cosmopolitan city – was changing too in appearance and mood from the place that was thought of simply as 'the real world' by Grillparzer's idealistic artist in *Der arme Spielmann* (a tale begun in 1831) to the place that the satirist Karl Kraus, who has been compared with Juvenal, made into a symbolic capital of doomed empire. When the Café Griensteidl, where 'Young Vienna', Viennese intellectuals and journalists, chose to meet, was pulled down in 1897 for road improvements, Kraus wrote a pamphlet entitled *Die demolierte Literatur*, which began: 'Vienna has been demolished into a big city.' The city grew most rapidly between 1846 and 1857, but by 1890, when the suburbs were incorporated by law, in its extended form the whole complex had reached a population of over 1,300,000. The old inner city had been 'ringed', and the old complex of churches and palaces complemented by parliamentary and administrative buildings, museums, theatres, and opera houses. There was – *pace* Kraus – less of a gulf between artists and bourgeoisie in imperial Vienna than there was in Paris. Some of the cafés, at least, belonged to both, and today they share the same faded photographs. As Carl Schorske has said, 'The democratization of culture, viewed sociologically, meant the aristocratization of the middle classes. Increasingly, from the age of Grillparzer to the age of Hofmannsthal, poets, professors and performing artists were valued guests, in fact, prize catches of the hosts and hostesses.'[62] Moreover, the different artistic and cultural circles criss-crossed. The musicians Mahler and Walter would meet and discuss Kant and Schopenhauer at the home of the Wittgensteins; the physicist and philosopher of science Boltzmann took music lessons from Bruckner.

Yet in Vienna – a crucible of many twentieth-century ideas and prejudices – there were intimations of decay as well as of change. Ferdinand von Saar, story writer and poet, recorded as early as the 1870s – for example, in his book *Die Steinklopfer* (The Stone Breakers) – the helpless misery of one section of the Viennese working class; and in his poem 'Proles' he dealt realistically with jerry-building in the new and poorer districts of the great city:

The first houses! Almost beginning to fall down,
although they have only just been built!
I saw dark smoke pouring from the chimneys,
and I heard the sound of the factories at work.
What air, oppressive and mephitic,
as I paced the streets! At every doorway and at every step,
half-naked children, anaemic and suffering from rickets.[63]

In an elegy to Stifter he exclaimed, 'I revere the memory of the poet who opened an Eden for me – an Eden which, alas, I have lost.'[64]

This mood became increasingly familiar to the younger generation at the turn of the century. It can be felt, for example, in the early poetry of Hugo von Hofmannsthal, born in the same year as Kraus, which evokes a cultural tradition while at the same time suggesting that disintegration is imminent. And it was: the breakdown of the poet's lyrical gifts – even, indeed, of his sense of language – is described in his famous Chandos letter (*Ein Brief*, 1902). The mood of cultural pessimism in most German-speaking poets of this generation was inspired by more, of course, than the mere size of cities. Nietzsche's apocalyptic prophecies of the doom of civilisation were undoubtedly influential, for instance; though these were rarely directed at city life as such, of which Nietzsche had not had much experience. Nor had the Salzburg poet Georg Trakl. Yet demonic images of steel and stone and ghastly cities loom up in his visionary landscapes of transcendent suffering and longing. 'O, the madness of the big city, where crippled trees stand by the black wall in the evening, and the spirit of evil stares out from a silver mask.'[65] This imagery contrasts, as we might expect, with more serene – though scarcely more realistic – images of villages, parks and gardens in Trakl's poetry.[66]

Carl Schorske, doubtless with Leo Marx's 'Machine in the Garden' in mind, has argued that in Vienna, where there was a conscious effort to bring the garden into the heart of the city throughout the nineteenth century, life proved too big for art. The expressionist artist Oskar Kokoschka, who violently broke into the garden, was expelled from it. In a city that prided itself on its civilisation – great though its social contrasts were in fact – Kokoschka acclaimed instinct; and a similar sense of elemental forces behind a false façade inspires much of Kraus's satire. It was in this city, which more than any other in Europe was to be dethroned from its glory by the cataclysms of twentieth-century history, that Freud explored the deep-seated discontents of civilisation itself, beginning with the family. Expressionism belongs as much to this setting and to this time as impressionism belonged to Paris a generation earlier. As Schorske has pointed out, 'in a rent society, with pent-up energies that could find no constructive outlet, prevailing culture appeared to a new generation not as a creative illusion but as a lie. In their prophetic explosion in the garden the Expressionists anticipated Europe's greater explosion, the new reality of world war and revolution.'[67]

There has been much debate about what stylistic or thematic features may be said to be common to the many writers and painters throughout Germany (and beyond) who have been dubbed Expressionists. Even their 'message', as interpreted by Kurt Pinthus in the famous anthology of their work, *Menschheitsdämmerung* (Berlin, 1920), is ambiguous; it could mean the half-light of a new dawn for mankind, or the twilight of its extinction. In the imagination of many artists of the time, it meant both. Similarly, the ever-recurrent imagery of city life in the poems of Heym, Stadler, Becher and Werfel wavers in mood between horror and hope, a sense of the depth of historical change and an equally deep uncertainty as to where it would lead.

IV

No one could have compared London with a garden in either the nineteenth or the twentieth century, although Englishmen, more than any other people in the world, dreamed of 'garden cities' combining 'all the advantages of the most energetic and active town life with the beauty and delight of the country'.[68] In England, indeed, there were many cities besides London – as we have seen, Manchester was one – that stimulated the imagination of writers and carried with them the sense of the city. It was only during the last few decades of the century that London established its dominance not only as the national capital but as 'the world city', and the English writing on cities of that period has much in common with parallel writing in other countries.

The size of London disturbed many Englishmen even during the early decades of the nineteenth century, when its population was less than 1 million; and William Cobbett's savage descriptions of the 'great Wen', as nasty as it was noisy, were accepted by many people who would have spurned Cobbett's Radicalism. Yet there were London poets (branded as 'the Cockney School') who sang its praises, and the Romantic Benjamin Haydon stated boldly that 'so far from the smoke of London being offensive to me, it has always been to my imagination the sublime canopy that shrouds the City of the World'.[69] Charles Lamb, an enthusiastic Londoner, catalogued its qualities impressionistically:

> Streets, streets, streets, markets, theatres, churches, Covent Gardens, shops sparkling with pretty faces of industrious milliners, neat seamstresses, ladies cheapening, gentlemen behind counters lying, authors in the

street with spectacles ... lamps lit at night ... noise of coaches, drowsy cry of mechanic watchmen at night, with bucks reeling home drunk; if you happen to wake at midnight, cries of Fire and Stop Thief; inns of court, with their learned air, and halls, and butteries, just like the Cambridge colleges; old bookstalls, Jeremy Taylors, Burtons on Melancholy, and Religio Medicis on every stall. These are thy pleasures, O London-with-the-many-sins.[70]

This is a good essay in associative imagery, but too 'literary' in tone – like much of the writing in *The London Magazine* founded in 1820 – to be entirely convincing; it links the eighteenth and nineteenth-century worlds of the metropolis. For all its size, London was still 'manageable', still a coherent entity; and this feeling of manageability persisted in writings thirty to forty years later – in, for instance, *Figaro in London* (1831-6), which reached a peak circulation of 70,000, and in *Punch*, which was founded in 1841.

As the nineteenth century went by, however, London became as unmanageable as it was for long ungovernable, and the statistician as explorer had to step in where the satirist had trodden before him. *Punch* made fun of statistics, but when, like Dickens, it turned to such pressing urban issues as public health, it could not itself dispense with statistics. Even Wordsworth, whose poems included vivid portraits of London, wrote to H.S. Tremenheere, the prototype of the Victorian inspector, that 'we must not only have knowledge, but the means of wielding it, and that is done infinitely more through the imaginative faculty assisting both in the collection and application of facts than is generally believed'.[71] Whereas in eighteenth-century London poverty and riches had existed side by side, during the nineteenth century different parts of the great city became increasingly segregated from each other in a society of 'two nations', an image that recurs time and again before, as well as after, Disraeli used it.[72] By the last decades of the century, West End and East End seemed separated by an un-bridgeable gulf. Although there was still poverty in the West End, it was hidden from view: in the East End, it was open and omnipresent. It was in an effort to discover the *terra incognita* of the socially submerged districts of London that Charles Booth set about his great survey of London life and labour in 1889, a survey that was to be imitated at other times and in other places, but never with such a strong sense of motivation.[73] Inevitably such a survey illuminated the varieties of life in London, and equally inevitably it turned attention away from the 'curiosities' of a big city to the more massive inequalities of social class. Some of the insights of Henry Mayhew's remarkable *London Labour and the London Poor* (1851-62) were missing, but the range and the power were formidable.[74]

The growth of the capital city turned attention throughout the whole of the century to the nature of change itself, to the tearing down and the building up, to the destruction and the construction, to the flux and the uncertainty of it all. By the last decades of the century there were vast areas of suburban London that were completely unknown to those Londoners who did not live there. Such was the combination of awareness of the spread of London and incapacity to explain its causes and its likely consequences, that the metaphors used to describe it were usually borrowed not from society but from nature. The words 'flood' and 'tide' were often employed, as they were in descriptions of the city crowds. 'A city', wrote Arthur Sherwell in 1901, 'is like a great hungry sea which flows on and on, filling up every creek, and then overspreads its borders, flooding the plains beyond.'[75] Less familiar images were also used. Patrick Geddes, who was to exert a powerful intellectual and moral influence on Lewis Mumford, one of the best-known and most influential of twentieth-century writers on cities, thought of London as 'a vast irregular growth without previous parallel in the world of life – perhaps likest to the spreading of a great coral reef'.[76]

Yet given the sense both of contrast and of change, there was also every kind of mixture of pride and prejudice, much of it localised even within London itself. If there was never any shortage of writings about the shortcomings of London, neither was there any shortage of appreciation of its delights. Henry James preferred London because it was more sophisticated than the American cities, all of which seemed alike.[77] Booth was drawn to city life in general, however horrifying some of his disclosures were, not least to himself. London for him was a stage rather than a laboratory, and because New York also seemed like a stage he found it as exciting as London. One of his helpers, H.L. Smith, made the point very clearly. What was it, he asked, that brought so many people to London? 'The contagion of numbers' was the answer, 'the sense of something going on, the theatres and the music halls, the brightly lighted streets and the busy crowds – all, in short, that makes the difference between the Mile End Fair on a Saturday night and a dark and muddy country lane, with no glimmer of gas and with nothing to do. Who could wonder that men are drawn into such a vortex [note the metaphor again], even were the penalty heavier than it is?'[78]

It is helpful to take all these impressions and expressions into account in reading Dickens on London, and it is important in understanding what he had to say to pay full attention to his letters and speeches as well as to his novels. It is important also, of course, to remember that his position was not simply that of an observer: he himself was an element in the changing scene, and how he chose to describe it depended both on his shifting memories and moods (or 'correspondences') and on his fleeting vantage points in time. He was fully aware of the flux. 'Scenes changed before his eyes, place succeeded place, and event followed event, in all the hurry of delirium'[79] we read in the early *Pickwick Papers,* in which only very seldom can Mr Pickwick himself stand back from what he sees: 'Mr Pickwick stood in the principal street of this illustrious town, and gazed, with an air of curiosity, not unmixed with interest, on the objects around him.'[80] Dickens later jotted a note in his Memorandum Book about 'representing London – or Paris, or any other great place – in the light of being actually unknown to all the people in the story, and only taking the colour of their fears and fancies and opinions. So getting a new aspect, and being unlike itself.'[81] This approach seems not very far removed from Baudelaire's 'bathing himself in the crowd';[82] and Hillis Miller, describing the role of the fog in the novel *Bleak House* (1853), draws a further pertinent comparison with Baudelaire: 'for Dickens, as for Baudelaire, the disorder of the outward particulars of the city world corresponds to a human condition of hallucinatory incoherence'.[83]

We should not turn to Dickens, therefore, for verbal photographs of London in Victorian times, although innumerable books have been written and continue to be written with titles such as 'The London of Dickens'.[84] We should rather seek to apprehend, even if we can never fully comprehend, his great city (which must be related to other great cities, and to clusters of symbols as well as of facts) through the welter of impressions interspersed with occasional set-pieces.

First, we can apprehend the contrasts, including, in many virtuoso passages, chains of contrasts within contrasts:

> Midnight had come upon the crowded city. The palace, the night cellar, the jail, the madhouse: the chambers of birth and death, health and sickness, the rigid face of the corpse and the calm sleep of the child: midnight was upon them all.[85]

Then we can apprehend the mutabilities:

> There was no such place as Stagg's Gardens. It had vanished from the earth. Where the old rotten summer-houses had once stood, palaces now reared their heads, and granite columns of gigantic girth opened a vista to the railway world beyond. The miserable waste ground, where the refuse had been heaped of yore, was swallowed up and gone; and in its frowsy stead were tiers of warehouses crammed with rich goods and costly merchandise.[86]

The intrusion of the railway was not a 'little event' to Dickens: it was a

catastrophic agency of total transformation, at its harshest an agency
of death. In *Dombey and Son*, as Kathleen Tillotson has pointed out,
'its appearance on each of four carefully spaced and placed occasions is
emphasized by a volcanic upsurge in the style, by description much
overflowing its narrative function. In these descriptions may be
discerned the fascination of the new as well as the horror of the
strange; but the tone is mainly that of dread.'[87]

Yet the city set-pieces in Dickens are by no means always laden with
dread. Some of them recapture the jollities of city life with immense
gusto: others reflect Dickens' interest in the curious and the strange,
an interest that was rooted in his childhood. Some deal with the old
parts of the London of his youth, others with the extended London of
his later years, far beyond Portland Place and Bryanston Square. In
Nicholas Nickleby (1839) there is one superb description of a busy city
scene, beginning with the water images we have already noted in other
writers:

> Streams of people apparently without end poured on and on, jostling each
> other in the crowd and hurrying forward, scarcely seeming to notice the
> riches that surrounded them on every side; while vehicles of all shapes and
> makes, mingled up together in one moving mass like running water, lent
> their ceaseless roar to swell the noise and tumult.

The passage ends with the curiosities and contrasts of the city:

> Nor were there wanting objects in the crowd itself to give new point and
> purpose to the shifting scene. The rags of the squalid ballad-singer
> fluttered in the rich light that showed the goldsmith's treasures; pale and
> pinched-up faces hovered about the windows where there was tempting
> food; hungry eyes wandered over the profusion guarded by one thin sheet
> of brittle glass – an iron wall to them; half-naked shivering figures stopped
> to gaze at Chinese shawls and golden stuffs of India. There was a
> christening party at the largest coffin makers, and a funeral hatchment had
> stopped some great improvements in the bravest mansion. Life and death
> went hand in hand; wealth and poverty stood side by side; repletion and
> starvation laid them down together.[88]

For the outer suburbs there are different images:

> They were in a neighbourhood which looked like a toy neighbourhood
> taken in blocks out of a box by a child of particularly incoherent mind, and
> set up anyhow; here, one side of a new street, there, a large solitary public
> house facing nowhere; here, another unfinished street already in ruins;
> there a church; here an immense new ware-house; there a dilapidated old
> country villa.[89]

No other nineteenth-century writer could describe so well the indeterminate tracts of countryside that were neither urban nor rural, tracts that have become a characteristic feature of twentieth-century landscapes:

> The neighbourhood in which it stands has as little of the country to recommend, as it has of the town. It is neither town nor country. The former, like the giant in his riding boots, has made a stride and passed it, and has set his brick-and-mortar heel a long way in advance; but the intermediate space between the giant's feet, as yet, is only blighted country, and not town.[90]

The real country meant different things to Dickens in different novels: a paradise of security in *Oliver Twist* with its 'jessamine honeysuckle'; in *Little Dorrit,* a closeness to heaven that is, in the last resort, not close enough. Arthur Clennam could feel 'that sense of peace, and of being lightened of a weight of care, which the country awakens in the breasts of dwellers in towns',[91] but the only real escape from 'the contradictions, vacillations, inconsistencies, the little peevish perplexities of this ignorant life', was the escape identified by Baudelaire – death. Then, however, there could be a transcendence.

> The beauties of the sunset had not faded from the long films of cloud that lay at peace on the horizon. From a radiant centre over the whole length and breadth of the tranquil firmament, great shoots of light streamed among the early stars like signs of the blessed later covenant of peace and hope that changed the crown of thorns into a glory.[92]

There are so many facets of Dickens that it is difficult to turn easily from a passage of this kind – and they are to be found in almost every chapter of *The Old Curiosity Shop* as early as 1841 – to the practical writings and speeches about the immediate, urgent, and often intractable problems of the growing nineteenth-century city as it was. He knew how to appeal to civic pride and to stir rich men after dinner. Yet the theme of public health, which to many other reformers was associated with 'getting behind Fate' through the introduction of more effective machinery of social control,[93] was directly related by Dickens to the drama of individual retribution and redemption. In *Bleak House* the filth of Tom-all-Alone's affects everyone, rich and poor, devoted and indifferent alike:

> There is not an atom of Tom's slime, not a cubic inch of any pestilential gas in which he lives, not one obscenity or degradation about him, not an

ignorance, not a wickedness, not a brutality of his committing, but shall work its retribution, through every order of society, up to the proudest of the proud and to the highest of the high. Verily, what with tainting, plundering, and spoiling, Tom has his revenge.[94]

This passage was written after the passing of the first English Public Health Act of 1848. One year after the publication of *Bleak House*, however, the General Board of Health set up under the Act was dissolved. Throughout Dickens' lifetime the health problems of London were never fully solved, and writers of a new generation, such as William Morris, following in the footsteps of John Ruskin, were to project their dreams of a clean London far outside the nineteenth century. It was in Utopia that Morris saw the London scene transformed:

The soap-works with their smoke-vomiting chimneys were gone; the engineer's works gone; the lead works gone; and no sound of riveting and hammering came down the west wind ... Both shores had a line of very pretty houses and there was a continuous garden in front of them.[95]

Although Humphry House was right to point out that it was in London, the London of his own times, that the pulse of Dickens must be taken,[96] Dickens was nevertheless interested in other cities, too. When he visited Paris in 1847 he wrote of 'wandering into hospitals, prisons [prisons were always a *must* in Dickens itineraries], dead-houses, operas, theatres, concert-rooms, burial grounds, palaces, and wine-shops ... Every description of gaudy and ghastly sight has been passing before me in rapid panorama.'[97] When he visited the United States he wrote memorable accounts of each of the great cities he visited, sometimes finding the perfect phrases, as in his description of Washington:

It is sometimes called a City of Magnificent Distances, but it might with greater propriety be called the City of Magnificent Intentions; for it is only on taking a bird's eye view of it from the top of the Capitol that one can at all comprehend the vast designs of its projector.[98]

Finally, in *Hard Times* (1854), he painted a picture of a new industrial city, Coketown, with such powerful strokes of the brush that the name 'Coketown' was chosen by Mumford as the symbolic name of all new nineteenth-century industrial cities, whatever the aliases behind which they masqueraded.[99]

It was a town of red brick, or of brick that would have been red if the smoke and ashes had allowed it; but as matters stood it was a town of unnatural red and black like the painted face of a savage. It was a town of machinery and tall chimneys, out of which interminable serpents of smoke trailed themselves for ever and ever, and never got uncoiled. It had a black canal in it, and a river that ran purple with ill-smelling dye, and vast piles of buildings full of windows where there was a rattling and a trembling all day long, and many small streets all very like one another, inhabited by people equally like one another, who all went in and out at the same hours, with the same sound upon the same pavements, to do the same work, and to whom every day was the same day as yesterday and tomorrow, and every year the counterpart of the last and next.[100]

Although Dickens thought of Coketown as 'a triumph of fact', a critic writing from a twentieth-century vantage point must regard his version of Coketown rather as a triumph of fancy. Dickens did not know this new kind of industrial community (described by a different writer as 'a system of life constructed on a wholly new principle'[101]) as well as he knew London. Not long before writing *Hard Times* he had described a factory as 'a grand machine in its organization' in which 'the men, the fingers, and the iron and steel, all work together for one common end';[102] but in the novel itself he had to deal not with the common end but with the implications of industrial conflict. He had touched on similar themes in *The Old Curiosity Shop*, where there were passages which anticipated what A. O. J. Cockshut has called 'a new pastoral tradition ... in which the Industrial Revolution can really share':

They walked on across the fields and down the shady lanes, sometimes getting over a fragment of a fence so rotten that it dropped at a touch of the foot, sometimes passing near a wreck of bricks and beams overgrown with grass, marking the site of deserted works. They followed paths and tracks, however slight. Mounds where the grass was rank and high, and where brambles, dockweed, and such like vegetation, were confusedly heaped together, they always avoided: for dismal stories were told in that country of the old pits hidden beneath such indications.[103]

In some ways Mrs Gaskell understood more of the tang of the new industrial North, country and town, than Dickens did, but in novels such as *Mary Barton* (1848) and *North and South* (1855) it is clear that her understanding, if not her sympathy, was limited by the facts of her own social position. She could write skilfully about working-men, the new products of an industrial society, but she could not fully comprehend their thoughts and feelings. There are no outstanding nineteenth-century novels in Britain that deal convincingly with industrial-isation from the inside, from the standpoint of the industrial worker himself; and, as Raymond Williams has noted perceptively, even when sympathy was present, it was often transformed, 'not into action, but into withdrawal.'[104] For the *critique* of industrialism we have to turn to Ruskin, to Morris and to the writers of socialist essays and poems during the late Victorian revolt of the last decades of the century.

In the meantime, George Gissing and the young H. G. Wells made the most of London. Gissing was a great admirer of Dickens, about whom he wrote an illuminating biographical study, but he pointedly contrasted Dickens' desire to please as many of his readers as possible with his own unflinching determination to tell the truth whatever the cost. He collected as many facts about London as Zola collected about Paris, and wrote sensitively, often painfully, about both its inner core and its outer suburbs, where 'bits of wayside hedges still shivered in fog and wind'. Wells got nearer than any other British writer to having a theory of London. It was set out most fully in *Tono-Bungay* (1909), where George Ponderovo thinks he can discern 'lines of an ordered structure' out of which the confusion of London has grown and can 'detect a process that is something more than confusion of casual accidents, though indeed it may be no more than a process of disease'.[105] At the end of what many of his contemporaries called 'this wonderful century'[106] Wells was as critical of the course of past progress as Morris. Indeed, in *The New Machiavelli* (1911) he dismissed the whole Victorian epoch as 'a hasty trial experiment, a gigantic experiment of the most slovenly and wasteful kind'. 'Will any one, a hundred years from now', he asked, 'consent to live in the houses the Victorians built, travel by their roads or railways, value the furnishings they made to live among or esteem, except for serious or historical reasons, their prevalent art and the clipped and limited literature which satisfied their souls?'[107]

By then there were many new voices, outside even more than inside Britain. In Britain itself, D. H. Lawrence had almost the last word. 'The English are town-birds through and through, today, as the inevitable result of their complete industrialization. Yet they don't know how to build a city, how to think of one, or how to live in one.'[108] Henry James, by contrast, could be invincibly matter-of-fact. 'When a social product is so vast and various', he said of London, 'it may be approached on a thousand different sides, and liked and disliked for a thousand different reasons.'[109]

NOTES

1   R. Vaughan, *The Age of the Great Cities* (1843); B. Disraeli, *Coningsby* (1844). See also, for the beginnings of this literature, T. Chalmers, *On the Christian and Civic Economy of Large Towns* (1821-6).

2   A. F. Weber, *The Growth of Cities* (1899); P. Meuriot, *Des agglomérations urbaines* (1897).

3   See, for example, M. and L. White, *The Intellectual versus the City: from Thomas Jefferson to Frank Lloyd Wright* (1962); K. Bergmann, *Agrarromantik und Grosstadtfeindschaft* (1970); and R. Williams, *The Country and the City* (1973).

4   See R. E. Park, E. W. Burgess and R. D. MacKenzie, *The City* (1926); D. Read, *Press and People* (London 1961).

5   K. Davis, 'The Origin and Growth of Urbanization in the World', *American Journal of Sociology*, vol. IX (1955); P. Hauser and L. Schnore (eds), *The Study of Urbanization* (1965).

6   See F. M. Jones, 'The Aesthetic of the Nineteenth-Century Industrial Town', in H. J. Dyos (ed.), *The Study of Urban History* (1968); W. Z. Hirsch (ed.), *Urban Life and Form* (1967); K. Lynch, *The Image of the City* (1960); A. L. Strauss (ed.), *The American City, a Sourcebook of Urban Imagery* (1968), and *Images of the American City* (1961).

7   R. Kipling, 'How I Struck Chicago and How Chicago Struck Me', *From Sea to Sea* (1914), pp. 230-48.

8   See B. L. Pierce, *As Others See Chicago* (1933).

9   For London see, for example, D. M. Low (ed.), *London is London* (1949). For New York, see B. Still, *Mirror for Gotham* (1956).

10 Quoted in A. Briggs, *Victorian Cities* (1968), p. 56.

11 ibid., p. 93.

12 J. J. Rousseau, *Émile, ou de l'education* (1854 edn), Book I, p. 36.

13 See H. N. Brailsford, *Voltaire* (1935).

14 William Blake, *Songs of Experience* (1793). Cp. P. Egan, *Life in London* (1821).

15 R. Williams, *The Long Revolution* (1961). See also his earlier study, *Culture and Society* (1958).

16 N. Frye, 'The Critical Path. An Essay on the Social Context of Literary Criticism', *Daedalus* (1969).

17 A. M. Schlesinger, *The Rise of the City* (1933), pp. 76, 79. See also his essay on 'The City in American Civilization', in *Paths to the Present* (1949); B. McKelvey, *The Urbanization of America* (1967); C. N. Glaab (ed.), *The American City. A Documentary History* (1963).

18 H. N. Smith, *Virgin Lane* (1950); R. Hofstadter, *The Age of Reform* (1962); L. Marx, *The Machine in the Garden* (1964).

19 Marx, *op. cit.*, p. 6.

20 Quoted ibid., p. 125. For the echoes, see Briggs, *Victorian Cities*, pp. 80 ff.

21 Marx, *op. cit.*, pp. 31 f.

22 W. Whitman, *Passage to India*, VII, 171 ff. (Published with *Leaves of Grass*, 1871.)

23 H. James, *English Hours*, A.L. Lowe (ed.) (1960), p.10.
24 Quoted in A. Briggs, *Victoria People* (1954), p.76.
25 See above, vol. I, pp.90ff.
26 E. Zola, *Paris*, trans. by F.A. Vizetelly (1898), pp.xi and xiii f.
27 C.Campos, *The View of France* (1965), p.6.
28 *Journal des débats* (Paris), 8 February 1843.
29 London Statistical Society, *Fourth Annual Report* (1838), Cp. the *Tenth Annual Report* (1844): 'The pursuit of statistical enquiries has already made such progress ... as henceforth to be a necessity of the age, and one of its most honourable characteristics.'
30 For the background, see the Introduction by M. W. Flinn to his edition of *The Sanitary Condition of the Labouring Population of Great Britain* (1965).
31 See below, p.56. Cp. C. Kingsley, 'Great Cities and their Influence for Good and Evil' (1857).
32 For the term and its historical significance, see L. Chevalier, *Classes laborieuses et classes dangereuses à Paris* (1958). A good contemporary account of the parallel group in the United States is in C. L.Brace, *The Dangerous Classes of New York* (1872).
33 Quoted in L.James, *Fiction for the Working Man* (1963), p.143.
34 H.Heine, *Französische Zustände* (1832).
35 J.Neré, 'The French Republic', *The New Cambridge Modern History*, vol. XI, F. H.Hinsley (ed.) (1962), p.322.
36 Oliver Wendell Holmes made the remark famous by quoting it in *The Autocrat of the Breakfast Table* (1858), Chapter 6.
37 F. Harrison, 'Historic Paris', reprinted in *Thoughts and Memories* (1926), p.331. See also E. Levasseur, *La population française* (1891), pp.397-407.
38 See Georg Lukács, *Studies in European Realism*, E. Bone (trans.) (1950), p.85.
39 See V.Klotz, *Die erzählte Stadt* (1969).
40 C. F.Schorske, 'The Idea of the City in European Thought: Voltaire to Spengler', in O. Handlin and J. Burchard (eds), *The Historian and the City* (1963), p.23.
41 Martin Turnell, *Baudelaire, a Study in his Poetry* (1953), p.193.
42 A. M.Boase, *The Poetry of France*, vol. III (1964), p.1xv.
43 See Harry Levin, *James Joyce* (1960), p.23.
44 Matthew Arnold, 'Lines Written in Kensington Gardens' (1852). Arnold never referred to Baudelaire, although he professed himself interested in French literature.
45 Rainer Maria Rilke, *Das Buch von der Armut and vom Tode* (1903). In his diatribe *Degeneration* (1895), Max Nordau had written of cities robbing even the richest citizens of their 'vital powers'.
46 J. J.Sheehan, 'Liberalism and the City in 19th-Century Germany', *Past and Present*, no. 51 (1971).
47 For population movements, see R. Heberle and R. Meyer, *Die Grossstädte im Strome der Dinnewanderung* (1937), and R. Hartog, *Stadterweiterungen im 19 Jahrhundert* (1962).

48   H. Holborn, *A History of Modern Germany*, 1840-1945 (1969), p. 370.
      See also T. S. Hamerow, *The Social Foundations of German Unification*
      (1969).
49   R. Heberle, 'Ferdinand Tönnies' Contributions to the Sociology of
      Political Parties', *American Journal of Sociology*, vol. LXI (1955);
      E. G. Jaccoby, 'Ferdinand Tönnies: a centennial Tribute', *Kyklos*, vol.
      8 (1955).
50   G. Rümelin, 'Stadt und Land', *Reden und Aufsätze*, vol. I (1875).
51   There are some notable exceptions in the works of Wilhelm Raabe, for
      instance in his *Pfisters Mühle* (1884) (*Pfister's Mill*), where the idyllic
      waters of an old millstream are polluted by industrial effluvia; but in
      this, as in many other stories, the focus of contrast between past and
      present is in personal reminiscence and nostalgia.
52   N. Fuerst, *The Victorian Age of German Literature* (1966), p. 118.
53   See R. Dahrendorf, *Society and Democracy in Germany* (1968).
54   For such writing, see G. L. Mosse, *The Crisis of German Ideology* (1966).
55   J. G. Fichte, *Reden an die deutsche Nation* (1921), pp. 125 ff.
56   Quoted in Fuerst, *op. cit.*, p. 66.
57   ibid., p. 65.
58   ibid., p. 73.
59   See K. Ziegler, 'Die Berliner Gesellschaft und die Literature', in
      H. Rothfels (ed.), *Berlin in Vergangenheit und Gegenwart* (1961).
60   Letter of 9 May 1888 to his son Theodor.
61   *Frau Jenny Treibel*, Chapter VII.
62   C. Schorske, 'The Transformation of the Garden: Ideal and Society in
      Austrian Literature', *American Historical Review*, vol. LXXII (1967).
63   Ferdinand von Saar, *Gedichte* (1904), p. 247.
64   Ferdinand von Saar, *Sämtliche Werke*, vol. III (1909), p. 77.
65   Georg Trakl, 'An die Verstummten' (1913), *Dichtungen* (1917).
66   See, for example, 'In der Heimat' (1913), and 'Im Dorf' (1913).
67   Schorske, *op. cit.*, *Amer. Hist. Rev.* See also his *Fin de Siècle Vienna*
      (1961).
68   Quoted in Briggs, *Victorian Cities*, p. 75. London itself had a powerful
      influence on the international movement to create parks. See G. F.
      Chadwick, *The Park and the Town* (1966).
69   Quoted in Briggs, ibid., p. 311. For London, see Chapter 8 of this book
      et passim.
70   Letter to Thomas Manning, 28 November 1800, quoted in R. W.
      King (ed.), *England from Wordsworth to Dickens* (1928), p. 151. See also
      Lamb's article for *The Londoner*, first published in 1802. 'I was born, as
      you have heard, in a crowd. This has begot in me an entire affection for
      that way of life, amounting to an almost insurmountable aversion from
      solitude and rural scenes.' 'The very deformities of London', he went
      on, 'which give distaste to others, from habit do not displease me.'
      (Quoted in G. Gordon (ed.), *Charles Lamb* (1921), pp. 75 f.)
71   See *I Was There, the Memoirs of H. S. Tremenheere* (1965).
72   It was used, for example, by W. E. Channing, the Unitarian preacher,
      in Boston in 1841: 'A Discourse on the Life and Character of the Rev.

Joseph Tuckerman'. For the expression of similar ideas in the city of Liverpool, the link city between Britain and the United States and Britain and Ireland, see M.B.Simey, *Charitable Effort in Liverpool in the Nineteenth Century* (1951).

73   Charles Booth, *Life and Labour of the People of London*, 17 vols. (1889-1903). See also T. S. and M. B.Simey, *Charles Booth* (1960).

74   See E. P.Thompson and E. Yeo, *The Unknown Mayhew* (1971) for a recent assessment.

75   Quoted in Briggs, *Victorian Cities*, p. 313.

76   ibid., p. 12. For the various nineteenth-century influences on Mumford, see his bibliographies in *The Culture of Cities* (1938), and *The City in History* (1961).

77   The theme is developed in Morton and Lucia White, *The Intellectual Versus the City: from Thomas Jefferson to Frank Lloyd Wright* (1962), and in Morton White, 'Two Stages in the Critique of the American City', in Handlin and Burchard, *op. cit.*, pp. 84 ff.

78   Charles Booth, *op. cit.*, vol. III (1892), p. 75.

79   Charles Dickens, *The Pickwick Papers* (1837), Chapter 21.

80   ibid., Chapter 7.

81   Charles Dickens, *Memorandum Book* (1855-65), quoted in J. Hillis Miller, *Charles Dickens, the World of his Novels* (1958), p. xv.

82   See Turnell, *op. cit.*, p. 193.

83   Hillis Miller, *op. cit.*, p. 163.

84   See H. House, *The Dickens World* (1941), pp. 12-14, 147.

85   Charles Dickens, *Oliver Twist* (1838), Chapter 46.

86   Charles Dickens, *Our Mutual Friend* (1865), Chapter 15. Cp. *Household Words*, 11 October 1851, for the disappearance of 'our school'.

87   Kathleen Tillotson, *Novels of the Eighteen-Forties* (1954), p. 200.

88   Charles Dickens, *Nicholas Nickleby* (1839), Chapter 32.

89   Charles Dickens, *Our Mutual Friend* (1865), Book II, Chapter 1.

90   Charles Dickens, *Dombey and Son* (1848), Chapter 33.

91   Charles Dickens, *Little Dorrit* (1857), Book I, Chapter 28. Note also in this novel the unforgettable account of a Sunday evening in London (Book I, Chapter 3). For a recent study of Dickens and the city that concentrates on 'death' as a unifying theme, see A. Welsh, *The City of Dickens* (1971).

92   ibid., Book III, Chapter 31.

93   See, for example, B. W.Richardson, *The Health of Nations*, 2 vols (1897) and below, p. 150.

94   Charles Dickens, *Bleak House* (1853), Chapter 46. Throughout this novel Dickens emphasises how city characters of all types were being trapped in an apparently impersonal system. For examples of his interest in public health outside his novels, see *All the Year Round* vol. IV (1860), pp. 29-31; vol. V (1861), pp. 390-4, 423-7, 453-6, 470-3 and 486-9; also K. J.Fielding (ed.), *The Speeches of Charles Dickens* (1960), pp. 127-32; and House, *op. cit.*, pp. 194-9.

95   William Morris, *News from Nowhere* (1891), Chapter 2.

96   House, *op. cit.*, p. 146.

97 See U. Pope-Hennessy, *Charles Dickens* (1945), Chapter 22.
98 Charles Dickens, *American Notes* (1842), Chapter 8.
99 Mumford, *The City in History*, Chapter 15, 'Paleotechnic Paradise, Coketown?'
100 Charles Dickens, *Hard Times* (1854), Chapter V.
101 *Bentley's Miscellany*, vol. VII (1840).
102 *Household Words*, 5 February 1853.
103 A. O. J. Cockshut, *The Imagination of Charles Dickens* (1961), pp. 141 ff.
104 Williams, *Culture and Society*, p. 119.
105 See Briggs, *Victorian Cities*, pp. 343-55, for a fuller account of the significance of Gissing and Wells in this context.
106 See, for example, A. R. Wallace, *The Wonderful Century* (1898).
107 H. G. Wells, *Experiment in Autobiography*, vol. I (1934), p. 277. For his forecast of 'coming cities', very different from the old, see his *Anticipations* (1901).
108 D. H. Lawrence, 'Nottingham and the Mining Countryside', *Adelphi* (June-August 1934); *Phoenix* (1936), p. 139.
109 Henry James, *op. cit.*, Chapter 1.

2   Ebenezer Elliott,
The Corn Law Rhymer

In 1949 Basil Willey suggested that the whole course of English thought and letters in the nineteenth century would have been different if this island had not contained the 'mountain paradise' of Westmoreland and Cumberland. 'The Lake District was part of its religious creed.'[1] If so, the new industrial towns, not very far away, were certainly part of its plain economic facts. To set the dirt and clamour of industrial Sheffield against the freedom and quiet of Wordsworth's Grasmere, and the news of 'bread at three half-pence a mouthful' against 'the authentic tidings of invisible things' is merely to introduce the two familiar sides of early nineteenth-century England. Neither was complete without the other, and it was Robert Southey, who knew something of both, who did much to introduce Ebenezer Elliott, the Sheffield poet, to the literary world.[2] They first corresponded in 1808, when Southey wrote of Elliott's 'couplets' that they had 'great point and vigour', although they did not meet until 1823.

Elliott was born in 1781 at the New Foundry, Rotherham, but when he wrote his first poems, foundries played little part in them: indeed, if they had done, Southey would never have read them. His father was a Radical, whose parlour was adorned with portraits of Cromwell and Washington.[3] Elliott's pretensions were then 'gothick' rather than economic or political. 'The Vernal Walk' (1798), printed at Cambridge,[4] contained, in his own words, 'some poetry stolen from Ossian and Thomson' and some theology stolen from his schoolmaster. It was the first of a series of Romantic poems, many of them dealing with ballad themes and telling, like the appropriately named *Rejected's Song*, of young brides, murdered sisters, newly-born babes, age-bent strangers, sailor husbands and grey Yorkshire ghosts.

The Elliott of these poems might never have been remembered at all, or at best he would have taken his place with a host of forgotten local poets, whose work is only interesting when it touches their own experience or throws light on their social background. As Southey wrote in a critical article, the early volumes, 'which continued "no political seasoning"', were carried to a market overstocked with poetry'.[5] Elliott was peeved by their reception, and talked of the monthly

reviewers as 'the men-milliners of literature'.[6] He used the language of
the foundry too, and spoke of his feelings being 'hammered until they
have become cold-short'.

Fortunately for the young poet, not only were fashions changing,
but so also was the whole economy. Southey, with his fear of industry,
became outdated, while Elliott became the poet of economic revolution. 'I claim to be a pioneer', Elliott wrote, 'of the greatest, the most
beneficial, the only crimeless Revolution, which man has yet seen. I
also claim to be the poet of that Revolution – the Bard of Freetrade;
and through the prosperity, wisdom and loving-kindness which Freetrade will ultimately bring, the Bard of Universal Peace.'[7] The second
stage of his evolution as a poet produced no more success than the
first, although he was influenced now by George Crabbe and his *The
Village Patriarch* (1829) included Sheffield characters and scenes, with
lines like

> There draws the Grinder his laborious breath;
> There, coughing, at his deadly trade he bends.
> Born to die young, he fears not man nor death.

It is this conscious identification of Elliott with an age of change
which makes him so interesting to the social historian, for although
there were many politicians and prophets, essayists and experts who
claimed to have caught the spirit of their age and helped to direct it,
there were few poets. Elliott gloried in his preoccupation with the
workaday world.

> If my composition smells of the workshop and the dingy warehouse I
> cannot help it; soot is soot; and he who lives in a chimney will do well to
> take the air when he can, and ruralize now and then even in imagination.
> But we are cursed with evils infinitely worse than a sooty atmosphere. We
> are bread-taxed ... Should we not be better off without agriculture
> altogether than bread-taxed as we are?[8]

It is as of much interest to trace the inspiration which turned Elliott
from a 'gothick' imitator into a social poet as it is to trace the
influences which turned Southey from a Radical into a conservative.[9]
In both cases the transformation was complete. In the later stages of
his life Elliott delighted in adding the letters C.L.R. (Corn Law
Rhymer) to his name, and even had a seal made combining these
initials with his own. It is of interest also to note the response which
his new political poetry secured from his contemporaries, for of this
self-styled 'Bard of Revolution', W. S. Landor wrote:

> I may not live to hear another voice,

> Elliott, of power, to penetrate, as thine
> Dense multitudes.[10]

These were the dense and unordered multitudes which made Southey afraid; and although Southey could tap depths never reached by Elliott, it was Elliott, not Southey, who reached a huge public.

I

The clue both to Elliott's poetry and to his message is to be found in his life. He was often depicted as a 'red son of the furnace', a poor man writing for poor men, and most of the literary notices of his *Corn Law Rhymes*, which first appeared in 1830, emphasised his humble provincial background and his work in the forge. Thus, writing in the *Edinburgh Review*, Thomas Carlyle welcomed formally and officially 'the intelligible voice from the hitherto Mute and Irrational, to tell us at first hand how it is with him, what in very deed is the theorem of the world and of himself, which he in those dim depths of his, in that wearied head of his has put together.'[11] Elliott had given Carlyle some encouragement for this characteristic salutation, for he had described himself in his preface as 'one of the lower, little removed from the lowest class'. Yet Elliott was the son of a small ironfounder, not a wage earner, and although as a young man he had worked for a pittance before becoming a partner, he stands out, therefore, more as a representative example of Smiles' *Self-Help* [12] than of the deep silence of working-class aquiescence suddenly bubbling over at the surface. His real villain was the drone, his gospel the gospel of work:

> Idler, why lie down to die?
> Better rub than rust.

He knew poverty for a time but he attributed it to the operation of the Corn Laws – and was able to raise money from his wife's relatives, and to begin business on his own account in the iron trade in Sheffield. The peak of his prosperity came in 1837, when he later claimed he ought to have retired, but he was able to abandon commerce in 1842 with £6000 and a little country house at Hargate 'on the edge of a common, an expanse of turf and bracken, where ponies grazed, and occasional gypsy smoke ascended'.[13] His approach to the working classes was dictated by his own more comfortable position in life. A more characteristic example of an artisan poet of this period was John Nicholson, the Airedale poet, who revealed none of Smiles' virtues, and ended his life abruptly by walking into a canal on a dark night.

A visitor to Sheffield described Elliott as 'a burly ironmonger ... eulogizing American republicanism and denouncing British aristocracy'; and although he was an ironmonger with a difference, for there was a bust of Shakespeare in his warehouse and casts of Achilles, Ajax and Napoleon in his office, their presence would have delighted Smiles rather than shocked him. Smiles would have been delighted, too, by Elliott's vigorous championship of competition, 'the great social law of God', and his attack on socialism.

One day, when walking with a socialist, the poet saw a number of willow trees in a meadow all recently cut into one uniform state. 'Behold a society of ready-made Socialists,' he exclaimed.[14] In *Bully Idle's Prayer*, he described his hero praying,

> Lord, send us weeks of Sundays,
> A Saint's Day, every day;
> Shirts gratis, ditto breeches,
> No work and double pay.

Communism – and he confronted the term – involved either idleness or theft, and both were equally abhorrent to him:

> What is a Communist? One who hath yearning
> For equal division of unequal earnings:
> Idler, or burglar, or both, he is willing
> To fork out his penny, and pocket your shilling.

Not surprisingly, he refused to have anything to do with the Sheffield Regeneration Society, founded in 1834 by followers of Robert Owen, and he published one letter addressed to Owen himself in the same year seeking either to 'convert him or contradict him'.[15]

There was a bottom, therefore, not only to Elliott's thought but also to his revolutionary fervour. When he claimed that he was more proud of the name 'Rhymer of the Revolution' than he would have been if he had been made Poet Laureate, it was of the English 'Revolution' of 1846 and not of the French Revolution of 1848 that he was thinking. He always stopped short.

His religious views were more vague than his political opinions:

> 'Till earth is like the countenance of God.
> This is Religion!' saith the Bard of Trade.

Yet Ebenezer's father was a Calvinist Dissenter, and two of his sons – two of a family of thirteen – became clergymen of the Church of England. The political message Ebenezer preached was fiery enough, but it was the fire of *'Freetrade'* (he spelt it all as one word, without a hyphen, and even gave it a capital letter) which warmed him, and not the fire of 'Socialism' or of militant Chartism.

His own experiences taught him his politics, and his message was severely practical. 'Whilst the Corn Laws existed and Labour Famine went hand in hand together, he had no time for the dainty speculations of philosophy.' Consequently he had little concern for any version of abstract politics. He struggled hard for the Reform Bill of 1832, because he believed that it would more speedily secure the repeal of the Corn Laws by giving adequate representation to industry and commerce, and hoped that after its passing there would be a continuing pressure for reform: for this reason he was in touch with Francis Place in London. He went on also to support the drawing up of the People's Charter in 1838 and attended the Chartist Convention in 1838.

Elliott was less interested in universal suffrage than in Corn Law repeal, however: I am for your Charter, but I am not for being starved to death first.' As early as 1839, indeed, he broke away from the Chartist movement, criticising its leaders both for 'wild' talk and for their appeals to physical force.[16] He had been happy so long as the middle classes and working classes cooperated, as they did more easily in Sheffield, he thought, since there were fewer signs in that city of 'that marked line of difference ... between rich man and poor man, which is becoming annually more observable in other places'.[17] 'But then came Feargus, and his blarney; trades-unionism, fierce in its imitative glory; and chartism with its stone blind selfishness; all fighting for the enemy! Wisehead, at last, was born of Empty-Pocket, in a respectable neighbourhood; and from that moment Monopoly began to tremble.'[18] There was now a need, of course, to include the Whigs among the enemy, and in 1842 he attacked them in 'contemptuous and not very polite language'. They were men 'who could once have saved the State, and would not ... Their time is past.'[19] He added that he still had 'the remains of a forlorn hope in the Tories. Peel, I have long thought, understands our position, and will do his best to prevent the coming catastrophe, but he wants moral courage.'[20]

Cobden was Elliott's ideal, 'our "Man of Men", doing the work of ten'; and his hopes were pinned on free trade as Cobden's were, not merely because of its economic importance, but because it provided social solace, the inspiration of a crusade and the hope of a millennium. 'I look to Cobden as the Leader of the Advance Body Guard of Man.'[21] It was because of this hope that Elliott worked closely with the Quaker Joseph Sturge in the Complete Suffrage movement which attempted to bring together middle-class Radical repealers and Chartists in 1842.[22] He was on friendly terms also with W. J. Fox, Unitarian editor of the *Monthly Repository* and Anti-Corn Law League lecturer.

For a short period in history, there seemed to be both poetry and revolution in the English middle classes and their aspirations, and Elliott was not long in finding poetry in new industrial marvels like steam.[23] *Steam at Sheffield* discovers 'glorious harmony in this tempestuous music of the giant, Steam'. The poet writes that he 'loves the thunder of machinery', and in *Steam in the Desert* he asks:

> Steam! – if the nations grow not old ...
> Why dost not thou thy banner shake
> O'er sealess, streamless lands, and make
> One nation of mankind?

The heroes of steam-power are praised from the 'thoughtful engineer, the soul of all this motion' to the great 'pioneers of invention'.

> Burns toil'd, but Crompton (better still)
> Toil'd, and created might.[24]

There is a complete contrast between such panegyrics and the polemic of Chartists like Ernest Jones who thought of 'King Steam' as a Moloch:

> A giant had risen, all grisly and grim,
> With his huge limbs loud-clattering and vast!
> And he breathed his steam-breath through long channels
>   of death
> Till the soul itself died in the blast.

While Jones dwelt on exploitation and imminent social revolution, Elliott looked forward to further inventions in the future, and quoted Hazlitt with approval concerning 'the great world of electricity', which 'lies all undiscovered before us, like America, asleep for centuries'.

Yet for Elliott, optimism rested on ensuring that the structure of politics would conform to the requirements of an expanding industrial age. He poked fun at those who wished once more to 'plough over Sheffield town' and sow it with rye. If the same advances could be made in politics as had already been made in industrial technique, men could anticipate a golden age of confident achievement. This too deserved its prophetic poetry. Introducing one of his lyrics, set to the music of *Rule Britannia*, he claimed that he wrote it 'that it might be granted to me to popularize, at least in one tune, the heavenly principle which seems to epitomize Christianity itself, that free exchange of blessed equivalents is the secret of all useful progress'.[25]

Free trade was more than an argument. It was a dogma. Not surprisingly, therefore, Elliott's best, or at least his most dazzling, writing, is in the form of hymns. However vague his personal religious views might be, he had no doubts about the essentials of the Cobdenite credo. He dedicated *The Splendid Village* (1833) to Colonel Perronet Thompson, the author of the famous *Catechism of the Corn Laws*, 'who next after Bentham has by his writings done more good for mankind, than any man since Adam Smith'.[26] He wrote in *The Recording Angel* of a final retribution:

> King of Dear Corn! the dead have heard that name;
> They come.

Elliott's poems sprang from his own intense dissatisfaction with the England that was and from his confident hope that in the future it could change through middle-class action. 'Only in a sinking land, a land of taxation without representation, of castes and corn hills, of degradation, want and misery ... where destruction grows like a weed, and where capital and skill alike are profitless, could such a poem as *The Splendid Village* have been written or conceived,' he explained.[27] If his verse had been inspired by such unconventional muses, the fault rested with the landlord, and not with himself or with 'the rabble'.

It was the attack on the landlord which gave revolutionary fervour to Elliott's verse. Landlords were described as 'palaced worms', 'deaf reptiles', as at best 'amiable robbers'. 'If devils were lords in England, could they do more than tax our bread?' 'Havoc's torch' began to glow when men began to realise:

> Ye coop us up and tax our bread,
> And wonder why we pine;
> But ye are fat and round and red,
> And fill'd with tax-bought wine.
> Thus three rats starve while three rats thrive,
> (Like you on mine and me),
> When fifteen rats are caged alive,
> With food for nine and three.

The *Corn Law Rhymes* were full of passages like this, which introduced allegorical characters like 'The Titled Scoundrel' and 'The Mitred Priest', but alongside them were passages designed to tear pity out of the reader by a direct appeal to the heart:

> Child, is thy father dead?
> Father is gone!
> Why did they tax his bread?
> God's will be done ...

In both vituperation and pathos, Elliott was essentially direct and simple. He stole the emotional fervour of working-class as well as middle-class reformers and enlisted it in the cause of Corn Law repeal. Henry Dunckley, in his *Charter of the Nations*, an essay on free trade and its results, to which the Council of the National Anti-Corn Law League awarded its first prize after the struggles were over, described how 'even poetry' lent its aid to the movement for reform. 'The flashes of terrific ire which broke through the rugged verse of the Anti-Corn Law Rhymer, carried illumination to minds beyond the reach of logic, or kindled into burning sentiment the knowledge which reading and sad experience had accumulated in the bosoms of thousands.'[28]

II

Elliott's personality might have been more representative of the small industrialist than the skilled mechanic, but his poetry was always calculated to appeal to the working classes. His *Corn Law Rhymes* were written and published in 1830 in a cheap edition by order of the Sheffield Mechanics' Anti-Bread Tax Society. It only cost 9d, while of his earlier works, *Peter Faultless* cost 6s, and *Night* 7s 6d. At the time of printing, as he himself said, he could not find one respectable shop-keeper who thought the Corn Laws an evil.

> The merchants, to a man, thought them beneficial. Exactly in proportion to the plunder-power exercised on his fortunes by the aristocracy, did the would-be Squire idolize his destroyers; and I had discussed the question ten years in all ways – by speech and writing, in prose and verse – before I made my first Sheffield convert of the mercantile class.[29]

It was on the poorer sections of the community, therefore, that the *Rhymes* had most effect. 'I read the poems over', wrote a South Yorkshire artisan,

> one after another, first to myself, and then to my wife and children. As the subjects were chiefly suffering poverty, of which we had been and still were, large partakers, they suited us amazingly ... An honest-hearted old collier, worn out with a life of hard work, and who was then a pauper, and frequented my little shop as a place for pastime, wept again and again as I read the passages to them.[30]

Southey, who believed that the *Corn Law Rhymes* were inspired by the 'Demon of Anarchy', was justified in saying that when Elliott was 'possessed by Radicalism, God forbid that there should be many who in such a spirit should write so well!'

The appeal of the poems was enhanced by the fact that many of them were set to familiar tunes, like *Robin Adair, Ye Banks and Braes, Rule Britannia* and even *God Save the Queen*. Elliott would sometimes read them in public at meetings and demonstrations, rather in the same way as Mayakovsky would read to mass audiences in the post-Revolution Russia of the 1920s, but he was not an impressive orator. 'I am told by my fireside critics that I do not *read* poetry, but sing it to a bad tune ... Why should rhymes be written, if they are not to be made sensible to the ear?'[31]

Community singing of his works often hid their crudities of expression, as in the case of his famous *People's Anthem*, written specially for music, and beginning with the well-known lines

> When wilt thou save the people?
> Oh, God of Mercy, when?

Although this hymn made its way both into the *Congregational Hymnal* and the socialist song-books, it interpreted 'the people' in the very broadest terms. 'Who are the people?' Elliott pertinently asked in a footnote, and replied: 'All those persons who, by honestly maintaining themselves, and perhaps earning a surplus – or by honestly living on the precious earnings and savings of others – prove their right to govern the community through their representatives.'[32]

The definition was important, for although it was true that the main appeal of the *Corn Law Rhymes* as verse to be recited or sung was to the poor, the better-off people could sing the ditties as fervently as their less fortunate brethren on the right occasions. Indeed, Elliott's verses, like the prose writings and poems of Samuel Bamford across the Pennines in Lancashire,[33] were powerful emotional instruments bringing the classes 'together'. Yet there were working men who did not wish to see the classes brought together, and not all working men retained their enthusiasm for corn law repeal in what came to be called 'the hungry forties'.

The shift of the campaign for the repeal of the Corn Laws away from the workshops to the respectable neighbourhoods diminished Elliott's hold on the working classes, and the successful repeal of the Corn Laws in 1846 finally repealed the *Corn Law Rhymes*. Ernest Jones' *Chartist Songs* were written in a different form, and expressed a completely different philosophy. Even as early as 1833, it had been prophesied that once the price of corn fell, Elliott's fame would fall in proportion. When there was a new Corn Law controversy in the early twentieth century, a writer claimed that 'not even the re-enactment of the corn laws could give renewed life to Elliott's songs'.[34] Both the poetry and the revolution had by that time fallen flat.

'Yet a foreign audience survived the early decline of Elliott's popularity in England. In the United States James Russell Lowell had praised 'the poor man's poet' as a 'man of great genius' as early as 1838.[35] So, too, did J. G. Whittier, who maintained that Elliott was to the artisans of England what Burns was to the peasantry of Scotland.[36] Whittier even wrote an obituary eulogy to him.

> Back, puny lordling! darest thou lay
> A hand on Elliott's bier?
> Alive, your rank and pomp, as dust,
> Beneath his feet he trod:
> He knew the locust swarm that cursed
> The harvest-fields of God.[37]

French interest in Elliott was of a rather different kind. L. C. Étienne, writing in the *Revue des Deux Mondes* in 1856, deliberately set Elliott's writing against the writing of the Lakeland poets as a specifically English product of the new industrial towns. 'This is the poetry of Sheffield and Manchester in contrast to the poetry of the Lakes. It is in England, in particular, that there is a poetry of the poor. France is too fond of the ideal in literature for the real to please it in its nakedness.'[38] The medium of fact in France was prose: in England poetry itself was 'nourished on fact', and popular poetry was bound up with 'the history of popular agitations'. There was a gulf, the reviewer went on, between the 'poor man's' poetry of Crabbe and that of Elliot, although in his 1833 Preface to a new edition of *The Village Patriarch*, Elliott had written that he might truly be called 'an unfortunate imitator of Crabbe, that most British of poets; for he has long been bosomed with me: and if he had never lived, it is quite possible that I might never have written pauper-poetry'. For the reviewer the gulf was wide. Crabbe's 'poor man' kept out of politics: Elliott's 'poor man' turned to politics. And religion might encourage the shift of stance. Thus, Miles Gordon, *The Ranter*, denounces oppressive taxation and social inequalities from under a Gospel Tree. Elliott's work, like his life, had struggle as its keynote, and the poor men he described were 'victims' of the Corn Laws only if they refused to act:

> Hail, England of my children! – not this den
> Of vermin, and their victims, nick-nam'd free –
> Isle of the Future! – will thy sons be men
> Or Corn-Law bipeds?

Elliot's poems reveal much private melancholy — he was preoccupied with the thought of death, 'for all must go where no wind blows' – but he never lost his public optimism. He denounced all acquiescence in things as they were. When the Wesleyans were luke-warm in supporting the agitation for the repeal of the Corn Laws, Elliott denounced the Wesleyan Methodist Conference 'as perhaps the most corrupt body of men in the world',[39] and he justified such vituperation with the question, 'Is it strange that my language is as fervent as a welding heat, when my thoughts are passions, that rush burning from my mind, like white-hot bolts of steel?'

Such lively industrial images present Elliott at his most natural and his best. Yet he could fall into cliché and into sentimentality. The real reason why the *poésie des pauvres* could never provide a satisfctory counterbalance to the poetry of the Lakes had nothing to do with uncouthness of expression or coarseness of style. It lay in the in-adequate quality of ideas and feelings in Elliott and all that he stood for. His evident poverty of thought reflected other kinds of poverty, and his self-advertisement was not peculiar to himself: it was part of his age and his class.

III

Elliott could read Wordsworth's ode on the *Intimations of Im-mortality* and find nothing in it, but in one of his own poems he could make Love sing of James Watt, inventor of the steam-engine, as well as of the struggling eighteenth-century poet, Chatterton. He could love a primrose, he said, just because it was a primrose and nothing more. That was all that Nature meant to him. Yet he might have been just as unself-critical when he wrote in this vein as he was when he wrote of working-class politics. He was far removed from Wordsworth in thinking and feeling, but he was drawn to Nature as relentlessly as Wordsworth was. The site of Sheffield had once been one of the most beautiful places in England, and not very far away to the south in the Peak District were hills and streams as beautiful as those in the Lake District. Yet when Cobbett visited it in 1830, he could state simply 'They call it black Sheffield, and black enough it is.'[40] Elliott, who believed that he could find no 'pure unmixed pleasure in Nature', never forgot that industry was new and Nature was there before it. He believed too that man had to refresh himself from its source:

> God blames not him who toils six days in seven,
> Where smoke and dust bedim the golden day,
> If he delight beneath the dome of Heaven
> To hear the wind and see the clouds at play,
> Or climb the hills among the flowers to pray.

In one of his last poems, 'Lyric for my Daughters', he tried to answer the riddle which lay behind all his political meditations:

> Ask not the unreplying tomb
> 'Where are the dead?'
> But ask the hawthorn-bloom
> Returning still ...

Perhaps the hawthorn blossom is a better memorial to him than the world of time-bound northern industry that he knew so well but that always walled round his experience.

NOTES

1 B. Willey, *Nineteenth-Century Studies* (1949), p. 69.
2 For Southey/Elliott letters, see C. C. Southey (ed.), *Life and Correspondence of the late Robert Southey* (1850), vol. IV, pp. 18-19, and E. R. Seary, 'Robert Southey and Ebenezer Elliott, some new Southey Letters', in the *Review of English Studies*, vol. XX (1939).
3 See A. A. Eaglestone, in *Ebenezer Elliott, A Commemorative Brochure* (1949), p. 4.
4 Printed by and for Benjamin Flower, editor of the liberal *Cambridge Intelligencer* (1st edn, 1801; 2nd edn, 1802).
5 'Critique printed by the late Robert Southey', printed in *More Verse and Prose by the Cornlaw Rhymer* (1850), vol. I, pp. 81-116.
6 *Peter Faultless to his Brother Simon, Tales of Night, in Rhyme and Other Poems* (1820), p. 44.
7 *More Verse and Prose* (1850), vol. I, p. v.
8 Introduction to *The Village Patriarch.* (1831 edn).
9 See G. Carnall, *Robert Southey and his Age, the Development of a Conservative Mind* (1960).
10 'On the Stature of E. Elliott', in *Complete Works*, vol. XV, pp. 173-4.
11 *Edinburgh Review*, vol. 55 (1832).
12 Smiles commented on Elliott's work and character in his *Autobiography* (1905), pp. 143-55, and in several other places in his works.
13 A. A. Eaglestone, *op. cit.*, p. 9.
14 G. S. Phillips [January Searle, pseud.], *Memoirs of Ebenezer Elliott, the Corn Law Rhymer* (1852), p. 144.
15 Letter to the *Morning Chronicle*, 19 January 1834.
16 Letter resigning from the Sheffield Working Men's Association, 6 May 1839. 'The conservatives, by defending monopoly and advocating physical force, are fighting the battle of the aristocracy under the people's colours.'
17 *A Statement of the Population of the Town of Sheffield* (1830). Cp. the position in Birmingham. See above, vol. I, pp. 139-40.

18 *More Prose and Verse*, vol. I, p. vi.
19 Letter to Rodgers, Secretary of the Sheffield Mechanics' Institute, 7 May 1842 (quoted in Phillips, *op. cit.*, pp. 103-4).
20 Compare this with his amusing poem, 'Queer Bobby in 1837', printed in *More Prose and Verse*. John Watkins, his Chartist son-in-law, dedicated his *Life, Poetry and Letters of Ebenezer Elliott* (1850) to Sir Robert Peel.
21 Phillips, *op. cit.*, p. 141.
22 See L. Brown, 'The Chartists and the Anti-Corn Law League', in A. Briggs (ed.), *Chartist Studies* (1960), pp. 343-5.
23 See A. Briggs, *The Power of Steam* (1982), Chapter 3, 'The Gospel of Steam'.
24 *More Prose and Verse*, vol. I, p. 53.
25 ibid., p. 8.
26 *The Poetical Works of Ebenezer Elliott* (1840), p. 82.
27 Preface to *The Splendid Village, Corn Law Rhymes and other Poems* (1833).
28 H. Dunckley, *The Charter of the Nations* (1854), p. 57.
29 *More Prose and Verse*, vol. I, p. vi.
30 Quoted by Eaglestone, *loc. cit.*
31 *A Lecture on the Principle that Poetry is Self-Communion'*, written for the Hull Mechanics' Institute.
32 *More Prose and Verse*, vol. I, p. 81.
33 See S. Bamford, *Passages in the Life of a Radical*, 2 vols (1844).
34 H. C. Shelley, 'Ebenezer Elliott, the Poet of Free Trade', in *The Fortnightly Review*, vol. 85 (1906).
35 C. E. Norton (ed.), *Letters of James Russell Lowell* (1893), vol. I, p. 34.
36 J. G. Whittier, *Personal Poems* (n.d.), p. 59.
37 *Collected Poems* (1919), p. 203.
38 L. Étienne, 'Les poètes des pauvres en Angleterre', in *Revue des deux mondes*, vol. XXIII (1856). See also P. Charles, 'De la poésie Chartiste en Angleterre', ibid., vol. XII (1845).
39 W. Odom, *Two Sheffield Poets* (1929), p. 88.
40 A. Briggs (ed.), *Rural Rides*, Northern Tours, 31 January 1830 (1957), p. 217.

3 *Middlemarch* and the Doctors

Victorian novels have long been accepted as useful source books for the social historian. Unfortunately, in sifting them to illustrate theses – a dangerous procedure – much of their charm and most of their meaning are usually lost. R. H. Tawney wisely warned against historians turning to the great works of the past and subordinating them to the lesser ends of the historian's art.[1] Yet his and other warnings have not prevented several nineteenth-century novelists, Dickens outstanding amongst them, from being grievously mistreated.

George Eliot was only in the process of being rediscovered and reassessed in 1948, when the first version of this essay was published in *The Cambridge Journal*, brilliantly edited by Michael Oakeshott.[2] Of course, there had long been a circle of devoted Eliot readers, who lingered as affectionately over *The Mill on the Floss*, for example, as George Eliot herself did over her own memories of childhood in writing it. Such readers reaped their own reward. In addition, there was a group of distinguished twentieth-century admirers of *Middlemarch*, in particular, with one of the most distinguished of them, Virginia Woolf, describing it as 'one of the few English novels written for grown-up people'.[3] Finally, there were already signs that the number of serious students of Eliot would soon increase. A year earlier, Gerald Bullett's study had appeared,[4] and in 1948 itself Joan Bennett's *George Eliot* was followed by F. R. Leavis's *The Great Tradition*, which included the reassessment of George Eliot which had been announced in *Scrutiny* articles of 1945 and 1946.[5] George Haight's influential edition of the *Letters* was not published until 1954-5,[6] but in my essay I forecast that given the quest for the lost secrets of Victorian 'stability' a 'real Eliot revival' would soon begin. In this case, I went on, the social historian should join in at the start and not at the finish, for there were special reasons for a closer study of Eliot's work, and no serious social historian would be any more satisfied than George Eliot herself would have been by an exclusive emphasis on 'stability'. She herself, too, would have approved of a serious examination not only of her craftsmanship but of her ideas, for she took both equally seriously.

I

The 'world' of Eliot's novels – and, perhaps, of *Middlemarch* in particular – is a world far more 'convincing' than the world of Dickens or
Disraeli. Dickens selected particular traits under the inspiration of his
unique experience, and the mixture of impression and fantasy in his
novels should suggest to social historians that there was some truth in
Chesterton's characteristic dictum that the world of Dickens was 'the
best of all impossible worlds'.[7] Disraeli, although he ransacked blue
books and turned statistics into stories, was never content with the
stories themselves. He worked both to entertain and to convert. He
chose the novel as his art form, he once stated, because it 'offered the
best chance of influencing opinion'.[8] As in *Felix Holt* (1866), Eliot, in
Middlemarch, which was published in eight half-volume parts in 1871
and 1872, set out to offer neither a poetic mythology nor a political
philosophy but a picture of the world as it was 'five and thirty years
ago', when 'there were pocket boroughs, a Birmingham unrepresented
in Parliament and compelled to make strong representations out of it,
unrepealed corn laws, three and sixpenny letters, a brawny and many-
breeding pauperism, and other departed evils'.[9]

Within the framework of this reconstructed world, Eliot's characters are neither puppets nor caricatures. They are people who develop
naturally, obeying the inner logic of their personalities and not the
outer manipulations of their author. Eliot had read – very critically –
the historian W. E. H. Lecky's *History of European Morals* which
appeared in 1869 and in which he emphasised that 'life is history, not
poetry. It consists mainly of little things, rarely illumined by flashes of
great heroism, rarely broken by great dangers or demanding great
exertions. A moral system to govern society, must accommodate itself
to common characters and mingled motives.'[10]

Eliot devoted a scrupulous industry to the task of establishing
veracity. She set her backgrounds with meticulous care. In writing
Felix Holt, she went through the arduous task of reading through *The
Times* files of 1823 to 1833 in order to correct childhood memories of
the period.[11] In *Middlemarch*, to which she gave the sub-title 'a study
of provincial life', she put to good use a wealth of knowledge about
the provinces, gleaned from personal reminiscence and from reading.
Her characters are at home in their environment, and Eliot sees their
background afresh from their own vantage points. Her knowledge is
always alive with understanding.

We now know a great deal more in detail than we did in 1948 about
the construction of *Middlemarch* which she started writing in 1869,[12]
and which she conceived of then as a novel of provincial life with that
title – though without Dorothea, Casaubon and Will Ladislaw.[13] From

the start she was deeply interested in medical themes within a provincial context – her first 'hero' of 1869, already called Lydgate, was a
physician – but it took time and effort to enrich her first fictions. 'Any
number of writers could have written George Eliot's notebooks; only
she could have written *Middlemarch*.'[14]

Lord Acton, who had a very high opinion of Eliot's novels and of
Middlemarch above the rest, thought that she was superior to many of
the greatest writers, both of poetry and of prose, not only in

> reading the diverse hearts of men, but of creeping into their skin, watching
> the world through their eyes, feeling their latent background of convic-
> tion, discerning theory and habit, influences of thought and knowledge, of
> life and of descent, and having obtained this experience, recovering her
> independence, stripping off the borrowed shell, and exposing scientifically
> and indifferently the soul of a Vestal, a Crusader, an Anabaptist, an
> Inquisitor, a Dervish, a Nihilist, or a Cavalier without attraction, pre-
> ference, or caricature. And each of them should say that she displayed him
> in his strength, that she gave rational form to motives he had imperfectly
> analysed, that she laid bare features in his character he had never realized.[15]

Eliot had the gifts of a historian, and this is one reason why
historians willingly turn to her. Even Henry James, who accused her of
proceeding 'from the abstract to the concrete' and of evolving her
figures and situations 'from the moral consciousness', noted also her
'solidity of specification' and in his unsigned review of *Middlemarch* in
1873 asked in conclusion, 'If we write novels so, how shall we write
history?'[16] The prelude to *Middlemarch* begins 'Who that cares much
to know the history of man, and how the mysterious mixture behaves
under the varying experiments of Time', and in Chapter 2 we are told
that 'to reconstruct a past world, doubtless with a view to the highest
purposes of truth' is wonderful work even if one is only employed as 'a
lamp-holder'. Eliot's return to sources was followed by a faithful
reconstruction. This is the clue to Acton's praise of her novels: her
method, rather than her thought, was what attracted him. 'You
cannot think how much I owed her,' he wrote to Mary Gladstone.

> Of eighteen or twenty writers by whom I am conscious that my mind has
> been formed, she was one. Of course I mean ways, not conclusions. In
> problems of life and thought, which baffled Shakespeare disgracefully, her
> touch was unfailing. No writer ever lived, who had anything like her power
> of manifold, but disinterested and impartially observant sympathy.[17]

This was high praise. Others found that Eliot's *forte* lay in her preoccupation with ideas as well as with people. If this was one of James's critical points, it is necessary to remember that Eliot in her own (or in the next) generation was felt to offer a contribution which was 'profound, not superficial; ethical, rather than sensational; and coherent and sustained instead of fragmentary and spasmodic'.[18] 'Her genius combines the powers of the telescope and microscope: it sweeps the wide horizon of events and forces which have moved the world; it ... reveals the microcosm of a single water drop.'[19] Her characters were just as much influenced by ideas and by systems of religion, politics, philosophy or science as they were by their friends or relations, and there could be a tug between the two. As the lawyer and historian A. V. Dicey wrote, again in an unsigned review of 1873, the flaw in Lydgate's nature and the ultimate source of his fall was a certain 'commonness' in his views of everything unconnected with science.[20] Some of Eliot's own sentences are concerned directly with the tug. 'In the British climate there is no incompatibility between scientific insight and furnished lodgings. The incompatibility is chiefly between scientific ambition and a wife who objects to that kind of residence.'

II

Middlemarch is set in the years 1829 to 1832, and tells of a life in the provinces, which is in constant movement. Institutions and people are changing. There is no stability.

> Some slipped a little downward, some got higher footing; people denied aspirates, gained wealth, and fastidious gentlemen stood for boroughs; some were caught in political currents, some in ecclesiastical, and perhaps found themselves surprisingly grouped in consequence; while a few personages or families that stood with rocky firmness amid all this fluctuation, were slowly presenting new aspects in spite of solidity, and altering with the double change of self and beholder.

It is to such a society that Lydgate, a promising young doctor, comes. He brings to the small provincial town great schemes which he has learnt in a wider world. His ambition is to 'pierce the obscurity of those minute processes which prepare human misery and joy, those invisible thoroughfares which are the first lurking-places of anguish, mania and crime'.

For him, this ambition expresses itself in a lively enthusiasm for medical reform. This is his only Radicalism. He hopes to restore to the medical profession its sense of responsibility, and to add to its scientific apparatus for the conquest of disease. *Middlemarch* tells a tale of disillusionment. His 'scientific conscious got into the debasing company of money obligation and selfish respect'. His dream had been that he would become a second Jenner, working in solitude far from the capital, discovering by himself important new principles. Instead of this, he has to leave Middlemarch for an excellent practice 'between London and a continental bathing place'. Instead of unravelling the mysteries of typhus or cholera, he writes a treatise on gout. To the outer world he has become a success. To himself he is a failure. 'He had not done what he once meant to do.'

There was one particular flaw in his character, which Eliot reveals to us when we are first introduced to him – his dislike of doing something disagreeable to himself. In his medical duties 'he cared not only for "cases", but for John and Elizabeth, especially Elizabeth'. He finds his Elizabeth in Middlemarch and, step by step, at first almost imperceptibly, but always relentlessly, his courtship and marriage with Rosamond Vincy dissolve the high-minded aspirations with which he had begun his professional career. Attempting to insulate his interest in the opposite sex from his serious interests, he finds that there can be no watertight division. It is marriage, and not any professional deficiencies, that provides the key to his failure. The failure is known to himself alone. 'The most terrible obstacles', he tells us, 'are such as nobody can see except oneself.' The most terrible failure is that

> I must do as other men do, and think what will please the world, and bring in money; look for a little opening in the London crowd, and push myself; set up in a watering place, or go to some southern town where there are plenty of idle English, and get myself puffed, – that is the sort of shell I must creep into and try to keep my soul alive in.

This is a wise paradox of the novel, that deficiencies of character may lead not to utter ruin, but to what the world judges as success. The banker Bulstrode's whited sepulchre crumbles to dust before our eyes, but he had his day of pride in the first seven books of *Middlemarch*. Lydgate's whited sepulchre is still left to shine when the novel is done.

There are many themes in *Middlemarch*, and the Lydgate theme is only one. Yet it was his story that first figured in 1869 in Eliot's notebooks for *Middlemarch*, and only by the end of 1870 was she working on a second story – that of 'Miss Brooke' – which was gradually interwoven and finally very intricately interwoven with it (along with other stories) in the published text of the completed novel. As Leslie Stephen has pointed out, *Middlemarch* is not a story, but a combination of at least three stories. 'The various actions get mixed together as they naturally would do in a country town ... The individuals are shown as involved in the network of surrounding interests which affects their development.'[21] With extraordinary skill, Eliot draws the three stories together in the last book. In deciding finally to leave Middlemarch, Lydgate confides in Dorothea Brooke, the central figure of the novel. Like Lydgate, she too has known the blighting of young hopes and the challenge of circumstance. Her secrets, too, she had hidden away in her heart. Both Lydgate and Dorothea represent

> the mixed result of young and noble impulse struggling amid the conditions of an imperfect social state in which great feelings will often take the aspect of error, and great faith the aspect of illusion. For there is no creature whose inward being is so strong that it is not greatly determined by what lies outside of it.[22]

If this is the 'moral', or one of the morals, of *Middlemarch*, it seems to be a very tame one; yet it is a clue to the Victorian sense of duty, which pushed forward social effort at a time when the individual and not the state was modelling a new society. The individual responds to the challenge of his environment through integrity of character. Private and public life interact. 'There is no private life, which has not been determined by a wider public life.'[23] There is no public life which can blossom out unless it has deep roots. The career of Lydgate illustrates, as H. G. Nicholas pointed out in a radio talk of 1948, 'the intensity with which the Victorian Age sought to combine material development and public probity'.[24] This was the foundation of its 'institutional morality'. 'The new morality of public institutions became, in effect, only the application to public life of a more rigorous code of personal behaviour.'

At the centre of the picture was a sense of service. George Eliot herself once wrote that the only hope she had of a future life was 'to have given to me some woman's duty, some possibility of devoting myself where I may see a daily result of pure blessedness in the life of another'.[25] She puts the same sentiment into the hearts of Dorothea and Lydgate. *Middlemarch* describes the England of 1829 to 1832[26], when provincial families were 'still discussing Mr Peel's late conduct on the Catholic question', but it was written forty years later, when the Victorian age had passed through its growing pains, and had established most of the principles which were to buttress its society. Lydgate has his head in the 1820s, but his heart is in the 1860s. For all George Eliot's realism in painting a scene, she could not eliminate – any more than Victorian historians could – the influence of the inter-vening years of self-examination and standard-setting which linked

Lydgate's period with her own. The problem she sets Lydgate and Dorothea is in its essence a mid-Victorian problem. Their vision and their struggle are the same as her own.

In a sense this point was made clearly in 1873 in a discussion of *Middlemarch* in the *Fortnightly Review*, by Sidney Colvin, one of George Eliot's regular visitors at her house, the Priory. 'She has worked between two epochs, upon the confines of two worlds, and has described the old in terms of the new. To the old world belong the elements of her experience, to the new world the elements of her reflection on experience.'[27] She was certainly aware herself of the chronological ordering of events since the period she was describing, setting it out carefully in her note-books. A recent historian has described the period from 1830 to 1858, the year of medical registration under a new Medical Act, as 'a decisive turning point in the development of medical education in England'.[28]

It is impossible to understand Lydgate – or Eliot – except within this perspective. Nor is it a necessary consideration only in relation to medical education or organisation. Eliot could not improve the development of thought itself. Though she concentrates in *Middlemarch* on the thought of the 1820s and 1830s, 'the more evolved situation of forty years later is present in hints about cell-theory' and 'more generally in the very quality of "knowledge" that *Middlemarch* itself displays'.[29]

III

If Eliot's choice of the problems reflects the standards of the 1860s, the colour is all of an earlier age. The story of Lydgate centres on the fight for medical reform, which provided the first of the great battles for public health in the nineteenth century. *Middlemarch* tells us far more about the significance of medical reform, which provided the first of the great battles for public health in the nineteenth century, than most twentieth-century academic monographs. In order to discuss this question, Eliot had to devote herself to much specialised reading. 'This morning I finished the first chapter of *Middlemarch*', she wrote in her Journal in August 1869. 'I am reading Renouard's History of Medicine.'[30] Study of the *Lancet*, the fascinating and then polemical medical magazine founded by Thomas Wakley in 1823, led her to the dispute concerning medically and legally trained coroners which was to figure in Chapter 16, and other reading led her to pre-Nightingale nursing.

From the beginning, medical history, partly the history of ideas, had to be related to hospital history, largely the history of institutions, and Eliot turned for guidance to individuals as well as to documentary sources. Thus, she asked Mrs Michael Congreve, wife of the Positivist leader, for information about provincial hospitals, 'necessary to my imagining the conditions of my hero'.[31]

Medicine, for George Eliot, was a profession with tremendous possibilities. It offered a world of pioneer enterprise to a young man of ability and enthusiasm. 'About 1829', she wrote, 'the dark territories of Pathology were a fine America for a spirited young adventurer.' She referred in particular to 'the brief and glorious career of [Marie François Xavier] Bichet [1771-1802]', and although she may have got the significance of his work wrong[32] she was right to relate the Paris scene to that of Middlemarch. In 1879, after the death of Lewes, Eliot showed that she was as interested in medicine in real life as she had been in the pages of *Middlemarch*. She chose as his most suitable memorial a Studentship in Physiology to be given to a young man qualified and eager to carry out research, but without the necessary means of doing so. She attached great importance to the Studentship. It was for her the best way of prolonging Lewes's life, the sort of memorial he himself would have chosen.[33]

Eliot was not alone in giving health reform a central place in her thoughts. While her interests lay primarily in medicine, the interest of many of her contemporaries lay in 'the health of towns and populous districts'. Among an active band of Victorian writers who were fascinated with what was called the 'sanitary idea', Charles Kingsley was the best known. 'I see one work to be done 'ere I die', he wrote to a friend in 1857, 'in which nature must be counteracted, lest she prove a curse and a destroyer, not a blessing and a mother; and that is Sanitary Reform.'[34] Kingsley's novels reflect his social purposes. *Yeast* describes waste and worry as clogging forces in a healthy society. *Two Years Ago* describes a cholera outbreak, and the incompetence of a local Board of Health. The greatness of Eliot emerges the more incontestably from a comparison of her handling of such themes and the methods of Kingsley. He never allowed his characters to develop naturally. They are always held in a vice-like grip. They are either mere mouthpieces of his own ideas, or caricatures of his own dislikes. Eliot, by focusing attention on character and the influences which mould it, illuminated the social problems of an age of change far more effectively than Kingsley could do through his naked didacticism. The preface to *Yeast* baldly states a social problem: 'Cottage improvement and sanitary reform, throughout the country districts, are going on at a fearfully slow rate, and must be speeded up.' The prelude to *Middlemarch* tells us only of Saint Theresa.

Nonetheless, however different they were in their approaches, Eliot and Kingsley shared the same conviction of the necessity for grounding all social effort in personal integrity. Public health was a major problem for them because an annual burden of disease and death, 'the endemic and not the epidemic pestilence', represented a failure of social control and kept England weighted down with 'a permanent overhanging mist of infection'.[35] The easy way out was to offer prayers to ward off typhus and cholera, or to stand still in the belief that 'suffering and evil are nature's admonitions', and could be got rid of neither by benevolence nor by legislation.[36] Palmerston, perhaps an unlikely supporter of public health reform, provided the best answer to those who resigned themselves to prayer, when he told the Edinburgh Presbytery in 1853 that 'when man has done the utmost for his own safety, then is the time to invoke the blessing of heaven to give effect to his exertions'.[37] The health reformers refused to bow down before the altar of fate. For them, the 'sanitary idea' implied that 'man could by getting at first principles ... get behind Fate itself and suppress the forces which led up to it at their prime source'.[38] Such a response would bring with it a new liberation, and the liberation would affect not only health, but social thought and social control as a whole.

In talking about cottages and doctors, Eliot was deliberately discussing one of the key problems of Victorian progress, and by setting her story in the provinces, she was choosing that particular environment where the battle for public health was waged most intensely. Indeed, the historian of public health in the nineteenth century must go back to Middlemarch with or without George Eliot. He needs his Middlemarch just as much as the American sociologist needs his Middletown. It was in the small towns of England that the warring interests struggled for mastery and fought for improvement either in the name of science, like Lydgate, philanthrophy, like Bulstrode, or sound administration, like Dorothea. In 1829, when Lydgate arrived in Middlemarch, philanthropy was uppermost as a softening influence, and he was frequently described as 'a sort of philanthropist'. The replacement of philanthropy by science was a much later development. When Eliot wrote *Middlemarch*, cholera was still a hotly debated mystery, and it was not until 1880 that the bacillus of typhoid was discovered, and English public health began to pass from the soap and water to the scientific phase. The first Public Health Act was passed in 1848, but it was not until 1875 – the year when Charles Kingsley died – that the Health Act of that year laid the foundations of an efficient national sanitary administration.[39]

If we can trust George Eliot as a guide, we can go back again to the Middlemarch of 1829 and explore its mazes with confidence, and in exploring Middlemarch, we shall be learning how to explore England as well. George Eliot puts a different metaphor into the mouth of Will Ladislaw in *Middlemarch* – 'that is the common order of things: the little waves make up the large ones, and are of the same pattern'. Elsewhere she wrote, 'For want of real minute vision of how changes came about in the past, we fall into ridiculously inconsistent estimates of actual movements.'

The topography of Middlemarch was directly based on Coventry,[40] and the combination of urban and rural, industrial and agricultural, is the one that Eliot herself knew at first hand. She rightly contrasts Middlemarch in one place in the novel (Chapter 76) with 'some southern town where there are plenty of idle English'. Yet it is a major theme of the novel – and one which links up with J. S. Mill – that 'opinion' in Middlemarch, closely related to prejudice and to interest, makes for a distressing conformity.[41] Lydgate was 'altogether foreign to Middlemarch' (Chapter 12), and this, of course, was one reason why Rosamond was attracted to him. 'It is always some new fellow who strikes a girl.' Ideas as well as people come from outside. Middlemarch is a microcosm but it is not the universe, which includes Paris, where Lydgate studied science, and Rome, where Dorothea studied works of art. Bulstrode goes to Middlemarch to hide his past: Lydgate leaves it for the same reason. There are always strangers and exiles. Such creatures are so close to Eliot herself that her interest in them transfuses and often transcends her interest in medicine or public health.

IV

The two main characters of Middlemarch – Lydgate and Dorothea – bounded by the limitations of life in the provinces, look out at the wider world, and find their ideas which guide them in their daily conduct. Like Saint Theresa and her brother walking out to seek martyrdom in the country of the Moors, they too have hearts which 'are already beating to a national idea'. Dorothea, hidden away in Tipton Grange, had a mind which was 'theoretic', and yearned by its nature after some lofty conception of the world which might frankly include the parish of Tipton and her own rule of conduct there'. Lydgate was more precise in his objectives, and less steady in his pursuit of them. 'To do good small work for Middlemarch, and great work for the world' was his main purpose.

Both Lydgate and Dorothea believed in practical reform. Lydgate held unflinchingly that 'the medical profession as it might be was the finest in the world; presenting the most perfect interchange between science and art; offering the most direct alliance between intellectual conquest and the social good'. Dorothea dreams of healthier cottages. 'Life in cottages might be happier than ours, if they were real houses fit for human beings from whom we expect duties and affections.' When her sister taunts her about her peculiar *'fad* to draw plans', Dorothea is annoyed. 'The *fad* of drawing plans! What was life worth – what great faith was possible when the whole effect of one's actions could be withered up into such parched rubbish as that?'

Dorothea's profound conviction survives the drab desiccation of life with Casaubon. Eliot revels in the contrast between Casaubon's arid pursuit of an academic dream and Dorothea's fresh, practical enthusiasm. She also contrasts Dorothea's work with Brooke's talk about political reform – Whig speeches at the hustings and dirty cottages on the estate. 'We all know the wag's definition of a philanthropist: a man whose charity increases directly as the square of the distance.' The portraits of Casaubon, an object lesson for all dons, and of Brooke, an object lesson for all politicians, throw into relief Dorothea's outstanding qualities. 'The idea of some active good within her reach haunted her like a passion.'

Dorothea and Lydgate come together in various ways, and Eliot shows all her penetrating skill in unravelling the tangle of personal relationships which twists about them. Lydgate's scheme for a new hospital is the most important external factor drawing them together. It is far more than a mere local institution: it becomes a symbol of the meeting of their minds.

The new hospital was in the process of being built when Lydgate first arrived in Middlemarch. It had been sponsored by Bulstrode, the Evangelical banker, who soon saw the possibility of employing Lydgate's talents to make the new institution work. For Lydgate, this seemed to be heaven-sent opportunity. 'A fine fever hospital in addition to the new infirmary might be the nucleus of a medical school here, when once we get our medical reforms; and what would do more for medical education than the spread of such schools all over the country?'

What Lydgate did not realise at the time was that the problems of running a hospital are not restricted to medical organisation nor to smooth administration. Politics and personalities intrude perpetually. Bulstrode did not build the hospital for the same reasons that inspired Lydgate. Lydgate wanted new treatment for fever and possibilities of preparing for the approach of cholera: Bulstrode wanted moral welfare to be the objective, and his own personal influence the agency. 'I will boldly confess to you', he told Lydgate frankly, 'that I should have no interest in hospitals if I believed that nothing more was concerned therein than the cure of mortal diseases.' Such a divergence was no proof of incompatibility, but it was dangerous because the two men did not begin their relationship with equal advantages. Lydgate had brains and dreams, Bulstrode money and power. As their relationship developed, Lydgate lost more and more of his independence. He began by closing his ears to Bulstrode's talk of religion. 'As Voltaire said, incantations will destroy a flock of sheep, if administered with a certain quantity of arsenic. I look for the man who will bring the arsenic, and don't mind about his incantations.' Gradually the tables were turned, and Lydgate was used to accomplish Bulstrode's purposes. The break-up of Bulstrode's reputation and the bursting of his pride broke Lydgate with them. The new hospital crumbled among the ruins. 'Let the new hospital be joined with the old infirmary, and everything go on as it might have done if I had never come.'

When Bulstrode fell ill, it was Dorothea who helped Lydgate to find sufficient courage to tie his life together again. She alone understood the extent of his disillusionment, expressed in his unwilling yielding to that 'pale shade of bribery which is sometimes called prosperity'. Lydgate, of course, saw it in a different light. In a passage in Chapter 81, written as a later insertion, Eliot says of him he had 'accepted his narrow lot with sad resignation. He had chosen this fragile creature, [Rosamond] and had taken the burthen of her life upon his arms. He must walk as he could, carrying that burthen pitifully.'

Such a treatment of the effect of our 'imperfect social state' on young and noble impulses makes *Middlemarch* a deeply moving novel. There are difficulties, however, with the comparison between Saint Theresa and Dorothea and in the case of Lydgate with the placing of all the weight on character. The first set of difficulties was brilliantly identified by a Roman Catholic reviewer of *Middlemarch*, who showed that Saint Theresa was 'much more of the ordinary woman than George Eliot, with a novelist's love, makes her heroine'.[42] The second set of difficulties was not identified at the time, because while medicine was becoming more 'scientific', it could not be pretended, as it can now, that skill can compensate for defects of character, or for lack of care. There was a sense in which, as Lord Acton realised, Eliot was writing of and for a transitional time in the history of the world.

If ever religion or science reigns alone over an undivided empire, the books of George Eliot might lose their central and unique importance, but as the emblem of a generation distracted between the intense need of believing and the difficulty of belief, they will live up to the last syllable of recorded time.[43]

In the early nineteenth century, in an age which had not yet produced its Chadwick or its Lister, personal integrity and unflinching determination were at a premium. At the same time, few people in England knew what a saint really was. The transition had begun.

In writing *Middlemarch*, George Eliot had no doubt read her

Samuel Smiles, very much the popular writer of the age of transition. *Self Help* was published fourteen years before *Middlemarch*. Jenner was one of its heroes. Having worked alone, and in face of great difficulties, he refused to return to London when his labours were crowned with success. 'No! in the morning of my days I have sought the sequestered and lowly paths of life – the valley and not the mountain – and now in the evening of my days, it is not meet for me to hold up myself for fortune and for fame.' Smiles ends his tale of Lydgate's hero by stating the moral: 'If vaccine were the only dis-covery of the epoch, it would serve to render it illustrious for ever; yet it knocked twenty times in vain at the doors of the Academies.'[44] Eliot cared as little about 'the Academies' as Smiles. At best, they would have been the places to which Casaubon, not Dorothea or Lydgate, would have turned.

V

Eliot has much to tell us not only about the leading figures in the story, but also about local reactions to them in the community which was so different from an Academy. Medical reform was not a popular cry in Middlemarch, and Lydgate met with two distinct lines of criticism, first from his fellow doctors, and second from the general public.

In describing both of these counter-movements, Eliot writes as usual with a well-informed intelligence. It was not only in Middle-march that old doctors attacked new-fangled methods and the young fanatics who employed them. Not all the profession followed Thomas Wakley, the proprietor of the *Lancet*, who was pushing a vigorous programme of reform. Eliot knew her Wakley. She makes her Dr Sprague say of him: 'I disapprove of Wakley, no man more: he is an ill-intentioned fellow, who would sacrifice the respectability of the profession, which everybody knows depends on the London colleges, for the sake of getting some notoriety for himself.' Wakley wanted to reform some of the 'venerable colleges which used great efforts to secure purity of knowledge by making it scarce.' When he was writing – in Lydgate's time – there was no registration of doctors. Their legal titles were, in Simon's phrase, 'as various as snuffs and sauces'. Attempts at reform, official or unofficial, met with bitter opposition. Sir James Graham's attempts to carry out a reform from the Home Office in 1843-4, for example, 'set the whole medical profession in a ferment, sowing the seeds of a vigorous and perennial animosity in every section of it'.[45]

Some of the best passages in *Middlemarch* describe Lydgate's fellow doctors. Firmly planted in local society, this motley assortment looked upon Lydgate with suspicion from the day that he announced that he did not intend to adminster drugs. However much they disagreed among themselves, they 'were willing to combine against all innovators'. 'What I contend against', said Mr Wrench, 'is the way medical men are fouling their own nest, and setting up a cry about the country as if a general practitioner who dispenses drugs can't be a gentleman.' They did not like Lydgate's methods. His use of the stethoscope was in advance of his times. He even had new ideas about the treatment of *delirium tremens* and cholera. He had irritating ways of challenging the diagnosis of his rivals. What Dr Wrench diagnosed as 'a slight derangement' Lydgate saw at once to be the pink-skinned stage of typhoid fever. Later on, Nancy Nash's tumour was re-diagnosed by Lydgate as cramp, and all the barbarian remedies previously prescribed were cast away. Although the patient made a marvellous recovery, Dr Minchin had been sufficiently provoked to call the whole affair – privately, of course – 'a disagreeable inattention to etiquette'.

Minchin's reaction was typical. Afraid of fighting openly on professional grounds, the doctors preferred to talk in corners about Lydgate's arrogance. They even let loose the word 'charlatan', which once out, soon strayed far beyond the ranks of the doctors to the general public.

In describing popular reactions to Lydgate and his methods, Eliot explores a strange and half-forgotten world, where medicine and magic meet, and where historians join hands with anthropologists. (They do so now far more willingly than in 1948.) Lydgate was not long in finding his non-professional admirers. They ranged from Lady Chettam, who discovered with joy that he 'confirmed her view of her own constitution as being peculiar by admitting that all constitutions might be called peculiar, and he did not deny that hers might be more peculiar than the others', to Brooke who liked all experiments, medical or political, provided that they were administered in small doses.

But if Lydgate had such friends, he also had his enemies. Many people believed with Mrs Dollop of the Tankard Inn in Slaughter Lane that he meant to let the people die in the hospital, 'if not to poison them, for the sake of cutting them up'. Others were wedded to popular remedies or to superstitious prejudices. 'I should like him to tell me how I could bear up at Fair time, if I didn't take strengthening medicines a month before hand', said the grocer's wife, 'but what keeps me up is the pink medicine, not the brown.' George Eliot's picture of a drug-ridden community is confirmed by the great medical and health reports of the 1840s, which were probably among her sources. She was far more successful than they were in making the worst abuses sound plausible.

Both of these two minor elements – the rivalry of his fellow doctors and the ignorance of the public – played their part in Lydgate's downfall. Indeed, the climax of the novel hangs around an experimental prescription given by Lydgate to Bulstrode for the treatment of the one man who stands in Bulstrode's way, a constant threat to his respectability and happiness. Lydgate recommends 'no liquors of any sort'. Bulstrode is weak enough and ruthless enough to let the patient have brandy. The patient dies. Bulstrode and Lydgate are both targets for local gossip. The doctors, like a Greek chorus, expose the weaknesses of their colleague. The public follow Mrs Dollop. 'It's a mercy they didn't take this Doctor Lydgate on to our club. There's many a mother's child might ha' rued it.' Lydgate is tortured neither by the doctors nor by the public, but by himself. 'Is there a medical man in Middlemarch', he asks, 'who would question himself as I do?' The central theme of the novel is reiterated. 'Only those who know the supremacy of the intellectual life – the life, which has a seed of ennobling thought and purpose within it – can understand the grief of one, who falls from that serene activity into the soul-wasting struggle with worldly annoyances.'

VI

It has not always been the fashion to admire the dexterity and judgement with which George Eliot handles her theme in *Middlemarch*. Her later novels were once dismissed as lifeless and uninspired, and G. W. E. Russell in 1896 called *Middlemarch* too long and too ponderous; a census overcrowded with figures; more of a study of character thrown into narrative form than a genuine novel.'[46] George Saintsbury went further in the same year, calling her later novels works of erudition not of genius – 'of painful manufacture not of joyous creation', relying too much on 'a most portentous jargon borrowed from the not very admirable lingo of the philosophers and men of science in the last half of the nineteenth century':

> Constructed no doubt with much art and material not seldom precious, they were not lively growths, and they were fatally tinged with evanescent 'forms in chalk' fancies of the day and hour, not less ephemeral for being grave in subject and seeming, and almost more jejune or even disgusting to posterity on that account.[47]

This is a pontifical judgement, one of many, which rings even more hollow when it is compared with Saintsbury's fulsome praise of Kingsley. *Alton Locke* and *Yeast*, he says, are 'a little crude, immature and violent, but of wonderful beauty and power as literature'.[48] Saintsbury missed in *Middlemarch* all those qualities which Lord Acton most admired, and which the historian must take account of as a first claim on his attention.

But he missed more than this. He took for 'forms in chalk', 'fancies of the day and hour', what we are now beginning to consider as vital forces in the making of Victorian society.[49] He missed the 'intellectual fermentation' which had impressed Alexander Kingslake, the historian of the Crimean War, who told Eliot's publisher that it was this which made 'works like *Middlemarch* very interesting'. Kingslake, as we have seen, was not the only historian to 'envy the process of disciplined thought which after all the "simmering" passes at once into the irrevocable'.[50]

For a proper understanding of the historical force at work both during the 1830s and the 1860s, the historian will find George Eliot's novels of far more value than many other well-established sources, and in the process of analysing them, he need not feel, as he is often accused of in other explorations, that he is treading on holy ground. Eliot herself will tread the ground with him, and in the course of the journey will reveal all the finer points of psychological insight and imaginative sensibility that made her a favourite not only of Acton, but also of Proust.

NOTES

1   See his 1949 lecture to the National Book League, 'Social History and Literature', reprinted in R. Hinden (ed.), *The Radical Tradition* (1964).
2   My essay appeared in the twelfth number of the first volume of *The Journal* in September 1948. The first piece in the number was a sermon preached in Westminster Abbey by Canon Charles Smyth, 'An Apology for Scholarship'. 'The scholar learns two things', Canon Smyth wisely remarked, 'the discipline of his craft, and its limitations.'
3   *The Times Literary Supplement*, 20 November 1919.
4   G. Bullett, *George Eliot: Her Life and Books* (1947).
5   J. Bennett, *George Eliot: Her Mind and Art* (1948); and F. R. Leavis, *The Great Tradition* (1948).
6   G. S. Haight (ed.), *The George Eliot Letters*, 7 vols. (1954-5). In 1948 the Eliot student had to rely on J. W. Cross, *George Eliot's Life as Related in her Letters and Journals* (1885). Haight's magnificent biography did not appear until 1968.
7   See G. K. Chesterton, *The Victorian Age in Literature* (1913).

8 General Preface to the *Novels* (1870). For a more recent survey of the role of the novel in the 1840s which is invaluable to historians, see K. Tillotson, *Novels of the Eighteen-Forties* (1954).

9 Introduction to *Felix Holt*.

10 W. L. H. Lecky, *History of European Morals*, vol. I (1865), p. 204.

11 Leslie Stephen, *George Eliot* (1902), p. 149. She also read *Shirley*.

12 She had been thinking of an 'English novel' since March 1867. (*Letters*, vol. IV, p. 355.)

13 See A. T. Kitchel, *George Eliot's Quarry for 'Middlemarch'* (1950); J. Beaty, *'Middlemarch' from Notebook to Novel* (1960); and J. C. Pratt and Victor A. Neufeld, *George Eliot's 'Middlemarch' Notebooks* (1979). Eliot students owe an immense debt to American scholarship.

14 Beaty, *op. cit.*, p. 84.

15 *Letters of Lord Acton to Mary, Daughter of the Right Hon. W. E. Gladstone* (1904), pp. 60-1.

16 *Galaxy*, vol. XV, March 1873, pp. 424-8. For other James reviews, see the excellent anthology by D. Carroll (ed.), *George Eliot, The Critical Heritage* (1971).

17 *Letters of Lord Acton*, p. 57.

18 M. G. Fawcett, 'George Eliot Revisited', in the *Contemporary Review*, March 1896, p. 361.

19 ibid., p. 369. See also S. Shuttleworth, *George Eliot and Nineteenth-Century Science* (1984).

20 *Nation*, 30 January 1873.

21 Leslie Stephen, *op. cit.*, p. 174.

22 Recognition of the similarity between the careers of Lydgate and Dorothea – and the underlying implications of the two stories – may have led Eliot to join them together. See Beaty, *op. cit.*, pp. 9-10.

23 *Felix Holt*.

24 H. G. Nicholas, 'The New Morality', in *The Listener*, 18 March 1948.

25 Quoted by V. Sackville-West in her essay on 'George Eliot' in *The Great Victorians*, vol. I.

26 The accuracy of Eliot's version of the history of the period, often presented indirectly, is discussed briefly by J. Beaty, 'History by Indirection', in *Victorian Studies*, vol. I (1957); and by R. D. Altick, 'Anachronisms in *Middlemarch*', a note in *Nineteenth-Century Fiction*, vol. 33 (1978).

27 *Fortnightly Review*, 19 January 1873.

28 See the important, wide-ranging article by S. W. F. Holloway, 'Medical Education in England, 1830-1858: a Sociological Analysis', in *History*, vol. XLIX (1964). The early period is covered by B. Hamilton, 'The Medical Professions in the Eighteenth Century', in *The Economic History Review*, vol. IV (1951). See also A. B. Erickson, 'An Early Attempt at Medical Reform in England, 1844-1845', in the *Journal of The History of Medicine* (1950), and R. G. Hodgkinson, The Social Environment of British Medical Science and Practice in the Nineteenth Century', in W. C. Gibson (ed.), *British Contributions to Medical Science* (1971).

29 M. Y. Mason, '*Middlemarch* and Science: Problems of Life and Mind', in the *Review of English Studies*, (1971).

30 *George Eliot's Life as Related in her Letters and Journals* (arranged and edited by J. W. Cross), vol. III, p. 97. Renouard's two-volume book was written in 1846. It was not translated into English. J. R. Russell's *History and Heroes of the Art of Medicine* appeared in 1861, and the two volumes of J. Thomson's *Life, Lectures and Letters of William Cullen* in 1832 and 1859. One book she did not mention here was Émile Littré's *Médecine et Médicins* (1871), which, as Pratt and Neufeld state (*op. cit.*, p. xxv), 'provided not only dates but compatible doctrines as well'.

31 Journal entry of 21 September 1869, quoted in Pratt and Neufeld, *op. cit.*, p. xxxvii. See also ibid., p. xx, for a later letter to Mrs Congreve. Thomson's *Life of Cullen* stressed the importance of hospital work for a doctor wishing to acquire 'that most valuable kind of knowledge which is derived from experience' and attacked 'absurd and disgraceful trade in drugs' (vol. I, pp. 663-4).

32 See Holstead, *op. cit.*, for her possible misunderstanding of his tissue theory. He refers to the English translation of Bichet's *General Anatomy Applied to Physiology and Medicine*, 3 vols (1892). For a summary of what happened to pathology between Bichet and *Middlemarch*, see W. H. McMenemey, 'Cellular Pathology', in F. N. L. Poynter (ed.), *Medicine in the 1860s* (1968), pp. 16 ff. The critical invention was that of the compound achromatic microscope. The work on cells of Theodore Schwann was not translated into English until 1847.

33 Letter to Mme Bodichon, 8 April 1879. Quoted in Cross, *op. cit.*, vol. III, p. 355. See a further letter to Charles Lewes, ibid., 382. Lewes had always been interested in physiology, and in its relation to science as a whole.

34 Quoted by Guy Kendall, *Charles Kingsley and his Ideas*, p. 75. A useful summary of Kingsley's views can be found in a paper he read 'on certain obstacles to Sanitary Reform' to the National Association for the Promotion of Social Science in 1858 (*Transactions*, pp. 428 ff.).

35 Viscount Morpeth's speech introducing the Public Health Act of 1848. *Hansard*, vol. XCVI, pp. 385-424.

36 *The Economist*, 13 May 1848.

37 Quoted by Sir John Simon in his classic work, *English Sanitary Institutions*. Simon himself wrote in his first Sanitary Report on the City of London that 'in the great objects which sanitary science proposes to itself – in the immense amelioration, which it proffers to the physical, social and indirectly to the moral condition of an immense majority of our fellow creatures, it transcends the importance of all other sciences, and in its beneficent operation seems most nearly to embody the spirit and to fulfil the intentions of practical Christianity'.

38 Sir Benjamin Ward Richardson, *The Health of Nations: A Review of the Works of Edwin Chadwick*, Introduction. It is interesting to note that Eliot in introducing the fear of cholera into her novel changed her first proposed composition of the meeting which exposed Bulstrode from a

vestry meeting to a public meeting. For cholera, see also below, pp. 153 ff.

39 See below, p. 50.

40 See J. R. Prest, *The Industrial Revolution in Coventry* (1960), esp. Appendix I, 'The Historical Value of *Middlemarch*'.

41 See W. L. Burn, *The Age of Equipoise* (1964), Chapter 3.

42 The Stories of Two Worlds: *Middlemarch* and *Fleurange*', in the *Catholic World*, September 1873.

43 See his *Letters to Mary Gladstone* (Daughter of the Rt Hon. W. E. Gladstone) (1904), pp. 60-1.

44 Samuel Smiles, *Self Help; with Illustrations of Character, Conduct and Perseverance* (1859), pp. 138-40.

45 Health of Towns Association, *Report of the Committee to the Members of the Association on Lord Lincoln's Bill* (1846), p. 11.

46 Russell, *op. cit.*, p. 362.

47 George Saintsbury, *A History of Nineteenth Century Literature 1780-1895* (1896).

48 ibid.

49 For a recent criticism, see G. Steiner, 'A Preface to "Middlemarch"', in *Nineteenth Century Fiction*, vol. IX (1955), in which he argues (p. 243) that it 'falls decisively short of that immense stature associated with some French and much Russian fiction in the nineteenth century'. There is a gap between 'thought and style' and a 'lack of unified texture'.

50 Letter from Kingslake to William Blackwood, 19 November 1874, quoted in Beaty, *op. cit.*, p. 107. Cp. the not entirely favourable reviewer in *The Saturday Review*, 21 December 1872: 'The mind works on every page.'

4   Private and Social Themes in *Shirley*

I consider it a great honour to address the Brontë Society. The *Transactions* of the Society reveal the variety of approaches to the work of the Brontës and the continuing relevance and freshness of their creative achievement. There are still new things to say and new ways of saying them. I suppose that my best qualification for giving this lecture is a birth qualification – always a point on which Yorkshire folk pride themselves. Before I knew anything about nineteenth-century Haworth I knew twentieth-century Haworth. Before I had heard of the Keighley Mechanics' Institute in the days of the Brontës, I was sitting at a desk in the present Mechanics' Institute. Before I had heard of *Wuthering Heights* I knew the moors. Before I read *Shirley*, I had read Frank Peel's fascinating little book *The Risings of the Luddites, Chartists and Plugdrawers* in the Philip Snowden Collection in the Keighley Public Library.[1]

In a sense I grew up with the Brontës and accepted them naturally as a part of my own background, an exciting and provocative part. I feel today that I am making my own humble homage to the Brontës as a native of this neighbourhood rather than attempting as a mere historian to evaluate a fragment of their work. *Experientia docet.* Unless there is a sense of personal encounter the historian can make little of creative achievement. He can ransack novels for texts in the same way that Victorian preachers ransacked the Old Testament; he can illustrate trends and movements and problems in social history by apt quotations; he can dabble in sociology and talk of the reciprocal interactions of writer and reading public. But left to himself he can neither understand nor appreciate. Works of art must be taken as wholes; their public themes must be seen in relation to their private themes. Even close textual criticism can be no substitute for imaginative response which at its best involves imaginative exchange.

I have chosen in this lecture to focus my attention on *Shirley* as a complete work of art, first, because I prefer to consider one novel carefully rather than to survey several generally; second, because its social theme – the Luddite disturbances – only one of its themes, which has often been considered as mere underpinning, interests me in itself as a fascinating theme in English history;[2] and third, and not least, because *Shirley* is an avowedly Yorkshire novel, perhaps the first impressive regional novel in the English language. The landscape is unmistakably one which all Yorkshire folk – all Haworth folk – know. How different it is from every other landscape in the world:

> There is only one cloud in the sky; but it curtains it from pole to pole. The wind cannot rest; it hurries sobbing over hills of sullen outline, colourless with twilight and mist. Rain has beat all day on that church tower: it rises dark from the stony enclosure of its graveyard; the nettles, the long grass, and the tombs all drip with wet.

The descriptions of the exterior of Hollow's mill in the valley (Charlotte knew far less exactly of what happened inside it) or the Stilbro' iron-works on the horizon are realistic pointers to the strong contrast between Industry and Nature in the West Riding of the early industrial revolution – and now.

The accents too are often outspokenly Yorkshire, although at least one London critic called them 'slang'. Mr Yorke – note the name – often preferred 'his native Doric to a more refined vocabulary'. 'A Yorkshire burr', he affirmed, 'was as much better than a Cockney's lisp, as a bull's bellow than a ratton's squeak.' His family was a real Yorkshire family, like many other such families,

> here and there amongst her hills and wolds – peculiar, racy, vigorous: of good blood and strong brain; turbulent somewhat in the pride of their strength, and intractable in the force of their native powers; wanting polish, wanting consideration, wanting docility, but sound, spirited and true bred as the eagle on the cliff or the steed in the steppe.

Even the fire that burned in his grate was a Yorkshire fire. It was such, Charlotte tells the reader, 'as, if you be a southern, you do not often see burning on the hearth of a private apartment'. The Yorke family, modelled on the Taylors of Gomersal, represents one side of Yorkshire life: Joe Scott, Moore's overlooker, and the Luddites another. 'I reckon 'at us manufacturing lads i' th' north is a deal more intelligent, and knaws a deal more nor th' farming folk i' the' south,' Joe Scott tells Moore, and for all Moore's foreign ways he had a Yorkshire father, which as Joe tells him 'maks ye a bit Yorkshire too'.

The Luddites in the novel may have lacked that intelligence of which Joe spoke, but they were Yorkshire to the marrow. Describing their activity on one occasion, Charlotte writes: 'A yell followed this demonstration – a rioter's yell – a North of England – a Yorkshire – a West Riding – a West Riding-clothing-district-of-Yorkshire rioters' yell.' Moses Barraclough is based directly on a Joseph Barrowclough described in the *Leeds Mercury*.[3] There were, of course, Luddites in Lancashire just across the border and in Nottingham, where everything began, but for Charlotte – with her strong sense of local identity (inside Yorkshire as well as between Yorkshire and other places) – even revolt was Yorkshire.

Some of the early reviewers and critics of *Shirley* challenged Charlotte's presentation of the regional characteristics of Yorkshiremen. They disliked her relative assessment of Northerners and Cockneys. 'Taken as they ought to be, the majority of lads and lassies of the West Riding are gentlemen and ladies, every inch of them; it is only against the weak affectation and futile pomposity of a would-be aristocrat they turn mutinous.' 'This is very possible', G. H. Lewes commented, in the *Edinburgh Review*, 'but we must in that case strongly protest against Currer Bell's portraits being understood to be resemblances; for they are, one and all, given to break out and misbehave themselves upon very small provocation.' For another unsigned reviewer in the *Spectator*, the sketches of workmen, masters and other social groups who 'forty years ago went up to make the society of an obscure place in Yorkshire' were done 'with a somewhat exaggerated style and coloured too much by the writer's own mind'.

There is little doubt that in this connection Charlotte was right and her London critics wrong. As she wrote to Mr Smith in March 1850, when *Shirley* had already been acclaimed in the North and the people of Haworth were drawing lots to take copies of it out of the Mechanics' Institute Library,

> While the people of the South object to my delineation of Northern life and manners, the people of Yorkshire and Lancashire approve. They say it is precisely the contrast of rough nature with highly artificial cultivation which forms one of their own characteristics ... The question arises, whether do the London critics, or the old Northern squires understand the matter best.

It is significant that Mrs Gaskell did not criticise Charlotte on this score, nor did knowledgeable admirers of *Shirley*, like James Kay Shuttleworth. Indeed, Mrs Gaskell, in her own novel *North and South*, published six years after *Shirley* in 1855, assumed that the ways of the North and its language would be quite unfamiliar to readers south of the Trent, and demonstrated more sensitively than Disraeli the existence of two nations within the same island. (One reviewer thought *Shirley* 'to some extent a reminiscence of *Mary Barton*'.) A proper understanding of the conflict between North and South in nineteenth-century English history is as important, indeed, for all historians of the period, as is an understanding of the conflict between North and South for historians of the United States of America.

Now with all its weaknesses – and as a novel *Shirley* has many – it is an important contribution to the literature of regional interpretation. It may be true, as Margaret Lane has written, that *Shirley* is based on 'a foundation of acquired fact', that before Charlotte sent to Leeds for a file of the *Leeds Mercury* of 1812, 1813 and 1814, describing the Luddite risings, she had deliberately looked around for 'a subject for her next work', yet there is a note of authenticity in what Charlotte says which was the product not of research but of understanding.[4] She was anxious, as Mrs Gaskell noted, to write of 'things which she had known and seen; and amongst that number was the West Riding character'. There is a difference between Charlotte consulting the old files of the *Leeds Mercury* and George Eliot consulting the old files of *The Times* when she wrote *Felix Holt* and *Middlemarch*. Charlotte knew more or less what she would find.

I do not agree with Margaret Lane when she remarks that Charlotte's imagination was 'not one that could be nourished on social history'. It is true that like most great novelists she could not live on history alone, and that she lacked George Eliot's power of historical and sociological synthesis – George Eliot had the makings of a great historian – but she was familiar with those elements in the social history of the North, which she described and discussed in *Shirley*, and she could relate the Northern social background she knew to the older heroic history and legend which had fascinated her in her childhood – the Wellington theme and the Napoleon theme which influenced *Shirley* also.[5] Her views had changed, however, by the time *Shirley* was written. 'I have now outlived youth', she wrote in March 1848,

> and, though I dare not say that I have outlived all its illusions ... yet many things are not what they were ten years ago, and, amongst the rest, 'the pomp and circumstance of war' have quite lost in my eyes their fictitious glitter ... Convulsive revolutions put back the world in all that is good, check civilisations, bring the dregs of society to its surface; in short, it appears to me that insurrections and battles are the acute diseases of nations, and that their tendency is to exhaust by their violence, the vital energies of the countries where they occur.[6]

Charlotte deliberately set out to make *Shirley* like a piece of actual life. 'Something real, cool, and solid lies before you', she warned her readers on page 1, a page in a chapter which several reviewers strongly disliked, 'something unromantic as Monday morning ... it shall be cold lentils and vinegar without oil; it shall be unleavened bread with bitter herbs and no roast lamb.' Charlotte was incapable of living up consistently to this sober sense of purpose, but it represented her mood at the beginning of the venture, a mood conditioned in part by the reception given to *Jane Eyre*, in part no doubt by the circumstances of the late 1840s. Society novels were giving way to novels about society; it was difficult to be as detached as Jane Austen had been from the mood of public preoccupation; and Charlotte had Chartists in mind before she thought of Luddites.[7] Critics found it just as difficult to remain detached as authors did. You will no doubt remember the *Quarterly*'s hostile review of *Jane Eyre*.

> Pre-eminently an anti-Christian composition ... a murmuring against the comforts of the rich and against the privations of the poor, which, as far as each individual is concerned, is a murmuring against God's appointment ... We do not hesitate to say that the tone of mind and thought which has overthrown authority and violated every code human and divine abroad, and fostered Chartism and rebellion at home, is the same which has also written *Jane Eyre*.

The reaction of the *Quarterly* was perhaps not typical, but other reviewers also conceived of it as a voice from the dangerous North, and the *Christian Remembrancer* protested vigorously that 'it burns with moral Jacobinism'.

Shirley is the nearest that Charlotte got to writing a social novel, but it is not, *pace* nineteenth-century reviewers, a social novel which falls into the same category as Mrs Gaskell's *Mary Barton* or *North and South*. As many writers have pointed out, notably Dr Phyllis Bentley, it is not concerned with one theme but with a bundle of loosely connected – sometimes unconnected – themes.[8] It lacks compactness and integration: the interest is too much diffused.[9] Lewes, whose review in 1850 so angered Charlotte, said many strange, arguable and exaggerated things, but he was surely right when he compared *Jane Eyre* and *Shirley* as follows:

> The unity of *Jane Eyre* in spite of its clumsy and improbable contrivances, was great and effective: the fire of one passion fused the discordant elements into one mould. But in *Shirley* all unity ... is wanting. There is no passionate link: nor is there any artistic fusion, or intergrowth, by which one part evolves itself from another. Hence its falling-off in interest, coherent movement and life. The book may be laid down at any chapter, and almost any chapter may be omitted. The various scenes are gathered up into three volumes – they have not grown into a work.

In this respect, as in others, *Shirley* is remote from the *Middlemarch* which was to be written in Lewes's household.

II

Right though I believe Lewes was in this respect, this cannot be the last or the only word, and I would like in my lecture this afternoon to discuss three themes in *Shirley* and in conclusion to touch on a few others. First, I want to examine the Luddite background, second to consider very briefly the governor-governess theme, and third to comment on the passionate feminine protest which convinced most people at the time that Currer Bell was a woman, albeit a very unusual one.

Charlotte was not alone in choosing a period of time for the setting of her novel which was neither historical nor contemporary but lay in a period from twenty to sixty years earlier. In her stimulating survey, *The English Novel in the 1840s*, Kathleen Tillotson has suggested that there were two main motives for choosing the recent past as a period to discuss and to describe: 'that the past, being past, can be possessed, hovered and brooded over, with the story teller's supposed omniscience; and that the past, being not the present, is stable, untouched by the winds and waves which rock the present'. The opening of *Shirley* is quite explicit, although the recent past was far from stable. 'But out of late years are we about to speak; we are going back to the beginning of this century: late years – present years are dusty, sunburnt, hot, arid.'

The story of *Shirley* begins in 1812, four years before Charlotte was born, but the main scene of the Luddite disturbances was not far from Miss Wooler's school at Roe Head. As Mrs Gaskell writes, 'every place surrounding that house was connected with the Luddite riots – and Miss W[ooler] herself, and the older relatives of most of her [Charlotte's] schoolfellows must have known the actors in these grim disturbances.' So did the Rev. Patrick Brontë. The Taylors' home (Oakwell Hall) was the original of Field Head, the home of the Yorkes in *Shirley*, and I believe that the Brontë Society has made at least one *Shirley* pilgrimage there. This was not the Yorkshire of *Wuthering Heights*, of course, but it was very much the Brontës' Yorkshire.[10]

In trying to understand the background of the Luddite riots, I made a recent pilgrimage, not to Birstall but to Rudding Park, a handsome early nineteenth-century house far from the factory smoke and near to Harrogate. There the Radcliffe family, formerly of Huddersfield, have lived since 1824, and there in the muniment room is a priceless parcel of documents about the Yorkshire Luddites which fills in many of the details given by Mrs Gaskell in her admirable Chapter VI of *The Life of Charlotte Brontë*. The first baronet, Sir Joseph Radcliffe, was given his title for his services in helping, as chief magistrate at Huddersfield, to suppress the Luddite risings, and the bundles of his papers, hitherto unexamined, throw light on some of the personalities described in *Shirley*.

There are letters to and from William Cartwright, the owner of the Rawfolds factory, near Liversedge – within walking distance of Roe Head. Cartwright had foreign blood in his veins, spoke French well, was tall with dark eyes and complexion and lodged in his mill. He had much in common with Robert Moore, though I hasten to add there was a Mrs Cartwright. There are details of the background and repercussions of the murder on Crossland Moor of William Horsfall of Marsden, a prominent owner of shearing frames, on his return from the market on 28 April – he had no Mrs Yorke or a nurse like Mrs Horsfall (interesting choice of names) to restore him to health – and he died two days after the attack on him. There is a fascinating letter from the Rev. Hammond Hoberson of Heald's Hall, a friend of the Rev. Patrick Brontë, and the prototype of the Rev. Helstone. Mrs Gaskell describes him briefly but vividly: he lived to a ripe old age, and remained 'war-like' to the last, the year 1841, an uneasy year to die.

Before quoting from a few of these documents, let me first put the bare facts in their chronological order. The Luddite movement, which began in the neighbourhood of Nottingham during the winter of 1811-12, soon spread to other parts of the country, including the West Riding. It was a complex movement which still lacks a historian.[11] It was largely a protest against the introduction of the machine, but also, and in some areas, predominantly, it served as a violent form of pressure on employers, 'collective bargaining by riot'. Scarcity of work and high prices of provisions provided the impetus to action. On 23 March 1811, textile mills at Rawdon, eight miles from Leeds, were attacked by a body of armed men, who seized the watchmen, entered the premises and destroyed the machinery. On 9 April about 300 men attacked mills at Horbury near Wakefield and destroyed machinery and property. They were seen some time before this on the road, marching in regular sections, preceded by a mounted party with drawn swords, and followed by the same number mounted as a rear guard. On the night of Saturday 11 April, Cartwright's Rawfolds factory was attacked. Cartwright, supported by four of his own workmen and five soldiers, barricaded themselves inside the mill, and met the assailants with a vigorous and sustained discharge of musketry. In the course of the engagement, several desperate attempts were made to break down the doors and to force a way into the mill, but none of them proved successful, and after a battle of twenty minutes, during which two of the assailants were killed and a considerable number wounded, they withdrew in confusion. The bravery displayed by Cartwright in the defence of his premises won the praise of other mill owners less brave than he was, and a subscription of £3000 was conferred upon him and his family.

The failure of this last attempt spurred the Luddites, led by a man called George Mellor, to try to shoot mill owners rather than to attack mills, and William Horsfall, who had expressed himself freely and in forcible language as an implacable enemy of the workmen, was attacked and murdered on 28 April. Cartwright himself was twice shot at, several attempts were made to kill General Campbell, who was in charge of troops at Leeds, and a young woman was assaulted in the streets of Leeds because she had been seen near the spot where a murder was committed and might have been able to give evidence which would lead to the discovery of the murderers. In general, however, Leeds was far more quiet than smaller towns and villages. So, too, was Halifax.[12]

There was no effective police force to secure the maintenance of law and order in the West Riding, and the mill owners had to depend on their own initiative and on the support of the army. Indeed, the 12,000 troops employed against the Luddites exceeded in size the army which Wellington took into the Peninsula in 1808. The magistrates, key figures in the story and more often representative of the squirearchy rather than of the mill owners, were usually driven to ask for more and more military protection, although in addition they swore in special constables and relied heavily on spies and informers. Gradually the violent protest movement was worn down; sixty-six persons were arrested and committed to York gaol for a variety of offences, and finally at a Special Commission in York early in 1813 eighteen of the prisoners, including three of Horsfall's murderers, were convicted of capital offences and fourteen of them were executed on 16 January 1813. Of the others, six were convicted of simple felony and transported for seven years, and the remainder were either liberated on bail or acquitted. It was not always easy to distinguish between 'Luddism' and 'crime', particularly in its later stages, as Mr Justice Le Blanc stated at the York Assizes.

The Radcliffe documents, which fill in some of the background of this story, begin with a letter from Radcliffe to the Home Office on 17 March 1812, describing 'dirty pieces of paper' which had been thrown into one of the mills near Huddersfield and notices being posted by the Luddites on doors and walls offering 100 guineas for the Prince Regent's head. Radcliffe asked for 'Infantry as well as Cavalry' to cope with the disturbances, and 'one or two Bow Street officers' to help to discover the culprits. The 'mob', he said, had 'executed their destruction' on one of the mills near Huddersfield 'before the Cavalry guard having their horses at Huddersfield [near two miles off] could get to their ... quarters'. One of the dirty pieces of paper reads as follows (The spelling in all the letters is given in its quaint nineteenth-century confusion, confusion which always extended to Radcliffe's name, and no attempt has been made to tidy up the grammar):

We give Notice when the Shers is all broken the Spinners shall be the next if they be not taken down[:]Bickerman taylor mill ... has had his garded but we will pull all down som night and kill him that Nave and Roag.

On 28 March 1812, Radcliffe himself received a letter from a man signing himself 'Solicitor to General Ludd'. It purported to have been sent from Ludd's headquarters in Nottingham, and deserves to be quoted in full:

Sir,
Take notice that a Declaration has this day been filed against you in Ludd's Court at Nottingham and unless you remain Neutral judgement will immediately be signed against you for Default. I shall thence summon a Jury for an Inquiry of Damages take out Execution against Both your Body and House and then you may Expect General Ludd, and his well organised army to levy it with all Destruction possible.
                    And I am Sir your
                              Solicitor to General Ludd

Nottingham
March 20, 1812.

You have Sir rather taken an active part against the General But you are quiet and may remain so if you Chuse (and your Brother Justices also) for him, but if you either convict or countinance the other side as you have done (or any of you) you may expect your house in Flames and your Self in Ashes in a few days from your next move, for our Court is not Governd by (?) Terms but Equity.

N.B. In showing the General the other side for Inspection he orders me to inform you how the Cloth Dyers in the Huddersfield District as spent £700 in Petition Government to put the Laws in force to stop the Shearing Frames and Gig Mills to no purpose so they are trying this method now, and he is informed how you are afraid it will be carried into another purpose but you need not be apprehensive of that, for as soon as the obnoxious is stopped or Destroyed the General and his Brave Army will be disbanded and returned to their Employment like other Liege Subjects.

A few weeks later Radcliffe was sent a warning from a 'friend', who signed himself 'Love Good'. It ran:

This comes from a friend. I fained myself to be and got into the Secrets of the Ludites and knowing the dreadful plots that is going forward I send this to you there is dreadful preparation going forward for great destruction. It is reported you Back Thos. Atkinson it was ordered a wile a go for your place and Bradley Mill to be burnt one Night But I Pled it of with great to do. When that time comes foot nor Horses will be of any use there will be a great Destruction. You must not compell Watching and Warding you must side with the Luds if you Live I should a spoak Personally to you But Darst not if this was known it is deth to me.

From Mr. Love Good.

The kind of destruction which was being planned and the attitude of the Luddites to the 'sacrifices' they were making is graphically described in a letter put into the post at Dobcross by a George Wilson on 19 April 1812, and sent to James Middleton of Nottingham. The letter was intercepted by the authorities, and for a time they considered prosecuting its sender:

There has an engagement been betwixt the Luds & the Army which the Luds was defeated which was owing to Halifax Luds not coming up as they was apointed there was 16 men stormed the Plaice which they had two killed there wounded men was carried of and none of them as been taken since which the two men was buried on Thursday last at Othersfield which the Corps was put in a Dark room with six mold Candles which the friends of the Luds folowed them every man in morning with a silk apron edged with black which the ministers refused to Burie them but the Luds insisted on them being Buried in the Church which are to have a grand stone he live fore and twenty hours after he was taken ... He refused to invulge anything.

A more literate but no less chilling document was a letter from A. B. to Radcliffe on 27 April 1812:

I thought it my duty as a friend to address you with a few lines upon the Perilous situation in this Country; as you are the principle Magistrate for this District, they look to you, and only you for some Redress. If this Machinery is suffer'd to go on it will probably terminate with ... War, which, I could wish to be avoided, therefore as you are not interested by Machinery and the spirit of the People appear so resolute in the Cause, that if some measures be not adopted and immediately, it will be attended with great Distruction, and particular those who are our greatest Persecutors. With respect to this Watch and Ward Act you are not aware of the additional oppression you are bringing upon your Tenants, and other occupiers of Lands and all for the sake of two Individuals in this District, which I am not afraid to subscribe their Names, Mr. Th. Atkinson &

Mr. Wm. Horsfall, who will soon be number'd with the dead, and summoned before the awfull Tribunal, and that God who will judge every Man according the Deeds done in the Body.

The Watch and Ward Act was an Act extending the death penalty to machine-wreckers. That high hopes were placed in it by the manufacturers is shown by a letter from John Harrop, of Dobcross, on 26 April 1812:

I am in hopes when the Watch and Ward Act is put into full execution, we may consider ourselves safe, but until that time we may consider ourselves in very great danger, the Rioters knowing that the present time is the only one for a probability of success.

At this point the Rev. Hammond Hoberson emerges as a 'strong man' on the side of the manufacturers. A Helstonian letter of 30 April 1812, to William Cartwright of Rawfolds Mill, reads:

I am decidedly of opinion that the Troopers in this Neighbourhood are too few – That it is of importance to the preservation of order and security that there should be an Intelligent active officer near this place, to keep the Military alert, and to give a prompt direction to their Movements. Such an officer might extend his attention to Dewsbury. This valley is of considerable importance. Mill Bridge is central, and any riotous assemblage which might collect towards Halifax, or even on this side of Leeds or Bradford would probably pass this way to Dewsbury towards Wakefield ... The Corn Mills at and near Mirfield, and the property at Birstall would I think be greatly secured by the military here. There is not an inhabitant in this Neighbourhood that I know of, that is at all alive to the situation of the country, or rather perhaps *that is able* and that *dares* to take any decisive part in directing the operations of the Military besides himself. Were it possible for me to devote my *whole* time to the military I would do my best.

Radcliffe himself felt at the beginning of May 1812 that it was the time to press for military re-inforcements, and on 2 May he wrote to Major Gordon – in charge of troops at Huddersfield. Three days earlier Gordon had himself written to General Gray, the Commander-in-Chief of the Northern District at York, stating that it was his opinion that 'Huddersfield requires a much larger force than I have under my command for the protection of the property'. Radcliffe's request is more colourful:

Having been told by several friends that I am one of the marked for destruction, I trust to your goodness in affording me a guard of five privates and a non-commissioned officer, to be here night and day; I have ordered 5 Barrack Beds to be got ready with all expedition, & a better one for the non-commissioned officer to be placed in two rooms adjoining my stables & opposite to my house.

The necessary re-inforcements arrived. In the meantime, Radcliffe asked a friend to buy him blunderbusses in London. That Yorkshire businessmen were not losing their business canniness in the moment of danger was shown by his friend's reply:

I have bought you a pair of Blunderbusses which I hope you will approve of on sight. I was asked nine guineas for them, but obtained them at eight which I do not think dear.

The tactics for dealing with the Luddites had an element of subtlety about them, however, and spies and informers were as important as non-commissioned officers and blunderbusses. On 27 June 1812, the Rev. William Hay, chief of the Manchester Magistrates (and later a key figure in the events leading up to the Massacre of Peterloo), sent the following message to Radcliffe by a special orderly:

I have just received Information, on which I think I can rely, that a very extensive meeting is to be held on Sunday between 4 and 10 in the afternoon and evening at a place called Cross Pipes, Denby Moor . . . I have consulted with General Acland (the General in Manchester) upon the subject and our very anxious wish is that this meeting may not on any account be prevented – We hope to have some friends there – I have a two-fold object in writing this – the first is, that if there should be any disposition in the troops at Huddersfield . . . to prevent or to disperse this meeting you would do all that you can to prevent it. The next is, that if you have one or two people whom you can depend upon, to send amongst them to make observation you would exercise your discretion in doing so – as by this means we may set off our informers as checks on each other.

The atmosphere remained tense in the early autumn of 1812, and Radcliffe had another warning on 21 October, when a letter was sent to him with the grim message: 'I most assuredly will make myself another Bellingham and I have the pellet made that shall be sent in your Hart.' Bellingham was the deranged murderer of the Prime Minister, Spencer Perceval, and there are signs that he was being viewed as a public hero by the Luddites at this time. Maitland at the War Office in London had written to General Gray in York on 12 May 1812, immediately after hearing of Perceval's murder:

Poor Perceval was *shot dead* in the lobby of the House of Commons on the 11 instant. There is every reason to believe it was done from motives of personal Revenge ... It may however be advisable for you to circulate this information to the people about you, that they may be placed upon their Guard.

During the shortening days of the early autumn there were mounting fears for the safety of property, and Earl Fitzwilliam, the Lord Lieutenant of the County, wrote to Radcliffe on 20 October:

Hitherto the whole band of Luddites of our Riding have escaped untouched; their system of Oaths and Terror apparently renders them intangible; an appearance much to be lamented ... that is productive of most serious evil and that may possibly become productive of still greater in the course of the long nights. Examples of detection, conviction and punishment, can alone avert these evils. [13]

The arrests and conviction of the Luddites duly followed, and Radcliffe was made a baronet for his services to the cause of law and order. In the Radcliffe home at Rudding Park, there is a gun which bears this inscription:

This gun was found hid in the Elland Hall Great Park Wood after the York Special Assizes in January 1813 together with many others stolen and cut down in the like manner by the Luddites who took them from the owner by forcibly breaking into their houses in the night time. All the rest were owned but this being from its value supposed to have belonged to a gentleman who was ashamed at having wanted resolution to resist the robbers was left in the custody of Sir Joseph Radcliffe before whom all the rest were brought and delivered to the owners as by them demanded and proved so to be.

This was not quite the end of the Luddite story. As late as 12 March 1815, Radcliffe was warned: 'Luddite is going to start here again ... Ludders this time will die to a man ... determined to have blood for blood.'

These documents are a more valuable source for a study of the Luddites than the files of the *Leeds Mercury* which Charlotte ordered from Leeds. [14] It is necessary, however, to pay tribute to Charlotte for the way she handled the Luddite material, particularly since some writers on the Brontës – including some who have had the honour of addressing this annual meeting – have claimed that she treated it quite inadequately. She did not confuse the Luddites and the Chartists. She was peculiarly sensitive to the ambivalent attitude of the mill owners she was describing, men who opposed the war against Napoleon and the policies of the British Government (symbolised in the Orders-in-Council) while at the same time they demanded stricter government intervention to suppress machine wrecking and attacks on property. She could distinguish between 'food riots' and factory disturbances. Historians have still not caught up with her. Not only is there no satisfactory history of the Luddites, but there is no scholarly monograph on the Orders-in-Council, one of the main focal points of business grievance.[15]

Charlotte was wise, too, to distinguish between the courage of men like Moore and the supineness of the manufacturers as a class. 'Most of the manufacturers seem paralyzed when they are attacked.' There is good evidence for this. Here is a note from Hoberson in the Rudding Park papers: 'Some of your neighbours are afraid they should be saddled with great expense with these soldiers. [Given the danger] I do not understand why they should think so.'

It was only after the event that many of the manufacturers paid tribute to the resolute stand made by a minority against them, and even then their tribute – satirised in Chapter 30 of *Shirley* – easily turned into obsequious flattery.

The most extreme criticism of Charlotte's approach to social problems in *Shirley* has been concerned not with atmosphere or with detail but with her inability to offer any kind of answer to the social question. If she had been a better social novelist, it has been suggested, she would have had an answer or at least a judgement. I do not believe that this criticism can be sustained. There was no obvious answer to the Luddite agitation except more jobs, a fall in the price of food and a rise in the standard of living. This long-term answer lends itself to statistical treatment, but it hardly provides material for a novel. All that Charlotte could do was to state the issues as seen both by employers and workers, to measure the social distance between them – she could be quite explicit about 'class' – and to point to the healing influence of time and experience, the kind of experience that affected Moore. The issue as seen by the employers is clearly stated in one of Moore's replies to Barraclough in Chapter 8.

You desire me to quit the country: you request me to part with my machinery: in case I refuse, you threaten me. I *do* refuse – point blank. Here I stay; and by this mill I stand ... What will you do? The utmost you *can* do – and this you will never *dare* to do is to burn down my mill, destroy its contents, and shoot me. What then? Suppose that building was a ruin and I a corpse, what then? Would that stop intervention or exhaust science? Not for the fraction of a second of time! Another and better gig mill would rise on the ruins of this, and perhaps a more enterprising owner come in my place.

The same view was stated categorically by John Harrop, a real-life Northern manufacturer, one of whose letters has already been quoted. He wrote bluntly in May 1812: 'I consider the protection of our machinery absolutely necessary for the public good. It is our determination to support it as long as we are able.'

A recognition of the grim necessity of this situation did not prevent Charlotte from sympathising with the distress of the working population and the hunger they endured. She was completely uninfluenced by political economy – the political economy that Harriet Martineau, the admirer of *Shirley*, so fervently accepted. She concentrated on the human plight of the poor, and in one terse and famous sentence at least expressed its chief social implication, 'Misery generates hate.'

It is as powerful a phrase as any coined by Carlyle, Disraeli or Engels, and it was as relevant to the 1840s as the 1810s. Fittingly, Sir William Beveridge, as he then was, made it the motto of his influential wartime book *Full Employment in a Free Society*, published in 1944. I do not know how familiar Brontë lovers are with Beveridge's two references to *Shirley*. 'This text', he says, 'is my main text. The greatest evil of unemployment is not physical but moral, not the want which it may bring but the hatred and fear which it breeds.' He goes on to quote another passage in *Shirley*, from the same conversation between Moore and Moses Barraclough, in which the workers' case is clearly set out. 'Invention may be all right,' says Barraclough, 'but I know it isn't right for poor folks to starve. Them that governs mun find a way to help us ... Ye'll say that's hard to do – so much louder mun we shout then, for so much slacker will t' Parliament men be to set on a tough job.' 'Worry the Parliament-men as much as you please', replies the employer, 'but to worry the mill-owners is absurd.'

That was a fair nineteenth-century statement, though Moore – or his successor in the 1840s – would probably have disagreed with Beveridge's comment, 'To look to individual employers for maintenance of demand and full employment is absurd. These things are not within the power of employers. They must therefore be undertaken by the State, under the supervision and pressure of democracy, applied through the Parliament men.'

I have quoted this passage because it shows that a statement in *Shirley* can be made the starting point for a serious argument not about nineteenth- but about twentieth-century society. Charlotte cannot be blamed for not giving a clearer answer than she did. For an example of complete helplessness in face of the social situation of her time, turn not to a novel but to the *Report of the Royal Commission on the Handloom Weavers*, published in 1841:

The power of the Czar of Russia could not raise the wages of men so situate. He might, indeed, order a scale of prices to be paid for them for the work which they did, but in such cases the manufacturer would soon cease to give out work, as it would be against his interest to do it. The Czar of Russia, either by fixing on a high scale of wages, or by a direct command, might put an end to the occupation altogether; and such would be a most merciful exercise of his unlimited power; but the authority of the government of a free country cannot thus control the subjects, even for their own good; and all that remains, therefore, is to enlighten the handloom weavers as to their real situation, warn them to flee from the trade, and to beware of leading their children into it as they would beware of the commission of the most atrocious of crimes.

III

I have left myself very little time to comment on the tutor-governess theme or the passionate feminine protests in *Shirley*, both of which have been discussed by many Brontë scholars.[16] To put what I have said about the Luddites in proper perspective, however, I must emphasise that most of the reviews of *Shirley* which appeared in 1849 and 1850 scarcely touched on the Luddite theme. The famous, hostile *Times* review, which appeared on 7 December 1849, and was read by Charlotte while she was staying in the 'big Babylon' of London – it brought tears to her eyes – does not mention the Luddites at all. Lewes's review in the *Edinburgh Review* in January 1850 only referred to the subject once. *Fraser's Magazine* thought that she had exaggerated 'the alarm and distress of the times', but passed on quickly to the judgement that Currer Bell 'knows women by their brains and hearts, men by their foreheads and chests'; having complained memorably that with 'nearly a hundred characters to be disposed of', not even Covent Garden could have found the right resources, it praised Charlotte for being 'always good on the topic of governesses, their rights and wrongs'. *The Times* dwelt on the more general feminine protests, while Lewes, to Charlotte's intense annoyance, concentrated likewise on such problems as 'the mental equality of the sexes – question mark'; female literature; 'sins against Truth and Nature'; and 'the Pride and Nobleness of Woman'.

The governor-governess themes are treated with eloquence and insight. They were at the same time public and private in *Shirley* in a way that the relationship between employer and employee was not. When Charlotte talked of the dependence of the private tutor or the governess on his or her master, she explored the implications of 'dependence' far more thoroughly than when she turned to the dependence of 'hands' or manufacturers. It was a form of exploitation that she knew at first hand. Even Mrs Pryor – whom *The Times* reviewer dismissed, probably rightly, with the remark 'a drearier gentlewoman it has seldom been ours to meet' – has powerful sentences about governesses put into her mouth. 'It was intimated that I must live alone, and never transgress the invisible but rigid line which established the difference between me and my employers.' Good Tory that she was – 'the last person to wish to instil into your mind any feeling of dissatisfaction with your lot in life, or any sentiment of envy or insubordination to your employer,' she warned Caroline against the perils of a governess's career. Even Shirley, depicted so sympathetically, is forced by the circumstances in which she finds herself, to try to exercise power over Louis, and Caroline is driven to ask her, 'are you impatient at what you perhaps consider his social position?'

The governess theme looms too large in *Shirley* to be ignored – it is a binding element in the plot in a way that no other theme is – and some extremely interesting remarks are made about it. It is not related at all, however, to the Luddite background, and the remarks are better put alongside parallel statements in Charlotte's other novels than considered in relation to other themes in *Shirley*.

The same is true of most of the striking but sometimes rhetorical passages concerning women's place in a rightful scheme of social relations. There is nothing 'cool' about the way Charlotte's women talk – and behave – in this novel of the male world. Indeed, Shirley herself feels passionately that she ought to enjoy male prerogatives. She wears men's clothes and moves through the novel – until near the end – as freely as a man. 'I am an esquire! Shirley Keeldar Esquire ought to be my style and title. They gave me a man's name; I hold a man's position: it is enough to inspire me with a touch of manhood.'

Shirley's feminine assertiveness speaks for itself: it does not require long speeches. Caroline's speeches by contrast often seem inconsistent with the drawing of her character. The best and most convincing passages are Charlotte's own, sometimes satirical:

> It is good for women, especially, to be endowed with a soft blindness: to have mild, dim eyes, that never penetrate below the surface of things – that take all for which it seems: thousands, having this, keep their eyelids drooped on system; but the most downcast glance has its loophole, through which it can, on occasion, take its sentimental survey of life.

It is interesting that Charlotte looks for loopholes rather than expects solutions – except of a romantic kind – in talking both of governesses and tutors on the one hand, and of women on the other. The good works of an 'old maid' are deemed inadequate fully to satisfy. 'Old maids, like the houseless and unemployed poor, should not ask for a place and an occupation in the world: the demand disturbs the lazy and rich: it disturbs parents.' The only escape for

Louis Moore, before he proposes to Shirley, lies not in society but
in nature. When Shirley tells him in one of her provocative and
imperious moods, 'my roses smell sweet to you, and my trees give you
shade,' Louis replies, 'No caprice can withdraw these pleasures from
me: they are mine.'

Sometimes a curate is used as a stalking horse – they have no other
purpose in the novel. Thus Mr Donne talks of lapdogs as 'something
appropriate to the fair sex.' 'Perhaps I am an exception,' Shirley
replies.

'Oh! you can't be, you know,' Donne goes on, 'All ladies are alike in
these matters: that is universally allowed.'

Charlotte's detestation of self-conscious male dominance did not
imply, however, that she saw 'solutions' here any more than in
economic and social matters influencing employment. In 1850, she was
to write to Mrs Gaskell of an article in the *Westminster Review* on
'Woman's Mission' that while there 'are evils which our own efforts
will best reach ... there are other evils deep-rooted in the foundations
of the social system – which no effort of ours can touch; of which we
cannot complain; of which it is advisable not too often to think.'[17]
She laid more emphasis on suffering than on action.

Shirley herself is willing ultimately to submit to her 'master'. She is
defined as a 'lady' and Charlotte is forced to consider in the novel the
problem of the unlady-like lady as well as the problem of the woman in
chains. For this reason the reader and the critic too are forced back to
the question: What is *Shirley* really about? The fatal absence of focus
which prevents it from being a successful novel derived from an initial
uncertainty in Charlotte's mind, an uncertainty which was not
resolved – it was rather accentuated – as the work took shape. She
changed her mind several times about the title and wanted her
publishers to decide. The uncertainty was immediately seized upon by
the reviewers. To one of them, 'the authoress never seems distinctly
to have made up her mind what she was to do; whether ... to paint
character or to tell a love story.' *The Times* reviewer was somewhat
cocksure in implying that the second of these objects had been
uppermost in Currer Bell's mind, but he argued that there was not one
love story but several. 'Love-making', he said, 'in one shape or
another, is going on from the first page to the last, and as soon as one
couple quits the scene another comes on to entertain the spectators.'[18]
Charlotte was probably less disturbed by this remark than by his
devastating conclusion. 'The infrequent brilliancy seems but to make
more evident and unsightly the surrounding gloom. *Shirley* is not a
picture of real life ... it is a mental exercise.'

I would not wish to be so harsh. As the friendly *Morning Chronicle*
put it,

> *Shirley* is totally free from cant, affection or emotional tinsel of any kind;
> genuine English in the rough originality of its conception of character:
> genuine English in style and direction. It is a tale of passion and character
> rather than an incident.

It certainly remains readable, interesting and full of imaginative
vitality.

The Times reviewer did not know the saddest of all the underlying
themes that darkened the days of composition – the deaths of
Branwell, Emily and Ann. Flippantly he suggested that the novel was a
product of the recent pestilence – the cholera outbreak – and that this
might explain the 'multiplicity of sick-bed solutions'. In fact, *Shirley*
was written, as the title of Chapter 24 proclaims, in 'the valley of the
shadow of death'. What shape it would have taken in different
circumstances it is impossible to say. It begins with curates, and more
of its pages might have been devoted to their antics – that would have
been a loss: alternatively it might have acquired greater unity as a
regional study – that would have been a gain. As it was, to quote Mrs
Gaskell, 'Charlotte went on with her work steadily. But it was dreary
to write without anyone to listen to the progress of her tale.' The sick-
bed solutions, the miracles of recovery, were only for the printed page.
The reality was different, and it broke through at more than one point
in the novel.

> Till break of day, she wrestled with God in earnest prayer. Not always do
> those who dare such divine conflict prevail. Night after night the sweat of
> agony may burst dark on the forehead; the supplicant may cry for mercy
> with that soundless voice the soul utters when its appeal is to the Invisible.
> 'Spare my beloved,' it may implore. 'Heal my life's life. Rend not from me
> what long affliction entwines with my whole nature. God of heaven – bend
> – bear – be clement.' And after this cry and strife, the sun may rise and see
> him wasted.

Inexorably, however, the novel passed through the valley of the
shadows to the happy ending – a double marriage, a new cinder-block
highway, cottages and cottage gardens, a mighty mill, and a chimney as
ambitious as the Tower of Babel. This was not quite the ending,
however, for in the last two paragraphs Charlotte seems to express her
own doubts first about the realism of her story, then about its
meaning. In her penultimate paragraph she goes back before her tale
began to the time when there was no mill in existence and it was
whispered that there were fairies in Fieldhead Hollow. As for her last
paragraph, it reads like this:

The story is told. I think I now see the judicious reader putting on his spectacles to look for the moral. It would be an insult to his sagacity to offer directions. I only say, God speed him in the quest.

NOTES

1   This study, first published in 1888, and recently much quoted, should not be taken as an impeccably authentic source. Its main interest is that it collects living oral traditions in the West Riding and stitches them together.

2   More recently, it has been suggested, as was hinted at the time, that the unspoken subject of the novel was Chartism, see T. Eagleton, *Myths of Power: A Marxist Study of the Brontës* (1975).

3   *Leeds Mercury*, 11 July 1812.

4   For Margaret Lane's highly intelligent Brontë studies, see M. Lane, *The Brontë Story* (1953), and her introduction to the Everyman edition of *Shirley* (1955). See also W. Gerin's invaluable *Charlotte Bronte – the Evolution of Genius* (1967), which describes the tragic family circumstances against the background of which *Shirley* was written.

5   See F. Ratchford, *The Brontës' Web of Childhood* (1941), pp. 180-1, 214-21.

6   T. J. Wise and J. A. Symington (eds), *The Brontës, Their Lives, Friendships and Correspondence*, vol. I (1932), p. 202.

7   See an interesting note written after this lecture by I. Holgate, 'The Structure of Shirley', in the *Brontë Society Transactions*, part 72 (1962).

8   Phyllis Bentley, who was present when I delivered this lecture and whom I met and talked to on several occasions, had a magnificent sense of place. See her book, *The Brontës* (1947).

9   I do not agree with Eagleton that the weakness of the novel lies in its failure to deal adequately with 'the working class'.

10   The local sources for *Shirley* have subsequently been noted in the introduction to the Oxford standard edition, edited by M. Rosengarten and M. Smith (1979). It does not deal, however, with the themes of this lecture or draw on the work of historians concerned with the Luddites.

11   Since 1958 several historians have attempted to write one. See, in particular, for published accounts, E. P. Thompson, *The Making of the English Working Class*, 2nd edn (1968), Chapter XIV: M. I. Thomis, *The Luddites* (1970); and J. Dinwiddy, 'Luddism and Politics in the Northern Counties', in *Social History*, vol. 4 (1979).

12   This situation should be related to what was said above (see vol. I, pp. 214-15 about cities as centres of subversion.)

13   When I gave this lecture, I had not studied the Fitzwilliam Papers which have been used by later historians. As a Whig Lord Lieutenant, Fitzwilliam was neither sympathetic towards nor secured the confidence of the Home Office during the Luddite disturbances.

14   It is interesting to speculate on what Charlotte would have thought or written had she consulted the *Leeds Intelligencer* as well as the *Leeds Mercury*, which usually drew no distinction between Luddism and crime, but which made the most of the theme of political subversion and even of 'French gold'.

15   The gap has been partially filled by the excellent French study in two volumes by F. Crouzet, *L'Économie britannique et le blocus continental* (1958).

16   The most recent discussions have taken place within the context of 'women's studies'. Marxist discussants have tried to relate Charlotte's views on 'class' to her views on 'gender'.

17   Wise and Symington, *op. cit.*, vol. II, pp. 49-50. The Radical feminist, Mary Taylor, asked Charlotte, 'has the world gone so well with you that you have no protest to make against its absurdities?' (ibid., vol. I, p. 235).

18   Of young Yorke he wrote, 'the didactics of the precocious twelve-year-old would do honour to John Stuart Mill himself'.

5   Trollope the Traveller

Trollope's *Travelling Sketches*, published in 1866, is not mentioned in his *Autobiography* (1883): it consisted of short pieces which first appeared in the *Pall Mall Gazette*, none of which attracted much attention from contemporaries. Yet Trollope did discuss in his *Autobiography*, with comments of unequal length and interest, how and why he had come to write his one-volume *The West Indies and the Spanish Main* (1859), his two-volume *North America* (1862), his two-volume *Australia and New Zealand* (1876), and, not least, his *South Africa* (1878).

Trollope was characteristically self-critical, greatly as he savoured each of his travels. The first of the four specialised travel studies he regarded as the best book that had come from his pen, 'short, amusing, useful and true':[1] it included large parts of Central America and ended not in the West Indies, but in Canada, which figured in *North America* too. The second, more ambitious, he thought of as 'not a good book', 'tedious and confused' and 'hardly likely to be of future value to those who wish to make themselves acquainted with the United States'.[2] The third was put quietly in its place in proper Trollopian language as 'a thoroughly honest book ... the result of unflagging labour for a period of fifteen months'.[3] The fourth was written too late in his life for him to attempt a judgement: all he stated in his *Autobiography* was the amount of money he received for it, £850, less than half of the amount he received in the same year for *Is He Popenjoy?*[4] The book was well received however. 'On so very dull a subject as South Africa,' wrote the *Saturday Review*, 'there is scarcely a dull page.'[5]

As always, Trollope attached supreme importance to 'truth', but, since he wanted to entertain as well as to inform, he was concerned in his four major travel books to extend his readers' imagination as well as their knowledge.[6] He knew that the public was increasingly drawn to travel books. 'That men and women should leave their homes at the end of summer and go somewhere – though only to Margate', he wrote in the first of the *Travelling Sketches*, 'has become a thing so fixed that incomes are made to stretch themselves to fit the rule.'[7] Trollope stretched *his* travels into the most distant places to include Kingston, 'of all the towns that I ever saw ... perhaps, on the whole, the least

89

alluring'; Cincinnati, 'slow, dingy and uninteresting, but with an air of substantial civic dignity'; Ballaarat [sic], 'very pleasant to the sight, which is, perhaps, more than can be said for any other "provincial" town in the Australian colonies'; Wellington, about which he said little except that it was 'built only of wood' and reminded him of St Thomas in the Virgin Islands, 'but in appearance only';[8] and Bloemfontein, about which he said much – 'not peculiarly beautiful' but 'complete and neat', with an air of 'contentment and general prosperity which is apt to make a dweller in busy cities think that though it might not quite suit himself it would be very good for everybody else'.[9]

After re-reading Trollope's travel books and studying in retrospect the immediate reactions to them, it is possible to qualify at the same time some of his judgements on their relative merits and some of the judgements of his contemporaries. *The West Indies* does not stand out so prominently as he thought either in content or in organisation, and is riddled with what often seems like prejudice. *South Africa* has similar qualities. *Australia and New Zealand*, while packed with 'much valuable information', is neither more nor less perceptive than *North America*, although it lacks colour.[10] As for *North America*, for all its weaknesses, including those recognised by Trollope and his contemporaries, it has a special significance in relation to his life and work. Because it was intended by Trollope to make late amends for his mother's 'somewhat unjust' book about 'our cousins over the water', it is a necessary element in his biography.[11] Because, as he put it in his first chapter, 'it had been the ambition of my literary life to write a book about the United States',[12] it is inevitable that its claims and weaknesses should be subject to independent critical tests. It was, moreover, one out of more than 200 somewhat similar books on North America produced by fellow Englishmen during the previous forty-five years.[13]

'For a dozen years we have been surfeited with descriptions of rambles by Englishmen through the United States,' wrote one reviewer, 'and it must be confessed that, so far as mere narrative description is concerned, we have read more instructive books than Mr Trollope's.' The itinerary of their 'tours' was often more interesting, and when the itineraries converged 'not even he' could 'give charm to the *crambe repetita* of so many predecessors'.[14]

I

There is one basic point about which there can be no doubt. Trollope enjoyed travel. It was also a necessary part of his youth and of his work.[15] After his first spell in Ireland, which played a key part both in his experience and in his imagination, he was called upon to explore 'a considerable portion of Great Britain' on horseback with 'a minuteness which few have enjoyed'.[16] His rural (and urban) rides were writing as well as seeing trips, for, as Frederick Page remarked, 'from the mere number of his books one might have thought that Trollope must have been writing all the time, at home, in railway carriages, on board ship.'[17] He had made three visits to Italy by the end of 1857, visited Egypt in the following year, where he finished the very English *Dr Thorne*, went on to the Holy Land and returned via Spain. The West Indies and Central America followed in 1858. Once again Trollope wrote as he travelled: 'the descriptions come hot on the paper from their causes.'[18] Not surprisingly, he thought of himself as belonging to 'the travellers' guild'.[19] He went round the world twice.

His American trip in 1861 was distinctive in two respects – first, in that he obtained leave from the Post Office to undertake it, and, second, in that he intended from the start to write a book about it. 'No observer', he said of his mother, 'was ever less qualified to judge of the prospects or even of the happiness of a young people. No one could have been worse adapted by nature for the task of learning whether a nation was in a way to thrive.'[20] It was for this reason that he was determined to make amends. It mattered little to him that his visit coincided with the American 'War of Secession', though he was interested in it, and he did not visit the South. 'A man might as well be in Westminster Abbey during the Coronation of her Majesty', *Fraser's Magazine* complained, 'and not look at the ceremony.'[21]

The popularity of travel books during the 1850s and 1860s was perfectly compatible with 'Podsnappery'. *Travelling Sketches*, on the lines of his earlier *Hunting Sketches*, deliberately pandered to the public. It described types rather than characters, characters with common names like Smith, Robinson and Miss Thompson, the kind of names Trollope had spurned in his early novels. It also introduced classes of characters, like 'unprotected female tourists' or 'the united Englishmen who travel for fun'. It is neither better nor worse than the many travel articles in *Punch*, like an article of 1858 with the title 'Why Englishmen Are So Beloved upon the Continent'. 'Because they never foster the delusion', the *Punch* writer explained, 'that by letting their moustache grow they may succeed in passing themselves off as natives of the Continent.'[22] And referring to Trollope's hero, Palmerston, who died one year before *Travelling Sketches* appeared in book form, the writer added, 'Because whatever grievance they may fancy they have sustained, they never more than twenty times *per diem* swear Lord Palmerston shall hear of it.'[23]

Trollope went on a second visit to the United States, this time a 'mission', in 1868.[24] While welcoming the private hospitality and saluting the grand public efforts 'made by private munificence to relieve the sufferings of humanity', he nonetheless dwelt as he had done – and as he was to dwell in some of his later novels – on the fact that 'at the top of everything ... the very men who are the least fit ... occupy high places.'[25] Yet the novel he finished in Washington, *He Knew He Was Right*, scarcely reflects this preoccupation.[26]

Australia and New Zealand was the record of travels originally intended by his wife and himself to see their 'shepherd son',[27] but, before going, he signed on with a newspaper, the *Daily Telegraph*, to write a series of articles.[28] 'If the travelling author can pay his travelling bills', he told his readers, 'he must be a good manager on the road.' He had also ensured equally prudently that if the *Great Britain*, the ship in which he travelled to Australia, sank, 'there would be new novels ready to come out under my name for some years to come.'[29] He was writing all the time on the journey, which he found very tiring,[30] returning, nonetheless, via America from San Francisco to New York through Salt Lake City, where he met Brigham Young. Both Australasia and America were to figure in his later work,[31] although it is doubtful whether he would have needed to travel there to write *Harry Heathcote of Gangoil*, the Christmas number of the *Graphic* in 1873, or *The American Senator* (1877), which, as a reviewer in the *Athenaeum* said, 'might just as well have been called "The Chronicle of a Writer at Dillsborough" ... The Senator might have been cut out of the book almost without affecting the story.'[32]

Trollope travelled to the last – he made a long trip to Italy in the late winter and spring of 1881 – and returned to the source, Ireland, twice in 1882. It was Ireland more than any other place on his itineraries which brought together the 'real world' of fact and the world of fiction which he created, and, if he never wrote a travel book about it, he felt deeply about all its problems. Trollope's Irish novels, according to T.H.S.Escott, an early and knowledgeable critic, presented 'a true picture of the country, a true insight into its people';[32] and the last of these novels, *The Landleaguers*, unfinished when Trollope died, has been described as 'the closest he ever came to writing documentary fiction'.[33]

In Trollope's travel books we get only rare glimpses of his 'inner life', carefully kept out of his *Autobiography*. In *Travelling Sketches* he dwelt more on nature than on society: 'to be able to be happy at rest among the mountains is better than a capacity for talking French in saloons.'[34] Likewise, in *Australia and New Zealand*, he compared eighteenth-century 'grand tours' with nineteenth-century expeditions: 'in the last century Englishmen travelled to see cities, and to see men, and to study the world – but in those days mountains were troublesome, and dark valleys were savage, and glaciers were horrible.'[35] He admired the members of the Alpine Club, who went on very different and more perilous journeys from his own.[36]

Sometimes these glimpses are related to a broader perspective. He begins one chapter of *The West Indies*, for example, with the words 'How best to get about this world which God has given us is certainly one of the most interesting subjects which men have to consider, and one of the most interesting works on which men can employ themselves.' Comparing the development of transport to the development of a child, he claims that men have so far reached only the learning-to-use-a-knife-and-fork stage, 'though we hardly yet understand the science of carving'. 'We know that the world must be traversed by certain routes, prepared for us originally not by ourselves, but by the hand of God.'[37] Given such an interesting perspective, the chapter is curiously uninteresting, although it hints at the futuristic concerns which were to be expressed in *The Fixed Period* (1882). Trollope criticised the French way not only of promoting transport ventures but of discussing such issues.

> When has truly mighty work been heralded by magniloquence? ... If words ever convey to my ears a positive contradiction of the assertion which they affect to make, it is when they are grandly antithetical and magnificently verbose. If in addition to this, they promise to mankind 'new epochs, new views, and unlimited horizons', surely no further proof can be needed that they are vain, empty and untrue.[38]

It is partly because of such a desire to deflate that it is not this chapter out of Trollope's three important travel books which lingers in the mind, but Chapter 14 of *North America*, where he deals not with canals or railways but with hotels. 'I consider myself as qualified', he exclaimed with feeling, 'to write a chapter on hotels – not only on the hotels of America but on hotels generally. I have myself been much too frequently a sojourner at hotels. I think I know what an hotel should be, and what it should not be; and am almost inclined to believe, in my pride, that I could myself fill the position of a landlord with some chance of social success, though probably with none of satisfactory pecuniary results.'[39]

Trollope did not like American hotels – either their methods of management or the services they offered – but he did recognise that American hotels of the future would create a new demand. 'The hotel itself will create a population – as the railways do. With us railways run to the town; but in the States the towns run to the railways. It is the same thing with the hotels.'[40] By contrast, English hotels – or inns – looked to the past. 'The worst about them is that they deteriorate from year to year instead of becoming better.' There was only the slightest touch of nostalgia in his statement that 'since the old days are gone, there are wanting the landlord's bow, and the kindly smile of his stout wife.' The new railway hotels, he added, were 'frequently gloomy, desolate, comfortless and almost suicidal'.[41]

While praising Swiss hotels as the best in the world, Trollope reserved special criticism for those he thought the dearest – the French. Running through his travel books, despite his professed cosmopolitanism,[42] there is a strong anti-French note, which applies to things as well as to people. 'Cotton-velvet sofas and ormolu clocks stand in the place of convenient furniture, and logs of wood at a franc a log fail to impart to you the heat which the freezing cold of a Paris winter demands.'[43] One of Trollope's main complaints against New York hotels was that they were full of French furniture. 'I could not write at a marble table whose outside rim was curved into fantastic shapes' or sit on '*papier mâché* chairs with small velvety seats'. When he complained to the landlord, he was told that his house had been 'furnished not in accordance with the taste of England, but with that of France'.[44]

Passing from descriptions of things (to which Trollope was always sensitive) to the framing of ambitious generalisation was always rather too easy for Trollope the traveller, as it is, perhaps, to most intelligent travellers, and rather more of Trollope the deflating self-critic might have been salutary. 'All America', he went on, 'is now furnishing itself by the rules which guided that hotel-keeper. I do not merely allude to actual household furniture – to chairs, tables and detestable gilt clocks. The taste of America is becoming French in its conversation, French in its comforts and French in its discomforts. French in its eating, and French in its dress, French in its manners and French in its art.'[45]

II

Some generalisations in the important travel studies went deeper, and some of them have been subjected to sharp criticism. Two, in particular, deserve further examination. The first related to the West Indies, the second to the United States.

Throughout *The West Indies*, which, as we have seen, Trollope considered his 'best book', there is an open distrust of the negro, even of his religion: 'I think', Trollope wrote of the negro in Chapter 4, 'Jamaica-Black Men', 'that he seldom understands the purpose of industry, the object of truth, or the results of honesty.'[46] It was not that Trollope dwelt for long on 'the black skin and the thick lip' – those, he said, the visitor got quickly used to: he lingered rather on psychological qualities which he held that negroes shared with children or dogs. 'They best love him who is most unlike themselves'; 'the more they fear their masters, the more they will respect him.'[47]

The generalisations multiply, although Trollope was aware of the differences between the islanders.[48] 'They have no care for tomorrow, but they delight in being gaudy for today.' 'They are greedy of food, but generally indifferent to its quality.' They would be 'altogether retrograde if left to themselves'. 'These people are a servile race, fitted by nature for the hardest physical work, and apparently at present fitted for little else.' Yet they had little inclination to work. 'Without a desire for property, man could make no progress. But the negro has no such desire; no desire strong enough to induce him to labour for that which he wants.'[49]

Trollope did not condemn the emancipation of slaves, but he held that 'we expected far too great and far too quick a result from emancipation'.[50] 'The negro's idea of emancipation was and is emancipation not from slavery but from work.'[51] Trollope strongly criticised 'philanthropists' of the Exeter Hall variety[52] who objected to the importation of 'coolie labour' into the West Indies, believing that this importation would force negroes to work in order to compete. Trinidad was judged favourably in comparison with Jamaica because it had imported 10 or 12,000 immigrants from Madras and Calcutta during the previous eight years and had in consequence reached a far higher level of work and prosperity. 'There is at present in Port of Spain a degree of commercial enterprise quite unlike the sleepiness of Jamaica or the apathy of the smaller islands.'[53]

It is fitting, perhaps, that Trollope's most persistent West Indian critic this century has been the late Prime Minister of Trinidad, Eric Williams. Curiously, however, Williams, a historian himself, said little of Trollope's relatively favourable views of Trinidad and concentrated on his unfavourable views of Jamaica.[54] He noted how Trollope in drawing a contrast between Jamaica's 'past glory' in the eighteenth century and its economic decline, following the abolition of slavery, had nothing to say about export of new crops or of 20,000 freeholders owning less than 10 acres. Trollope's gloomy picture was certainly unrelieved – for it embraced both economics and politics. 'Are Englishmen in general aware', he asked, 'that half the sugar estates in Jamaica, and I believe more than half the coffee plantations, have gone back into a state of bush ... that chaos and darkness have swallowed so vast an extent of the most bountiful land that civilisation had ever matured?'[55] And, he went on, the continued existence of 'Queen, Lords and Commons' in Jamaica (though not in Trinidad, where legislative power was entirely in the hands of the Crown[56]) made a mockery of representative institutions.

The House of Assembly is not respected. It does not contain men of most weight and condition in the island, and is contemptuously spoken of even in Jamaica itself, and even by its own members ... Let any man fancy what England would be if the House of Commons were ludicrous in the eyes of all Englishmen ... In truth, there is not room for machinery so complicated in this island. The handful of white men can no longer have it all their own way; and as for the negroes – let any warmest advocate of the 'man and brother' position say whether he has come across three or four of the class who are fit to enact laws for their own guidance and the guidance of others.[57]

Trollope wanted Jamaica to adopt the British nineteenth-century gospel of work, therefore, but to dispense with its seventeenth-century British-type constitution. He was more sensitive than some visitors to the role of coloured (as distinct from black) people in the West Indies,[58] but very insensitive to the long-run effects of importing Indian (or Chinese) labour. 'The blood of Asia will be mixed with that of Africa', he prophesied, 'and the necessary compound will, by God's infinite wisdom and power, be formed for these latitudes, as it has been formed for the colder regions in which the Anglo-Saxon preserves his energy, and his works.'

God was not left out of this prophecy. 'Providence has sent white men and black men to these regions in order that from them may spring a race fitted by intellect for civilisation: and fitted also by physical organisation for tropical labour.' Trollope spoke too, in what was to become familiar late nineteenth-century language, both about Britain's 'noble mission' and 'the welfare of the coming world' being in the hands of 'the Anglo-Saxon race'.[59] Yet the mission for him was not Imperial. If it were 'fated' that the West Indies should pass into the hands of 'another people', this would not worry him.[60] He said nothing of their becoming genuinely 'independent',[61] but he welcomed American independence and viewed with 'composure' 'the inevitable, happily inevitable, day when Australia shall follow in the same path.'[62] 'The mother country in regarding her colonies', he stressed, 'should think altogether of this welfare, and as little as possible of her own power and glory ... If we keep them, we should keep them – not because they add prestige to the name of Great Britain, not because they are gems in our diadem, not in order that we may boast that the sun never sets on our dependencies, but because by keeping them we may best assist in developing their resources.'[63] And in a letter he stated firmly that since the condition of a colony was 'inferior', it would certainly be shaken off 'when the power of shaking off will come'.[64]

Trollope disliked Disraeli, whose version of 'Imperialism' seemed to him as dangerous as his political opportunism in Britain itself. The tone of his writings, therefore, was very different from that of J. A. Froude, who later in the century was to cover much of the same ground.[65] He objected, too, to the vacillations of the Colonial Office, which reflected 'the idiosyncracies of the individual ministers who have held the office of Secretary of State rather than a settled course of British action'.[66]

Nonetheless, Eric Williams was right to describe *The West Indies* as 'merely an expurgated version' of Thomas Carlyle's *Occasional Discourse upon the Nigger Question*, published in 1849, which for Williams stands out as 'the most offensive document in the entire world literature on slavery and the West Indies'.[67] It is easy to trace the parallels, despite Trollope's distaste for the writings of Carlyle, which Williams does not note;[68] and when the two men met for the first time in 1881 at G. H. Lewes's house, Carlyle told Trollope he had 'read and agreed with the West Indian book'.[69] There is one reference to Carlyle in the book which bears out Williams' assessment.

> As far as I am able to judge, a negro has not generally those gifts of God which enable one man to exercise rule and mastership over his fellow men. I myself should object strongly to be represented, say in the city of London, by any black man that I ever saw. 'The unfortunate nigger gone masterless', whom Carlyle so tenderly commiserates, has no strong ideas of the duties even of a self-government, much less of the government of others. Universal suffrage in such hands can hardly lead to good results.[70]

In referring to the City of London, Trollope was moving his imagination homewards, and it is important to remember, of course, first that there was no universal suffrage in Britain in 1859, and second that Trollope was not in favour of introducing it. When he arrived in San José, Costa Rica, he felt as 'if he were riding into a sleepy little borough town in Wiltshire'. There were hard-working Germans there as well as Spaniards and Indians, but the images of home returned again when, before climbing Mount Irazu, he recalled 'clambering to the top of Scafell Pike'.[71]

Trollope was not usually, however, the kind of traveller who referred everything back to the places he knew best or to the kind of people he knew at home. If the latter had been his bent, he would have preferred white society in Jamaica, where the planter has 'so many of the characteristics of an English country gentleman that he does not strike an Englishman as a strange being'. There was scope there, also, for a country gentleman, Trollope argued. 'They have their counties and their parishes ... They have county society, local balls, and local race meetings. They have local politics, local quarrels, and strong old-fashioned local friendships. In all these things one feels oneself to be much nearer to England in Jamaica than in any other of the West Indian islands.'

It was because this society of 'gentlemen' – or 'near gentlemen' – was under threat that Trollope did not care to linger there. 'Not only coloured men get into office, but black men also.' 'If we could, we would fain forget Jamaica altogether,' he wrote. 'But there it is; a spot on the earth not to be lost sight of or forgotten altogether, let us wish it ever so much. It belongs to us, and must in some sort be thought of and managed and if possible governed.'[72]

The warning was necessary, for six years later insurrection in Jamaica disturbed the peace which Trollope had identified with torpor; and on this occasion British intellectuals divided dramatically on the issue of whether or not to support Governor Eyre (ex-explorer of Australia), who had ruthlessly put down a negro rebellion.[73] Carlyle and Ruskin were on one side; Mill and most 'intellectuals' on the other. Between 1859 and 1865 the Jamaican sugar economy had prospered, but between 1866 and 1876 in the aftermath of the crushed rebellion elected assemblies disappeared not only in Jamaica but also in several other West Indian islands. Trollope would doubtless have approved of the outcome, including a statement in the report of a Royal Commission which visited the Windward Islands in 1884 and praised non-representative government for 'new endeavours ... to supply the benefits and appliances of civilisation'.[74]

In 1859 Trollope looked with hope rather than with fear at the conclusion of his journey not to the West Indies – or to Costa Rica – but to the United States. It was there, he felt, that contemporaries could discover 'the best means of prophesying ... what the world will next be, and what men will next do'.[75]

III

'I have ever admired the United States as a nation', Trollope wrote in *North America*. 'I have loved their liberty, their prowess, their intelligence, and their progress. ... I have felt confidence in them, and have known, as it were, that their industry must enable them to succeed as a people, while their freedom would insure to them success as a nation.'[76] And in one of his letters he went further still. 'I was thinking today that nature intended me for an American rather than an Englishman. I think, I should have made a better American.'[77]

Trollope's attitude to the United States, therefore, was radically different from his attitude to the West Indies before he visited either place; and if he ended *The West Indies* with a reference to the United States, he could not complete *North America* without making a few cross-references to the West Indies. In particular, in one disturbing passage he looked forward to the gradual extinction of the negro population of the United States and their possible replacement by 'coolies from India and China' as in Guiana and the West Indies.[78] He also reiterated his belief in 'the intellectual inferiority of the Negro', emphasising that he restricted his belief to 'those of pure Negro descent'. He saw a difference between the intellectual and social status of the 'coloured', stating that, whereas he had never met 'in American society any man or woman in whose veins there can have been presumed to be any taint of African blood', in Jamaica they were 'daily to be found in society'. Trollope was no de Tocqueville, as he admitted, and he presumably meant Society with a capital S.[79]

There were the same references to 'the Creator' in *North America* as there had been in *The West Indies*. God was the real author of 'Development' in which Trollope put his trust. There was an old story, 'told over and over again through every century since commerce has flourished in the world; the tropics can produce – but the men from the North shall sow and reap and garner and enjoy'. The 'cosmopolitan' Trollope could be very non-parochial in his generalisations.

> If we look to Europe, we see that this has been so in Greece, Italy, Spain, France and the Netherlands; in England and Scotland; in Prussia and in Russia; and the Western world tells us the same story. Where is now the glory of the Antilles? Where the riches of Mexico and the power of Peru? They still produce sugar, guano, gold, cotton, coffee ... but where are their men, where are their books, where are their learning, their art, their enterprise?[80]

Trollope immediately pitted New York, Boston, Philadelphia, Chicago, Pittsburgh and (his mother's) Cincinnati against New Orleans, Charleston, Savannah, Mobile, Richmond and Memphis.

The same attitude towards 'Development' dominates *South Africa*. 'The progress to be most desired is that which will quickest induce the Kafir to put off his savagery and live after the manner of his white brother.'[81] In the diamond fields of Kimberley, where blacks outnumbered whites, higher wages were doing more to raise black fortunes than religion – the spasmodic energy of missionaries – philanthropy or even educational – the unalluring attraction of schools'. 'Who can doubt but that work is the great civiliser of the world – work and the growing desire for those good things which work only will bring?[82] Trollope was 'realistic' enough to note that the great black majority was sceptical about such civilising forces. 'Were it to be put to the vote tomorrow among the Kafirs whether the white man should be driven into the sea or retained in the country, the entire race would certainly vote for the white man's extermination.'[83]

Unlike the United States, divided South Africa offered few hopes of long-term political unity. Yet if Trollope saw South Africa after the annexation of the Transvaal – and this gave political point to his book – the fact that he saw the United States during the Civil War forced him to consider at least the relationship between 'Development' and political aspiration.[84] In *South Africa* he criticised the 'political confusion' in the South following the victory of the North, adding that 'we are all convinced that in one way or another a minority of white men will get the better of a majority of coloured men.'[85] The problem of South Africa could not be settled by leaving a small pocket of independent black power. 'Of what real service can it be to leave to the unchecked dominion of Kaffir habits a tract of 1600 square miles when we have absorbed from the Natives a territory larger than all British India? ... Whether we have done well or ill by occupying South Africa ... we can hardly salve our consciences by that little corner.'[86]

Trollope had not foreseen a war between the States of the American Union in 1859 or, as he called it, a 'disruption'.[87] Nor, as we have seen, was it his main theme in his two travel volumes. He could not avoid it, however, and the war weaves its way through the book.[88] He had four points to make, and they all involved considerable generalisation. First, 'I do not see how the North, treated as it was and had been, could have submitted to secession without resistance.'[89] Second, 'The North and the South must ever be dissimilar.'[90] 'The Southern States of America have not been able to keep pace with their Northern brethren ... they have fallen behind in the race.'[91] Trollope's sympathies, unlike those of many (though not all of) his fellow countrymen, were with the North. Third, 'the preaching of abolition [of slavery] during the war is to me either the deadliest of sins or the vainest of follies': 'it is the banner of defiance opposed to secession'.[92] None the less, 'every Englishman probably looks forward to the accomplishment of abolition of slavery at some future day. I feel sure of it as I do of the final judgement. When or how it will come I cannot tell.'[93] Fourth, secession would be 'successful'; 'I cannot believe that the really Southern States will ever again be joined in amicable union with those of the North.'[94] 'I think that there will be secession, but that the terms of secession will be dictated by the North, not by the South.'[95]

There was an element of irony in the fact that while Trollope had long wanted to write a book about the United States unlike his mother's or, so he felt, to 'add to the good feeling which should exist between two nations which ought to love each other so well, and which ... hang upon each other so constantly',[96] when he actually got there

American feeling against England was very bitter. 'All Americans to whom I spoke felt that it was so.'[97] Trollope believed that this was a mistaken as well as an unfair reaction: 'it seems to me that a great nation should not require an expression of sympathy during its struggle. Sympathy is for the weak rather than for the strong.'[98] Nevertheless, he ended his book uneasily, recognising that it would need more than books to guarantee future transatlantic 'good feeling'. 'When this war be over between the northern and the southern states, will there come upon us Englishmen a necessity of fighting with the Americans? If there do come such necessity ... it will indeed be hard upon us, as a nation, seeing the struggle that we have made to be just towards the States generally, whether they be North or South.' And he then drew a European parallel. 'In that contest between Sardinia and Austria, it was all but impossible to be just to the Italians without being unjust to the Emperor of Austria.'[99] This was not his only European parallel. He added a characteristically Trollopian supplement. 'If we must fight, let us fight the French, "for King George upon the throne". The doing so will be disagreeable, but it will not be antipathetic to the nature of an Englishman.'[100]

Trollope was not allowed by his critics to get away with any of his generalisations in 1861 – or his supplement – although, of course, the critics contradicted each other. The fact that the American constitution did not refer specifically to secession did not mean that there was no case for secession: 'to assert that whatever the constitution does not sanction is illegal, is to call it an abominable despotism.'[101] 'Before discussing the ineradicable differences between North and South, Mr Trollope should have visited the South.'[102] 'Nothing throughout this book impresses us so constantly as the consciousness of how little Mr Trollope knows about the South.'[103] In any case, Northern sympathies were dangerous. *Fraser's* believed 'after long observation of this deplorable struggle' that 'there is very little wisdom and very little worth on either side.'[104] On slavery and its implications, Trollope had been unfair to the negroes. He had neglected 'some elements of the Negro character which seem to give a better promise for any future'.[105] 'It is not for the black man that our fears arise. Can any man familiar with the South fail to see that whatever slavery may be for the black man, it is ruin materially and morally for the white?'[106] The forecast that the terms of secession would be dictated by the North was as unproven as the forecast that the North would prove to be very strong. 'There is no man, either American or English, whose ratiocinations on these subjects are worth the paper they are written on. ... As well might one endeavour to bale the vast Croton reservoir at New York with a lady's thimble as to gauge the dimensions and prospects of the vastest convulsion the world has ever seen.'[107] As for possible war – and the relative merits of war with the United States or with France – 'we do not believe that English people generally give Americans as a nation the preference over other foreigners, nor have they any reason to do so'. 'The blood relationship is a mere sentimental dream, conjured up for the purpose of fine writing.'[108]

The critics, some of whom praised the writings of other commentators on the United States and the war,[109] posed questions which Trollope did not ask and made generalisations of their own. In particular, they asked what North American experience revealed about 'the real merits of democracy' and 'wherein it undoubtedly failed'.[110] Trollope had praised the Americans of the North on two grounds – 'they were educated and they were rich'. Yet the education nourished small men at the expense of great men – 'the average of political intelligence ... may be much higher in the American States than in European countries, but it is an average which is gained by depression as well as by elevation'[111] – and the quest for riches was at best only loosely related to happiness. One critic of Trollope quoted John Stuart Mill, who 'confessed' that he was not 'charmed by the ideal of life held out by those who think that the normal state of human beings is that of struggling to get on'. Mill had concluded that while the Northern and Middle States of America had obtained the Six Points of Chartism (not true) and there was no poverty, 'all that these advantages seem to have done for them' was that 'the life of the whole of one sex is devoted to dollar hunting, and of the other to breeding dollar-hunters.'[112] The review of *North America* in *Fraser's* was followed immediately by John Ruskin's 'Essays on Political Economy', the sequel to his *Cornhill* papers, challenging the whole mid-Victorian approach to wealth.

Not all the critics concentrated on such problems of values, while the *Cornhill* itself did not disapprove of Trollope defending with 'great good humour and strong good sense the real virtue of money-making'.[113] In other places *North America* was condemned more for its verbosity, for its lack of organisation, for its little inaccuracies than for its argument.[114] It seemed a mistake, too, that Trollope had included 'the inevitable Declaration of Independence' in an appendix, even though he might never have read it.[115] 'Character and manners', however, the critics usually felt that he handled well.[116] They quoted little directly in Trollope's words, although one of them selected for his readers a remarkable Trollopian passage on the American corn trade (which eventually was to transform Trollope's England more than the Civil War):

Statistical accounts do not bring any enduring idea ... I was at Chicago and

Buffalo in October 1861. I went down to the granaries, and climbed up to the elevators. I saw the wheat running in rivers from one vessel into another, and from the railroad up into the huge bins on the top stores of the warehouse. I saw corn measured by the forty-bushel measures with as much ease as we measure an ounce of cheese, and with greater rapidity. I ascertained that the work went on weekday and Sunday, day and night incessantly; rivers of wheat and rivers of maize ever running. I saw the men bathed in corn as they distributed it in its flow. I saw bins by the score laden with wheat, in each of which bins there was space for a comfortable residence. I breathed the flour, and drank the flour, and I felt myself to be enveloped in an ocean of breadstuff.[117]

Trollope placed himself in the middle of the picture. Yet even here he was no prophet. He saw the corn feeding the millions of the American East and the coming millions of the American West, but he did not foresee it (as Cobden did) pouring across the Atlantic Ocean and ruining English farmers. He rested content with a contemporary reaction. 'Events in these days march so quickly that they leave men behind, and our dear old Protectionists at home will have grown so sleek upon American flour before they have realised the fact that they are no longer fed from their own furrows.'[118]

The critic in *Blackwood's* attacked Trollope's method of arguing, as much as the content of his argument. He personified too much and when excited or in difficulty resorted to metaphor. 'Abstract questions or metaphysical discussions which would have worn a very dry aspect ...become bright, piquant, and interesting when personified and seen through the medium of familiar imagery.'[119] Sometimes the personification (of a drunken husband, for example, or a 'small chimney sweeper' or a 'Billingsgate heroine') led him – and his readers – completely astray: sometimes the metaphors clashed with each other. He was particularly misleading when he discussed national relationships. What consolation was there, for instance, in the statement that 'the States of America will master their money difficulties because they are born of England not of Austria. What! Shall our eldest child become bankrupt by its first trade-difficulty – be utterly ruined by its first little commercial embarrassment? The child bears much too strong a resemblance to its parent for me to think so.'[120]

This review described Trollope as 'among the most amusing and popular of our novelists' who had established 'agreeable relations with his audience'. 'It is not often that a good novelist makes a good politician', however, he went on. Bulwer did, but Trollope was no exception. 'We think that his just and fairly-earned reputation will continue to rest upon his clever and always entertaining novels.'[121] 'We shall grudge the time he may spend in writing any more books of travel, or politics', he concluded, 'if they deprive us of one of the brilliant successors of *Barchester Towers*.'[122]

IV

In considering Trollope's travel reflections it is always necessary to remember, as he himself put it, that he was well aware that his own muse was not Clio: 'I appeal to her frequently, but ever in vain.'[123] Historians appeal to Trollope – and he certainly appeals to them – but they would be wrong (and some of them are) to take everything he says at face value, as 'evidence'. As the travel books show, the evidence always requires to be interpreted.[124] Literary critics will be more tempted to relate Trollope's travel books to his fiction than to the writings of recent historians or of his historically-minded contemporaries. They may argue negatively, as an early critic did, that to include the American Declaration of Independence as an appendix to *North America* is no more odd than to insert into *The Three Clerks* long passages on the organisation and promotion system of the British civil service.[125] More positively, however, they will ask questions about the relationship of Trollope's 'travel material' to his novels.

Four aspects of the relationship are interesting. First, however tempted Trollope was to generalise in his travel books, he also showed exceptional interest in and a capacity to deal with particulars. It is the particulars, above all the particulars of encounters and conversations, which will command most interest for critics of the novels. Second, he showed from time to time – though seldom as strikingly as Dickens – that he had a remarkable gift for phrase, not least when he conveyed a sense not of perspective but of immediacy, or when the note of irony, so strong in the *Autobiography*, gives a twist to the obvious.[126] Third, he was forced in his travel books to consider his 'public', and his asides to them can and should be compared with the asides (and the less explicit devices) in his novels. Fourth, he very occasionally touches on the art (and problems) of the novelist in his travel books, for example in his chapter on 'Literature' in *North America*,[127] and, like his comments on Post Offices, these constitute a distinctive 'source'.

One of the best instances of Trollope's concern for particulars is his delightful description in *The West Indies* of his meeting in Port Antonio, Jamaica, with a coloured girl whose lover had left her.[128] 'Whence she came or who she was I did not know and never learnt.' The meeting might have been awkward for two reasons. She was coloured, and the lover who had abandoned her was not a Christian but a Jew. She was a Baptist. Trollope had Sterne in mind as he told the story to his readers. Yet the flavour is entirely his own. He also brings himself directly into the conversation not as observer but as active participant. 'Now I hate Baptists', he remarks *en passant*, 'as she did her lover – like poison; and even under such pressure as this I could not bring myself to aid in their support.'[129] The conversation – and it was unsolicited – ends with the girl saying, 'I don't t'ink I'll be happy no more. 'Tis so dull: goodbye'; and Trollope adds, 'Were I a girl I doubt whether I also would not sooner dance with a Jew than pray with a Baptist.'[130] He also clearly establishes his own stance, doubtless to reassure his readers. 'I am not a very young man; and my friends have told me that I show strongly that steady married appearance of a paterfamilias which is so apt to lend assurance to maiden timidity.'[131]

This is by no means the only record of a specific conversation in *The West Indies*, and it is fair to add that whatever Trollope might have thought about the general prospects for negroes in the future he had no inhibitions about talking to particular negroes freely and generally. He had lively accounts to give also of dancing and bathing. He recognised that 'in the West Indies it is absolutely necessary that these people should be treated with dignity. . . . They like familiarity but are singularly averse to ridicule; and though they wish to be on good terms with you, they do not choose that these shall be reached without the proper degree of antecedent ceremony.'[132] Trollope was the best possible judge of 'the proper degree' in Kingston as in London. He also showed conspicuous curiosity about everything, not least food. Avocado pears make their way into his list of food preferences at a time when there could have been little idea of eating an avocado pear in London.[133]

There are lively personal encounters also in *North America* (though not in *Australia and New Zealand*). A chapter which deals *inter alia* with 'The Frontier Man'[134] is free from unnecessary abstraction as it proceeds to reveal a man with 'romance, high poetic feeling, and above all manly dignity'. 'All the odious incivility of the republican servant has been banished.' Trollope, always interested in talking to women, reveals the frontier wife too, in this case a wife deserted by her husband. 'I have known what it is to be hungry and cold, and to work hard till my bones have ached. I only wish that I might have the same chance again. If I could have ten acres cleared two miles from any living being, I would be happy with my children.'[135]

It was when he passed from particulars to generalities again that Trollope reached barriers to thinking. 'That women should have their rights no man will deny. To my thinking neither increase of work nor increase of political influence are among them.'[136] There are parallel passages in *Australia and New Zealand*. 'Women all the world over are entitled to everything that chivalry can give them. They should sit while men stand. They should be served while men wait. They should be praised – even without desert. They should be courted – even when having neither wit nor beauty. They should be worshipped – even without love.'[137] How much irony is there here in what seems at first sight to be such a conventional, if eloquent, presentation of Victorian attitudes? However little or much, it is difficult to consider Trollope 'a feminist'.

Trollope was not able to convert his impressions of a different society (with the exception of Ireland) into a novel of the kind that Dickens wrote in *Martin Chuzzlewit*, where, as has been suggested, Dickens 'turned his limitations as a traveller into novelists' gold'.[138] Yet, like Dickens, he had an often impressive turn of phrase, particularly when there was an explicit or implicit cross-reference. 'The unfinished dome of the Capitol will loom before you in the distance, and you will think that you approach the ruins of some Western Palmyra.'[139] 'A man may lose himself in the streets, not as one loses oneself in London between Shoreditch and Russell Square, but as one does in the deserts of the Holy Land, between Emmaus and Arimathea.[140] A list of the names of gold mines in Victoria – 'New Chums', 'Old Chums', etc. again recalling mining passages in *The Three Clerks* – ends with 'the Gladstone'. 'Indeed, there are five or six Gladstone Companies', he concludes, 'and to be fair ... a Disraeli Company. I do not, however, find it quoted among those that are paying dividends.'[141]

None of these passages compares in quality, however, with the memorable poetic passages in Dickens' *American Notes*, such as his descriptions of Washington – 'It is sometimes called the City of Magnificent Distances, but it might with greater propriety be called the City of Magnificent Intentions'[142] – or of Boston – 'When I got into the streets upon this Sunday morning, the air was so clear, the houses were so bright and gay; the signboards were painted in such gaudy colours ... that I never turned a corner without looking out for the clown and the pantaloon, who, I had no doubt, were hiding in a doorway or behind some pillar close at hand.'[143] By contrast, Trollope's Boston was a pale imitation of London. 'There is an Athenaeum, and a State Hall, and a fashionable street – Beacon Street – very like Piccadilly, as it runs along the Green Park – and there is a Green Park opposite to this Piccadilly, called Boston Common.'[144] In 'melancholy' Washington Trollope walked unimpressed through its 'ragged collection of unbuilt broad streets'; Dickens was more involved in the scene when he wrote, 'after walking about it for an hour or two, I felt that I would have given the world for a crooked street.'[145]

Dickens and Trollope each visited the manufacturing town of Lowell, and in their accounts of this fascinating community both their strengths are plain. That they both went there is a sign of the interest taken by early or mid-nineteenth travellers in visiting industrial places. 'Lowell and its Factory System' was Dickens's sub-title, and he was impressed above all else by the factory girls, all of whom had the 'deportment of young women, not of degraded brutes of burden'. The rooms in which they worked were as clean and 'well ordered' as they were, and they lived in pleasant boarding houses, where there were 'joint stock pianos' and books from circulating libraries. The town itself had 'quaintness and oddity of character', once again associated in Dickens's imagination, as Boston had been, with the sparkle of newness: 'the very river that moves the machinery in the mills (for they are all worked by water power) seems to acquire a new character from the fresh buildings of bright red brick and painted wood among which it takes its course; and to be as light-headed, thoughtless, and brisk a young river, in its murmurings and tumblings, as one would desire to see'.

Dickens 'carefully abstained from drawing a comparison between the factories and those of our own land', although he adjured his readers to ponder on the differences between Lowell and 'those great haunts of misery' in their own country. He suggested too that the 'large class' of his readers who would feel that the work people of Lowell were thinking 'above their station' should think again for themselves. 'Are we quite sure that we in England have not formed our idea of the "station" of working people from accustoming ourselves to the contemplation of that class as they are, and not as they might be?'

The title of Trollope's chapter on Lowell, 'Cambridge and Lowell', itself suggests an unusual contrast. Cambridge with Harvard was to New England what Oxford and Cambridge were to all England; Lowell was 'in little what Manchester is to us in as great a degree'. Like Dickens, Trollope began with the factory girls, 'neat, well-dressed, careful, especially about their hair, composed in their manner, and sometimes a little supercilious in the propriety of their demeanour'. And then he thought again of Harvard. They had been admitted, 'as it were, to a philanthropical manufacturing college'. 'This is all very nice and pretty at Lowell, but I am afraid it could not be done at Manchester.' Dickens would not have made that judgement. Nor would he have gone on to deal in some detail (adding quotations from documentary sources) with the economics of water power as compared with steam or with the history of Lowell. For Trollope Lowell was 'a commercial Utopia': it could not be duplicated. Chicago, not Lowell, offered an example of what would happen elsewhere in the United States, for it had grown fast and was beyond control. There were things that philanthropy could not do. Moreover, the philanthropists of Lowell had learnt from the mistakes of England, where industry had developed first. 'In our thickly populated island any commercial

Utopia is out of the question.' Once again Trollope had reached the frontiers of conventional thinking.

It is clear from his travel books that he never wanted to distance himself too far from his public, however, even when he was far away from them in space. He draws his public in from the start. 'On reaching Sydney', he begins *Australia and New Zealand*, 'the traveller should remember that he is visiting the spot on which our Australian empire was commenced, amidst difficulties of which we in England in these days think very little.'[146] He ends *North America* with a contrast between begging in Ireland and working in the United States, a land of 'self-asserting, obtrusive independence', and here he only just distances himself from those members of his public whose attitudes to Ireland were significantly different from his own. 'I myself am fond of Irish beggars. It is an acquired taste – which comes upon one as does that for smoked whisky, or Limerick tobacco. But I certainly wish that there were not so many of them at Queenstown.'[147]

It is in *North America* that he has most to say of 'literature', devoting a whole chapter to it.[148] 'As consumers of literature the Americans are certainly the most conspicuous people on the earth.'[149] Dickens sold more than Tennyson and Buckle – men and women after their day's work are not always up to the *Civilization*' – and (here we have the characteristic Trollopian gloss) 'as a rule they are generally up to *Proverbial Philosophy*, and thus perhaps, may have had something to do with the great popularity of that very popular work.'[150]

Before turning to copyright, a subject which preoccupied Dickens,[151] Trollope once more emphasised his sense of obligation to a broad public, drawing India into the picture as well as Australia and New Zealand and the United States. 'The English author should feel that he writes for the widest circle of readers ever yet obtained by the literature of any country.'[152] Wherever Trollope travelled to see the world, he knew that he had readers. And he knew how they often looked to what he had to say more than to the books of their own writers. 'General literature is perhaps the product which comes last from the energies of an established country. ... The production of books must follow the production of other things and the growth of literature will be slow.'[153]

There was no sign, however, that Trollope expected his travel books to be read *in situ*, although he referred at the end of *North America* to 'his readers on either side of the water';[154] and the *Cornhill Magazine*, which by a coincidence printed its review of *North America* next to a paragraph on Buckle's death – and an exalted section on 'the profession of literature' – noted that it would 'give pain' in America. 'Everyone who has winced under the severities of blame would sympathise with the Americans if they are angry at this exposure of their faults. But the castigated author, when he has any true metal in him, extracts its virtue from the bitter medicine. ... Will not the energetic Americans do the same?'[155] Trollope would not have worried too much provided that there were 'energetic' people to read him. It is a final irony that, for all his eagerness to travel busily around the world, and to comment freely on men, women, manners and events, many of the people who have gained the greatest satisfaction from his work are those who have always preferred to stay comfortably behind – not necessarily at home, in Barsetshire, a place where, unlike most of the places Trollope visited, dreams can come true.

NOTES

1   *An Autobiography* (1950 edn), p. 129.
2   ibid., pp. 164, 166.
3   ibid., p. 349.
4   ibid., p. 364.
5   *Saturday Review*, 23 February 1878.
6   The author's first duty, Trollope wrote, is that 'he shall tell the truth, and shall so tell that truth that what he has written may be readable' – *North America* (1862) 1.3. For Trollope's sense of the 'real' and his capacity to create the 'illusion of reality', see J. M. Cohen, *Form and Realism in Six Novels of Anthony Trollope* (1976).
7   'The Family that Goes Abroad', first published in the *Pall Mall Gazette*, 3 August 1865.
8   *The West Indies and the Spanish Main* (1859), p. 11; *North America*, II.108; *Australia and New Zealand* (1876 edn), p. 101.
9   *South Africa* (1879 edn), pp. 388-9.
10 'No doubt the story of the Maori may be told with poetry,' he writes (*Australia and New Zealand*, II.39), but 'such an attempt is not my way.' 'As far as I have told it, I have endeavoured to tell it with truth.'
11 *Autobiography*, p. 161. See Frances Trollope, *Domestic Manners of the Americans* (1832).
12 *North America*, I.1.
13 See J. S. Whitley and A. Goldman (eds), *Charles Dickens: American Social History as Recorded by British Travellers* (1934).
14 *Fraser's Magazine*, vol. LXII (1862), p. 256.
15 *An Autobiography*, pp. 27-8, describes his early 'banishment' to Belgium.
16 Chapter 4 describes his appointment in Ireland: 'since that time who has had a happier life than mine?' (p. 61).
17 Preface to *An Autobiography*, p. xii.
18 ibid., p. 129.
19 *North America*, II.391.
20 ibid., pp. 23 ff.

21 *Fraser's Magazine*, vol. LXVI, p. 256.

22 *Punch*, XXXIV (1858), p. 8. The first of the *Travelling Sketches*, 'The Family that Goes Abroad', appeared in the newly-founded *Pall Mall Gazette* on 3 August 1865. The others appeared in its pages irregularly, except for 'Tourists who enjoy their work' which appeared only in the published volume which *Punch* did not review.

23 For Trollope on Palmerston, see the biography (1882) which he wrote of him. Curiously he did not mention him in his *Autobiography*. See Asa Briggs, 'Trollope, Bagehot and the English Constitution', *Victorian People* (1954).

24 *Autobiography*, Chapter 17. For the invitation to go, see a letter from John Tilly to Trollope, 12 December 1967, quoted in N. J. Hall (ed.), *The Letters of Anthony Trollope* (1983), vol. I, p. 416.

25 ibid., pp. 314, 315.

26 It does, however, include a 'conventional Yankee woman'. For Trollope's views on American women, see *North America*, I, 295-302.

27 *Autobiography*, p. 341. See also p. 326 for Frederic's resolve to follow 'a Colonial career', a not unfamiliar Trollopian theme.

28 They were signed 'Antipodean' and appeared at irregular intervals between 23 December 1871 and 28 December 1872.

29 *Autobiography*, p. 345.

30 'I cannot be at ease with all the new people and the new things,' he wrote, complaining also that he found himself 'too old to be eighteen months away from home.' See Bradford Allen Booth (ed.), *The Letters of Anthony Trollope*, (1951), pp. 290-1.

31 *Athenaeum*, 16 June 1877. Nonetheless, there is one interesting passage in the novel about travel (Chapter 77): 'When an intelligent Japanese travels in Great Britain or an intelligent Briton is in Japan, he is struck with no wonder at national differences. He is on the other hand rather startled to find how like his strange brother is to him in many things.' Curiously, he went on, English-American human relations were more difficult.

32 See T. H. S. Escott, *Anthony Trollope* (1913).

33 R. C. Terry, *The Artist in Hiding* (1977), p. 193.

34 'Tourists Who Don't Like Their Travels', which first appeared in the *Pall Mall Gazette*, 6 September 1865.

35 *Australia and New Zealand*, p. 100.

36 'The Alpine Club Man', first published in the *Pall Mall Gazette*, 2 September 1865. For controversy about the death of four members of Edward Whymper's Alpine party in July 1865, and its significance, see *inter alia* D. Robertson, 'Mid-Victorians Amongst the Alps', in U. C. Knoepflmacher and G. B. Tennyson, *Nature and the Victorian Imagination* (1977), pp. 113-17.

37 *The West Indies*, pp. 335-6 (Chapter 21). *South Africa* is full of references to transport also, and to its effects.

38 ibid., p. 349.

39 *North America*, II.390.

40 ibid., II.396. Cp. I.59: 'I cannot say that I like the hotels in those parts or indeed the mode of life at American hotels in general.' On railways, see *South Africa*, p. 259: 'The question of a railway is of all the most vital to the new colony [of the Transvaal].'

41 *North America*, II.393-4.

42 See, for example, a well-known passage in his *Letters*: 'There is much that is higher and better and greater than one's country. One is patriotic only because one is too small and weak to be cosmopolitan' (*Letters*, pp. 178-9).

43 *North America*, II.392-3.

44 ibid., I.303-4.

45 ibid., I.304.

46 *The West Indies*, p. 57.

47 ibid., p. 59.

48 This is one of the strangest features of his book. He preferred British Guiana to the rest: 'when I settle out of England ... British Guiana shall be the land of my adoption' (ibid., p. 168); and had good words for Barbados, 'so respectable a little island' (p. 163 and Chapter 13). 'Little England as it delights to call itself ... owes no man anything, pays its own way and never makes a poor mouth' (p. 216).

49 ibid., pp. 62-3. In slave-owning Cuba Trollope noted more 'evidences of capital' than in Jamaica (p. 136). In Bermuda he generalised again that 'no enfranchised negro entertains an idea of daily work' (p. 374).

50 ibid., p. 63. He also condemned the current attitudes of the Anti-Slavery Society (pp. 187, 220 ff.).

51 ibid., p. 92.

52 For Exeter Hall and its influence, see B. Semmel, *The Governor Eyre Controversy* (1962), esp. pp. 18-22. In *South Africa* Trollope noted how the Boers were completely uninfluenced by such philanthropy.

53 *The West Indies*, p. 219.

54 E. Williams, *British Historians and the West Indies* (1966), pp. 90-101.

55 *The West Indies*, pp. 104-5.

56 Trollope liked British Guiana because it had 'no noisy sessions of Parliament as in Jamaica, no money squabbles as in Barbados .... The form of government is a mild despotism tempered by sugar' (ibid., p. 170). Bermuda would have been better also 'without a constitution of its own' (p. 377).

57 ibid., pp. 122-3. He also criticised the system in the Windward Islands (p. 158).

58 See ibid., Chapter 5, 'Coloured Men', where he called the coloured people and not the whites 'the ascendant race' (p. 73). 'That the mulatto race partakes largely of the intelligence and ambition of their white forefathers, it is I think useless, and moreover wicked, to deny' (p. 78). Trollope had no vision of black power. 'The West Indian negro knows nothing of Africa except that it is a term of reproach' (p. 56).

59 ibid., pp. 75, 76, 84-5.

60 ibid., p. 83. The 'appointed work' (whatever that was) would have been done.

61 He was contemptuous of 'farces' in Haiti and such-like lands' (ibid., p. 118) and had this to say of the twentieth century: 'It may be that after all we shall still have to send out some white Governor with a white aide-de-camp and a white private secretary ... to support the dignity of the throne of Queen Victoria's great-grandchild's child. Such may or may not be. To my thinking it would be more for our honour that it should not be so' (p. 84).

62 ibid., pp. 84-5. Trollope's anti-Imperial position is very clearly set out in C. A. Bodelson, *Studies in Mid-Victorian Imperialism* (1960), p. 50 ff. For Trollope and the Boers in South Africa, see C. J. Eys, *In the Era of Shepstone* (1933).

63 *Australia and New Zealand*, I.22.

64 Letter to G. W. Rusden, 23 July 1873, printed in Hall, *op. cit.*, vol. II, p. 594.

65 See *The English in Ireland* (1872); *Two Lectures on South Africa* (1880); *Oceana* (1886); and *The English in the West Indies* (1888). He also wrote *Lord Beaconsfield* (1890).

66 *South Africa*, Chapter 20. Cp. p. 182, where he argues generally and reaches for once a prophetic conclusion. 'Having absorbed the Transvaal in 1877 and Cyprus in 1878, should we now in 1879 weld Zululand to Afghanistan? The task grows to such an extent that a new acquisition will be required to satisfy the ambition of each three months .... We are powerful, we are energetic, we are tenacious: but may it not be possible that we shall attempt to clutch more than we can hold? When once the subject peoples shall have begun to fall from our grasp, the process of dropping them will be very quick.'

67 Williams, *British Historians and the West Indies*, pp. 90, 80.

68 'We do not put very much faith in Mr Carlyle – nor in Mr Ruskin and his other followers .... It is regarded simply as Carlylism to say that the English-speaking world is growing worse from day to day' (*An Autobiography*, p. 354). When he read Carlyle's *Latter Day Pamphlets* in 1851 he concluded that a 'grain of sense' was 'smothered up in a sack of the sheerest trash'. (Hall, *op. cit.*, vol. I, p. 29.)

69 G. Haight (ed.), *George Eliot's Letters*, vol. III (1955), p. 287.

70 *The West Indies*, p. 253. Cp. ibid., p. 89. 'Where white men and black men are together, the white will order and the black will obey, with an obedience more or less implicit according to the terms on which they stand.'

71 ibid., pp. 273, 389.

72 ibid., pp. 94-5, 102.

73 Semmel, *The Governor Eyre Controversy*, surprisingly does not mention Trollope once.

74 Quoted in W. L. Burn, *The British West Indies* (1951), p. 144.

75 ibid., *The West Indies*, p. 389.

76 *North America*, II, 430-1.

77 Letter of 23 August 1861 in Hall, *op. cit.*, vol. I, p. 193. He added, however, that 'I hold it higher to be a bad Englishman, as I am, than a good American – as I am not.'

78 *North America*, II, 88-9.

79 ibid., vol. I, p. 3., where he compared himself with de Tocqueville and other 'philosopho-political' or 'politico-statistical' writers. He described himself as 'a man who professes to use a light pen and to manufacture his article for the use of general readers.' Somewhat similar points were to be made in *South Africa*. The coloured people of the Cape 'though idle, are not as apathetic as savages, not quite as indifferent as Orientals' (p. 4).

80 *North America*, II, 65.

81 *South Africa*, p. 316.

82 ibid., p. 317.

83 ibid., p. 23. Later in the book Trollope somewhat qualified this statement when he drew contrasts between British and Boer attitudes and the attitudes of blacks to each (e.g. p. 226). He also distinguished between Zulus and Kafirs as 'Natives' (Chapter 10). 'I liked the Zulu of the Natal capital very thoroughly' (p. 169).

84 See *South Africa*, p. 292. 'That Englishmen should live under a policy devised or depending on Negroes I believe to be altogether impossible.'

85 ibid., p. 22.

86 ibid., p. 94.

87 *North America*, I, 1.

88 For *The Times* on the war, see H. Brogan (ed.), *The Times Reports the American Civil War* (1975).

89 *North America*, I, 10. Cp. p. 272: 'The South chose violence, and prepared for it secretly and with great adroitness. If that be not rebellion, there never has been rebellion since history began.'

90 ibid., I, 12. See also vol. II, Chapter 3, 'The Causes of the War'.

91 ibid., II, 65-6.

92 ibid., II, 85-6.

93 ibid., II, 89.

94 ibid., II, 452.

95 ibid., II, 454.

96 ibid., I, 3.

97 ibid., I, 268. 'The name of an Englishman has become a by-word for reproach' (p. 282). See also pp. 364ff. and II, 457ff. Nonetheless, he never detected 'any falling off in the hospitality and courtesy generally shown by a civilised people to passing visitors' (II, 171).

98 ibid., II, 281.

99 ibid., II, 455.

100 ibid., II, 462. He thought of Canada as a possible *casus belli* (p. 460) and here his anti-imperialism came out strongly. He always envisaged Canadian independence.

101 *Blackwood's Edinburgh Magazine*, vol. XCII (1862), p. 374.

102 *Home and Foreign Review*, vol. I (1862), p. 116.

103 *Fraser's Magazine*, vol. LXII, p. 257.

104 ibid., p. 260.

105 *Home and Foreign Review*, vol. I, p. 117.

106 *Fraser's Magazine*, vol. LXII, p. 264.

107 ibid., p. 259.
108 *Blackwood's Edinburgh Magazine*, vol. XCII, p. 378. The critic added that Trollope himself used a better argument against a war with the United States – that 'sixty millions sterling of stock – railway stock and such like' – were held there by Britain.
109 Among the books and articles praised were J. Stirling, *Letters from the Slave States* (1857) and H. Martineau's 'Brewing of the American Storm' in the June issue of *Macmillan's*. There was no reference to Dicey's articles in the same periodical. In a letter to the *Spectator*, 16 August 1862, Dicey used the phrase 'a people's war'.
110 *Blackwood's Edinburgh Magazine*, vol. XCII, p. 373. The argument about the 'lessons' of American democracy was of key importance in the debates on parliamentary reform later in the 1860s. See *Essays in Reform* (1867).
111 *Home and Foreign Review*, vol. I, p. 127.
112 ibid., p. 128.
113 *Cornhill Magazine*, vol. VI (1862), p. 106. 'I do not believe', Trollope had written, 'that Dives is as black as he is painted or his peril is so imminent'.
114 See, in particular, *Fraser's Magazine*, vol. LXII, p. 256.
115 *Home and Foreign Review*, vol. I (1862), p. 110.
116 ibid., p. 113. 'It seems like cutting blocks with a razor', therefore, 'when he devotes time and space to telling us that all the States of the Union return an equal number of senators.'
117 *North America*, I, 231-2, quoted in *Home and Foreign Review*, I, 114. The title of Trollope's Chapter 11, from which the passage came, was 'Ceres Americana'.
118 *North America*, I, 234. Trollope had no high opinion of Cobden. 'He is no statesman', he wrote in a letter of 1862. 'As for Bright ... if he or any other man will re-echo American ideas, Americans will return the echo .... But he has been alone in England.' (Letter of 4 January 1862 in Hall, *op. cit.*, vol. I, p. 169.)
119 *Blackwood's Edinburgh Magazine*, vol. XCII, p. 374.
120 ibid.
121 ibid., pp. 372-3.
122 ibid., p. 390.
123 *North America*, II, 435.
124 R. Foster, 'Appreciating the Usual', in the *Times Literary Supplement*, 27 March 1981, touches on some of these themes.
125 *Home and Foreign Review*, vol. I, p. 110.
126 Nonetheless, *Blackwood's*, vol. XCII, p. 389, found the style of *North America* 'slipshod', like the argument.
127 *North America*, II, Chapter 15.
128 *The West Indies*, p. 32 ff.
129 ibid., p. 36.
130 ibid., p. 38.
131 ibid., p. 33
132 ibid., p. 22.

133 Avocados are mentioned twice – on pp. 21 and 28 along with bread-fruit and mangoes. See *The American Senator* (1877), Chapter 27. 'Men care more for what they eat than anything else.'

134 *North America*, I, Chapter 9.

135 ibid., I, 198-200.

136 ibid., II, 408.

137 *Australia and New Zealand*, II, 99.

138 J. S. Whitley and A. Goldman, Introduction to *American Notes*, p. 23.

139 *North America*, II, 3.

140 ibid.

141 *Australia and New Zealand*, II, 56-7.

142 Dickens, *North American Notes* (1842), Chapter 8. A cheap edition of this appeared in 1859.

143 ibid., Chapter 3.

144 *North America*, I, 26.

145 ibid., II, 2-3; *North American Notes*, Chapter 8. In his *Memorandum Book, 1855-1865*, Dickens had written revealingly of 'representing London or Paris or any other great place – in the new light of being actually unknown to all the people in the story, and only taking the colour of their fears and fancies and opinions.' See also the illuminating chapter on *Bleak House* in J. Hillis Miller, *Charles Dickens: The World of His Novels* (1959). Edward Dicey (*Macmillan's Magazine*, vol. VI, p. 285) saw Boston in a completely different light from Dickens.

146 *Australia and New Zealand*, p. 3.

147 *North America*, II, 464.

148 ibid., II, Chapter 15.

149 ibid., II, 411.

150 ibid., II, 414. For Martin Tupper, author of *Proverbial Philosophy*, see the excellent study by D. Hudson, *Martin Tupper, His Rise and Fall* (1949).

151 See *The Letters of Charles Dickens*, vol. III (1974), p. 232, for a particularly strong statement. For Trollope's involvement with American copyright questions, see his *Autobiography*, Chapter 17; and Hall, *op. cit.*, vol. I, pp. 193-8, a most important letter to J. R. Lowell on the subject.

152 *North America*, II, 415.

153 *Australia and New Zealand*, II, 107. Trollope was concerned with newspapers as well as books (see ibid.), and he shared Dickens's view of the low quality of the American press. A rather different line was taken by Edward Dicey in his article in *Macmillan's Magazine*, vol. VI, pp. 150-1.

154 *North America*, II, 441.

155 *Cornhill Magazine*, vol. VI, p. 106.

6 The Appeal of William Morris

With the development of the interest in the Victorians at every level – serious and trivial – it was inevitable there should be a growth of interest in William Morris. Born in 1834, three years before Victoria came to the throne, Morris died in 1896, five years before the Queen. His own experience, therefore, as boy and man was what we would now call Victorian. In the background was the industrial revolution, with an unprecedented growth in material wealth. Yet there were continuities with the pre-industrial past and movements of discontent and protest seeking to shape a very different future. It was not a settled time, though the myth persists that it was, and if Queen Victoria had not lived for so long we would not have been tempted to treat everything that happened between 1837 and 1901 as being of one piece.

The Victorians were their own best critics. They were particularly critical of what they regarded as their two major national weaknesses – cant and complacency. Morris was more sharply critical than most. He described the society of his own age as 'hateful' and its so-called 'civilisation' as 'ugly', 'silly' and 'wrong'. 'Apart from my desire to produce beautiful things,' he exclaimed, 'the leading passion of my life is hatred of modern civilisation.' When he visited the Crystal Palace in 1851, at a time when the word 'Victorian' was first beginning to be used, he called it 'wonderfully ugly'. Later in his life, when he became a socialist, he wrote to a friend in 1885 that the only hope for the future lay in revolution, adding 'now at last when the corruption of society seems complete, there is arising a definite conception of a new order.'[1]

Morris came from a comfortable background and most of the people who read his first poems and bought the first beautiful objects he and his partners produced, came from a comfortable background too. Yet, like many Victorians, Morris criticised the middle classes of his day for hypocrisy, cowardice and joylessness. When he turned to the submerged working classes, he looked for virtues that were missing in the ranks 'above'. He distinguished himself from many other Victorian critics, however, in participating directly – and fervently – in working-class movements from 1883 onwards, sharing in the toil as well as in the excitement. While he was not alone in urging that after a century of so-called progress men should 'forgo some of the power over nature . . .

116

in order to become more human and less mechanical', few other critics who shared his philosophy drew from it the same practical conclusions as Morris. Joining in the class struggle, which is how Morris perceived it, gave him new hope for the future. Without it he would, he claimed, have despaired:

> There I was in for a fine pessimistic end of life, if it had not somehow dawned on me that amidst all this filth of civilisation the seeds of a great change, what we call Social Revolution, were beginning to germinate. The whole face of things was changed for me by that discovery, and all I had to do then in order to become a Socialist, was to hook myself onto the practical movement.

That 'practical movement' had registered only a few successes when Morris died or indeed when Queen Victoria died five years later. Yet as far as Morris himself was concerned, socialism came as a personal fulfilment as well as a conversion. As G.M. Young, not a socialist, put it in 1936, 'his socialism was the final synthesis of all his purposes: and without it his character would have been unfinished, his life incomplete.'[2] G.B. Shaw had said the same years before – with reference to his mind rather than his life. 'Morris's writings about socialism really called up all his mental reserves for the first time.'[3]

G.M. Young had much to do with the development of scholarly interest in the Victorians, an interest which soon widened outside intellectual circles, and by 1936 had sketched a brilliant portrait of Victorian England compared with which Morris's sturdy indictment seemed a rough caricature. In fact, Morris's relationship with the rediscovered nineteenth century is more complicated than he could possibly have been aware himself.

His appeal in the middle years of the nineteenth century had nothing to do with socialism. When *The Earthly Paradise* was published in 1868, the *Saturday Review*, itself not given to cant, noted how popular it was among people who as a rule did not care to read any poetry, and it singled out not working men, but 'political economists and scientific men to whom Shelley is a mystery and Tennyson a vexation of the spirit.' Morris was then, in his own words, a 'dreamer of dreams, born out of my due time' – and there were other mid-Victorians who felt as he did. When his eventually famous 'Firm' came into existence in 1861 – producing all the 'beautiful things' desirable for a house (and some for a church or a palace), including as the years went by glass, wallpapers, textiles, fabrics and furniture – the people who bought the products were rich, not poor. Moreover the Firm was a commercial success. It was another socialist, Walter Crane, who insisted that the great advantage of the Morrisonian method [was that it led] either to simplicity or splendour. You might have an oak trestle table, rush-bottomed chairs and a piece of matting or gold and lustre . . . jewelled light and walls hung with rich arras tapestry.[4]

It was Morris's own restlessness of spirit that made him dissatisfied with worldly tokens of success or with escape, as in *The Earthly Paradise*, into a dream world far removed from the realities of the nineteenth century. There was an element of personal tension, including estrangement from his wife, which drove him from within. Before he became a socialist in 1883 he wrote a new kind of poem 'Sigurd the Volsung' (1876-7), in which he showed how much he preferred the Vikings (and their values) to the Victorians (and theirs). He also took charge of the Firm and moved into liberal politics. In 1883, the year when he joined the Democratic Federation, describing himself simply on his membership card as a designer, he gave a lecture on 'Art under Plutocracy' in Oxford, with Ruskin in the chair, in which he recommended the members of his privileged audience to 'cast in their lot with the working men . . . Do not hold aloof from us, because we have not attained that delicacy of manners . . . which the long oppression of competitive commerce has crushed out of us.'

Morris by then had crossed what he called 'the river of fire',[5] and he wanted everyone to know it. Yet some of his most powerful statements of personal commitment came not in public lectures but in private letters. To the Austrian Marxist socialist Andreas Scheu, for example, he wrote that, 'in spite of all the success' he had enjoyed, he had concluded that:

> The art I have been helping to produce would fall with the death of a few of us who really care about it, that a reform in art which is founded on individualism must perish with the individuals who have set it going. Both my historical studies and my practical conflict [note his use again of the adjective 'practical'] have forced on me the conviction that art cannot have real life and growth under the present system of commercialism and profit-mongering.

'I would like to be able,' he also told Scheu, 'to make a good fitting boot or a pair of clothes, not only those things that are the toys of rich folk.'

Andreas Scheu has left a vivid pen portrait of Morris at this time, which should be contrasted with the pen portraits of Morris as a young Pre-Raphaelite thirty years before, by turns fidgety and boisterous. Already by then Morris had grown the great beard that he never lost, and had begun to wear flappy, unfashionable clothes. On Scheu, 'the fine, highly intelligent face of the man, his earnestness, the half-

searching, half-dreaming look of his eyes, his plain unfashionable
dress, made a deep impression'. That was the personal magnetism, a
part of Morris's contemporary appeal, associated closely with a quest.
The young Leeds socialist, Alf Mattison, described a visit to Kelmscott House in Hammersmith in 1892, four years before Morris died, as
follows:

> What a pleasant time we had; there was Morris at the head of the table;
> May Morris at my side, and about six or eight more comrades. Morris was
> in hearty and jovial mood ... Tales were told and songs were sung.

Another place of great fellowship was Kelmscott Manor, Morris's
country home in Oxfordshire from 1871 until his death.

Morris was more at ease with the concrete than the abstract,
although his 'half-dreaming look' could not be ignored. (He was to
make the most of his dreams in his writings, not least in *News from
Nowhere*, 1890.) To try to place him among his contemporaries,
however, we must go beyond appearances and inclinations, and trace
three crucial relationships, two of which are concerned with ideas, and
one of which was concerned with the context within which he worked.
The first two are the relationships between Morris and Ruskin and
between Morris and Marx, and the third is the relationship between
Morris and the visual environment of his time, a changing environment which still included a rich, if persistently threatened, historical
heritage.

Morris's life might have followed roughly the same outline had there
been no Ruskin. Yet it is impossible to understand the English
nineteenth century as it actually was without understanding Ruskin,
one of its greatest critics, although a man who clearly belonged to it
and to no other century. Ruskin, born in 1819, the same year as Queen
Victoria, died in 1900, only one year before she did. He was not alone
in favourably comparing past with present, particularly the lost past of
the middle ages, in extolling the Gothic and, above all, in relating the
visual - buildings and objects - to the social.[6] Yet no one, except
Thomas Carlyle, stood out so prominently as prophet as well as sage.
Ruskin encouraged people to look in order to understand, and Morris
always acknowledged his debt to him. He had warmed to Ruskin's
indictment of the human and social failings of the century long before
he had heard of Marx or felt attracted by socialism. Indeed, key
passages in Ruskin (some of them with echoes of Carlyle before him)
relate directly to what Morris came to feel with passion:

> You must either make a tool of the creature or a man of him. You cannot
> make both. Men were not intended to work with the accuracy of tools, to

be precise and perfect in all their actions ... It is verily this degradation of the operative into a machine, which, more than any other evil of the times, is leading the mass of the nations everywhere into vain, destructive struggling for a freedom which they cannot explain the nature of to themselves ... It is not that men are ill fed, but that they have no pleasure in the work by which they make their bread, and therefore look to wealth as the only means of pleasure. [7]

Ruskin, like Marx, was a sharp critic of the division of labour when it carried with it the cramping of men.

The critique of commercialism and industrialism preceded Morris, therefore, nor was it specifically Marxist: its roots lay deep in a romanticism which preceded the full development of industry, and it had as much to do with a sense of nature as with a sense of society. Morris knew this. When once a socialist criticised Ruskin in the pages of *Commonweal*, the journal of the Socialist League, Morris himself added the note that, however much damage might have been 'done to his influence by his strange bursts of fantastic perversity', his 'feeling against commercialism' had been 'absolutely genuine' and 'his expression of it most valuable'. He had been able to stir disciples too, and Morris went on to suggest that through his writings, which in his view had stopped short of socialism, he had 'made many socialists'.

There were, however, important differences between the two men, and the relationship between them was never the simple one of master to disciple. There was an inquisitorial element in Ruskin that was missing in Morris. The novelist Henry James once described Ruskin's world of art as being 'like a sort of assize court in perpetual session'. Morris's world of art by contrast was a true garden of delight. Before he became a socialist he dreamed of a palace of art, open to all. After he became a socialist, the image of the garden seemed more natural. Morris wanted people to live in an uninhibited way, enjoying themselves both at work and at play. With Morris, who like many Victorians could contemplate even with some satisfaction the prospect of the onslaught of barbarism, there was always hope in education as a guiding force; there was always a returning to keel. With Ruskin, there was a 'darkening glass', ending in madness. Young referred to his 'wiry outline', a phrase of William Blake's, and compared Ruskin's and Morris's behaviour before a Royal Commission: 'Ruskin, having said his piece, is all at sea; Morris knows what he is about from the first question to the last.'

The biggest difference of all, of course, was that while Ruskin drew and painted as well as he talked and wrote, Morris actually made *things* – with other people working by his side. He used his hands. 'What is irresistible in Morris', a German observer explained, 'is the tangible character of his productions. Here culture takes a visible form and becomes reality: one sound mind working for the comfort of other sound minds.'

The relationship between Marx, who was neither artist nor craftsman, and Morris, who was neither economist nor historian, has recently received far more detailed attention than that between Morris and Ruskin, although Morris's first biographers left it unconsidered. Such attention goes back to the 1930s, when the first signs of the Victorian revival, with different causes, can be traced. It was two years before Young reviewed May Morris's *William Morris: Artist, Writer, Socialist* in 1936 that Robin Page Arnot produced his little book *William Morris: A Vindication* which re-asserted Morris's Marxism. Edward Thomson's *William Morris, Romantic to Revolutionary*, a massive book with a similar thesis, did not appear until 1955, and even then it was relatively little noticed when it was first published. Since then, Paul Thompson has produced his admirably comprehensive study *The Work of William Morris* (1967) and Paul Meier, in a huge two-volume French study translated into English in 1978 as *William Morris, the Marxist Dreamer*, has set out to assess in meticulous detail Morris's debt to Marx and Engels. In what is now mainstream Morris criticism, *News from Nowhere*, to the distaste of others besides Thompson,[8] is usually treated as orthodox Marxist description of the Communist future, though there are differences of opinion about the extent of Morris's originality.

Morris was certainly excited when he read parts of Marx, was directly involved with Engels, who did not fully appreciate him, in the tangled London socialist politics of the late 1880s, and echoed (or paralleled) much Marxist language in his speeches and writings. There is much in common between the thoughts of the young Marx and the middle-aged Morris. Yet Morris followed his own line of development in many of his pre-socialist lectures and had got near to the critique of industrialism which was given Marxist underpinning after his conversion. When he became a revolutionary, he knew from the start what commitment meant. The 'happy days' that lay on the other side of the 'river of fire' would be secured only after organised (and, if need be, bloody) action. It was at this point that Morris separated himself unequivocally from most of the other Victorian critics of Victorianism, such as Matthew Arnold. 'No rose water will cure us: disaster (and if need be bloody) and misfortune of all kinds, I think, will be the only things that will breed a remedy.'

Meier is right to emphasise both the unity of Morris's thought and its essential creativity. He is right, too, to note how Morris had broken earlier with what he called 'the rights of property, the necessities of morality and the interests of religion', treating them thereafter as 'sacramental words of cowardice that silence us'. These were the necessary props of Victorianism, not all of which other British non-Marxist socialists even wished to pull down. Yet there were many differences between Marx and Morris apart from the obvious fact that one was grounded in Hegel and the other in Ruskin, and that Marx studied, analysed and gave orders, while Morris made things.

Marx was an intellectual in a sense that Morris never was, although both men wished to relate ideas to action, transforming action. Marx was a highly original political economist too, able to move from insight to system, while Morris never found political economy easy, though he recognised its importance, and had serious reservations about 'system'. Nor did Morris advance a distinctively Marxist approach to history, although he saw the weaknesses of Sidney Webb's version of history without Marx.[9] Marx would never have idealised the middle ages as Morris sometimes did,[10] or dismissed sweepingly the Renaissance and all that followed it, as Morris always did. Indeed, he would willingly have conceded many of the triumphs of the industrial revolution, one of the major themes of the *Communist Manifesto*. Not least important, Morris did not regard the future triumph of socialism as inevitable, scientifically demonstrable. It depended on will more than on logic. Hopeful though he was that socialism would win, with the working classes in the vanguard, he was too imaginative to take it for granted. 'The revolt against capitalism may be vanquished.' He once wrote:

The result will be that the working class – the slaves of society – will become more and more degraded, that they will not strive against overwhelming force, but stimulated by that love of life which Nature ... has implanted in us, will learn to bear everything – starvation, overwork, dirt, ignorance, brutality.

To combat apathy as well as ignorance, Morris insisted on socialist education and set out to provide it himself, addressing no fewer than 249 meetings between 1885 and 1890 in what must have been one of the busiest of all socialist calendars:

So I began the business, and in street corners I spake,
To knots of men. Indeed, that made my very heart ache.
So hopeless it seems, for some stood by like men of wood.
And some, though fain to listen, but a few words understood.
And some hooted and jeered; but whiles across some I came
Who were keen and eager to hear; as in dry flax the flame
So the quick thought flickered among them; and that indeed was a feast.

There must have been many occasions when by natural inclination

Morris would have chosen to feast at Kelmscott rather than in the back streets of England's cities.

His relation to his environment is the third relationship that needs to be understood. Morris hated the smoke and noise and dirt of the cities. He did not like an economic system based on coal and iron, and he also despised the engineering triumphs of the nineteenth century, dreaming of a return to an England where everything was on a more intimate human scale. As Young pointed out more perceptively than some recent writers, before Morris became aware of the significance of class antagonisms, he appreciated the sharp Victorian contrasts between town and countryside. 'He was educated nominally at Marlborough, and really in Savernake and on the Marlborough Downs.' He loved landscape before he learned to love buildings: this was part of the appeal of Iceland. Young notes too how he wrote of the ridge of hills near Faringdon that 'the hills are low but well designed', which he rightly observes was 'a proper compliment from one artist to another'. There was certainly a link between *The Earthly Paradise* and *News from Nowhere*, and even when he was once writing in militant language on the need for industrial action, he remarked sensitively that 'when the day comes that there is a serious strike of the workmen against the poisoning of the air with smoke or the workers with filth, I shall think that art is getting on indeed and that schools of art have had a notable success.'

Old buildings he preferred to new ones. Nor did he like what nineteenth-century architects were prepared to do with old buildings. That was why he played such an important role in the founding in 1877 of 'Anti-Scrape', the Society for the Protection of Ancient Buildings. 'These old buildings do not belong to us only; they have belonged to our forefathers', he wrote, 'and they will belong to our descendants unless we play them false. They are not in any sense our property, to do with as we like. We are only trustees for those that come after us.' Once again, however, his aesthetic and historical interests led him to a political answer.

> You cannot abolish the slums of our great cities: you cannot have happy villagers living in pretty houses among the trees, doing pretty looking work in their own houses, or in the pleasant village workshops between seedtime and harvest, unless you remove the causes that have made the brutal slum-dweller and the starveling field labourer.

It is largely because of what Morris had to say on such themes, which link concern for human relationships with that for natural and built environment – the two should never be separated and often are – that Morris has retained and in many ways strengthened his appeal in the late twentieth century. During the last few decades, indeed, interest in his work has grown substantially, not least outside circles sympathetically drawn to the Victorians. Thus, the William Morris Society, harassed though it is by a majority of Morris Trustees, includes many members who are not members of the Victorian Society. Some are more interested in his politics than in his craftsmanship. Others are interested in both and in the sense of design which links them. For these reasons, the appeal of Morris straddles two contrasting centuries and two contrasting segments of the divided world of this century. As our own world changes, different aspects of his work are singled out. Yet increasingly there is a desire to find out about the whole man.

How can we place all this in perspective? There are many people, loved or revered by their own contemporaries, who are forgotten by posterity, and there are some people who influence posterity far more than they ever influenced their contemporaries, Marx outstanding among them.

When Morris died in 1896, Robert Blatchford, socialist pioneer, wrote a moving obituary notice which revealed how interested he was in the relationship between contemporary judgements and the likely judgements of posterity. 'He was our best man and he is dead', he began, but he added at once: 'it is true that much of his work still lives and will live.' And then he went on to amplify his judgement:

> Great as was his work, he himself was greater. Many a man of genius is dwarfed by his own creations ... Morris was of a nobler kind. He was better than his best. Though his words fell like sword strokes, one always felt that the warrior was stronger than the sword. For Morris was not only a genius, he was a man. Strike at him where you would, he rang true.[11]

This was an incomplete, if memorable, judgement for by concentrating on the words it left out the objects, and these had and can still have their own appeal. It was a somewhat misleading judgement too, in that one sentence at least would have irritated Morris, the sentence referring to 'genius'. Morris associated art not with genius but with fellowship, and wanted above all to belong to a society of equals; and he was willing to labour to secure the necessary social and cultural transformation. Where Blatchford's words would have appealed to Morris most was when he was speaking of Morris ringing true, whether he was being stricken or, he might have added, which was more likely, when he was striking others himself. He wanted to ring true, and he did. The appeal persists.

The reason why the appeal persists in 'east' and 'west' is that in both segments of the world, the development of twentieth-century socialism has followed lines which would not have appealed to Morris. He hated bureaucracy, militarism and the stifling of the human spirit. And he did not confuse socialism and welfare measures. He was not taken in by slogans. He tested societies not by what they said about themselves, but by their quality of life. There are essential features of his critique of industrialism which are as pertinent in 'communist' countries as they are in 'capitalist' ones. And he would have insisted on their relevance to the life of the individual as well as of the society. 'Art cannot be the result of external compulsions', he claimed, 'the labour which goes to produce it is voluntary.'

The nineteenth century allowed more than an accepted place for that 'voluntary' drive than the twentieth century, and Young was wise to include in his essay on Morris the words of a Regius Professor of Divinity in Oxford, words he feels Morris would have accepted, even though they were printed in the Tory *Quarterly Review*:

> There is a tendency deeply implanted in our best impulses, by which men are moved to make others partners of whatever good they themselves possess, to abnegate all superiority and disclose the very secret spring of it.[12]

We know how Morris abnegated all superiority. We are less sure, perhaps, whether we have yet tapped 'the very secret spring'.

NOTES

1 For Morris see *inter alia* E. P. Thompson, *William Morris, Romantic to Revolutionary* (1977 edn); P. Thomson, *The Work of William Morris* (1967); and P. Meier, *William Morris. The Marxist Dreamer*, 2 vols (English trans., 1978). See also my selection of his works, *William Morris – Selected Writings and Designs* (1962).

2 G. M. Young, 'Topsy', reprinted in *Daylight and Champaign* (1957), p. 71.

3 May Morris, *W. Morris, Artist, Writer, Socialist*, vol. II, introduction by G. B. Shaw, p. xxvi.

4 Quoted in G. Naylor, *The Arts and Crafts Movement* (1971), p. 114.

5 See the brilliant chapter with this title in Thompson, *op. cit.*, Chapter 7.

6 See *inter alia, The Dream of Order*.

7 J. Ruskin, *The Stones of Venice* (1851-3), 'The Nature of Gothic'.

8 See his 1976 postscript in the 1977 edition of his book, p. 773: 'the important question might not be whether Morris was or was not a Marxist, but whether he was a Morrisist.' Even this is to over-emphasise the *ism* behind the *ist*.

9 See his review of *Fabian Essays* in *Commonweal*, 29 January 1890.

10 A key passage which cautiously suggests (and then not quite) the contrary was published late in his life in an article in *Liberty*, February 1894: 'We cannot turn our people into Catholic English peasants and guild craftsmen, or into heathen Norse bonders, much as may be said for such conditions of life.' At his funeral Morris's pall bearers, it was noted, were not Victorian working men but 'rustics' who might have figured in the Anglo-Saxon Chronicle.

11 *Clarion*, December 1896.

12 Quoted in Young, *op. cit.*, p. 69.

II
PROBLEMS AND POLICIES

In *Pickwick* a bad smell was a bad smell; in *Our Mutual Friend* it is a problem.

Humphrey House,
The Dickens World (1941)

A voluntary campaign of popular direction may, under the right circumstances, exert as much influence upon health conditions as would the development of an administrative programme.

Richard Shryock,
The Development of Modern Medicine (1947)

There is always, of course, the danger of statistical illusion when one compares the rate of increase of a smaller magnitude, such as welfare, with the growth rate of a larger magnitude, such as the gross national product.

Gaston Rimlinger
(1977)

A civilization ... ultimately has only the diseases it agrees to sustain.

F. Dagognet
(1970)

7   Public Opinion and Public Health in the Age of Chadwick

The battle for public health in the nineteenth century was fought on two fronts. On one front, the experts were fighting against misunderstanding and ignorance for a more complete mastery of their own developing professions. On the other, administrators and politicians were struggling against what Jeremy Bentham had christened 'sinister interests', elements actively opposing the happiness and well-being of the community, and behind them the forces of inertia, deep-rooted prejudices and popular apathy. In the long run, there was successful advance in both directions, along the two roads of 'scientific study' and 'political principle'. In the short run, there were both counter-attacks and inconclusive skirmishes. Yet as a writer in the *Quarterly Reveiw* put it as early as 1850, two years after the passing of the first national Public Health Act, 'it is as true of sanitary improvement as of human progress in all other kinds, that its successive steps are not fortuitous but determinate; each real advance, however apparently independent, being in fact but the logical extension of improvements already achieved'.[1]

The passing of the 1848 Act marked the climax of more than a decade of concern and increasing commitment – with a far longer prelude which has only recently been carefully investigated.[2] Many people were involved in the story, but if one individual character has to be singled out, it must still be that of Edwin Chadwick, so often at the centre of controversy in his own lifetime. In a real sense, this was 'the age of Chadwick', when both his authority – and the refusal of many people to accept it – preceded the development of new medical explanations and the rapid expansion of sanitary engineering. The first half of the nineteenth century saw the application of common sense to the sanitary problem, common sense backed by accurate observation, the compilation of relevant statistics and pressure to reform administration. The latter half of the century saw the exploration of the new fields of bacteriology and later of nutritional science, and the beginnings of the conversion of administration from an arena of controversy into an operational system of management.

Chadwick belongs to the pre-bacteria age. He depended in his analysis upon the evidence of his senses, of his own eyes and of his own nose. He saw dirt and he smelt decay. 'Pungent and offensive stinks', as he called them, led him to the centres of bad health: as he was to say in his old age, 'a man's own nose without any other direction will commonly indicate the chief seats of bad health.' He was more sophisticated than that, of course, in his analysis of the economy, of society, and of government, and it was both because of his views on these matters and his actions in relation to them that he was so controversial. 'Future historians who want to know what a Commission, a Board, whether working or Parliamentary, a report, a Secretary of State, or almost any other member of our system was in the nineteenth century', wrote *The Times*, in a well-known editorial in 1854, 'will find the name of Chadwick inextricably mixed up with his inquiries ... Ask – Who did this? Who made this index or that dictionary? Who managed that appointment, or ordered that sewer? and the answer is the same – Mr. Edwin Chadwick.'

Yet behind Chadwick were other historical forces of which he was the effective interpreter, and beside him were scores of other figures inside and outside government service, local and national, who co-operated with him in the building up of a public health system.

Behind Chadwick and many of his fellow pioneers was the driving force of Benthamite utilitarianism, and although the extent of the influence of Benthamism on nineteenth-century social legislation has been questioned in recent years[3] there is no doubt that Chadwick himself was one of Bentham's greatest disciples, seeking to apply in the wider sphere the doctrine of 'the greatest happiness of the greatest number.' Dr Southwood Smith also was a co-inheritor. He it was who received Bentham's body for dissection, and kept the skeleton enclosed in a mahogany cupboard in his consulting room. He it was who wrote for the first issue of the Benthamite journal, the *Westminster Review* in 1823, who became one of the first members of the Society for the Diffusion of Useful Knowledge set up in 1827; who popularised in lectures and in pamphlets the secrets of personal hygiene and individual good health. Both Chadwick and Southwood Smith saw the social implications of the new industrial community, its threats to life and to welfare. They shared the main values of the new world, but they refused to sit back passively and accept without challenge its chaotic wastes and worries. They refused to accept what many others regarded as the inevitable hand of fate. They believed, in Richardson's words, that 'man could, by getting at first principles and causes, mould life together into its natural cast, and beat what had hitherto been accepted by Fate by getting behind Fate itself, and suppressing the forces which led up to it at their prime source.'[4]

This was the Benthamite approach to the world of the early nineteenth century, a world of unparalleled advance, but a world also of incongruities and survivals where history often seemed to be an enemy, as it was to Chadwick. The Benthamites, with their test of expediency, laid all their stress on environment, on the framework of satisfactory living, and the sanitary reformers in their work of purification, were applying criteria which had far wider implications.

So much is quite general, and there is room for further debate on the extent of the Benthamite contribution to change. Passing from the general to the particular, we must note that as late as the beginning of the reign of Victoria in 1837 the statute book contained 'no general law of sanitary intention'. Yet long before this time, both Chadwick and Southwood Smith had traced the association of destitution and disease. In 1830 Southwood Smith, in his *Treatise on Fever* had attributed the impoverishment of the poor to epidemics of disease, and had pointed out how much of the trouble was preventable. Before 1830 Chadwick had begun to study typhus in the rookeries of East London, and in 1836 Parliament was persuaded to set up a General Registry Office to collect statistics on mortality rates and incidence of disease.

It was one year after Victoria came to the throne that the Poor Law Commissioners, inspired by Chadwick, sent a memorandum to the Home Secretary, stressing the need for a systematic improvement of sanitary conditions in the towns. This was the beginning of a burst of agitation, which culminated in the passing of the Public Health Act of 1848.

The agitation extended both from the centre – Chadwick's office – and the circumference – the local areas. From the heart of the metropolis, Chadwick launched his reports on sanitary inadequacies and abuses. In 1839, the Poor Law Commission was ordered to undertake a thorough inquiry into the sanitary conditions of the country, and to report on their findings. Soon afterwards, a Select Committee of the House of Commons, appointed on the initiative of R. A. Slaney, who was alarmed at the extent of popular discontent in the towns, was starting on the same sort of investigation, and Southwood Smith was one of its most forceful witnesses.[5]

The results of these and subsequent studies were embodied in the famous reports of the 1840s. Chadwick did not like the Slaney report because he felt that it placed all the stress on local action. The 1842 *Report on the Sanitary Condition of the Labouring Population*, however, was a special landmark in that it both exposed the terrible suffering of new industrial urbanisation on standards of communal living and demanded national action. 'Such is the absence of civic economy in some of our towns that their condition in respect to cleanliness is as bad as that of encamped hoardes or an undisciplined soldiery' or the 'worst prisons' ever visited by John Howard.

The further reports of 1843, 1844 and 1845 added to the catalogue of horrors. Such stories of the stagnant pools and social swamps of the new Britain could lead to one conclusion only. It was stated simply and clearly by Southwood Smith:

> The neglect of the decencies of life must have a debasing effect on the public mind. There is a point of wretchedness which is incompatible with the existence of any respect for the peace and property of others; and to look in such a case for obedience to the laws, when there is the slightest prospect of violating them with impunity, is to expect to reap where you have not sown.

Bad sanitation was, in fact, a symptom and a cause of the lack of social sense in the community; and for the first time in the 1840s a society which had been preoccupied with industrial advance and individual gain was beginning nationally and systematically to demand adequate social controls to maintain an orderly framework for civilised living.

The classic reports of the 1840s were invaluable agencies of civic education. They did their work more slowly and more selectively than the noisy propaganda of the Anti-Corn Law League, which was pouring out from Manchester during the same period, but in the long run their exposure of the social cost of dirt and disease proved completely unanswerable. They were aimed at the reading public, the members, for the most part, of only one of the two nations, who occupied Britain during these years; and the stories they told helped to build up an impression of the way the other half lived. Their effect can be compared with the effect of Dickens's novels or of Disraeli's *Sybil*, and indeed their moving narratives offered a wealth of effective illustrative material to any would-be novelist.

The reports were backed first by the statistics from the General Registry Office, described by Lord Morpeth as 'the most valuable documents in a statistical point of view which ever appeared in this or any other country', and second by the propaganda of the newly founded Health of Towns Association, set up in 1844, publishing its own cleverly contrived weekly sheets of facts and figures, organising the resources of platform and press, and taking the issue into the heart of the big cities. Chadwick was not a member of its Committee of sixty-nine, which included doctors like Southwood Smith and W.A. Guy,[6] as well as politicians, among them not only R.A. Slaney but Benjamin Disraeli. Because of his official position Chadwick stayed out of a public agitation. Yet he knew as much about its operations as he knew about backstairs official discussions. He knew that while he was writing private notes to the Duke of Buccleugh, Chairman of the

Health of Towns Association, the Association was producing cheap publications with titles like 'Why are Towns Unhealthy?' and 'Sanitary State of the Metropolis'. It was an advantage that the main sponsors of this central propaganda did not belong to one political group. Indeed, they relied as much on religion as on politics: their first meeting was held at Exeter Hall, centre of great religious demonstrations. The Evangelical leader, Lord Ashley, inspired by old impulses, spoke of what he called the dehumanising influences at work in the towns, 'weakening and destroying the feelings and affections', 'human faces retrograding, sinking down to the level of brute tribes.' There was fear there as well as hope. In 1840 he had observed 'the vast and inflammable mass that lies waiting day by day, for the spark to explode it into mischief', and described socialism and Chartism as 'two great demons in morals and politics'.[7]

The Evangelical Tory Ashley and the Whig magnate Normanby were first introduced to the slums of Whitechapel and Bethnal Green by Southwood Smith, and they were appalled at once by a glimpse of squalor and decay which they had never caught before. Ashley noted in his Diary of September 1841 (note the lateness of the date):

What a perambulation have I taken today in company with Dr. Southwood Smith! What scenes of filth, discomfort, and disease!... No pen nor paint brush could describe the thing as it is. One whiff of Cowyard, Blue Anchor or Baker's Court, outweighs ten pages of letter press.[8]

The sanitary evils of the towns were not always so apparent at first sight. When Chadwick and his colleagues visited the fever-ridden homes of the poorer classes in the large cities, it was frequently declared by the inmates that they had 'never for many years witnessed the approach or presence of persons in that condition near them'.

The stirring of the Christian conscience gave moral impetus to the movement for change. Chadwick's grandfather had been a friend of John Wesley, and Southwood Smith had himself been a Unitarian minister. The Bishop of London, Charles Jones Blomfield,[9] lent all his aid to the movement, both in and out of Parliament. Clergymen were everywhere among the vanguard of reformers. Their regular duties took them into the heart of what Morpeth described in the Commons as the 'chambers of death'. At times they faced dangers comparable with those on the field of battle, and they had their own dead, men like Standon and Riddell of Newcastle, 'martyrs to their self-denying devotion to the cause of suffering humanity'.

The work of the clergy reminds us that the fight for public health was not fought merely from behind government desks, nor merely from London. The same pattern of local action can be traced in many different parts of the country. The Health of Towns Association had provincial branches, one of the first of them in Liverpool, and they sometimes published magazines like the *Liverpool Health of Towns Advocate*.[10] The pioneers of change were those who had seen for themselves the worst evils – not only ministers of religion, but also medical practitioners, relieving officers and lawyers. Thus, in Huddersfield Clough, a local solicitor, told a public meeting in 1848 how he first became interested in the sanitary question after reading a report made by a constable to the local magistrates, giving details of appalling living conditions:

> Timothy Corcan in a dwelling of but two rooms, four yards square, had twenty inmates, and but four beds, being five to a bed. Of these inmates, two were sick of fever: ... Dennis Scully in a cellar dwelling of one room had nine inmates and no beds. In this dwelling, two were laid dead of the fever. The privies and cesspools in the yard were in the most disgusting and offensive state.

Clough was profoundly shocked, and was even more shocked when the Huddersfield magistrates went on to reply that they had no jurisdiction in the matter. His horror impelled him to set out on a tour of inspection himself, and he found that there was no exaggeration in what the constable had said. Yet a Catholic priest in the neighbourhood, to whom he spoke, told him that he had seen but a few of the many black spots of the district, and that beneath the surface there were even worse features than those which were immediately apparent. Clough concluded his remarks to the meeting by showing how 'these facts and others of a similar kind induced him to see if a means of remedy could not be found'. A further speaker drove the lesson home:

> Such masses of putrefaction would cause them to wonder at there being as much health in the town as there was. Had they been in the dirty avenues and seen the sights he had seen, they would never have slept in their beds till they were removed.

That was the logic of informed opinion – a glimpse of horror and a righteous zeal to eradicate it. The same story is true of most of the large towns of the country during these years, although if we are to believe Palmerston, speaking in 1854, there still remained in every town a clean party and a dirty party side by side.

Local indignation was reinforced by local reports, which were just as important in stimulating opinion as the national reports which have passed into history.

In almost every large town and populous locality, boards had been formed for the purpose of making periodical reports and exciting public interest in the subject, all beginning with one and the same complaint, the utter inadequacy of the law for the removal of the great and pressing evil [then] endured.

There are too many to mention in detail, but some stand out – Dr Neil Arnot's reports on Edinburgh and Glasgow, where there were people, in his phrase, worse than wild animals; Cooper's reports on Southampton; Shafto's on Exeter; Playfair's on Lancashire; Smith's on the West Riding; Martin's on the Midland manufacturing towns, like Coventry and Leicester; Robinson's on Newcastle on Tyne; and Dr Kay's and Dr Simon's on the metropolis.

Many of the reports were very powerfully written. They usually began with a statistical base, for example:

The deaths of infants in Preston under one year were – in well-conditioned streets, 15 deaths to a 100 births; in middling-conditioned streets, 21 deaths to a 100 births; ill-conditioned streets, 38 deaths to 100 births; worst conditioned streets, 44 deaths to a 100 births.

Yet statistics were given colour and life by stories. One, not taken direct from a report, but from a letter to Morpeth written by Dr Parkes on the death of his foreman's mother, read:

She was buried yesterday. She was a nice, clean, hardworking woman, and what is very vexing about her death is, that a nasty, filthy town drain that runs under their house has been the cause of it ... Such deaths are really awful, and are of very common occurrence.

The effect of the local reports was to spread more widely what the eye-witnesses had seen at first hand. They did much to counteract what Dr Robinson described at Newcastle on Tyne as 'the disinclination to active exertion', a more formidable enemy of change than any 'personal antipathy to sanitary improvement'. Inertia was always an enemy of health, private or public. The classic story in this connection dates from 1844:

A man had to fetch water from one of the public pumps in Bath, the distance from his house being about a quarter of a mile. 'It is as valuable', he said, 'as strong beer. We can't use it for cooking, or anything of that sort, but only for drinking and tea.'

'Then where do you get water for cooking and washing?'

'Why, from the river. But it is muddy, and often stinks bad, because all the filth is carried there.'

'Do you then prefer to cook your victuals in water, which is muddy and stinks, to walking a quarter of a mile to fetch it from the pump?'

'We can't help ourselves you know. We could not go all that way for it.'

The witness quoting the story went on to give his theoretical explanation, and there was usually a tag at the end, often revealing the gap between one set of class attitudes and another, a gap in understanding as well as in information:

> With the poor ... no privation is felt as little as that of cleanliness. The propensity to dirtiness is so strong, the steps so few and easy, that nothing but the utmost facilities for water can act as a counterpoise; and such is the love of uncleanliness, when once contracted, that no habit, not even drunkenness, is so difficult to eradicate.

This background of social habit certainly helps to explain Chadwick's famous dictum – 'If a great epidemic were to occur again, I would proclaim and enforce the active application of soap and water as a preventive. I have had frequent opportunities of observing this plan as a factor of sanitation.' Soap and water meant much in an age when 'the people of Britain were being thrown back in continually closer crowds upon the city gates.' Scrubbing was a priority. Ashley re-echoed Wesley's aphorism 'cleanliness comes next to godliness' when he wrote that he attached 'unparallelled value' in public and in private movements to sanitary questions: they were second only to the religious and, in some respects, inseparable from it. The Health of Towns Association claimed comprehensively that it would 'substitute Health for Disease, cleanliness for filth, order for disorder, economy for waste, prevention for palliation, justice for charity, enlightened self-interest for ignorant selfishness, and bring home to the poorest and meanest amongst us, in purity and abundance, the simple blessings which ignorance and negligence have long combined to limit or to spoil – *Air, Water, Light.*'[11]

Vis inertiae in private health was, of course, accompanied by a similar and magnified unwillingness to budge in matters of public health. The education of opinion took years to realise, and it was finally accomplished only with the momentum of the motive of fear, particularly fear of the mass-murderer epidemics of cholera and typhoid that started in the overcrowded alleys and tenements and spread so alarmingly that the danger often 'hung over the whole land'. In one of his most powerful passages, Ashley described passionately how the poorer folk looked with terror on the approach of fine weather, bringing with it the crescendo of disease. 'What was a blessing to others', he declared, 'was to the poor a positive curse.' And Chadwick often reminded him of the consequences of the failure of Parliament to act. 'Pray look over the enclosed mortality bill with its account of the slaughter of fifteen thousand above the average for the quarter,' he told him in the autumn of 1846, 'and you will see how true it is that if we are idle, death is not.'[12]

Ignorance and fear side by side generated misery and insecurity, and misery and insecurity in turn generated much of the hate and the suspicion that darkened the social history of early Victorian Britain. If it is true, as Dicey tells us, 'that circumstances are the creators of most men's opinions ... that public opinion is far less the result of reasoning and of argument than of the circumstances in which men are placed', then this darker side of the 'Bleak Age' is of paramount importance in explaining the quickened interest in public health in the 'hungry Forties'.[13]

The incentives which moved the pioneers and the ways in which they spread their ideas, have had to be studied before turning to the arguments they used.

The first argument was an economic one. Classical 'Political economy' was as much of a force in the public health movement as Benthamism or Christian benevolence, and it dwelt both on cost and interdependence: 'the negative condition of health, immunity from disease, was not an end which could be wholly achieved by individual action.'[14] Attention was focused from the start on the high cost of disease. The cost was measured absolutely in terms of wastage of labour, expenses of sickness, funeral charges, orphanage responsibilities, relief for widowhood and poor law assistance. Morpeth pointed out that it would be difficult to say 'what these barbarisms cost, but no reasonable man could doubt that they amounted to several millions a year.' His own estimate was in the region of £15 million a year. Local authorities often made their own estimates. Clough at Huddersfield, for instance, reckoned that in the year ending December 1845, £466 was spent out of the local rates on expenses directly connected with ill-health brought about by bad sanitation. Most of this expense might have been saved, he argued, 'had the places these poor creatures were obliged to crowd into not been such as engendered disease and death.'

Unnecessarily large charges on the rates have always been anathema to audiences of northern businessmen, and this sort of argument was beginning to convince people, though it was not finally accepted until a much later date. As *The Times* put it: '£20 expended in the sewerage of a blind alley would save £50 to be otherwise raised by the overseers of the poor' or, as it was stated in its more general form in an article in the *British and Foreign Medico-Chirurgical Review*:

One broad principle may be safely enunciated in respect of sanitary economics – that it costs more money to create disease than to prevent it;

and that there is not a single structural arrangement chargeable with the production of disease, which is not also in itself an extravagance.[15]

The *Edinburgh Review* stated firmly that in 'the economic sense of the term a short-lived population is generally a surplus population'.

The economic argument was further elaborated, as economic arguments generally are, by social considerations. Disease took a heavy yearly toll of deaths. In 1840, the crude death rate was 23 per 1000, slightly more than that of India today. The average age of death was twenty-nine. One child in six died before the age of one. The Health of Towns Association estimated an annual death roll of 40,000 due to sanitary causes, and the provincial press focused attention on the relevant detail in items like the 'March of Death' – 'Five funerals left Sibbridge on Sunday last within ten minutes of each other.'

These regular figures were beginning to impress. In introducing the 1848 Health of Towns Bill, Morpeth argued from the start that the purpose of the Bill was not to 'provide against any temporary evil, any transient visitant', but against 'the abiding host of disease, the endemic and not the epidemic pestilence, the permanent overcharging mist of infection, the annual slaughter doubling in its ravages our bloodiest fields of conflict'. In the first month of that year, the *Chronicle* in Bolton had headed a long article on the subject with the words 'Delay of Sanitary Reform, A Proof of the Weakness and Dishonesty of the Government'.[15a]

The assault on the 'abiding host of disease' gained momentum, when it was realised beyond all doubt that the sectors of battle varied considerably, that different sets of social conditions produced different sets of death tolls, that the towns were worse than the country, the rich far better off than the poor, the overcrowded districts more badly hit than the prosperous districts. Chadwick soon reached the terrible conclusion that by knowing the general layout of a town, he could deduce where the worst epidemics would occur. Southwood Smith reached the same conclusion too:

If you trace down the fever districts on the map, and then compare that map with the map of the Commissioners of Sewers, you will find that wherever the Commissioners of Sewers have not been, there fever is prevalent, and on the contrary, wherever they have been, there fever is comparatively absent.

In Sheffield, James Heywood and William Lee told how:

after the first few days' experience in our recent inspection, we were able, with an awful precision, not only to detect the unhealthy parts of the town, but the portions of the streets, and the particular houses in streets and courts, especially liable to febrile and other diseases. The result of our inspection is a conviction which nothing can ever remove or weaken, that ... a thousand at least are destroyed every year in this town, by diseases, which would have no existence under complete sanitary arrangements.[16]

It merely needed a little more sharpening to draw out the correlation of disease and squalor on the one hand and crime and civic irresponsibility on the other. Here the Chaplain of Preston Gaol put the issue very clearly:

Filthiness of person and sordidness of mind are usually united ... If you would banish squalor and sickness from the labourer's cottage, you must remove ignorance and corruption from his head and heart. Amidst the dirt and disease of filthy back courts and alleys and yards, vices and crimes are lurking together, unimagined by those who have not seen such abodes.

What lasting benefit, asked Ashley, could be obtained from public education, until home environment was made more healthy and more respectable?

The economic argument had its special appeal for the businessman. The social argument appealed to the church- and chapel-goer, and the honest Radical. What of the working man? Many speakers in the 1848 debate called the Health of Towns Bill a working man's measure, specially designed to protect above all others 'the children of poverty and toil', whose only capital consisted of their health and strength. There were in different parts of the country working men's associations pledged to sanitary reform. Morpeth quoted a petition from a group of working men:

The wealthy, the easy classes can build themselves commodious houses; they can select healthy situations, they can in most instances command unfailing supplies of water and fresh air; if health fails them in one place, they may pursue it in a thousand others; but for the children of poverty and toil, if legislation does not interfere to bring it to them, it will become as unattainable a blessing as the rarest gifts of fortune.

The phrase 'if legislation does not bring it to them' reminds us that this was an age of limited suffrage with powers of voting still in the hands of a few. It is important in studying the criticism of Chadwick in 1854, when the General Board of Health fell, to remember that he was being attacked by Members of a Parliament which still claimed to represent not numbers but interests. Some speakers in 1848 stressed the need of public health legislation to 'rally the [working classes] round the institutions of the country'. 'If they neglected these improvements, the people would be discontented that nothing had been done for them. By a measure of this nature, they would do much to increase the security of property ... and to make large bodies of the population of great towns contented and cheerful.'

This was a time when the attitudes of the working classes to social questions were changing, although the changes remain to be charted, and their extent carefully assessed. In 1836, a medical officer in the Midlands had described appalling living conditions in the home of a family of thirteen, and had ended his report by saying: 'I have never heard, during the course of twelve years' practice, a complaint of inconvenient accommodation.' By 1848, it is certain that at least among certain individuals – it is difficult to go further than that – this indifference was being blown away. The Metropolitan Working Classes Association for Improving the Public Health had been founded in 1846, claiming that 'the working classes have lately become aware that they suffer much disease and misery, both in body and mind from the pressure of causes, many of which might be removed, and others lessened.' It drew attention to 'ventilation, warming, and bathing', as well as drains and sewers, and when Morpeth introduced his Public Health Bill in 1848 he was able to quote at least one letter that he had received from a working man:

I do not agree with those who would leave everything to regulate itself, or to the exertion of private individuals, however well-meaning, lacking that information, which is at the command of a government, would never be able to do it as effectually as it should be done.

The objective of the Bill in his words was to discover 'how best to overcome the prevalence of disease, to narrow the bounds of death, and to promote human happiness and comfort', and this very noble but none too precise goal met with widespread approval by 1848. Speaker after speaker in the debates paid at least lip-service to the ideal. So much so that *The Times* asked for a lively opposition to stir the reformers.

O for a pettish and personal opposition [to the Bill] just enough to quicken Lord Morpeth's energies! Would that there was a fever party in Palace Yard, or 'Protection of British Diseases' in New Bond Street. Will Mr Shaw hold a brief for the typhus or the Duke of Richmond take his stand on diarrhoea? There will then be the early prospect of a good sanitary law, too late for last summer but in time for the next.[17]

There was an element of rhetoric in the demand for an opposition to effective legislation, an opposition if not to 'sanitary reform' at least to the particular Bill Morpeth introduced. It was an opposition which, in fact, was usually inarticulate, working behind the scenes, but at other times it reached powerful heights of self-expression in Parliament and on the platform. Moreover, the opposition was not quelled with the passing of the 1848 Act, and the same elements of discontent and opposition were to become even more prominent in the break-up of the much criticised Board of Health in 1854, and the withdrawal of Chadwick from public life. There was no finality about the Health of Towns Bill in 1848. It was a beginning rather than an end.

It is an over-simplification to suggest that the only counter-forces to the health agitation came from what Bentham was wont to describe as 'sinister interests'. Yet certainly there were interests everywhere which had a stake in dirt and disease. The most extreme example was the private ownership of refuse heaps and dung hills. The 1842 Report on the Sanitary Condition of the Labouring Population mentioned the notorious case of Greenock, where

> in one part of the street, a narrow back street, there is a dunghill. I do not mistake its size, when I say it contains a hundred cubic yards of impure filth. It is the stock in trade of the person who deals in dung. He retails it by the cartful. To please his customers, he always keeps a nucleus, as the older the filth, the higher the price.

More subtle than this most blatant of all interests were the special interests of water companies, municipal and private markets and slaughter houses, gas companies, chimney owners, burial concerns, ward politicians, and even, ironically but commonly enough, existing Improvement Commissioners. And it was not only the fact that some of these interests were very powerful relative to the general interest that counted. Some of them could claim with or without reason that they were interested in public health themselves at the level of public concern which really mattered.

John Stuart Mill was writing realistically in his *Autobiography* when he explained that 'interest in the common good is at present so weak a motive in the generality, not because it can never be otherwise, but because the mind is not accustomed to dwell on it as it dwells from morning till night on things which tend only to personal advantage'.[18] It was only when individuals and interests could be persuaded that without a regular framework for public health they would be among the sufferers, that they could be persuaded to yield at all. There is a fascinating story from a northern town of the inadequacy of purely individual action by the property-owner. A person living in the upper part of the town had been obliged to spend money to build a drain to carry away sewerage which was getting into his kitchen. He got rid of the nuisance but, without his knowing, it was only removed thereby into the kitchen of the neighbouring local surveyor. Obviously in cases like this the application of the Benthamite principle of utility had to be superintended not by the individual but by 'the state'. A framework had to be built for the benefit of all, including the property-owners.

Yet for all the inevitable give and take, interests kicked and struggled, often with considerable success. The 1848 Bill was less a triumphant vindication of principle than a compromise between existing interests – Morpeth and his Prime Minister, Lord John Russell; the Government and the opposition; the water companies and the Ministry; Parliament and the City of London; other local authorities and the centre. Between March and May 1848, Morpeth, in his own words 'selected two or three practical persons in the House and out of it, who endeavoured to put [the Bill] into such shape that while the objectives, which had been urged against it could be met, it would still retain its original efficiency'. An unwillingness to offend and an eagerness to appease characterised the preparation and passage of the legislation. 'It was not intended', said its sponsor, 'to put anything into the Bill, which would unnecessarily raise objections and so frustrate the expedition of carrying the measure into effective operation. This temporising in 1848 could not produce a final equilibrium of forces. Most of the interests, quietened in 1848, burst forth again with renewed vigour against Chadwick in 1854, only to be destroyed themselves, beyond all recall, by the end of the century.

On the whole, however, the pure obstructionism of sectional interests was always masked by the screen of ideas. As Dicey reminds us, 'a delusion however largely the result of self-interest, is still an intellectual error, and a different thing from callous selfishness. It is at any rate an opinion.'[19] The mobilisation of opinion against the development of effective legislation on national sanitary policy begins towards the middle of the 1840s and reaches its vociferous climax in 1854.

The chief argument against the Bills of 1847 and 1848 was a political argument. Health could not be separated from politics. The Bills, it was said, were unconstitutional. They were un-English. They embodied an alien principle of centralisation, which could only do the country irreparable harm, and would finally land it in the same chaotic and reckless state as its neighbour across the Channel. 'By bringing local grievances into one focus, the government would be falling into the error of a neighbouring country, which in consequence of having for years centralised everything, ended in centralising discontent.' The leading exponents of this view in the House of Commons were David Urquhart, Member for Stafford, such an eccentric and unique figure that he was called by the *Examiner* 'The Great One', and Colonel Sibthorp, Tory Member for Lincoln. They were backed by a small but active group of Members, and if their arguments were sometimes shaky, their language was always vigorous and colourful. 'The Bill destroys every vestige of local pre-eminence, and reduces everything to a dull and level monotony.' 'It is imbued in every part with an objectionable assumption of power by the Government.' 'It has long been the pride of this country that the Government has little to do with the management of our own internal affairs.' The Bill is a 'usurpation by the Government of the powers of local bodies and a destruction by the general executive of local rights'. 'What are the crimes of our reformed municipalities that a reformed Parliament should propose to reconstruct the Court of Star Chamber?' The method was as bad as the substance. 'It is more like a Russian ukase than an English Act of Parliament.'[20]

This anti-centralist cry was buttressed by two arguments. First the localities had been libelled and misrepresented, particularly by the Health of Towns Association. 'The public mind', said one MP, 'had been drugged with the grossest misrepresentations in respect to the sanitary conditions of the United Kingdom.' All the time that 'language the most unseemly and propositions the most absurd' were enflaming the country, the towns were quietly cleaning themselves. 'The city which he had the honour to represent', argued Sibthorp, 'required no such Bill as this . . . they required no change. Why should the pure city of Lincoln be mixed up with the impure cities?' 'We are not surprised, though we regret', wrote the *Manchester Guardian*, 'that our town council should endeavour to have Manchester exempted from the operation of the Public Health Bill.'[21]

'The local authorities', shouted Pearson, 'were being deprived of that independent conduct and action, which was the glory of our Saxon institutions,' and 'like rickety children', they were to be placed under the control of central government. Urquhart went further. He moved an amendment to have his own borough of Stafford omitted from the Bill. This led to a short and sweet debate, which ended with the Member for South Staffordshire, Viscount Ingestre, confessing with feeling 'that he believed there was no town which so much required the cleansing process as the town of Stafford'.

The second political argument involved denunciation of those clauses in the Bill which suggested an extension of the administrative departments working under the government. This was the familiar contemporary raging against patronage. 'Many greedy people expected places from the Bill', said Sibthorp, 'friends not of humanity but of self.' 'Having got hold of the lawyers', argued Hanley, 'they were now going to get hold of the doctors and surveyors.' 'If these sanitary improvements were persevered with, the doctors would soon make their fortunes.' They therefore fought for this Bill with a zeal and an energy which they would not have exhibited in support of any more

abstract proposition for the improvement of the public good.'
Members professed to see the thin end of the wedge. 'If this Bill were
passed, other Bills carrying the principle still further would be speedily
introduced, and there would be a substitution of paid officers in every
department of state.'

These political arguments had their roots deep in English history, in
subjects far away at times from public health. The themes recurred
constantly in all the debates of the period, and are not entirely without
relevance today. In addition, economic arguments were put forward
against the 1848 legislation (as well as in its favour), on the grounds
that it cost far too much, more than the country could bear. 'The
whole Bill', raged Sibthorp, 'is a job. It is a desire on the part of the
Government to saddle the country with heavy expenses to feed and
fatten men who were poor and lean.'

Another MP stated bluntly that 'he for one was not prepared to
send down Commissioners into the towns of England with lavish and
extravagant salaries to do that which could be better done without
them.' A third MP argued closely that retail dealers and small traders
in particular would not be able to support the increased burdens of
expenditure; while a fourth, in horror, stated that the measure would
involve 'a new tax to be imposed on the people of England, equal
perhaps to the Income Tax'. (It was then 7d in the £.)

These were the main arguments against the 1848 Bill. On the right
flank, Sibthorp thundered, 'I hate all Commissions, I hate all jobs, I
suspect all Governments.' On the Radical flank, there was a loud
murmur for the abolition of the Window Tax, and a more democratic
system of voting in the new franchises for the local Boards of Health.
Urquhart went as far as Sibthorp in launching a frontal attack on the
whole edifice, clause by clause. The common law (if it were properly
applied), he argued, would solve all the problems of the day. 'I place no
trust in new doctrines. I believe that all good things were old.' 'The
reason why this country was at its lowest ebb ... was that [the] House
has passed laws which affected the labour and industry of man ...
Away with this mawkish philanthropy, which pretended to stop the
current of a fever by holding the pulse of the patient.'

This was *laissez-faire* with a vengeance, too much even for Radicals
like G.F.Muntz, who only went so far as to query the efficacy of
sanitary legislation to solve *all* the troubled issues of the day. There
were curious Tory-Radical alignments at times. Thus, while Sibthorp
confessed in the debate that he 'disapproved of the new patent water
closets' and 'much preferred the old system', solid Northern and
Midlands manufacturers disputed the wisdom of any smoke clause.
They felt that it would injure industry, and possibly even render
impossible the making of coke. John Bright boasted he had always

opposed every Smoke Bill on the grounds that it was impossible in practice for such a scheme ever to work.

Opposition opinion inside the House was a faithful mirror of opposition outside, although it was natural that the local-central issue roused most excitement in the constituencies, and was most commented on in the local Press.

National newspapers picked on major issues, as did the quarterlies. The *Morning Chronicle*, for instance, drew a sharp distinction between ends and means.

> The intention of this measure is worthy of the age and country in which we live. The practical methods by which it is proposed to carry out these measures are as unworthy of the political science of the age, that they must, if adopted, prove galling and intolerable to the English independence of spirit and hatred of perpetual interference.[22]

The Times favoured the Bill – 'if this Bill will not do', it asked, 'what will?'[23] The opposition papers thundered against it, the *Jurist* leading the way by branding the Bill 'a vast Political Inclosure Bill, a Bill to suppress and inclose all the open and common fields provided by our Saxon constitution for the exercise and enjoyment of those rights and privileges of self-government which have always been regarded as the root and firm basis of English liberties'.

In the North of England, where there had been such a fierce popular opposition to the Poor Law Amendment Act of 1834, and where local loyalties were powerful and London still a distant capital, there was considerable opposition in 1848. The Lord Mayor of Leeds complained that the Bill superseded municipal corporations, and set aside local self-government to a far greater extent than any other enactment which he had ever come across before. He pleaded for a different scheme. The *Leeds Mercury* echoed him. Why should all towns be placed under the control of a central board in London? Why should they be under the 'surveillance of an inspector and an over-ruling board 200 miles off?' 'While we are most anxious that every town in the kingdom should have the benefit of good sewerage and pure water ... we could not consent to purchase these blessings by a permanent infringement of the rights of municipal bodies, and through them of the people at large.'[24]

From Leeds itself came the answer to some of these doubts and queries. The *Leeds Intelligencer*, political rival of the *Leeds Mercury*, congratulated Morpeth on the results of his labours. Its editorial line was to hail the march of legislation 'which laid down the principle that the health, cleanliness, and purity of the poor man's street and dwelling just as much as the rich man's are to be the primary concern of the state,'[25] instead of being 'aristocratic appendages and elegant luxuries. It was so much concerned with what it called 'the road to true democracy' that it welcomed central control to destroy local filth and disorder.

The conflict between these two local papers brings me to the climax of my lecture – the clash between the protagonists and the opponents of the Health of Towns Bill, the swing and the counter-swing of argument, the ebb and flow of opinion. In Leeds, Manchester, Bradford, London, or where you will, there was the same clash of opinion reflected in rival newspapers. And there is little doubt that this political controversy, reaching its peak in 1854, did much to make public health a lively issue at a time when, despite all the noise of the informers, lack of interest and popular apathy were very widespread.

If controversy quickened the public health issue, certainly fear of cholera speeded up the passage of the Bill through its final stages. While the Lords were debating, cholera was sweeping westward across the continent. Lord Brougham, in opening the discussion on the Bill in the Lords, pointed out that while such a measure was always worthy of favourable consideration

> at no time was it more desirable than at the present moment, when there was but too much reason to apprehend that . . . the Cholera, was making a steady, systematic and rapid progress towards the shores of England. It was in their interest, as it was their manifest duty, to promote as much as possible the progress of the only conceivable measure, which would give check to that dreaded scourge of humanity . . .It was right that the true position should be properly understood. Alarm ought not to be raised except on the principle stated by Mr. Burke, that the fire bell alarmed our slumbers, but it prevented us from being burned in our beds.

With this alarm, the progress of the Bill gained speed, but it is important not to exaggerate the influence of the fear of cholera outbreak in 1848 on the passage of legislation. After all, the 1848 Bill was only the climax of a series of earlier abortive Bills in the 1840s, beginning with Normanby's attempts in 1841, and ending with the failure of Morpeth's first measure in 1847. The 1848 Bill must be seen against a wider panorama than the hot and exciting summer of 1848, year of European revolutions and tottering of thrones. By 1848, there was a substantial body of opinion actively in favour of legislation for public health. Even the opponents of the Bill could not deny that the 'electors wanted sanitary reform'.

The MP for Dover for instance, recollected 'that in the hustings of the last election, there was not a more popular question'. This view was underlined by the Member for Bristol. At Huddersfield, a speaker described the *volte-face* of public opinion between 1820 and 1848. In 1820, it was hostile; by 1848, a 'flood of light had been let in as it were, on those sanitary questions, and the results were a general desire to promote improvements'.

In 1820, the first of the two dates, Sir Robert Peel had described public opinion as 'the tone of England, that great compound of folly, weakness, prejudice, wrong feeling, right feeling, obstinacy, and newspaper paragraphs'.[26] All these elements were still there in 1848. Yet there was more right feeling than in 1820. Industrial England was now producing its prophets, like Carlyle, to plead before the captains of industry:

> Men are brothers and sisters, not mere warring atoms. A Scotch widow left free to starve in a slum according to economic law contracts the typhus and kills seventeen other human beings thus proving her sisterhood.

But if there was right feeling, there was still plenty of wrong feeling, folly, prejudice, obstinacy, and newspaper paragraphs. The newspaper paragraphs were indeed more important than they had been twenty-eight years before, but, just as eloquent as their fiery editorials for or against the Bill, was the conspicuous silence of some sections of the press which did not deign to mention the sanitary debates at all. In estimating the significance of 1848 in English history, we must not forget the deep silence that spoke volumes. 'Although the *Annual Register* devoted 259 pages to the proceedings of Parliament in 1847, and 194 pages in 1848, the debates on the Public Health Bills were completely ignored.'

Perhaps this was merely a recognition of the fact that the rising statesmen of the House of Commons – like Gladstone and Disraeli, for all the fact that the latter patronised the Health of Towns Association – did not deign at this time to speak about drains and sewers. They were prepared to fight long and hard about the Corn Laws and the Charter, but as *The Times* put it 'we are not to be persuaded that stench and smoke could have preserved that which corn and sugar lost, if they had but been attacked with half the same determination'.[27]

Few people were genuinely satisfied with the settlement of 1848 which neither pleased the Radical reformers nor appeased the sectional interests. In particular, the fact that the City of London was left out was criticised from the start. As the *Westminster Review* put it in 1848 itself,

> the questionable policy of excepting the metropolis from the provisions of the Public Health Bill has not had the effect, which was hoped for by the Government, of diminishing the hostility of interested parties ... In this, as in all cases of proposed reforms ... postponement only affords time to those who profit by abuses to organize an opposition, and perhaps to

render it effective, by the usual arts of private influence and misrepresentation.[28]

The first hint of the main opposition line of attack came in a speech by Mr Divett in the 1848 debates. He told the House 'that the electors did not object to sanitary improvement, but they did not choose to be ordered how to set about it'. The England of Palmerston did not want to be ordered to do anything, and for this reason, if for no other, the new Public Health Board, with its assiduous zeal and its hurrying energy, offended more by its activity than it would have done by its lethargy. The 'three kings of Somerset House' – Ashley, Chadwick, and Southwood Smith – were branded as interlopers and interferers, pushing their noses into everybody's business, and not even succeeding in dealing adequately with the epidemics of cholera, which swept the country with considerable force in 1849 and 1853. Before cholera arrived, the *Morning Chronicle* asked pointedly, 'Was there ever a better bureaucrat than Mr Chadwick; Is not this gentleman a perfect model of what a man should be, who has to regulate all the drains and sewers from his writing desk?'[29]

The most vocal opposition in the country came from bodies like the 'Private Enterprise Society' and more important Toulmin Smith's 'Anti-Centralisation Union', which operated between 1854 and 1857. The lawyer-geologist Smith wrote two influential attacks on the 1848 Act and the system it embodied first in his *Local Self Government and Centralisation*, which appeared in 1851, and second in *The Parish, its Obligations and Powers: Officers and their Duties*, which came out three years later. Smith popularised these books by lecture tours and letters to the press, setting up against the experience of the new, centralised Public Board, 'scrubbing and cleaning the whole national community', the ideal of local action for local health, carried out through the traditional organs of British local government, the parish and the township. Smith appealed to history: Chadwick appealed to efficiency. Smith said that no new statutory powers were needed. The magic of goodwill was the only requirement, and this could grow more easily in the hearts of individuals, living together in small groups, than be manufactured and exported by the edicts of a central state department. Chadwick's supporters argued that this might have been the ideal solution for a model parish like Hornsey, where Smith lived and worked, but it was hardly the answer for a new industrial community, where, as shown by the Census of 1851, half the population was now urban, and was still in movement.

Beneath this clash of ideas, there was the constant burrowing of interests underneath. In 1853, Ashley gave a list in his diary of his chief enemies. They were varied and powerful:

We roused all the dissenters by our burial bill. The Parliamentary agents are our sworn enemies, because we have reduced expenses, and consequently their fees within reasonable limits. The Civil Engineers also, because we have selected able men, who have carried into effect new principles, and at less salary. The College of Physicians and all its dependencies, because of our independent action and singular success in dealing with the cholera. ... All the Boards of Guardians, for we exposed their selfishness, their cruelty, their reluctance to meet and relieve the suffering poor in the days of the epidemic. The Treasury besides [for the subalterns there hated Chadwick: it was an ancient grudge and paid when occasion served]. Then came the Water Companies, whom we laid bare, and devised a method of supply, which altogether superseded them. The Commissioners of Sewers, for our plans and principles were the reverse of theirs; they hated us with a perfect hatred.

This conjunction of hatreds led to the fall of the General Board of Health in 1854, and its replacement by a new body, with a paid President sitting in Parliament. 'Æsculapius and Chiron in the form of Mr. Chadwick and Dr. Southwood Smith', wrote *The Times*, which was now on the other side, 'have been deposed, and we prefer to take our chance of cholera and the rest than be bullied into health.' 'After five years of intense and unrewarded labour,' wrote Ashley in his diary, 'I am turned off like a piece of lumber. Such is the Public Service. Some years hence, if we are remembered, justice may be done to us, but not in our lifetimes.'

I have tried to concentrate in this paper less on personalities than on issues and on the background to them and not on structures, laws, constitutions or commissions, but on incentives, ideas, interests, pressures. This sort of study of the dynamics of change is essential if the early nineteenth century is to live again for the citizens of the twentieth.

Certain broad conclusions are clear. In this 'age of Chadwick', public health could not be separated from politics. The creation of adequate health machinery, involved political fights about the nature of British Government. That is why the historian must turn to questions of poor law and public health if he is to understand the making of the modern constitution.

By 1854, it was clear that there could be no absolute *laissez-faire*. Chadwick himself distinguished between economic and social *laissez-faire*, the former based on a contrast between 'obstruction and interchange', the latter implying 'letting mischief work, and evils go on which do not affect ourselves' and thereby serving as a destructive and revolutionary doctrine, undermining the cohesion and progress of the community. By 1854, it was recognised that public health was impossible without some sort of legal apparatus. Even though the 1848 mechanism was inadequate, a new mechanism would have to be found. The age of fact-finding would have to give way to the age of administration.

The inadequacy of the arrangements of 1848 sprang from three fundamental circumstances, over which the health pioneers had little control – first, the lack of a regular civil service, both as a department of state and as a group of responsible, trained servants. This defect began to be remedied very soon afterwards, but it did not reach a really satisfactory solution until much later. Much new machinery had to be set up, and new devices instituted, particularly the device of the grant-in-aid. Second, there was a limited franchise in 1848. The series of enactments from 1867 onwards, with the parallel development of national education, were the landmarks in this direction. Without them, the making of social policy would have been very different indeed. Third, there was an inadequate system of medical and sanitary knowledge in 1848. Sanitation was conceived of too simply, and medicine lacked its modern scientific base. These gaps in knowledge, too, were to be filled in, at least in part, before the end of the century.[29]

These three developments take us from the age of Chadwick into the heart of the modern world, with its own wealth of problems and controversies. We can hunt for parallels and differences if we wish. What I would like to stress in conclusion is the element of continuity. The successful exploitation of the sanitary idea in the age of Chadwick, brought with it a transformed environment, and in its wake, a new liberation. To go back to Richardson's words, it implied 'that man could, by getting at first principles ... get behind Fate itself, and suppress the forces which led up to it at their prime source'. This liberation had far bigger applications than the merely technical. It remoulded public opinion.

As for the role of public opinion, it was very eloquently stated by Ashley, Earl of Shaftesbury, in 1848:

> We wish to beget ... to create and to sustain a true, firm, paramount, and wise public opinion .... It is not by law, it is not by individual efforts, it is not by the desultory attempts of a few benevolent people [that improvement would come, but by] a wise, benevolent and instructed public opinion.[30]

NOTES

1   *Quarterly Review*, vol. 87 (1850), p. 468.
2   See *inter alia*, M. W. Flinn's introduction to Chadwick's *Report on the*

Sanitary Conditions of the Labouring Population of Great Britain (1965); E. P. Hennock, 'Urban Sanitary Reform a Generation before Chadwick?', in the *Economic History Review* vol. X (1957) and B. Keith Lucas, 'Some Influences affecting the Development of Sanitary Legislation in England', in ibid., vol. VI (1954).

3   The first revisionist in a protracted historical controversy was O. MacDonagh who led the way in his detailed *A Pattern of Government Growth* (1961) and in an important article 'The Nineteenth Century Revolution in Government: A Reappraisal', in *The Cambridge Historical Journal*, vol. XIX (1958). An earlier article of importance was J. L. Brebner, 'Laissez-faire: State Intervention in Nineteenth-Century Britain', in *Journal of Economic History Supplement*, vol. VIII (1948). I gave a version of this paper to Professor Brebner's postgraduate seminar at Columbia University in 1953.

4   See B. W. Richardson, *The Health of Nations*, vol. II (1887). The subtitle of the book was 'A Review of the Work of Edwin Chadwick with a Biographical Dissertation'.

5   See P. Richards, 'R. A. Slaney, The Industrial Town and Early Victorian Social Policy', in *Social History*, vol. IV (1979).

6   Guy was the author of *Public Health – A Popular Approach to Sanitary Science* (1874).

7   'Infant Labour', in *Quarterly Review*, vol. LXVII (1840).

8   Quoted in E. Hodder, *The Life and Work of the Seventh Earl of Shaftesbury* (1887), pp. 195-6.

9   Blomfield had worked on the Poor Law Commission and was allied with him on many occasions. See G. Kitson Clark, *Churchmen and the Condition of England, 1832-1885* (1973), pp. 163-5.

10 The first number appeared on 1 September 1845.

11 Quoted in B. L. Hutchins, *The Public Health Agitation, 1833-1848* (1900), p. 114.

12 Draft letter from Chadwick to Ashley, 3 November 1846 (Chadwick Papers).

13 See A. V. Dicey, *Lectures on the Relation between Law and Public Opinion during the Nineteenth Century* (1914 edn), Lecture II. The phrase 'Bleak Age' was coined by J. L. and B. Hammond. See their *Age of the Chartists* (1930); a shorter version of this was published as *The Bleak Age* (1935).

14 L. Robbins, *The Theory of Economic Policy in English Classical Political Economy* (1952), p. 144.

15 Quoted by Lord Morpeth, *Hansard*, vol. XCVI (1848), cols 385-424.

15a *Bolton Chronicle*, 15 January 1848.

16 For 'health mapping', see E. W. Gilbert, 'Some Early English Maps of the Geography of Health and Disease', a paper read to the International Geographical Congress (1952). In Leeds in 1852 Dr Robert Becker had illustrated his *Report of the Leeds Board of Health* with a 'cholera plan'.

17 *The Times*, 18 June 1848.

18 J. S. Mill, *Autobiography* (1873), p. 100.

19 Dicey, *op. cit.*, p. 200.
20 *Hansard*, vol. XCVIII, cols 71 ff.
21 *Manchester Guardian*, 25 March 1848.
22 *Morning Chronicle*, 15 May 1848.
23 *The Times*, 16 May 1848.
24 *Leeds Mercury*, 15 March 1848.
25 *Leeds Intelligencer*, 16 March 1848.
26 Quoted in C. S. Emden, *The People and the Constitution* (1956), p. 200.
27 *The Times*, 15 May 1848.
28 *Westminster Review*, vol. XXIII (1848).
29 *Morning Chronicle*, 15 April 1848.
29 For the very different politics of the next phase, see R. Lambert, *Sir John Simon* (1963).
30 Address to the National Association for the Promotion of Social Science (1858).

8 Cholera and Society in the Nineteenth Century

There were several world outbreaks of 'Asiatic Cholera' during the nineteenth century, the first striking Britain in 1831, the last in 1893. The Asian centre of the disease was said to be India, where it exercised 'habitual dominion'. From the 'alluvial swamps and malarious jungles' of Asia it passed through Russia and the Middle East to the teeming cities of Europe and from Europe across the Atlantic.[1] Nor was Africa immune.[2] The disease 'mastered every variety of climate, surmounted every natural obstacle, conquered every people'.[3]

In Europe, cholera was thought of pre-eminently as 'a disease of society'.[4] 'It attacks towns, multitudes of men rather than sporadic dwellers in the wilderness.' The seas and oceans of the world were an imperfect barrier, and it was through large ports, like Hamburg, that it followed its grim course. In Asia and Africa, too, it was thought of as a disease of the great thoroughfares of trade and commerce. It seemed, indeed, to have the 'predilection of an alderman for easy travelling or the empressement of a courier for rapid movement' since it almost invariably selected the 'best roads' for its 'dreadful invasion'. 'Like man', it was claimed, 'it travels along the high roads from town to town, gradually, and attacks the most populous and commercial first. In its visits to an uninfected country, it selects the principal port or frontier town, and from there it takes the most frequented thorough-fare to reach the largest cities.'[5]

Cholera was a disease of society in a more profound sense also. It hit the working poor particularly ruthlessly, thriving on the kind of conditions in which they lived, and although it was not unique in this respect, it created a unique sense of shock. Moreover, it threatened the better-off too, sometimes directly. It would not be segregated.[6] Whenever it approached European countries, therefore, it quickened social apprehensions, and wherever it appeared, it tested the efficiency and resilience of local administrative structures. It exposed relent-lessly vested economic interests, political abuses and social and moral shortcomings. It prompted rumours, suspicions and at times violent social conflicts. It was a favourite subject for the Press, which was often accused of magnifying or sensationalising the dangers it brought with it – 'dismaying the timid and perplexing and astonishing the ignorant'[7] – yet it also inspired not only sermons but novels and works of art.

Through the centuries other epidemic diseases had produced more victims. Cholera was far less of a killer, for example, than the plague, which wiped out whole communities: even in the nineteenth century deaths directly attributable to it were never as numerous as deaths attributable to other diseases, like typhoid, or to ever-present tuberculosis. As R.J. Morris has written in an admirable detailed study of cholera in England in 1831 and 1832, its demographic impact was small but significant.[8] Although during the period from 1838 to 1868, when there were four outbreaks, the Registrar-General's statistics throw into relief the cholera years as peak years in mortality statistics, the impact of cholera in 1849, for example, only just exceeded that of the typhus which was brought to England by refugees from the Irish famine and over a five-year period around 1849 deaths from common diarrhoea exceeded deaths from cholera.

Yet such comparisons produce a somewhat spurious sense of perspective. A study of the history of cholera in the nineteenth century is something far more than an exercise in medical epidemiology, fascinating though such exercises are in themselves; it is more, too, than an exercise in historical demography. The *Surgeon-General's Catalogue* alone records 777 expert works on cholera published in London – including articles in medical journals – for the years 1845-56,[9] and these were the medical part only of a huge international literature, which is far too voluminous to sift. Until the 1950s cholera was an important and somewhat neglected chapter in social history.[10] More recently, however, historians have devoted theses and monographs to it. In some respects, indeed, it may well have had the same shocking and disproportionate influence on medical historians as it had on contemporaries.[11]

I

Professor Louis Chevalier was a pioneer in directing attention to certain aspects of the social significance of cholera during the later 1950s in his book *Classes laborieuses et classes dangereuses* and in a volume of essays which he edited called *Le Choléra, la première épidemic du XIXe siècle*.[12] In the former work the experience of cholera is taken as one particular example of the close relationship, dramatically displayed at moments of crisis, between biological and social and economic facts during the whole of the early nineteenth century. 'Biological drama should not be isolated from economic and political drama ... both of which lead to questions of life and death.'[13] By vividly demonstrating inequality in death, 'Asiatic Cholera', accord-

CHOLERAPHOBY.

Plate 2: Elliott's monument, Weston Park,
Sheffield

Harold, returned from Normandy, presents himself to Edward the Confessor.

Plate 3: Daniel Maclise depicts an episode in his *Story of the Norman Conquest* (Art-Union of London, 1866)

Plate 4: The first *Annales:* the prospect
for 1965 (1919)

ing to Chevalier, directed attention to inequality in life: moreover, the range and intensity of the reactions it inspired – scientific, sociological and popular – enable the social historian to recapture not only lost moods but lost value systems. Chevalier is certainly successful in recapturing lost moods and lost value systems, at least as far as Paris is concerned, but he goes further and makes interesting and challenging general suggestions about the whole scope of social history.

The book of essays *Le Choléra* was a by-product of Professor Chevalier's quest for a new historical synthesis, for social history with demography not at the margin but at the base. It includes essays on the first great cholera epidemic of the nineteenth century not only in Paris but in Lille, Normandy, Bordeaux, Marseilles, Russia and England. Unfortunately, like most collective works, the volume is extremely uneven. Given Chevalier's purpose it is perhaps surprisingly so, and far from standing out in retrospect as a landmark in social history, it has been supplanted by other works. Some of the essays have no footnotes; Chevalier himself is too sparing with these, and some of his references are consequently obscure. In a few of the essays demography plays little part even at the margin of the narrative. In others little detailed attention is paid to the contemporary social reactions to cholera which for the editor are the major element in the study.

The book as a whole has three other major general weaknesses. First, all comparisons in it are implicit. No attempt is made to pull together the scattered evidence about cholera from different places, to draw conclusions from it, least of all to test Chevalier's own hypotheses. The book needed a fuller and less general introduction or the addition of a tidy and systematic epilogue. Second, it has a curiously narrow range of reference. The first cholera outbreak, which began in India in 1817 and reached Britain and France in 1831 and 1832, is not related to other cholera outbreaks later in the century. Thus, no more advantage is taken of the comparative method in relation to time than in relation to space.

Given the huge changes in the course of the nineteenth century – in the expression of public opinion through the Press and other sources as much as in the revision of political processes and the reframing of administrative structures – this is a basic weakness. In *Classes laborieuses et classes dangereuses* brief reference is made to the cholera outbreak in Paris in 1848, but again Professor Chevalier prefers generalisation to comparison. He talks of the survivors of 1832 living to see renewed in 1849 the same experience of cholera 'under the same form and with similar violence': the lesson also was the same – 'that of a fundamental injustice and of a great popular fraternity unforgettably demonstrated in the fear of death'.[14] This comment is much too general. The political and social circumstances of the first and second cholera outbreaks were different in both France and England. Were reactions different too? Some of the British reactions in 1848 and 1849 have already been examined by writers on Edwin Chadwick.[15] What were reactions in France which Chadwick sometimes compared favourably with his own country? Even more interesting comparisons may be made of the first oubreak with later outbreaks in the century.

The third weakness affects the whole study. Reference is frequently made in Le Choléra to the role of doctors – both to the careful and suggestive surveys they often prepared of local manifestations of cholera and to the divided opinions they held about the nature of the disease and the mode in which it was transmitted. Too little is said, however, about the organisation of the medical profession,[16] and nothing concerning the light that is thrown by later medical conclusions about cholera on the experiences of 1831 and 1832 which remain at the centre of his preoccupation. There is no reference, for example, to John Snow, whose famous writings on the transmission of cholera remain invaluable sources for the social as well as the medical historian,[17] or to the works of Max von Pettenhofer, who continued to argue in 'environmental' terms against Snow in the last decade of the nineteenth century.[18] Several years after Robert Koch had identified *vibrio cholerae* (1883), Pettenhofer and a group of his pupils swallowed virulent cultures of the bacillus to try to prove that it could not cause cholera without other factors being present. The debate about 'other factors' seems as distant as the debates about 'miasma' and 'contagion' in the early nineteenth century, and modern writers prefer to argue about epidemiology in sophisticated terms of 'patterns of causes' or 'multiple causation'.[19]

The conclusions of later doctors are relevant, however, in that they do not reveal as simple a connection between misery and cholera as Chevalier and some of the other writers of essays in his volume suggest. Cholera was in a real sense 'the disease of the poor', but it was not the disease of *all* the poor. Many places with bad sanitary conditions escaped it, and in many places the rich (partly because of the mode of communication of the disease by water supplies) were not immune. 'It has attacked the palaces of princes', wrote an English commentator in 1832, 'and an English camp which may vie with these in cleanliness, equally with the filthiest habitations of the Tartar or the Polish Jew.'[20] When David Eversley in a useful and informative essay on cholera in England writes that 'misery was one of the principal causes of the disease',[21] his use of the word 'causes' needs a long gloss.

Surprisingly the gloss brings out points which are not uninteresting to social historians. Eversley does not mention, for example, that many of the cotton towns in Lancashire with very high 'normal' mortality rates were virtually untouched by cholera not only in 1831-2 but in 1849-50. They included Preston, Blackburn, Bury, Rochdale, Oldham, Bolton and Halifax. Wigan was left unscathed in 1831-2 although there were over 500 cases in 1848-50. Contemporaries noted that few factory hands caught the disease: some percipient workmen argued that the 'insects' which caused it could not survive factory temperature:[22] Snow gave other explanations.[23] Whatever the cause, the social consequences are interesting. In the most advanced industrial region of the world, the centre of the sharpest class conflicts, cholera was absent as a disturbing factor in many populous places outside Manchester which was not immune. Orator Hunt in the House of Commons talked not of the misery of Preston, his own constituency, but of Spitalfields.

Further there was virtually no cholera in Birmingham. It is very surprising that Eversley, writing from Birmingham about a period when Birmingham was in a position of almost undisputed leadership in the political reform agitation, does not mention Birmingham in his chapter at all and that he does not give the reason. Although the Black Country was particularly hard hit by cholera – Bilston alone had at least 693 deaths[24] – Birmingham was almost untouched not only in the cholera outbreak of 1832 (when there were twenty-one deaths)[25], but in the more serious outbreak of 1849, when there were only twenty-nine.[26] The comparative figures for Manchester were 706 and 878.[27] For Liverpool, the hardest hit of English cities, there were 1523 and 5308. More people died of cholera in Portsea Island in 1866 than in all the nineteenth-century epidemics in Birmingham. In talking of the unequal incidence of epidemics,[28] Eversley should surely have mentioned this kind of locational differentiation. The equation of dirt, disease and political disturbance is one that always needs careful and critical treatment.

France provides just as interesting a case as England. Among the cities which do *not* figure in the collection of essays on local cholera outbreaks in France is Lyons which, like Birmingham, was a key centre in the development of nineteenth-century social and political modes of action.[29] The reason for this – also not given – is that there was virtually no cholera in Lyons either. Pettenhofer, indeed, made a special pilgrimage to Lyons to examine the basis of its immunity. He rightly pointed out that for social reasons it should have had a cholera outbreak. It had highly insanitary districts, at least its fair share of *classes dangereuses*, and regular commercial intercourse with infected regions. Lyons puzzled Pettenhofer. 'I cannot believe', he once remarked, 'that the inhabitants of Lyons or Würzburg have intestines or privies any different from those of Marseilles, Paris and Rothenfels.'[30]

Cholera did not only create panic: it posed puzzles. It was characterised by what M. Guiral, the author of an excellent essay on

Marseilles, calls a certain 'bizarrerie'.[31] Nineteenth-century writers spoke of its 'eccentricity' or of its 'caprice'.[32] It struck hard, but it struck strangely. Some of the strangeness was the strangeness of coincidence. In 1830 and 1847, for example, it struck Moscow on exactly the same day of the year – 18 September. The first case in Britain in October 1831 was at Sunderland: two of the first British cases in October 1848 were in Sunderland also. Not every coincidence was accidental. In Leith, the first case in 1848 was in the same house as in 1832: in Bermondsey, it was near the same ditch. In Pollockshaws, the first victim died in the same room and even in the same bed as sixteen years before.[33] As early at 1832, a doctor argued that 'generally speaking, the disease fixed its residence in such places as medical men could have pointed out *a priori*'.[34] Out of the coincidences and the 'bizarrerie' – the fact that some houses were spared while neighbouring housese were devastated, one side of a street left untouched, another plague-ridden – Snow drew a skilful and commanding analysis. But he did not explain everything. 'The history of cholera', a recent writer has noted, 'teaches the epidemiologist to be humble.'[35]

Chevalier has done well to direct the attention of social historians to this difficult topic. The reasons for studying it carefully are self-evident. Yet it is scarcely mentioned in standard national histories,[36] and no attempt has hitherto been made to examine the response to it comparatively against an international background. It is through detailed comparative history that its chief features can best be understood. On the basis of the very full documentation which is readily available further studies would be useful and illuminating.

This paper is concerned with the scope of the subject rather than with detailed conclusions. It takes the material of Chevalier and his colleagues as given and seeks to consider more fully the three points discussed above – comparison, perspective and the use of medical evidence. All three are related and impossible completely to separate out from each other. Perspective must be considered first, however, since it influences the whole approach to the study.

II

Chevalier starts with Paris in the early nineteenth century. His background is 'the long crisis which lasted from the last years of the Restoration to the first years of the July Monarchy'.[37] He sees the cholera outbreak of 1832 not so much as a catastrophe as a culmination – 'the consequence of an earlier evolution and the revelation of a biological, economic and social condition'.[38] He refers on several occasions to 'the pathological condition of the city of which normal mortality and mortality from cholera have one single aspect'.[39] The choice of this particular point of entry to the subject – Paris in a period of demographic expansion and 'the lack of adaptation of the city system to the growth of population' – determines the treatment. Paris was a city of social conflicts. Cholera, if only because of its mode of communication (not touched on by Chevalier) was predominantly a disease of the poor. In metropolitan Paris not only did inequality of life and inequality of death move together but epidemic was closely identified with social conflict. 'Cholera makes precise the biological foundations of class antagonism.'[40] Contemporaries recognised this: cholera exacerbated class hatred.

The vivid demonstration of the social pathology of Paris which cholera provided is well discussed by Chevalier, but in other places and at other times cholera can provide different social demonstrations. Class hatred is a social not a biological phenomenon.[41] In colonial India, to take a different setting, cholera does not appear to have sharpened social conflicts, although there was an obvious contrast between the condition and vulnerability to the disease of the European and the Indian. A commentator in 1818 noted local Indian reactions rather in the same fashion as Camus noted social reactions to plague in his novel, *La Peste* (1947).[42]

> Those who are lucky to have escaped personal knowledge of the calamity of what it is like to live in 'the city of the plague' can with difficulty form an idea of the state of mind of its inhabitants; the first feeling of dismay, the reflux of levity, the agitation at the beginning, and the unconcern with all that is going on which follows immediately; the mild workings of charity – the cautious guarded contacts with others, sustained by selfishness – the active energies, in short, of the good, and the heartless indifference of the bad, are all presented in their several extremes.[43]

That light that cholera throws on the operation of charity – other light was being thrown on the same subject in Britain by writers on the Poor Law – is merely one aspect of its social significance. Charity, however, a facet of religion, and the relative appeal to the 'plague-stricken' of religion and politics (both interpreted in the broadest sense) obviously depended on local social conditions.

That conditions in Paris provide only one point of entry in relation even to early nineteenth-century France is well brought out in Guiral's study of Marseilles. The inhabitants of that city were reminded each year by religious ceremonies of the plague of 1720. The events of 1832 recalled the past and had the effect of stimulating a return to Catholic religion. The *Gazette du Midi* commented that the cholera epidemic had quickened the religious zeal of the inhabitants of Marseilles, a conclusion well amplified by Guiral.[44] In many other parts of the world cholera was not so much associated with 'failure to adjust the urban structure to the growth of population' as with the latest visitation in new form of an old scourge, with 'terrible and affecting circumstances which have arisen out of the dispensation of the Almighty'.[45] It is notable that in their brief study of Russia in *Le Choléra*, Mme Netchkina, K.V. Sivrov and A.-L. Sidorov dwell on the role of charity and of religion in the Russian situation of 1831 and 1832. It would be interesting to have available a fuller account of differences between Moscow and St Petersburg, for in the former city there were no 'cholera disturbances' at all.[46]

Religion plays an interesting part in the story of cholera in all parts of the world, not least in India where outbreaks were (and are) often associated with massing of crowds at religious festivals.[47] In Paris and London in 1831 and 1832 there might be signs of anti-clericalism sharpening class hostility during the epidemic, but in Dieppe and Le Havre, where there were heavy cholera casualties, fishermen began by attributing the cholera to divine displeasure threatening the end of the world and went on to declare that the divine displeasure was caused by the legitimate sovereign of France having been expelled from the throne.[48] In Ireland, where cholera seems to have played no part in social disturbance, lumps of smouldering peat were offered in lieu of medical assistance with the words, 'The plague has broken out; take this and while it burns up offer seven paters, three aves and a credo in the name of God and the holy St John that the plague be stopped.'[49]

Even in Britain the House of Lords, on the initiative of Bishop Blomfield of London, added the phrase 'whereas it has pleased Almighty God to visit these kingdoms ...' to the Cholera Morbus Prevention Bill of 1832. Bishop Blomfield's speech on this occasion is particularly interesting since he was a close friend and consistent supporter of Edwin Chadwick in the battle for public health. On this occasion he chose to look back rather than forward, recalling the plague of the seventeenth century when 'there was a devout acknowledgment that that calamity had been caused by the Providence of God'.[50]

The absence of such a reference to God in the draft Bill offered by the government to the Commons in 1832 had provoked strong opposition from a group of Members, and they were not appeased when the Cholera Prevention Bill (Scotland) included such a clause. The odd, if not unique, situation thereby arose that 'the Scotch seemed to be monopolising Providence to the exclusion of the English'.[51] The debates on this subject, briefly referred to by Eversley, are as interesting for the light they throw on religion as on politics. Philosophical Radicals, notably Joseph Hume, joined with popular Radicals, notably the group associated with the *Poor Man's Guardian*, in describing religious measures to combat cholera as 'cant, humbug and hypocrisy'.[52] Other Members, the great majority, claimed that in referring to God they were simply 'recognising the Divine power'. One Member said that he trusted it was not yet necessary for any gentleman to apologise for proposing such recognition.[53] Briscoe, the leader of this group, added in a later debate that 'whenever Ministers of the Crown ceased to lend the influence of their high station to support religion, from that hour the sun of the country's prosperity was set for ever'.[54] These debates should be set in the context not only of the struggle for the Reform Bill but of the debates on tithes and religious privilege.

There is room for a fuller study of the impact of cholera on religious opinion. Yet cholera touched other concerns as well. When neither class hatred nor religion entered the debate, there were other social irritants. The most powerful of them was the fear of bureaucracy. In Russia, for example, as in Camus's novel *La Peste*, great irritation was caused, as the Russian historians who have contributed to *Le Choléra* show, by the enforcement of *cordons sanitaires*. Differences of opinion about the value of *cordons sanitaires* tended to divide 'conservatives' (particularly conservatives with military experience) and 'reformers'. Yet the reformers themselves were often divided. In England, Hume tended to dismiss all cholera precautions as alarmist – he does not emerge well from the debates despite his professed concern for 'civil liberties' – while Henry Warburton, philosophical Radical and pioneer of medical reform, made it clear that enlightened *laissez-faire* was not the same as 'Turkish indolence'. When George Robinson pressed as hard as he could for 'gentle' control of cholera in the interests of commerce, Warburton retaliated that while 'the mercantile interest was no doubt of great moment ... the public safety was a matter of permanent importance'. In his view, it was because of 'mercantile activity and mercantile avarice and jealousy' that cholera had spread around the world.[55]

Since cholera tended to break out in 'great commercial marts',[56] merchant reactions to cholera are as interesting in this period of business expansion as the reactions of the poor. They can be traced fairly fully in many of the places described in this article. In Sunderland itself, for example, they exacerbated the situation during the early days of the epidemic. Lord Londonderry and the local shipping interest did their best to prove that it was 'a wicked and malignant falsehood' that there was Asiatic cholera in the town.[57] In Marseilles there were complaints of 'centralisation' from Paris as well as of bureaucratic interference.[58] It is impossible to tell from *Le Choléra* what were reactions in Bordeaux, for Dr Fréour in his brief note scarcely mentions them.[59] Reactions to the various nineteenth-century attacks in Hamburg would make a fascinating study in itself.

'Great commercial marts' and capital cities provide different insights into the significance of cholera. So too do small communities, particularly those which were very badly hit like Bilston in the Black Country. In Paris cholera might in a real sense be a 'culmination' – as Chevalier clearly shows, for instance, in his details of quinquennial mortality rates.[60] In Bilston it was an unanticipated calamity. Leigh described public health in Bilston as being 'in general good' before the outbreak. So too was political morale. Bilston was in the vanguard of the reform agitation. Despite a local 'depression in trade' (a more potent influence on popular Radicalism in England than cholera), the Bilston wake on 29 July 1832 was well attended and there were the 'usual orgies'. Cholera was brought into the community from Manchester by a canal boatman. It ravaged the community mercilessly. No fewer than 450 Bilston children under the age of twelve were left orphans by the cholera, and a special Cholera Orphan School was established by public subscription. It is scarcely surprising that religion was the main gainer from this terrible experience. 'A reformation of morals and revival of religion is said to have followed the scourge.'[61]

III

The story of later cholera outbreaks during the nineteenth century reflects not only changes in social structure, including the professional structure, increasingly sophisticated, but basic changes in social attitudes, particularly concerning the possibility of exercising 'social control'. Many comments were made, particularly in Britain, which qualify the view that cholera above all diseases was associated with 'class hatred'. In the first place, Edwin Chadwick did not want the drama of cholera to divert public attention from the habitual inequality of mortality rates: in particular, he objected to special quarantine measures and put his trust in new health legislation to cover all times. In the second place, there was increased emphasis on the way in which ill-health conditions among one section of the population could influence health conditions – including life and death – amongst the rest. 'The epidemic was no respecter of classes', wrote Dr Sutherland, one of the medical inspectors of the General Board of Health in 1849. 'Rich and poor suffered alike or escaped alike, according as they lived in the observance or violation of the laws of their physical well-being.'[62]

There was more emphasis, therefore, on the need for sanctions to secure the observance of these laws in 1849 than there had been in 1832. Indeed, it was strongly argued that these laws still held even if there were no large-scale cholera outbreak. The Public Health Act of 1848, which set up the General Board of Health, had been carried within the shadow of cholera in Europe. Chadwick, who was as aware as Chevalier of the parallelism – and relationship – between disease and crime, watched the progress of the disease and the progress of the legislation with equal attention. When cholera reached Moscow, he warned Lord Morpeth that

> if preparations be not soon made only the Sanitary Commissioners who have recommended them will be held blameless if it should reach us. You will remember the difficulty there was [in 1831] in forming a Board of Health at the Privy Council office. I fear that we might not now under existing circumstances get the voluntary service we might have done then. Will not the service fall to the new Board and be a means of introducing it to the country?[63]

It is the purpose of this article not to examine the administrative response of the Central Board of Health to the second cholera outbreak, which has been studied less thoroughly than the first,[64] but to set the outbreak and the reactions it inspired into perspective. The second great outbreak, like the first, had its origin in Lower Bengal. Indeed, between 1817, when cholera first burst out of Bengal to start its international career, it had never been absent from some part or other of the Indian Peninsula.[65] In 1847 it entered European Russia again, as it had done in 1829, and reached Britain, again by way of the Baltic, in 1848. The second outbreak was far more serious, at least as far as Britain was concerned, than that of 1831-2 and, as Sutherland wrote, it affected all sections of the population, 'cutting off many beyond the limits of the destitute and reckless class who were its most usual victims on the first occasion. Many of the respectable class of workmen and shopkeepers were among the victims.'[66] It also drew in London far more comprehensively than the 1831-2 epidemic, which meant that the London Press was deeply involved. There was consequently far less talk in 1848 than there had been in 1832 of cholera selecting its victims 'generally among the lower classes ... and chiefly from those who were most intemperate and dissolute in their habits'.[67] The barriers of class and character had been battered down. There was far more talk in the London Press, including *Punch*, of the need to tackle the public health problem more comprehensively through changes in both attitudes and institutions.

The same point was made in countries where even less attempt had been made than in England to improve 'sanitary institutions' – in Moscow, for instance, where the disease extended itself 'over the whole city' and attacked 'all classes' or in Constantinople when it attacked 'upper as well as lower classes'.[68] Lessons were learnt from other countries, including Britain, where there had been 'sanitary improvement'. There were popular complaints in St Petersburg, reminicent of 1831 and 1832, that the water had been poisoned by the upper classes, but in most places the epidemic was regarded as a universal lesson in the need for public health. (The 1866 epidemic reinforced the lesson.) Where endemic disease and statistics relating to it – including the terrible differential mortality statistics – could not convince people of the gravity of the problem of public health, cholera could. As a writer in the *Edinburgh Review* put it in 1850, 'Cholera is in truth a Health Inspector who speaks through his interpreter, the Registrar General, in a language which reaches all ears.'[69] A modern historian has made the point somewhat differently. 'Cholera, like plague, was a sensational disease, and it aroused the petty parochialism of the mid-nineteenth century as effectively as plague had aroused the corrupt bureaucracy of the eighteenth century.'[70]

It is interesting to note that in a country where there was no outbreak of cholera – Australia – sanitary reformers sometimes expressed a wish that there had been an outbreak to rouse public opinion. 'Epidemics', wrote a Melbourne doctor in 1861,

> are of signal service by procuring indirectly those sanitary reforms which offer a comparative immunity from their recurrence. It might savour of inhumanity to wish that this Colony, hitherto in a measure free from the devastating scourges which have periodically swept over Europe and Asia, shall become the scene of an unsparing pestilence; and yet, judging by the capacity of those who should be the first to move in bringing about the preventive conditions, it would seem that this terrible stimulus is required, in order that we may obtain them.[71]

For all the lessons of cholera in Europe, there were only limited improvements in urban health and housing conditions during the middle years of the century – the full story of improvements and resistances to them remains to be told – and the 'sanitary idea' was the crusade not of the majority but of an enlightened minority. The minority was not only enlightened but dedicated. It believed that the conquest of disease was the conquest of Fate, that where Asia acquiesced Europe should act. 'Man could by first principles ... get behind Fate itself, and suppress the forces which led up to it at their prime source.'[72] Cholera appears in this way as a catalyst of public opinion, an ally in the service of the sanitary reformers. It was not until the late nineteenth century that public health became an 'expert service', and it is only in the twentieth century that social control has become genuinely international.

The last two big British outbreaks of cholera in 1853-4 and 1866 were far less serious than the earlier epidemics, although once again London was affected far more than it had been in the first outbreak.[73] The 1853-4 outbreak followed further attacks of disease in the Baltic ports. These may have been caused either by 'a new approach from Asia' or, what seems more likely, a 're-kindling of smouldering fires' in Europe itself. Among the most interesting reactions to the outbreak was that of Lord Palmerston, then Home Secretary in Aberdeen's government. When the presbyters of Edinburgh asked him to proclaim a day of fasting and humiliation to check the progress of the cholera, he replied that only when Edinburgh freed itself of the 'gaseous exhalations' arising from overcrowded dwellings and undisposed filth, would it be time to ask the Maker of the Universe to interpose.[74]

This mood of practical concern may usefully be compared with the mood of 1831-2. So, too, can the reports published on the two occasions. One of the most interesting local reports about the 1853-4 outbreak was drawn up by H.W. Acland in Oxford. Acland emphasised the existence of 'sanitary laws which our Creator has imposed upon us'. 'The consequence of the violation of these laws is punishment to the *community* for its *common crime*; as it is in the case of the individual for his individual crime.' Acland compared the Oxford attacks of 1832, 1849 and 1854 and drew general social deductions from them. The deductions ranged widely over social questions – the need for improved housing and sewerage disposal – and moral questions – the need for better and wiser 'living'. He recognised that 'to enumerate the arrangements which a wise Community would adopt beforehand to mitigate the terrible scourge of coming Epidemics ... would lead the reader into questions of the most extensive nature – social, so called, political and religious'.[75]

Yet while the 1854 outbreak in Oxford inspired these relatively sophisticated reflections, parallel and later outbreaks in other parts of the world often duplicated earlier patterns of experience and response. The 1866 British outbreak entered Britain not from Russia and the Baltic, but from Egypt. It was kept carefully under control. In Egypt there was the same grim story of panic, flight of the rich (including the Viceroy), suspension of commerce, and mass-murder mortality among the poor, which had characterised the earlier outbreaks.[76]

The contrast of experience between Britain and Egypt was a foretaste of some of the international contrasts of experience in the twentieth century. In the Indian epidemic of 1937, for example, over 10,000 out of 442,000 Indian villages were infected with cholera, and there were 236,143 deaths, well over twice as many as in all the nineteenth-century British epidemics put together. Yet not one

British or Indian soldier in the Indian Army died of cholera in this terrible year.[77] In a post-war Egyptian outbreak in 1947, international action was immediately taken to deal with Egyptian problems. The action was medical as well as administrative. The World Health Organisation transported enough anti-cholera vaccine to inoculate one out of six persons in Egypt.

It did not need anti-cholera vaccine to dispel cholera from most of Europe in the late nineteenth century. In the three late nineteenth-century outbreaks of 1873, 1884 and 1892 Britain, for instance, was left virtually untouched. The 1884 outbreak in the Mediterranean was the result of maritime contact with the East: the 1892 outbreak in Hamburg was almost a laboratory proof of the conclusions of Snow's theories on the role of water in the transmission of the disease. The death rate in Hamburg was 13.4 per thousand: in the suburb of Altona it was 2.1 per thousand. Both the city and the suburb received their water from the Elbe, but in Altona there was an efficient infiltration plant.[78] It was this last great outbreak in Germany which stirred American authorities on the other side of the Atlantic to look to their public health apparatus. In New York the Hamburg outbreak was used to force the case for the establishment of a Division of Pathology, Bacteriology and Disinfection, 'perhaps the most important step in modernising public health practice in the United States'.[79]

IV

The vast store of material about cholera tempts the social historian to seek for comparisons. There certainly have been parallel phenomena in different parts of the world. The *Cholera Gazette* in England had its counterpart, for example, in the *Cholera Bulletin* in New York. Yet there have always been contrasts as well as parallels. The desire to publicise facts, which lay behind the issues of later publications, and the desire to conceal facts have often conflicted. One English Member of Parliament told the Commons that while serving in India 'his plan had been to keep the ways of the disease as much a secret as possible, and he had consequently prohibited every soldier from mentioning the very name of Cholera, though they were much inclined to make it a topic of conversation'.[80] He recognised that such a plan 'would not be practicable here'.

In every country where articulate opinions could be formed and expressed, the question always arose of the extent to which cholera would attack all sections of the community. In America, as in Europe, cholera was specifically associated in 1832 with 'the most miserable and degraded of our population – white, black and coloured' – and it was said to 'arise entirely from their habits of life'.[81] Yet in America and in Europe this familiar association did not check the flight of the rich when cholera threatened. Marseilles and Albany were alike in this respect. The rich were sometimes accompanied by the representatives of authority – the Prefect was conveniently away from Marseilles in 1835, for example, with an attack of gout.[82] Bishop Philpotts, the target of the reformers of Exeter, was away in Torquay during the terrible Exeter outbreak.[83] The Viceroy of Alexandria was absent on his boat for 'a few days of rest' during the 1865 Egyptian outbreak.[84]

It is scarcely surprising that given fear, verging on panic, cholera was associated with every kind of rumour, particularly with the two contradictory rumours leading to the same conclusion – the first that cholera was a fiction designed to suppress the rights of the poor and the second that the authorities had deliberately introduced cholera by poisoning as a means of attacking the poor.[85]

In Paris, as Chevalier shows, cholera had two distinct 'images' – one bourgeois, and one associated with the *menu peuple*. In all parts of the world the disease had its folklore and its songs and ballads. 'The cholera cometh', sang the Americans of the Mohawk Valley, 'take care – take care!'

> Look well to thy dwelling – beware – beware!
> He breatheth corruption, and loveth the spot
> Where offal is suffered to lie and to rot;
> Then look to thy cellar, thy closet and yard –
> For all kinds of filth he hath special regard.[86]

This was a moral song. It pointed to the connection between dirt and disease, which was the first preoccupation of the sanitary reformers of the nineteenth century. Not the least interesting comparison that can be drawn between cholera epidemics in different parts of the world concerns the language of the lists of precautions recommended by medical and administrative authorities. For many years more white-wash figured prominently near the head of the list. And what looked to be clean was often taken to be clean, particularly water. The General Board of Health in 1849 tried to deal with the evil smells of the sewers which they thought contributed to the disease by flushing the sewers regularly into the Thames. As one of Chadwick's biographers has written, 'the low districts of the capital might have been constructed by design to serve as a culture medium for the breeding and nourishment of the germs of the epidemic'.[87] Some of the implications of this set of attitudes have been well discussed by Margaret Pelling in her *Cholera, Fever, and English Medicine, 1825-1865* (1978).

Comparison of different national responses to cholera is revealing in illuminating general problems in comparative national history. There is an enormous amount of available literature, since doctors and administrators were at pains to travel widely to see how other countries tackled questions which they knew or feared would soon confront them. Dr Berry and Dr Russell were sent from Britain, for example, to examine the first great cholera epidemic in Russia. In Germany Dr Lichtenstädt translated the official Russian reports on cholera.[88] Sunderland, as has been shown, was a 'Mecca' of doctors during the first British epidemic, and Indian experience was drawn on very freely in most parts of the world, particularly (at an expert level) by Pettenhofer.[89] Comments made by foreigners usually concerned not only medical arrangements but such social factors as quarantine, the willingness of the local population to go into hospital, the efficiency of local charity, the creation of *ad hoc* administrative machinery, and the policy (or lack of policy) of central government.

A systematic comparison of the role of cholera in modern social history at different times and in different places is thus already possible on the basis of available evidence. It would have to take account of at least five sets of facts – first, the facts of demography, including antecedent and later mortality rates and the incidence of cholera in terms of area, occupation, age and so on; second, the facts of economic and social structure, and economic and social relations, including facts relating to the type and size of community and relations not only between rich and poor but between 'authorities' and 'subjects'; third, political circumstances, and the immediate context of the cholera outbreaks; fourth, the structure of government, administration and finance, and the relationship of government effort to voluntary effort, including charity, and help from outside; fifth, the extent of medical knowledge and popular attitudes towards that knowledge. Such comparison would be of general interest to historians. It would go further than the limited task Chevalier set himself and his colleagues – that of relating demography to history in the same way as demography is related to the study of contemporary societies, giving a quantitative foundation to the analysis of social life.

V

The chief merit of Chevalier's analysis is that it relates what contemporaries often thought of as an exceptional visitation of Providence to what many of them too readily accepted as the 'normal' facts of life and death. He draws heavily on the work of the French pioneers of medico-social surveys, devoting a half of his chapter on cholera in Paris to what he calls 'measurement of facts'.[90] Cholera encouraged the development of statistics, as did changing approaches to lunacy, so that medicine figured at least as much in the history of statistics as economics. The most important Parisian document from this point of view was one published in May 1834 by a Commission of ten members: it reveals not only the demographic significance of cholera but the social geography of Paris, and the composition of its population, including the large 'floating population' which Chevalier has studied so fully in other works.[91]

In Britain geography also was applied the nineteenth-century methodology of exploration and explanation. Indeed, what later in the century Dr Haviland called 'medical geography' was given a striking impetus.[92] Snow's famous map of the distribution of the deaths from cholera in the Broad Street (Golden Square) area of London in 1854 was by no means the first. In 1833 Dr Robert Baker illustrated his *Report of the Leeds Board of Health* with a 'cholera plan', showing that the incidence of the disease was the highest in the more densely populated area of the town. Dr Shapter included a detailed map in his *History of the Cholera in Exeter* published in 1849, while three years later Augustus Petermann of Potsdam, a Fellow of the Royal Geographical Society, brought out a *Cholera Map of the British Isles showing the districts affected in 1831-33*. Petermann vigorously upheld the claims of 'geographical delineation' in the investigation of 'the local causes' that might influence the progress of cholera and its 'degree of fatality'.[93]

Despite this close association between cholera and the development of medical geography, cholera probably played a smaller part in encouraging broader social investigation and demands for new social policies in Britain than Eversley suggests.[94] The study of occupational diseases in the industrial areas preceded the cholera outbreak,[95] and the extensive public inquiries into social conditions in the 1840s owed little to it.[96] The cholera outbreak of 1848-9 marked the culmination of a decade of enquiry, and the enquiry continued after the outbreak was over. The significance of differential urban mortality rates was understood if not always acted upon before the 1840s,[97] and it was the facts of typhus not cholera which induced the Poor Law Commissioners in 1838 to summon Drs Arnott, Kay and Southwood Smith to investigate the sanitary conditions of the towns. Some of the towns, like Preston, which were singled out in the famous 1842 *Report . . . on an Inquiry into the Sanitary Conditions of the Labouring Population of Great Britain*, had almost completely escaped the cholera: yet it was Preston which provided some of the most effective statistics of differential mortality rates in 'well-conditioned', 'middling-conditioned', 'ill-conditioned' and 'worst-conditioned streets'. Contemporaries were as clear as Chevalier that more commonplace and less dramatic diseases and more systematic policy-making were at the heart of the problem of the improvement in social well-being.

Too much emphasis on the social pathology of cities distorts the pattern of urban history in the nineteenth century. The forces of resistance to chaos and panic deserve as much attention at the chaos and panic themselves. A key theme in the history of the first cholera outbreak was the inability of doctors, despite their often heroic efforts in the sickroom, to reach agreement about the causes and the mode of communication of the disease. At best this approach was pragmatic: at worst their bitter disagreements promoted popular distrust and disapproval. In Russia public disapproval of the doctors was pushed so far that they were accused of trying to kill their patients.[98] In the United States a contemporary poetaster noted that

> Cholera kills and doctors slay
> And every foe will have its day.[99]

In Britain, as elsewhere, suspicion lingered late into the century. When in 1869 Snow urged the congress of the Social Sciences Association to press for an enlargement of machinery and the extension of governmental powers to achieve sanitary reform, *The Times* reported that the 'stage of universal consent' still had not been reached. 'What is needed is first information and then faith on the part of the public, and doctors must agree among themselves, if that be possible, before the outside world can be expected to agree with them.'[100] Snow himself was in frequent disagreement not only with some of his medical colleagues but with the more pragmatic supporters of sanitary reform – the foul, small, soap-and-water brigade. He urged that cleanliness should not be a cleanliness for mere appearance's sake: it should be 'a rational cleanliness, like that by which the chemist keeps his tests pure and distinct and the farmer his land free from weeds'.[101] The formulation of an articulate scientific approach was an important step forward in the history of the control of disease, but in Britain at least the practical effects of the application of scientific knowledge were not felt until the last quarter of the century. Cholera had already ceased to intrude when the Royal Sanitary Commission of 1868 was appointed, a Commission which included four medical men, among them H.W. Acland, the investigator of cholera in Oxford. The setting-up of the Local Government Board in 1871 and the Public Health Act of 1875 followed, but it was a medical journal, reporting a meeting called by Joseph Chamberlain in Birmingham, which warned Disraeli's government in 1875 that unless it aroused a national sense of 'sanitary evils', the motto *sanitas sanitatum* would have to be changed to *vanitas vanitatum*.[102]

Medical ideas might be shared or debated by doctors throughout the whole world, but sanitary institutions bore the stamp of their own national origin. There is room for further comparative work on this subject. The improvement of the means of resistance to the 'diseases of society', of which cholera was the most dramatic, provides just as interesting themes as the social pathology of the very different cities of Europe during the early nineteenth century.

NOTES

1 The phrases are those of Sir John Simon, the nineteenth-century pioneer of 'the sanitary idea'. See his 1853 Report as medical officer of the City of London. S. W. De, *Cholera: its Pathology and Pathogenesis* (1961) disputes the assertion that Asia is the original home of cholera.

2 See, for example, J. Christie, *Cholera Epidemics in East Africa* (1876). Cp. W. S. Smillie, 'The Period of Great Epidemics in the United States', in F. H. Top (ed.), *The History of American Epidemiology* (1952).

3 *Quarterly Review*, vol. XLVI (1832), p. 170.

4 *The Economist*, 20 January 1849.

5 *Quarterly Review, op. cit.*

6 Cholera is propagated by a micro-organism, *vibrio cholerae*, propagating only in the human intestinal tract. Infection is always oral, and the disease is disseminated by ingestion of excreta. The organism is easily killed either by carbolic disinfectants or the chlorination of filtered water. In bad living conditions, as C. V. Chapin, an American authority, bluntly puts it, 'it requires only a little observation to demonstrate that the path from intestines to mouth is not always a circuitous one'. See his *Sources and Modes of Infection* (1910). Cp. R. Pollitzer, *Cholera* (1959), N. Hirschhorn and W. B. Greenough, 'Cholera' in the *Scientific American*, August 1971, and D. Barva and W. Burrows (eds), *Cholera* (1974).

7 *Carpenter's Political Magazine*, part II (1831-2), p. 48.

8 R. J. Morris, *Cholera, 1832* (1976), p. 12.

9 M. Pelling, *Fever and English Medicine, 1825-1865* (1978), p. 4.

10 The classic account of British cholera outbreaks in the nineteenth century is that of C. Creighton, *A History of Epidemics in Great Britain*, 2 vols (1894). Vol. II, Chapter IX is concerned with 'Asiatic Cholera'. Creighton clearly recognised that epidemiology comes into 'close contact with social and economic history' (vol. II, p. vi). For a more recent account, see E. A. Underwood, 'History of Cholera in Great Britain', in the *Proceedings of the Royal Society of Medicine*, vol. 41 (1948).

11   See among published work in addition to the important books by
      Morris and Pelling, N. Longmate, *King Cholera* (1966); R. E. McGrew,
      Russia and the Cholera, 1823-1832 (1965); C. E. Rosenberg, *The
      Cholera Years: the United States in 1832, 1849 and 1866* (1962), and
      'Cholera in Nineteenth-Century Europe: a Tool for Social and
      Economic Analysis', in *Comparative Studies in Society and History*, vol.
      8 (1966). There are several detailed local studies, e.g. M. Durey, *The
      First Spasmodic Cholera Epidemic in York*, 1832 (1974).

12   L. Chevalier, *Classes laborieuses et classes dangereuses* (1958), and (ed.)
      Le Choléra, la première epidémie du XIXe siècle (1958).

13   *Classes laborieuses*, p. xvii.

14   ibid., p. xxii.

15   S. E. Finer, *The Life and Times of Sir Edwin Chadwick* (1952), Book
      VIII, 'The Cholera'; R. A. Lewis, *Edwin Chadwick and the Public
      Health Movement* (1952), Chapter IX.

16   See above, pp. 55 ff.

17   There is a convenient American reprint (1936) of his main works, *The
      Mode of Communication of Cholera* (1849, 2nd edn 1855) and *On
      Continuous Molecular Changes, more particularly in their relation to
      Epidemic Diseases* (1853).

18   For Pettenhofer's work, see C-E. A. Winslow, *The Conquest of
      Epidemic Disease* (1944).

19   See, *inter alia*, J. N. Morris, *Uses of Epidemiology* (1951).

20   *Quarterly Review, op. cit.*, p. 202.

21   *Le Choléra*, p. 170.

22   Creighton, *op. cit.*, vol. II, pp. 823 ff.

23   Preston and Oldham, for example, were supplied with water from
      surface drainage on the neighbouring hills.

24   There is a good account of the cholera in Bilston by W. Leigh, *An
      Authentic Narrative of the Melancholy Occurrences at Bilston ... during
      the Awful Visitation of that Town by Cholera* (1833). Leigh was
      incumbent of St Leonard's, Bilston and a county magistrate. He took
      the Chair at several reform meetings in 1832 when Staffordshire was not
      only hard hit by cholera but in the thick of the fight for reform. 'It is
      impossible to describe the enthusiasm which prevails in [these]
      districts,' a local writer noted. (*Reports of the Principal Staffordshire
      Reform Meetings*, 14 May 1832, Birmingham Reference Library.) Leigh
      trembled 'for the effect' burying cholera burials in family graves would
      'produce among the lower classes of my parishioners'.

25   Creighton, *op. cit.*, vol. II, p. 821, gives a number of basic statistics.
      These and all nineteenth-century cholera statistics should be used to
      the full but treated with caution. This was emphasised by contem-
      poraries. Thus the General Board of Health in its *Report on the
      Epidemic Cholera of 1848 and 1849* warned that 'there were in 1832 no
      means of obtaining an accurate return of the number of attacks and
      deaths; nor has there been any return that can be relied on of the
      number of attacks in the late epidemic. We adopted all available means
      to obtain such a return, but we know that the disease was prevalent in

several places from which no returns at all have been made, and that in others, the attacks and deaths have been much understated.' This kind of warning might have well been repeated by Chevalier.

26 Creighton, *op. cit.*, pp. 841 ff. There were 1365 deaths in the Wolverhampton area, including Bilston in 1849. On the immunity of Birmingham there are some interesting comments by Isaac Aaron, medical officer of the local Board of Health in 1831 and 1832, and later medical officer of Sydney in Australia. See *Sydney Magazine of Science and Art*, pp. 193 ff.

27 ibid. There is a full and interesting account of cholera in Manchester in 1832 by H. Gaulter, *The Origins and Progress of the Malignant Cholera in Manchester* (1833).

28 *Le Choléra*, p. 170-4.

29 See above, vol. I, pp. 214-23.

30 M. von Pettenhofer, 'Boden und Grundwasser in ihren Beziehungen zu Cholera und Typhus', in *Zeitschrift für Biologie*, vol. V (1869).

31 *Le Choléra*, p. 128.

32 *Westminster Review*, vol. 15 (1831).

33 General Board of Health, *Report on the Epidemic Cholera of 1848 and 1849*, p. 18.

34 W. R. Clanny, *Hyperanthraxis or the Cholera of Sunderland* (1832), p. 42.

35 H. Paul, *The Control of Communicable Disease* (1952), p. 383. Yet Snow noted much.

36 As Eversley points out (fn. 4, p. 158) cholera is not referred to by Halévy in his account of events in England between 1830 and 1832. Trevelyan even in his *English Social History* refers to it only in passing. *Vibrio cholerae* thrives best in salty water. Snow noted that Southwark water was saltier than Lambeth's. Lavisse and Rambaud's *Histoire générale* briefly mentions cholera in Paris in 1832, but associates its outbreaks not with social tension in the capital but with 'a sort of truce' in Parliament, 'most of the Deputies having fled' (vol. X (1898)). The fact that Casimir Périer, the French Prime Minister, died of cholera makes it difficult to avoid mention of the epidemic altogether. The drama of the situation has been brought out in a lively popular book by J. Lucas-Dubreton, *La Grande Peur de 1832, le choléra et l'émeute* (1932). It is impossible either from the *Peuples et civilisations* series or from the American series *The Rise of Modern Europe* to gain any knowledge of the chronology or social consequences of cholera in nineteenth-century Europe.

37 *Classes laborieuses*, p. xvi.

38 *Le Choléra*, p. 8.

39 ibid., p. 6.

40 ibid., p. 13.

41 See the interesting article by R. Baehrel, 'La haine de classes en temps d'épidemie' in *Annales*, vol. VII (1952), pp. 351-60.

42 *La Peste* is interesting in that it says little about social conflicts. The main influence of the plague, indeed, was to draw the town together as a

collective unit, with a sense of 'collective destiny'. For 'religion and morals', see Morris, *op. cit.*, Chapter 7, p. 129. 'Science could not provide ... certainty ... Therefore religious and moral explanations and imperatives played a greater part than in later industrial society.' Yet as Morris shows, 'the relationship between God and cholera was not a simple one'.

43 *Quarterly Review, op. cit.*, p. 171.
44 *Le Choléra*, pp. 136 ff.
45 *Quarterly Review, op. cit.*, p. 170.
46 *Le Choléra*, pp. 143-55.
47 Cp. Morris, *op. cit.*, pp. 118 ff., where English and Scots fairs are discussed. In Oxford the local Board of Health considered stopping St Giles' Fair, but realised that such a prohibition could never be enforced and had to be satisfied with warnings about the dangers of drink.
48 *Le Choléra*, p. 106.
49 Creighton, *op. cit.*, vol. II, pp. 186 ff, where he quotes the *Gentleman's Magazine*, June 1832.
50 *Hansard*, 3rd series, vol. X, cols 443-4.
51 ibid., col. 439. The phrase was Hume's.
52 ibid., col. 438. Archbishop Howlett composed a special prayer which was particularly keenly criticised in the Radical press by Cobbett, who was given the chance to attack together many old opponents whom he has hitherto attacked separately. See *Weekly Political Register*, 26 February 1832. 'The RICH are now raising money to supply the means of giving proper food, raiment, bedding, medicines and fuel, to the poor! ... Why was not this done *before*? Because before, *the rich were in no danger* from contagion existing amongst the poor.'
53 *Hansard, op. cit.*, col. 392.
54 ibid., col. 440.
55 ibid., cols 267-8. Both Blomfield and Warburton are historical characters who deserve further attention from historians of nineteenth-century Britain. For the idea of the *cordon sanitaire*, see A. T. Holroyd, *The Quarantine Laws* (1839), and J. C. McDonald, 'The History of the Bulletin of the History of Medicine', vol. XXV (1951).
56 *Quarterly Review, op. cit.*
57 See S. W. Hazlewood and L. Morley, *History and Medical Treatment of Cholera at Sunderland* (1832).
58 P. Guiral, 'Marseilles', in *Le Choléra*, pp. 121-40.
59 Dr Fréour (no initial given), ibid., pp. 109, 20.
60 ibid., p. 8.
61 Leigh, *op. cit., passim*; Creighton, *op. cit.*, vol. II, p. 823. It is interesting to compare a Black Country work cited both by Creighton and Eversley, – G. Girdlestone, *Seven Sermons Preached during the Prevalence of Cholera in the Parish of Sedgley* (1833) – with the two contrasting sermons preached by Father Paneloux in Camus's *La Peste*.
62 *Report of the General Board of Health on the Quarantine* (1849), p. 73.
63 Chadwick to Lord Morpeth, 24 May 1848. (Chadwick Papers, University College, London.)

64 There is much of value, however, in M. Pelling, *op. cit.*, esp. pp. 46 ff., though the book is concerned directly with a wide range of fundamental questions.

65 *The Report of the General Board of Health on the Epidemic Cholera of 1848 and 1849* claimed that according to parliamentary returns from 1825 to 1845 cholera caused the deaths of nearly one in eight of British soldiers and one in five of Indian soldiers who died in India.

66 Creighton, *op. cit.*, p. 841.

67 *Hansard, op. cit.*, col. 345.

68 *Report of the General Board of Health on the Epidemic Cholera of 1848 and 1849.*

69 *Edinburgh Review*, vol. CLXXXIV (1850), p. 389.

70 M. C. Buer, *Health, Wealth and Population* (1926), p. 230.

71 'The Public Health', in the *Australian Medical Journal*, October 1861.

72 B. W. Richardson, Introduction to *The Health of Nations: A Review of the Work of Edwin Chadwick* (1887).

73 Of 23,000 deaths in 1853-4, almost half, 11,000, were in London. In 1866, 5500 out of 14,000 deaths were in London.

74 See H. C. F. Bell, *Lord Palmerston*, vol. II (1936), p. 76.

75 H. W. Acland, *Memoir on the Cholera at Oxford* (1856), p. 105.

76 A brief account is given in D. S. Landes, *Bankers and Pashas* (1958), pp. 241-2.

77 J. S. Simmons, T. F. Whyayne, G. W. Anderson and H. M. Horack, *Global Epidemiology*, vol. I (1944), p. 119. For changes in perspective, see N. Howard-Jones, 'Cholera anomalies: the Unhistory of Medicine as Exemplified by Cholera', in *Perspectives in Biology and Medicine* (1972).

78 Paul, *op. cit.*, p. 385.

79 Winslow, *op. cit.*, p. 340. For appalling conditions in New York in the 1850s, see S. Smith, *Report on the Sanitary Conditions of New York* (1865).

80 *Hansard, op. cit.*, col. 387. The speaker was Sir James Malcolm.

81 There is a fascinating account of the cholera outbreak in New York State in the *New Yorker*, 18 October 1947, by S. H. Adams, 'That was Up-State New York: My Grandfather and the Plague'.

82 *Le Choléra*, p. 131.

83 Details are given in R. S. Lambert's useful study, *The Cobbett of the West* (1939).

84 Landes, *op. cit.*, p. 242.

85 The rumours were widespread in Paris (*Le Choléra*, p. 19), in St Petersburg (ibid., p. 148), and in England, where there was also the characteristic variant that it was a 'job' (ibid., p. 175). It was always easy in England to apply the term 'job' to projects of sanitary reform. Colonel Sibthorp, the eccentric Tory critic of the Public Health Act of 1848 and all other useful social legislation, had much in common with Cobbett. 'I hate the Commission, I hate all jobs, I suspect all Governments,' he declared. See above, pp. 142-3.

86 Adams, *op. cit.*, Cp. the poem cited by M. Guiral, A. Sapet, *Le Choléra Morbus à Marseille*.

87 Lewis, *op. cit.*, p. 202.

88 J. R. Lichtenstädt, *Die Asiatische Cholera in Russland* (1831).

89 Pettenhofer consulted Douglas Cunningham and Timothy Lewis in 1868 after they had returned from an official visit to India to study the cholera. He quoted James Cunningham's reports in his book on the spread of cholera in India in 1871.

90 See above, p. 117.

91 ibid. See also *Classes laborieuses et classes dangereuses* and *La Formation de la population parisienne au XIXe siècle* (1950).

92 A. Haviland, *Geographical Distribution of Disease in Great Britain* (1892), p. 3.

93 An account of 'Some Early English Maps of the Geography of Health and Disease' was given to the International Geographical Congress of 1952 by Professor E. W. Gilbert.

94 *Le Choléra*, pp. 170-1, where he says that the revelations of working-class conditions in Sunderland 'for the first time' provided 'authentic designation of the relationship between cleanliness, misery and malady'.

95 For example, C. T. Thackrah's *The Effects of the Principal Arts ... on Health and Longevity* (1831). Chadwick's first published work of note was on the misleading picture of social conditions presented by the out-of-date life tables of insurance agencies. (*Westminster Review*, February 1828.) Chadwick quoted Villermé, who is in turn referred to by Professor Chevalier. (*Le Choléra*, p. 11.) The *Westminster Review* also included in its early numbers searching articles by Dr Southwood Smith, on 'Contagion and Sanitary Law' and plague, typhus fever and quarantine (*op. cit.*, January, July 1825).

96 For the significance of these reports seen in proper perspective in relation to earlier ventures, see the important article by E. P. Hennock, 'Urban Sanitary Reform a Generation before Chadwick?', in the *Economic History Review*, vol. X, August 1957.

97 See Major Greenwood, *Some British Pioneers of Social Medicine* (1948).

98 *Le Choléra*, p. 150.

99 Adams, *op. cit.*

100 *The Times*, 5 October 1869.

101 Snow, *On Continuous Molecular Changes* (1893), p. 172.

102 *British Medical Journal*, 23 January 1875.

9 The Welfare State in Historical Perspective

The phrase 'welfare state' is of recent origin. It was first used to describe Labour Britain after 1945. From Britain the phrase made its way round the world. It was freely employed, usually but not exclusively by politicians and journalists, in relation to diverse societies at diverse stages of development. Historians also took over the phrase. Attempts were made to re-write nineteenth- and twentieth-century history, particularly British history, in terms of the origins and development of a welfare state.

Much of the political talk and the international journalism was loose and diffuse. The phrase welfare state was seldom defined. It was used, for example, to cover both social and economic changes, and sometimes it was conceived of as influencing the distribution of property as well as of income. Among the social changes the demand for more comprehensive social security – freedom from want – was linked, often with little thought, with the demand for greater equality of opportunity through educational reform. The differences between the two goals, differences which had been noted by earlier writers, were not usually stressed. It was only in the aftermath of change that the social implications of meritocracy were disentangled from the social implications of other aspects of legislation. There was confusion also on critical issues concerning social change and economic power. The most important economic changes which found a place in British definitions of the welfare state were those which seemed to entail direct and immediate social consequences – the 'abolition of poverty' and the 'conquest of unemployment'.

The historical writing dwelt primarily on the contrast between the nineteenth and twentieth centuries. The night-watchman state, condemned by Lassalle, had become as obsolescent, it was argued, as *laissez-faire* itself. Emphasis on political rights had given way naturally, as the nineteenth century went by, to the demand for social rights. The year 1848 stood out as a landmark on the continent: Chartism was a landmark movement in Britain. Democracy had become completely meaningful only as it had taken the form of social democracy. Welfare states were fruits of social democracy. One strain in this historiography was a modern counterpart of the Whig historiography of nineteenth-century Britain with the concept of welfare substituted for the concept of representative government. The past was seen as leading inevitably and inexorably along a broad highway – with the welfare state as its destination.

Already the early journalism appears dated and the history looks slanted. Increasing emphasis has recently been placed in Britain, the home of the phrase, on the contemporary social influence not of legislation but of an expanding market economy. Both critics and admirers of the welfare state have been driven to concern themselves with affluence. There has been talk of myths of the welfare state, including a myth of the welfare state for the working classes which has persuaded (against much factual evidence) both politicians and voters that most, if not all, contemporary social problems have been solved since 1945. The inhibiting effects of the myth have received as much attention from critics as the liberating effects of the legislation. At the same time, recent writings from all sides make it abundantly clear that the ideals which inspired the achievement of a welfare state are now no longer universally shared. Comprehensive notions of a welfare state based on complete equality of citizenship no longer receive universal assent (or lip-service). Against a background of recurring fiscal crises, paying for services has replaced fair shares for all as a current political slogan.

The switch may only be temporary and it has already met with resistance, but it is a sign that what only recently seemed to be fixed is far from fixed, that the post-1945 welfare state was not in itself a final destination. 'Beyond the welfare state' has already become a slogan for socialists. On the other side, a number of writers, some of them influential, have reverted to older and more limited ideas of a 'social service state' where limited services are provided for a limited section of the population. That section is the least well-off section of the community. The state services liquidate themselves, it is claimed, as more and more people rise above the level of a minimum standard of living to reach 'freedom' to buy for themselves the services (health, education, etc.) which they want.

While political attitudes have been changing not only in Britain but even more markedly in other parts of the world, a small number of British historians and sociologists have begun to make a more searching examination of the background and benefits of the welfare state. As a result of their continuing labours, the significance of each of the great 'turning points' of British welfare state history is already being re-assessed. The stark contrast between the nineteenth and twentieth centuries has been qualified. Legislation such as the National Health Insurance Act of 1911 or the Housing Act of 1919, which had hitherto been treated generally or symbolically, have been reinterpreted in the light of newly discovered or hitherto neglected evidence. The pressures have been more carefully scrutinised, and the setbacks have been examined as well as the successes.

Many of the 'reforms' were designed as remedies for specific problems: they were certainly not thought of as contributions to a trend or a movement. The sources of inspiration were multiple – socialism was only one, and not always the most important, of several strands – and this very multiplicity added to later complications and confusions. The old Poor Law, from which social services emerged both directly and by reaction, was not so much broken up, as its critics had wished, as eroded away by depression, war, unemployment and the introduction piecemeal of remedial legislation. The social welfare legislation of the Labour government of 1945-50, the climax of fifty years of social and political history, has itself begun to be viewed historically. The presuppositions which underlay it can now be seen to have been the products of a particular set of circumstances, circumstances which have already changed. Among those circumstances the experience of war seems to have been as relevant as the appeal of socialism in determining the practicability and the popularity of introducing comprehensive welfare proposals.

So far, however, the re-interpretation and the rewriting have largely been insular. Relatively little attention has been paid, in consequence, to the comparative history of welfare legislation. Specialists in social administration have collected comparative data, but they have naturally enough used them more frequently for practical than for historical purposes. The uniqueness of Britain has been emphasised to the neglect of the study of trends and tendencies in other countries.

In certain respects British experience has been unique, as foreign writers as different as Halévy and Schumpeter have recognised. The uniqueness can only be appreciated, however, when the experience of several countries is taken into account. The trends and tendencies which led journalists, politicians and historians to apply the label welfare state to Britain may be noted in all modern industrialised communities. They have influenced non-industrialised communities also. The 'causes' of the welfare state, as of nineteenth-century *Sozialpolitik*, are to be found, therefore, in far more general phenomena than the programmes of the British Labour Party or the persistent prodding of the British liberal conscience.

It was the International Labour Office, a mine of invaluable factual information and a source of inspiration in international social service development, which noted in 1950, at a time when the term welfare state was being generally applied to Britain, that a new conception was transforming the pre-war systems of social insurance in many countries. 'There is a movement everywhere', one of its reports stated, 'towards including additional classes of the population, covering a wider range of contingencies, providing benefits more nearly adequate to needs and removing anomalies among them, loosening the tie between benefit right and contribution payment, and, in general, unifying the finance and administration of branches hitherto separate.'[1] In other words, a 'quest for universality' was transforming the pre-war social service state into some kind of welfare state.

The new conception reflected changing attitudes towards citizenship as well as changing views about the proper role of the state. Some of these attitudes and views had taken shape during the Second World War when talk of 'four freedoms' was thought to have universal application, and the International Labour Conference at Philadelphia in 1944 dwelt on 'the deep desire of men to free themselves from the fear of want'. 'The meaning' which can be given to 'international society', it was argued, will be judged in terms of human benefit and welfare.[2] The ILO report of 1950 went on to state that

> the transformation of social insurance is accompanied by the absorption or coordination of social assistance, and there begins to emerge a new organization for social security, which we can describe only as a public service for the citizenry at large. This new organization now concerns society as a whole, though it is primarily directed to the welfare of the workers and their families. It tends, therefore, to become a part of national government, and social security policy accordingly becomes coordinated closely with national policy for raising the standard of welfare and, in particular, for promoting the vitality of the population.

This international report touches on matters which had already been discussed at length in British contexts. During the Second World War, the historian of British social policy writes,

> it was increasingly regarded as a proper function or even obligation of government to ward off distress and strain not only among the poor but among all classes of society. And because the area of responsibility had so perceptibly widened, it was no longer thought sufficient to provide through various branches of social assistance a standard of service hitherto considered appropriate for those in receipt of poor assistance.[3]

The disassociation of welfare from Poor Law stigmas inevitably meant a raising of standards. Concern for the citizenry at large meant both taking account of democratic demands and not simply seeking to satisfy assessed needs.[4]

There were many instances in Britain of changing notions of what was appropriate. One of the most striking was revolution in school meals policy. School meals had developed during the nineteenth century as a charitable service for 'necessitous children' (private charity outside the scope of the Poor Law). The private charities providing them were at pains to make sure that they were not catering for the children of 'undeserving and worthless parents'. The Education (Provision of Meals) Act of 1906, which brought the state directly into this area of social welfare policy, was a highly controversial measure. It drove A. V. Dicey, the noted British lawyer and writer, to complain that it was altogether wrong that fathers of children fed by the state should retain the right of voting for Members of Parliament. 'Why a man who first neglects his duty as a father and then defrauds the state should retain his full political rights', he went on tendentiously, 'is a question easier to ask than to answer.'[5]

Dicey, like a number of his Conservative contemporaries, was concerned that social service legislation would follow a slippery slope in which each generation would fall more sharply than its predecessor. The statesmen who had passed the Education Act of 1870, creating the first public-provided schools, would probably have been quite unwilling to have passed the 1891 Act relieving parents of the necessity for paying for any part of their children's elementary education. The people who passed the 1891 Act would in their turn have baulked at the School Meals Act of 1906. Dicey was right in implying that the men of 1906 would certainly have stopped far short of the school meals revolution of the Second World War. A Board of Education circular of 1941 completely abandoned old precepts that cheap school meals should be provided only to children who were both necessitous and undernourished. Already during the previous year the number of school meals provided had doubled. By 1945, 1,650,000 dinners were taken on every school day in England and Wales, about 14 per cent being free and the rest costing the parents a nominal sum. This figure compared with 130,000 in 1940 and 143,000 in the depressed conditions of the mid-1930s. In round figures, one child in three was fed at school in 1945 in place of one child in thirty in 1940.[6]

The distribution of milk, fruit juice and welfare foods was regulated on social grounds throughout the Second World War. The same principles were carried from nutritional policy to social security policy. 'In a matter so fundamental', a government White Paper of 1944 stated, 'it is right for all citizens to stand together, without exclusion based on differences of status, function or wealth'.[7] The argument was not simply that administrative problems would be simplified if structures were 'comprehensive' or 'universal', but that through 'universal schemes' 'concrete expression' would be given to the 'solidarity and unity of the nation, which in war has been its bulwark against aggression and in peace will be its guarantee of success in the fight against individual want and mischance'.

This White Paper, like the equally significant White Paper of 1944 (Cmnd. 6527) which accepted the need for social action to prevent unemployment, was the product of a coalition government, pledged to national unity. The strains and stresses of total war forced politicians to consider the community as a whole: the hopes of re-construction (the term was used with particular fervour during the First World War) were held out to inspire the public in years of trial. There was thus a close association between warfare and welfare. Moreover, the knowledge that large sums of money, raised through taxation at a level without precedent, were being used to wage war led without difficulty to the conclusion that smaller sums of money could produce a welfare state in times of peace. All parties were interested in this line of argument. The Conservative partner in the wartime coalition, the predominant political partner, published as late as 1949 a pamphlet, *The Right Road for Britain*, which stated unequivocally that

> the social services are no longer even in theory a form of poor relief. They are a cooperative system of mutual aid and self-help provided by the whole nation and designed to give to all the basic minimum of security, of housing, of opportunity, of employment and of living standards below which our duty to one another forbids us to permit any one to fall.

By 1949, when this pamphlet was published, the legislation introduced by the Labour government of 1945-50, particularly the health service legislation, was freely talked of as welfare state legislation. Much of it went beyond the ideas of 'comprehensiveness' or 'co-operation' as such and reflected socialist philosophies of equality. Attempts had been made to raise the standards of service to meet the claims of 'equal citizenship'. 'Homes, health, education and social security, these are your birthright,' exclaimed Aneurin Bevan. Sociologists as well as socialists explained the new policies in terms of the fabric of citizenship. Hitherto, they suggested, social service policy had been thought of as a remedial policy to deal with the basement of society, not with its upper floors. Now the purpose was extended. 'It has begun to re-model the whole building', T. H. Marshall wrote in 1949, 'and it might even end by converting a skyscraper into a bungalow or at least into a bungalow surmounted by an architecturally insignificant turret.'[8]

The changes in mood since 1949 have already been noted: they can be explained in narrowly fiscal or broadly sociopolitical terms, and they constitute the background of current controversies. The object of this paper is to go back beyond the current controversies, beyond the relatively recent experience of total war, to the historical matrix within which the idea of a 'welfare state' has taken form. Before going back in time, however, it is necessary to attempt a more precise definition of the term welfare state than has been common in recent discussions. And the definition itself will suggest certain interesting and relevant lines of historical enquiry.

I

A welfare state is a state in which organised power is deliberately used (through politics and administration) in an effort to modify the play of market forces in at least three directions – first, by guaranteeing individuals and families a minimum income irrespective of the market value of their work or their property; second, by narrowing the extent of insecurity by enabling individuals and families to meet certain social contingencies (for example, sickness, old age and unemployment) which lead otherwise to individual and family crises; and third, by ensuring that all citizens without distinction of status or class are offered the best standards available in relation to a certain agreed range of social services.

The first and second of these objects may be accomplished, in part at least, by what used to be called a social service state, a state in which communal resources are employed to abate poverty and to assist those in distress. The third objective, however, goes beyond the aims of a social service state. It brings in the idea of the optimum rather than the older idea of the minimum. It is concerned not merely with abatement of class differences or the needs of scheduled groups but with equality of treatment and the aspirations of citizens as voters with equal shares of electoral power.

Merely to define the term welfare state in this way points to a number of historical considerations, which are the theme of this article. First, the conception of market forces sets the problems of the welfare state (and of welfare) within the context of the age of modern political economy. In societies without market economies, the problem of welfare raises quite different issues. Within the context of the age of modern political economy an attempt has been made, and is still being made, to create and maintain a self-regulating system of markets, including markets in the fictitious commodities, land, money and labour. The multiple motives lying behind the attempt to control these markets require careful and penetrating analysis.

Second, the conception of social contingencies is strongly influenced by the experience of industrialism. Sickness, old age and death entail hardships in any kind of society. Ancient systems of law and morality include precepts designed to diminish these hardships, precepts based, for example, on the obligations of sons to support their parents or on the claims of charity, *obsequium religionis*. Unemployment, however, at least in the form in which it is thought of as a social contingency, is a product of industrial societies; and it is unemployment more than any other social contingency which has determined the shape and timing of modern welfare legislation. Before the advent of mass unemployment, 'unemployability', the inability of individuals to secure their livelihood by work, was a key subject in the protracted debates on poor law policy. The existence of 'chronic unemployment', structural or cyclical, has been a powerful spur from the nineteenth century onwards, leading organised labour groups to pass from concentration on sectional interests to the consideration of social rights of workers as a class. It has also influenced philanthropic businessmen wishing to improve the efficiency and strengthen the social justice of the business system; and politicians and governments anxious to avoid dangerous political consequences of unemployment. The memories of chronic unemployment in the inter-war years and the discovery of what it was believed were new techniques of controlling it reinforced welfare state policies in many countries after the Second World War.

Third, the idea of using organised power (through politics and administration) to determine the pattern of welfare services requires careful historical dating. Why not rely for welfare on the family, religion, charity, self help, mutual aid (guild, church, trade union, friendly society) or fringe benefits (business itself)? Whole philosophies of welfare have been founded on each of these ideas or institutions; and often the philosophies and the interests sustaining them have been inimical to the suggestion that the state itself should intervene. The possibility of using governmental power has been related in each country to the balance of economic and social forces; estimates of the proper functions and, true or false, of the available resources of the state; effective techniques of influence and control, resting on knowledge (including expert knowledge); and, not least, the prevalence (or absence) of the conviction that societies can be shaped by conscious policies designed to eliminate 'abuses' which in earlier generations had been accepted as 'inevitable' features of the human condition.

Not only does the weighting of each of these factors vary from period to period, but it also varies from place to place. It was Bentham, scarcely distinguished for his historical sense, who in distinguishing between *agenda* (tasks of government) and *sponte acta* (unplanned decisions of individuals) wrote that 'in England abundance of useful things are done by individuals which in other countries are done either by government or not at all ... [while] in Russia, under Peter the Great, the list of *sponte acta* being a blank, that of *agenda* was proportionately abundant'.[9] This contrast was noted by many other writers later in the nineteenth century, just as an opposite contrast between Britain and the United States was often noted after 1945.

If the question of what constitutes welfare involves detailed examination of the nature and approach to social contingencies, the question of why the state rather than some other agency becomes the main instrument of welfare involves very detailed examination of a whole range of historical circumstances. The answer to the question is complicated, moreover, by differences of attitude in different countries, to the idea of 'the state' itself. Given these differences, a translation of basic terms into different languages raises difficulties which politicians and journalists may well have obscured. For example, is the term *Wohlfahrtsstaat* the right translation of welfare state? British and German approaches to the state have been so different that they have absorbed the intellectual energy of generations of political scientists. In the nineteenth century there were somewhat similar difficulties (although on a smaller scale) surrounding the translation of the British term 'self help'. A French translator of Samuel Smiles's book of that title (1859) said that the term self help was almost untranslatable.

Fourth, the 'range of agreed social services' set out in the provisional definition of welfare state is a shifting range. Policies, despite the finalism of much of the post-1945 criticism, are never fixed for all time. What at various times was considered to be a proper range shifts, as Dicey showed, and consequently must be examined historically. So too must changing areas of agreement and conflict. Public health was once a highly controversial issue in European societies: it still is in some other societies. The sanitary idea was rightly regarded by the pioneers of public health as an idea which had large and far-reaching chains of consequences. It marked an assault on fate which would be bound to lead to other assaults. Public health, in the administrative sphere of drains, sewers and basic environmental services, has been taken outside the politics of conflict in Britain and other places, but personal health services remain controversial. There is controversy, very bitter indeed in the United States, not only about the range of services and who shall enjoy them but about the means of providing them. The choice of means influences all welfare state history. Welfare states can and do employ a remarkable variety of instruments, such as social insurance, direct provision in cash or in kind, subsidy, partnership with other agencies, including private business agencies, and action through local authorities. In health policy alone, although medical knowledge is the same in all countries of the West and the same illnesses are likely to be treated in much the same kind of way, there is a remarkable diversity of procedures and institutions even in countries which make extensive public provision for personal health services.

Fifth, there are important historical considerations to take into account in tracing the relationship between the three different directions of public intervention in the free (or partially free) market. The demand for minimum standards can be related to a particular set of cumulative pressures. Long before the Webbs in 1909 urged the need for government action to secure 'an enforced minimum of civilised life', the case for particular minima had been powerfully advocated. Yet the idea of basing social policy as a whole on a public commitment to minimum standards did not become practical politics in Britain until the so-called Beveridge revolution of the Second World War. The third direction of welfare policy, and the distinctive direction of the welfare state, can be understood only in terms of older logic and more recent history. The idea of separating welfare policy from subsistence standards (the old minima, however measured) and relating it to 'acceptable' standards ('usual work income') provides an indication of the extent to which primary poverty has been reduced in affluent societies. It may be related, however, to older ideas of equality, some of which would lead directly not to state intervention in the market but to the elimination of the market altogether, at least as a force influencing human relationships. A consideration of the contemporary debate is more rewarding if it is grounded in history.

II

Each of these five historical considerations deserves fuller treatment. The texture is often complex. There have been markedly different chronologies of development and different answers have been given in different countries to the same set of leading questions.

By the end of the nineteenth and the beginning of the twentieth centuries there had been a general reaction against attempts to maintain self-regulating systems of markets. This reaction has been variously described as the decline of liberalism, the advent of collectivism and the rise of socialism. Fabian writers, who are particularly illuminating on these themes, used all three labels, and after painting a grim picture of a period of capitalist anarchy in the early nineteenth century went on to show how

> in the teeth of the current Political Economy, and in spite of all the efforts of the millowning Liberals, England was compelled to put forth her hand to succour and protect her weaker members ... Slice after slice has gradually been cut from the profits of capital, and thereby from its selling

value, by strictly beneficial restrictions on the user's liberty to do what he likes with it ... On every side he is being registered, inspected, controlled, and eventually superseded by the community ... All this has been done by 'practical men', ignorant, that is to say, of any scientific sociology, believing Socialism to be the most foolish of dreams ... Such is the irresistible sweep of social tendencies, that in their every act they worked to bring about the very Socialism they despised ...[10]

In outlining this development of 'our unconscious Socialism', Sidney Webb directed attention to the efforts both of 'individuals' and of 'municipalities' before he turned explicitly to the state. The masses were kept in the background, vague and undifferentiated. So too were the trade unions, the importance of which he discovered only a few years later. The main emphasis was placed on the power of the ballot box, as it was by revisionists on the continent. It might have been foreseen, Webb remarked (and it had indeed been foreseen by men like Bagehot) that 'individualism could not survive their [the working classes'] advent to political power'. Unconscious or later conscious socialism was the necessary corollary of political democracy. The result would necessarily be the emergence of a more active state.

The analysis was historically significant but limited in depth. Another of the Fabian essayists, Hubert Bland, pointed out by implication three of Webb's superficialities. First, state control did not imply socialism, conscious or unconscious. 'It is not so much to the thing the State does as to the end for which it does it that we must look before we decide whether it is a Socialist State or not.' Sixpenny telegrams organised by a state-run Post Office had nothing to do with socialism or welfare in the welfare state sense. Second, and in writing in this way, Bland was exceptionally percipient about the shape of the future: 'it is quite certain that the social programme of our party will become a great fact long before the purely political proposals of the Liberals have received the royal assent'. Third, and here Bland was a better historian than Webb, there had been a far less sharp break than Webb had suggested between the 'period of anarchy' of the early nineteenth century and 'the present'. There was certainly no one single landmark, like Mill's *Political Economy* (1848), which provided a frontier post between an age of individualism on one side and an age of socialism on the other.

'There never has been as long as society lasts', Bland went so far as to argue, 'and never can be a *parti sérieux* of logical *laissez-faire*. Even in the thick of the industrial revolution the difference between the two great parties was mainly one of tendency – of attitude of mind.'[11] The simplicities of market political economy could never be consistently applied in practical politics. The attempts to plan *laissez-faire* was doomed from the start. If you had to refer to an economist, you would have to fall back upon Adam Smith, a pragmatist, rather than upon more systematic classical theoreticians. When the classical theoreticians were drawn into active politics, their theories immediately became hedged round by an intricate tangle of qualifications.

Bland was more subtle in his approach than Webb (and incidentally more direct in his demand for a new and 'definitely Socialist party'). It is clear from more recent academic writings first that there never was a completely negative state even in early nineteenth-century Britain, and second that even classical theoreticians were by no means unanimous about the merits of complete *laissez-faire*. 'The principle of *laissez-faire* may be safely trusted to in some things', wrote J.R.McCulloch, but in many more it is wholly inapplicable; and to appeal to it on all occasions savours more of the policy of a parrot than that of a statesman or philosopher'.[12] Nassau Senior, the architect of the Poor Law of 1834, a substitute for a social policy, yet an innovation from which many new social policies in health and education derived, maintained that

> it is the duty of a government to do whatever is conducive to the welfare of the governed. The only limit to this duty is power . . . it appears to me that the most fatal of errors would be the general admission of the proposition that a government has no right to interfere for any purpose except for that of affording protection, for such an admission would be preventing our profiting from experience, and even from acquiring it.[13]

Senior stressed, of course, that the power limit to the duty of the state was set not only by the coercive power of the law but by the effective power of the 'laws of political economy'. A knowledge of the laws of political economy was necessary to legislators, and the new Poor Law of 1834 with its abandonment of outdoor relief to the poor and its stress on making conditions for indoor relief in workhouses 'less eligible' than the worst employment outside was an attempt to rule the poor by the laws of political economy. Later critical writers were to dismiss these economic laws as 'gigantic stuffed policemen';[14] and even at the time there were passionate enemies of political economy who went far towards envisaging a welfare state where politics would have primacy over economics.

In early industrial Britain one of the most influential of the groups of anti-political economists was Richard Oastler whose religious and political conviction drove him to campaign against the Poor Law of 1834, and to lead a working-class agitation during the 1830s for legal limitation of the hours of work of women and children in textile factories. He was known in consequence as the 'Factory King'. To him, political economy was 'at total variance with every precept of our

Holy Religion, every principle of our Constitution, and every security to Rank and Prosperity'. The ideal state was what he called the social state. This state would seek 'to secure the prosperity and happiness of every class of society', but it would be particularly concerned with 'the protection of the poor and needy, because they require the shelter of the constitution and the laws more than other classes'. The social state was the 'true' state of history: it was the political economists who were the revolutionaries. Because, however, the actual state in the early nineteenth century was deviating further and further from the ideal (and historic) state, the defence of social rights would have to take the form, if need be, of rebellion.

> If governments are established in this land for the sole purpose of hoarding up large masses of gold and stamping down individual wretchedness, if *that* is the sole interest and sole object of our government, I declare myself a traitor to it, if I die tomorrow for using the word.[15]

Oastler's movement, grounded in Toryism, thus merged into Chartism, and the idea of the 'historic rights of the poor', undermined by 1834, provided a link between 'traditionalism' and modern working-class politics. Chartism was a movement with several distinct sources of inspiration: it nevertheless asserted clearly and unequivocally the case for the extension of the suffrage to the working classes in the name not only of political but of social rights.

What Marx called 'feudal socialism' was one source, therefore, of the revolt against the market economy, the laws of political economy and the night-watchman state. Indeed, the *Deutsche Allgemeine Zeitung* called Oastler a 'democratic Tory', a title adopted by his most recent biographer.[16] It is easy to see how close certain aspects of his thought were to the thought of John Ruskin, a social prophet of great influence, who went on (with Marx himself) to shape the thought of William Morris, and later of J. A. Hobson. Ruskin criticised orthodox political economy at greater length than Oastler, while seeking to evolve a system of political economy of its own, with his own definitions of wealth, 'illth' and value, and with a practical concern for the provision of a living wage. 'The first duty of the state', he urged, 'is to see that every child born therein shall be well housed, clothed, fed and educated until it attains years of discretion.' He added the rider that to do this the government must have an authority over the people of which we now do not so much as dream.[17]

Through Ruskin and others, Oastler points forwards as well as backwards. His immediate support, however, came from working men, organised in factory committees (he has his place, therefore, in the history of working-class organisation as well as of social thought) and from a motley group of clergymen, philanthropists, small squires and Tory Members of Parliament. Leading the latter for many years was Lord Ashley, later the seventh Earl of Shaftesbury, the main parliamentary spokesman for legislative interference with the working hours of women and children. It was Ashley's efforts which led to the passing of a number of Factory Acts, notably the Ten Hours Act of 1847, which marked a definite breach with *laissez-faire*. He was also associated with reforms in mining, housing and health. Like Oastler, Ashley would have argued that the breach with *laissez-faire* was less significant than the capitalist breach with the past. The welfare state was the true historic state.

The Fabians took up this point also. *Laissez-faire* was an aberration, 'an acute outbreak of individualism, unchecked by the old restraints'.[18] There had not only been a medieval order – unlike Carlyle, Ruskin and Morris, they did not dwell on this – but a mercantilist order, buttressed by custom and law. It had disappeared under the weight of the pressure for profit during the industrial revolution. According to the Fabians, it was the task of socialists to create a new order appropriate to democracy. The increasing state intervention during the previous forty years seemed to point (although, as Bland showed, not always indubitably) towards this destination.

Bland was right to imply that there were intricacies and complications. Ashley, for example, can only be properly understood if his work is related to that of Senior as well as of Oastler. The extension of the powers of the state had a Benthamite as well as a philanthropic or Tory inspiration. One of Senior's colleagues in the drafting of the new Poor Law of 1834 was Edwin Chadwick, Bentham's disciple and 'attached friend'. Chadwick went on to concern himself with public health and was the author of the important official publication, *The Sanitary Condition of the Labouring Classes* (1842), which had a profound effect on the evolution of British social legislation. When at last in 1848 a General Board of Health was founded under the first national Public Health Act (there had previously been a certain amount of local initiative and legislation), both Chadwick and Ashley were made members. Behind Ashley was the old dream of a traditional social state, grounded in responsibility and strengthened by charity: Chadwick, selecting from a number of possible Benthamite philosophies that which laid greatest emphasis on the active intervention of the state to suppress 'sinister interests' in the name of 'the greatest happiness of the greatest number', was a believer in a renovated 'administrative state'. Such a state would rest on uniformity of procedures and the kind of centralisation which Oastler abhorred. 'I care more for the good of the service', Chadwick once said in a revealing phrase, 'than for putting it in what is called Harmony with the House of Commons.'[19]

Ashley and Chadwick worked together closely before, to their mutual regret, the General Board of Health was destroyed by a coalition of enemies in 1854. Yet their sources of inspiration remained quite different. Ashley, Tory though he was, looked to the people: he liked crowds. Chadwick looked to the expert. There were, of course, far fewer acknowledged experts in the late 1840s and 1850s than there were a hundred years later when the twentieth-century welfare state was being fashioned. It is interesting to note also that Chadwick, like Senior, feared the extension of the suffrage to the working classes. Senior had warned against the advocacy of 'the political economy of the poor', their belief in the power of human institutions to subvert 'the laws of political economy' in the name of social rights and equality:[20] Chadwick feared something worse, that the 'quest for popularity' would lead rich men to subvert the poor at election times by offering lavish promises.[21]

These fears, shared by many people of property, were as important, and in some ways more incisive, than other men's hopes in determining the tempo and the pattern of state intervention during the first three-quarters of the nineteenth century. For Chadwick and the practical Benthamites, however, the fears were not completely inhibiting. They were constructive men who evolved useful new administrative devices, notably the device of inspection, without which social legislation would have been administratively ineffective. Although the coercive powers of factory, mining and school inspectors were severely limited and most of the early inspectors came from the upper middle classes, the inspectors exerted considerable influence, through their presence as well as through their reports, not only on the way in which existing legislation was administered but on the preparation of new legislative initiatives.[22] In the long run, moreover, Benthamism itself could be given a democratic tinge. As Professor McGregor has written, 'the greatest happiness of the greatest number is an invitation to a continuous review of economic policy; and the greatest number is always the working classes.'[23]

The complex detail of nineteenth-century British approaches to state action makes all attempts to divide the century neatly and tidily into phases or epochs seem grossly oversimplified. The most ambitious of such attempts was A.V.Dicey's large and stimulating *Law and Public Opinion in England in the Nineteenth Century* (1905). Originally a collection of lectures delivered in Harvard in 1898, Dicey's book had polemical as well as historical significance, particularly when it was re-issued in 1914 with a new preface attacking 'the trend towards collectivism' which had been especially pronounced, he thought, since the return of the Liberals to power before the general election of 1906. Dicey placed at 1865 or 'roundabouts' the beginning of 'collectivism', which he defined as 'faith in the benefit to be derived by the mass of the people from the action or intervention of the State'. Thereby he ignored the interventionist element in Benthamism, formalised statements both about philanthropy and *laissez-faire*, and confused his own hostility towards collectivism with an objective investigation of facts and policies. A recent critic of his work has replaced his tidy phases with a more complex picture of pressures and counter-pressures.

> Looking back across the nineteenth century in Great Britain, it is possible to tabulate the parallel developments of *laissez faire* and state intervention almost year by year. What must be kept in mind in spite of our tendency to polarize opposites is that both were exercises of political power, that is, instrumentalities of several kinds of interest. These interests strove to be the state, to use the state for economic and social ends.[24]

Against this background, the extension of the suffrage, which to Webb was decisive, was relevant primarily in that it provided the working classes with an instrument whereby they too *might* attempt to control the state. What Senior, Chadwick (and Bagehot) most feared, Webb, Bland and the Fabians most hoped. Bland noted 'the sort of unconscious or semi-conscious recognition of the fact that the word "state" has taken to itself new and diverse connotations – that the state idea has changed its content'. He argued that working people had themselves changed from fearing it as an enemy to regarding it as a 'potential saviour'.[25]

This comment was exaggerated, as we shall see, as a statement of fact, but it was a pointer to the politics of the future. In Britain, as in many continental countries, independent Labour parties emerged in the late nineteenth century and put forward demands for 'the socialisation of politics'. The demands included many of the measures which subsequently have been regarded as central to the welfare state. Just as eighteenth-century civil rights (freedom of meeting, for example, or of the press) were employed to ensure political rights (the right to vote and its corollaries), so political rights were to be employed to secure social rights. Bevan's claim after 1945 – 'Homes, health, education, and social security; these are your birthright' – would have seemed neither strange nor extravagant to the socialists of 1895. The long intervening period was a period of intermittently intense struggle to secure objects which had already been defined before the beginning of the twentieth century.

Reliance on the state (rather than on trade union or other kinds of voluntary action) to secure these objects was for a time controversial, as we shall see, yet, as the Fabians pointed out (the Marxists with their concern for the forms of economic power did not agree), the state against whose interference 'the popular party' waged 'such bitter war' in the first decades of the nineteenth century was 'an altogether different thing' from the state whose assistance 'the new democracy' was continually invoking and whose power it was bent on increasing. Bland recognised also that if Labour parties put forward welfare objectives in their electoral programmes, other parties working within a democracy would be forced, themselves, to put forward policies which would attempt to meet some at least of the Labour demands. Tories had advanced social policies earlier in the nineteenth century in the name of traditionalism or sometimes of paternalism: Liberals, some of whom were developing a positive theory of welfare of their own, would similarly be forced to advance welfare policies, if only in the name of political realism. 'The Liberals', he held (and he had a clear anti-Liberal bias) were 'traditionally squeezable folk' and 'like all absorbent bodies' they would be 'forced to make concessions and to offer compromises .... Such concessions and compromises will grow in number and importance with each successive appeal to the electorate, until at last the game is won.'[26]

This characteristically Fabian conclusion, which attached strategic significance to the working of the parliamentary system, was not shared by those socialists on the continent, and in Britain, who were sceptical about Parliament and drew a sharp distinction between 'palliatives' and 'fundamental economic and social transformations'. Four years before Bland wrote his essay, Joseph Lane in *The Commonweal* put the alternative point of view when he warned his socialist readers that although it was possible that 'the governing classes' might offer a 'normal working day of eight hours', free meals for children, and cumulative taxation on large incomes, 'their doing so would certainly put off the revolution which we aim at.'[27] The argument has been echoed ever since. In practice, however, non-Fabian socialists, like H.M. Hyndman, who believed not that the 'game would be won' but that there would be a 'final clash', were prepared to advocate 'palliatives', including, for example, free meals for children. Hyndman's Social Democratic Federation refused to take up an impossibilist position and instead talked of palliatives as stepping stones leading in the right direction.[28] The international socialist controversy on this subject, which reached its climax when two rival conferences were held in Paris in 1889, was never completely settled, but the palliatives generally agreed upon at the possibilist conference, the larger of the two, were all of a kind later to be associated with the welfare state.

It was argued, and has often been argued since, that the successful achievement of a programme based on individual palliatives would represent a victory for working-class values within a capitalist market society. Marx himself had claimed that the passing of the Ten Hours Act of 1847 was the first great occasion on which 'in broad daylight' the political economy of the middle class had 'succumbed to the political economy of the working class'. Certainly, the ten hours agitation, led by Oastler and supported by Ashley, marked a genuine stage in a process of conversion of values.

The social service state of the twentieth century, palliative state or not, in so far as it was a product of working-class efforts and aspirations was a different phenomenon from the social state of Oastler. Like the mercantilists, Oastler founded his theory of the state on a theory of society divided into 'proper stations and ranks'. 'God has appointed the proper stations and ranks for each. He has exhibited Himself in His Word and His Works as the God of Order, and has thus left man without excuse if he should be in want and destitution.' In this sense, Oastler's was a stationary view of pre-market society. It did not assume a future increase in national income, and it looked back to 'ancient corporations and guilds' as proper instruments of welfare. There were periods in the past when

> the labourer's wages were protected by statute, and the common foods of the working people ... were prohibited from being made articles of speculation. Care was then taken that the labourer's hope of reward should not to be cut off by the inordinate desire for gain in the capitalists.[29]

When Oastler attacked 'acquisitive society', he was speaking the same language which had been taken for granted as a basis of social morality until a long erosion of values gave way to fundamental shifts in outlook, organisation and not least in real wealth which we associate with the industrial revolution.

The ten hours movement and the later movements for nine hour and eight hour days increasingly became movements within the expanding (but fluctuating) industrial market, with *class* bargaining power being used. The late nineteenth-century British and continental labour groups were reacting against the individualism of orthodox political economy and capitalist economic organisation not by falling back on ideas of rank and order but by developing ideas of class and movement. The systems of regulation which they were anxious to establish were not copies of medieval or mercantilist models (although for a time these were familiar and some of them came into later prominence with guild socialism)[30] but new models appropriate to the new 'social nexus' of industrialism. Written into them was the ideal not only of fairness, a link between old and new, but of equality. The old system, both Fabians and trade unionists saw, was riddled with what Webb called 'status and permanent social inequalities'. The attack on status, which had been prosecuted by middle-class Radicals and Benthamite theorists, was now pursued by working-class socialists and Fabian theorists. There was a real link between Mill and the Fabians. Of course, the attack was local rather than general, intermittent rather than continuous, if only because of economic fluctuations, and subject to all kind of manoeuvres and diversions.

Once arguments for social reform had shifted from talk of rank and order, it was easier for a section of non-socialist Radical opinion to support them. The so-called new Liberals of the late nineteenth and early twentieth centuries argued the case for welfare from a democratic standpoint within the new market economy. They could condemn certain of the conditions of the market without condemning capitalism as a whole, and they could criticise, from a very different standpoint from that of Oastler, the theory of poverty which lay behind the Poor Law of 1834. They could thus reach substantial, though limited, agreement with trade unionists and socialists about particular social service measures, as was shown during the period of Liberal government from 1906 to 1914.

It is necessary to draw distinctions between the early and the late nineteenth century not only to arrive an historical truth but to dispose of current descriptions of welfare state policy in terms of neomercantilism. The enlargement of welfare is not adequately so described. 'There are elements in it which were not present in mercantilist phases of the history of civilisation .... It issues from a new phase in man's history.'[31]

The point is perhaps most clearly demonstrated from the history not of Britain itself, but of British settlements in the Antipodes, where there were striking examples before the end of the nineteenth century of what a French observer called 'socialism without doctrines'.[32] The early granting of universal suffrage in Australia and New Zealand was followed by the demand for social measures which would guarantee 'fairness'. Both Australians and New Zealanders had long boasted that they had no Poor Law – by that they meant that the conditions giving rise to a Poor Law and to workhouses were absent. In fact, however, they had by no means eliminated poverty, and in the last decade of the nineteenth century legislative measures were introduced which went further in certain respects than British legislation. There had been considerable dependence upon the state from the earliest period of colonisation (the older British middle-class fear of the state as an establishment was missing), and there was little serious challenge to the view that the state machinery was freely available to those groups able to secure possession of it. 'The more the state does for the citizen,' Pember Reeves, the first New Zealand Minister of Labour, remarked in 1895, 'the more it fulfils its purpose . . . . The functions of the state should be extended as much as possible . . . . True democracy consists in the extension of state activity.' It was Pember Reeves who coined the phrase 'colonial governmentalism'.[33]

There was nothing paternalistic, however, about this willingness to delegate powers to the state. The emphasis, though at times it may have been somewhat misplaced, was always egalitarian. There was talk along practical, if extended Benthamite lines, of 'the right to work, the right to fair and reasonable conditions of living and the right to be happy'.[34] The collective power of the state (not a remote, impersonal state but a close-at-hand, essentially personally manipulated piece of machinery) was to be used to support social rights. These attitudes were reflected in the social service legislation of the Ballance-Seddon-Reeves ministry in New Zealand from 1891 onwards, and in the legislation of the Turner government in Victoria from 1895.

Much of this legislation was concerned with the creation of effective departments of labour and the control of sweated industries paying low wages to their workers. In both Australia and New Zealand, however, pensions legislation was either introduced or just around the corner by the end of the nineteenth century. The New Zealand Old Age Pensions Act of 1898 was the first in a British Dominion. It provided at state expense pensions to people of good character, but with little or no means, above the age of sixty-five. New South Wales and Victoria followed the example of New Zealand in 1901, and the new federal constitution of Australia stated in the same year that the Commonwealth might legislate for old age and invalid pensions. A Federal Act of 1908 extended the old age pensions system to all Australian states and included also pensions for the blind and for permanently disabled persons. In the same year, Britain passed its first non-contributory Old Age Pensions Act after decades of pressure from philanthropists, societies and even politicians. It was an Act hedged round with moral qualifications,[35] but it nonetheless marked, as did Dominions legislation, an attempt to get away from the harshness of an all-embracing Poor Law. 'The state was making new provision for welfare, in piecemeal fashion, outside of and parallel to the Poor Law.' This, it has been argued, was 'the real beginning of the welfare state in its modern form'.[36]

Pember Reeves, who came to England from New Zealand, was a member of the Fabian Society. He divided old age pensions into three classes: 'First comes the socialists' ideal', he said,

of a universal and comfortable provision which shall supersede the necessity for petty thrift; next come the various schemes, more or less orthodox in principle, but complicated and burdensome in their nature, for the reward and encouragement of thrift and self-denial; in the third class may be placed the humanitarian proposals, the humble yet not ungenerous aim of which is to soften the bitterness of poverty to those aged who, while unfortunate, are not wholly undeserving.

The antipodean legislation, he believed, fell into the third class: 'it was designed to offer help to those who need it most'.[37] Its inspiration was neither a set of doctrines nor a cluster of ideas: it was a bundle of feelings about how people were treated. In Britain itself Hobson was to argue that the strongest solvent of the Poor Law of 1834 was 'a movement along the lines of the strongest human feelings'.[38]

It was Liberal rather than socialist governments that moved along the lines described above, abandoning in the process many of the ideas which had dominated Liberal thought earlier in the century, however much they had been qualified, as we have seen, on particular occasions or by particular writers. 'When I went up to Oxford', wrote Lord Milner of the early 1870s, 'the *laissez faire* theory still held the field. All the recognised authorities were "orthodox" economists of the old school. But within ten years the few men who still held the old doctrines in their extreme rigidity had come to be regarded as curiosities.'[39] One of the liveliest transforming influences was T.H. Green, who argued forcefully that the state ought to remove all obstacles to the development of social capacity, such as those arising from lack of education, poor health and bad housing.[40]

Hobson himself – and later L.T. Hobhouse – were sensitive students of the changes and initiators of new views. The issues with which late Victorian and Edwardian Liberal intellectuals were having to concern themselves were social issues, and the practical politics, as Bland had prophesied, was increasingly pivoting on social politics. 'It is not about details that the people care or are stirred', wrote R.B. Haldane, 'what they seem to desire is that they should have something approaching to equality of chance of life with those among whom they live'.[41] Even old Conservative principles of property were reinterpreted in Radical terms, and in Hobhouse's arguments were converted into instruments of social justice.[42] Individualism itself was increasingly associated with the freeing of the powers of 'underprivileged' individuals. In 1909 Hobson commented that

the whole conception of the state disclosed by the new issues, as an instrument for the active adaptation of the economic and moral environment to the new needs of individual and social life, by securing full opportunities of self-development and social service for all citizens, was foreign to the Liberalism of the last generation.[43]

The welfare measures of the Liberal governments of 1905-14,

culminating in the bitterly controversial 'budget against poverty' of 1909 and Lloyd George's national insurance schemes against ill-health and unemployment in 1911, were in sharp contrast to the Gladstonian Liberalism of only thirty years before. 'They are so far removed from the old Liberal individualism', one Liberal historian has written recently, 'that they may be called social democracy rather than pure Liberalism.'[44]

III

That was the British story, more complex than it is usually told, and revealing a multiplicity of motives and inspirations.

German experience in the nineteenth century was in certain important respects different from that of Britain. If before 1900 factory legislation was more advanced in Britain than in any other European country, Germany had established a lead in social security legislation which the British Liberal governments of 1906 to 1914 tried to wipe out. Bismarck's reforms of the 1880s – laws of 1882, 1884 and 1889 introducing compulsory insurance against sickness, accidents, old age and invalidity – attracted immense interest in other European countries. Just as British factory legislation was copied overseas, so German social insurance stimulated foreign imitation. Denmark, for instance, copied all three German pensions schemes between 1891 and 1898, and Belgium between 1894 and 1903. Switzerland by a constitutional amendment in 1890 empowered the federal government to organise a system of national insurance. In Britain itself a friendly observer noted in 1890 that Bismarck had 'discovered where the roots of social evil lie. He has declared in words that burn that it is the duty of the state to give heed, above all, to the welfare of its weaker members.'[45]

More recently, Bismarck's social policy has been described by more than one writer as the creation of a welfare state.[46] The term is very misleading. Bismarck's legislation rested on a basic conservatism which Oastler himself would have appreciated[47] and was sustained by a bureaucracy which had no counterpart in Britain except perhaps in Chadwick's imagination. The Prussian idea and history of the state and the British idea and history of the state diverged long before the 1880s, and it is not fanciful to attribute some of the divergences to the presence or absence a century before of cameralism, the idea of the systematic application to government of administrative routines.

Equally important, the history of political economy in the two countries diverged just as markedly. The development of a school of historical economics provided a powerful academic reinforcement in Germany for *Sozialpolitik*. The refusal of historical economists to isolate economic phenomena, including economic man, their distrust of laws of political economy covering all ages and all societies, their critique of the motives and institutions of contemporary capitalism and their underlying belief in a social order, distinguished them sharply from classical political economists in Britain. Their influence was considerable enough for Schmoller, the most important figure in the history of the school, to argue forcefully that no Smithian was fit to occupy an academic Chair in Germany.[48]

Even among the precursors of the historical school and among economists who stayed aloof from Schmoller and his circle, there was a powerful tradition linking social reform with conservative views of society.[49] J.K. Rodbertus was a conservative monarchist who combined dislike of the class struggle and belief in state socialism. Adolf Wagner, who stayed aloof from Schmoller and admired Ricardo as the outstanding economic theorist, acknowledged his debt to Rodbertus when he gave a warm welcome to Bismarck's legislation.

According to Wagner, Germany had entered a new social period, characterised by new economic ideas, new political views and new social programmes. National economy (*Volkswirtschaft*) had to be converted into state economy (*Staatswirtschaft*): the foundation of a new economy would have to be welfare. The idea of regarding labour power as a commodity and wages as its price was inhuman as well as un-Christian. Wagner proposed a number of practical measures, some of which went further than those introduced by Bismarck. Schmoller, too, advocated policies aiming at

the re-establishment of a friendly relation between social classes, the removal or modification of injustice, a nearer approach to the principles of distributive justice, with the introduction of a social legislation which promotes progress and guarantees the moral and material elevation of the lower and middle classes.[50]

Bismarck, for whom the idea of insurance had a particular fascination both in his domestic and foreign policies, did not envisage a social policy which would go anywhere near as far as some of the 'socialists of the chair' would have wished. He objected, for example, to the limitation by law of the hours of women and children in factories and he was at least as stubborn as any mill owner of the Manchester School when theorists talked of state officials interfering with private concerns in agriculture or industry. He also disliked extensions of direct taxation. He wanted the state, however, to be actively involved in the financing and administering of the insurance schemes which he proposed, and he defended the introduction of these schemes – against both right-wing and left-wing opposition – in terms of the 'positive advancement of the welfare of the working classes'. 'The state', it was laid down in the preamble to the first and unsuccessful Bill of 1881, 'is not merely a necessary but a beneficent institution'. Bismarck disagreed with Theodor Lohmann, who drafted his first social insurance legislation, about whether the state should contribute directly to the costs of insurance. Bismarck got his way that it should, but the political parties objected and his first attempts at legislation foundered. It was a measure of his recognition of political realities that the idea of state contributions was dropped in 1884 when his Accident Insurance Bill was introduced. The law of 1889, providing for disability and old age pensions, did entail a flat-rate contribution from the imperial Treasury of 50 marks for each person receiving a pension, but this was a small element in the total cost and fell far short of the amount Bismarck had originally envisaged.

Many of Bismarck's critics accused him, not without justification, of seeking through his legislation to make German workers depend upon the state. The same charges have been made against the initiators of all welfare (and earlier of Poor Law) policy often without justification, yet it was Bismarck himself who drew a revealing distinction between the degrees of obedience (or subservience) of private servants and servants at court. The latter would 'put up with much more' than the former because they had pensions to look forward to. Welfare soothed the spirit, or perhaps tamed it. Bismarck's deliberate invocation of subservience is at the opposite end of the scale from the socialist invocation of equality as the goal of the welfare state. It is brutally simple, too, when compared with sophisticated Liberal attempts to define the conditions in which liberty and equality may be made to complement each other.[51] The invocation was, of course, bound up with conscious political calculation. Bismarck was anxious to make German social democracy less attractive to working men. He feared class war and wanted to postpone it as long as possible. His talks with Lassalle in 1863 had ranged over questions of this kind,[52] and in 1884 he argued explicitly that if the state would only 'show a little more Christian solicitude for the working man', then the social democrats would 'sound their siren song in vain'. 'The thronging to them will cease as soon as working men see that the government and legislative bodies are earnestly concerned for their welfare.'[53] It has been suggested that Bismarck was influenced by Napoleon III's successful handling of social policy as an instrument of politics. He certainly spent time seeking an 'alternative to socialism', and it was this aspect of his policy which gave what he did contemporary controversial significance throughout Europe.

His policy also provided a definite alternative to Liberalism. During the last years of his life when he was prepared to contemplate insurance against unemployment and when he talked of the right to work as enthusiastically as any Chartist, he was reflecting that sharp reaction against economic Liberalism which could be discerned, in different forms, in almost every country in Europe. Disraeli's social policy in his ministry of 1874-80 had somewhat similar features. It also had the added interest of appearing to realise hopes first formulated by Disraeli in the age of Oastler and the Chartists. In 1874 also a royalist and clerical majority in the French National Assembly carried a Factory Act, limiting hours of work of children below the age of twelve, which went further than a law of 1848 on the same subject. A later and more comprehensive Act of 1892 was the work of conservative republicans. The nineteenth century closed with a British Money-Lenders Act which, Professor Clapham has argued, in effect revived the medieval law of usury, the last remnants of which had been swept away, it was thought for ever, in 1854.[54]

Medieval attitudes to welfare were echoed most strongly in Christian apologetics. Papal encyclicals, notably *Rerum Novarum* (1891), were not only manifestos in crusades against Liberalism or socialism but were also important documents in the evolution of *Sozialpolitik*. De Mun, von Ketteler and von Vogelsang were writers who advocated particular or general welfare policies: so did Heinrich Pesch, who has been singled out for special treatment by Schumpeter. Among Protestants also there was renewed call for a social gospel. It is not without interest that Lohmann, who had advised Bismarck and went on to advise William II in the formulation of the far-reaching Labour Code of 1891, was a deeply religious man, the son of a Westphalian Lutheran pastor. Canon W.L. Blackley, the pioneer of old age pensions schemes not only in Britain but in other parts of the world, and the founder of the National Providence League, was an honorary canon of Winchester Cathedral. On the Liberal side – and there was a close association in Britain between religious nonconformity and political Liberalism – Seebohm Rowntree, one of the first systematic investigators of the facts of poverty, was a Quaker. The whole attack on the limitations of the Poor Law was guided, though not exclusively, by men of strong religious principles.

IV

The complexity of the nineteenth-century background contrasts at first sight with the simplicity of the twentieth-century story. For a tangle of tendencies we have a trend, a trend culminating in greater order and simplification. In fact, however, the twentieth-century story has its own complexities, which are now in the process of being unravelled. Professor Titmuss has shown, for instance, that Lloyd

George's national health insurance legislation of 1911, a landmark in trend legislation, was the culmination of a long and confused period in which doctors had been engaged in a 'Hobbesian struggle for independence from the power and authority exercised over their lives, their work and their professional values by voluntary associations and private enterprise'. He has maintained that the legislation of 1911 can only be understood if it is related, as so much else in the twentieth century must be related, to the history of hidden pressures from established interests and a sectional demand for an 'enlargement of professional freedom'.[55] Many of the complexities of twentieth-century history certainly lie buried in the records of the network of private concerns and of professional groups which came into existence in the nineteenth century. There can be no adequate historical explanation which concerns itself in large terms with the state alone. Just as the administration of welfare is complicated in practice and can be understood only in detail, so the outline of welfare state legislation only becomes fully intelligible when it ceases to be an outline, and when it looks beyond parliamentary legislation to such crucial twentieth-century relationships as those between governments and pressure groups and experts and the public.

Yet there are five factors in twentieth-century welfare history (other than warfare, one of the most powerful of factors) which are beyond dispute and dominant enough to need little detailed research. They are, first, the basic transformation in the attitude towards poverty, which made the nineteenth-century Poor Law no longer practicable in democratic societies; second, the detailed investigation of social contingencies which directed attention to the need for particular social policies; third, the close association between unemployment and welfare policy; fourth, the development within market capitalism itself of welfare philosophies and practices; and fifth, the influence of working-class pressures on the content and tone of welfare legislation.

The first and second of these five factors can scarcely be studied in isolation. The basis of the nineteenth-century British Poor Law of 1834 was economic logic. That logic was strained when empirical sociologists, like Charles Booth and Rowntree, showed that a large number of poor people were poor through no fault of their own, but because of tendencies within the market system. They pitted statistics against logic by attempting to count how many people were living in poverty and by surveying the various forms that their poverty assumed.[56] Prior to Booth's 'grand inquest', Beatrice Webb wrote, 'neither the individualist nor the socialist could state with any approach to accuracy what exactly was the condition of the people of England'.[57] Once the results of the inquest had been published 'the net effect was to give an entirely fresh impetus to the general adoption of the policy of securing to every individual, as the very basis of his life and work, a prescribed natural minimum of the requisites for efficient parenthood and citizenship'.

Booth's thinking about economics was far less radical than his thinking about welfare, but Rowntree, who drew a neat distinction between primary and secondary poverty, the former being beyond the control of the wage-earner, went on to advocate specific welfare policies, ranging from old age pensions to family allowances, public-provided housing to supervised welfare conditions in factories. The policies which he urged at various stages of his long life became, indeed, the main constituent policies of the welfare state.[58] Like the welfare state, however, Rowntree stopped short of socialism. He separated questions of welfare from questions of economic power, and remained throughout his life a new Liberal. The main tenet of his Liberalism was that the community could not afford the waste, individual and social, which was implied in an industrial society divided naturally into rich and very poor. Poverty was as much of a social problem as pauperism. The roots of poverty were to be found not in individual irresponsibility or incapacity but in social maladjustment. Poverty, in short, was not the fault of the poor: it was the fault of society. Quite apart from socialist pressure, society had to do something about poverty once it was given facts about its extent, its incidence (Rowntree drew attention to the cycle of poverty in families), its ramifications and its consequences. All facts were grist to the mill. They included facts not only about wages but about nutrition: subsistence levels could only be measured when nutritional criteria were taken into account.

Sharp turns of thought about poverty were by no means confined to people in Britain. There were signs of fundamental rethinking, allied as we have seen to feeling,[59] both in Europe and the United States at the end of the nineteenth and the beginning of the twentieth centuries.[60] The survey method, which Booth and Rowntree depended upon, was capable of general applicability.[61] The limitations of systematic charity had been exposed at the beginning of the industrial age. It is no coincidence that in Britain and Sweden, two countries with distinct welfare histories, there was keen debate about the Poor Law at almost exactly the same time. In Sweden the Poor Relief Order of 1871, with its checks on poor relief, was criticised by the Swedish Poor Relief Association which was formed at the first General Swedish Poor Law Congress in 1906. A year later, the government appointed a committee to draw up proposals for fresh legislation governing poor relief and the treatment of vagrants. In Britain the Royal Commission on the Poor Laws, which was appointed in 1905 and reported in 1909, covered almost all topics in social policy. The issues were clearly stated and both the social contingencies and the necessary policies of social control were carefully examined. Although new direct legislation was slow to come in both countries, there was much indirect legislation, and in both countries there were demands for what Beatrice Webb called 'an enforced minimum of civilised life'.[62]

The main threat to that minimum in the later twentieth century came from 'mass involuntary unemployment'. This, of course, was a world phenomenon which strained Poor Law and social service systems in most countries and presented a threat – or a challenge – to politicians and administrators. In Britain, which was the first country to introduce compulsory unemployment insurance (1911, greatly extended in 1920), the system of relief broke down under the stresses of the 1930s. Insurance benefits, linked to contributions, were stringently restricted, and while tussles about the means test were leading to extreme differences of outlook between socialists and their opponents, an Unemployment Assistance Board, founded in 1934, was providing a second-line income maintenance service, centrally administered. In Europe there was an extension of unemployment aid schemes, whether by insurance (the Swedes, for example, introduced state-subsidised unemployment insurance in 1934), 'doles', or in certain cases positive state-run schemes of public works. In the United States and Canada, where there had been entrenched resistance to government intervention in welfare provision, new legislation was passed,[63] while in New Zealand, which had long lost its reputation as a pioneer of welfare, there was a remarkable bout of state intervention after the return of a Labour government to power in 1935. The Social Security Act of 1938 contained a list of health services and pension benefits which, while resting on previous legislation, were everywhere hailed as a bold and daring experiment. The Minister of Finance anticipated later welfare legislators in other countries by arguing unequivocally that 'to suggest the inevitability of slumps and booms, associated as they are with affluence for a limited number during a period, and followed by unemployment, destitution, hardship and privation for the masses, is to deny all conscious progressive purpose'.[64] According to the ILO, the 1938 New Zealand Act 'has, more than any other law, determined the practical meaning of social security, and so has deeply influenced the course of legislation in other countries'.[65]

Twentieth-century social security legislation raises many interesting general issues – the relevance of the insurance principle, for example; the relationship between negative social policy and positive economic policy; and, underlying all else, the nature and extent of the responsibilities of the state. Insurance principles, actuarially unsound though they may be and inadequate though they have proved as instruments of finance at moments of crisis, have been historically significant. They removed the stigma of pauperism from a social service, reconciled voluntary and compulsory approaches to provision, and facilitated public approval of state expenditures which otherwise would have been challenged. They thus served as a link between old ways of thinking (self help and mutual help) and new. Positive economic policy was in the first instance, as in Roosevelt's America, the child of improvisation: its systematic justification had to await revolutions in political economy (Keynes and after) which accompanied shifts in social power.

The difference in tone and content between two books by William Beveridge – his *Unemployment* (1909) and his *Full Employment in a Free Society* (1944) – is one of the best indications of the change in the world of ideas between the early and middle periods of the twentieth century. Beveridgism, an important British phenomenon during the Second World War, had sufficient popular appeal to show that the world of ideas and the world of practical politics were not very far apart. For the intellectuals and for the public the magnification of governmental power – and the enormous increase in government expenditure financed from taxation – were taken for granted.

The fourth and fifth factors are also related to each other. In all advanced industrial countries in the twentieth century there has been a movement towards welfare in industry – 'industrial betterment' it was originally called – which has been accompanied by the emergence of philosophies of human relations, welfare management and industrial and labour psychology.[66] The movement has to be explained in terms of both economics and politics. A managerial revolution, limited though it may have been in its economic effects, has accelerated the tendencies making for welfare capitalism. The need to find acceptable incentives for workers, to avoid labour disputes and to secure continuous production, to raise output in phases of technical change and (more recently) to hold labour permissively in a period of full employment has often driven where human relations philosophies have failed to inspire. Welfare, a word which was often resented by workers when it was applied within the structure of the firm, was, indeed, used in a business context before it began to be applied to a new kind of state. Within state schemes of welfare, employers have made, and are expected to make, sizeable contributions. In France and Italy, in particular, obligatory social charges as a percentage of assessable wages constituted the main source of welfare expenditure.[67] In the United States business rather than the state was, and is, expected directly to provide a network of welfare services. As in all such situations, the provision of welfare varies immensely from one firm (giant businesses are at one end of the scale) to another.

> In contrast to these countries, such as Great Britain, which appear to regard government (for reasons which have been stated above) merely as the most effective of several possible institutions for the administration of income security programmes or the provision of services, ... a society like the United States that distrusts its government is likely to seek to organise its social security services in such a way as to keep government activity to a minimum.[68]

American experience, fashioned more by economic growth than by depression, in contrast to the experience described in other countries, shows that this likelihood has been converted into fact.

It is not accidental that the labour movement in the United States has showed little interest in socialism and that its leaders have chosen of their own volition to bargain for fringe benefits at the level of the plant. In most European countries, particularly in Britain and in Scandinavia, there has been a tendency for working-class pressures to lead to greater state intervention. In Britain, nineteenth-century patterns of mutual dependence through voluntary action, which impressed so many observers from de Tocqueville onwards, have become less dominant, except in the field of industrial relations where they have very tenaciously survived.[69]

As we have seen, the demand for state action has been related to the rights of citizenship, to equality as well as to security. During the critical period between the two world wars, when economic and social conditions were very difficult, welfare measures were demanded and provided piecemeal with varying conditions of regulation and administration, 'a frightening complexity of eligibility and benefit according to individual circumstances, local boundaries, degrees of need and so forth'.[70] The Second World War, which sharpened the sense of democracy, led to demands both for tidying up and for comprehensiveness. It encouraged the move from minima to optima, at least in relation to certain specified services, and it made all residual paternalisms seem utterly inadequate and increasingly archaic. It was in the light of changes in working-class life within a more equal community that post-war writers noted the extent to which the social services of the earlier part of the century had been shaped by assumptions about the nature of man, 'founded on outer rather than on inner observation', on the 'norms of behaviour expected by one class from another'.[71] This period of criticism has already ended. The assumptions which shaped the welfare state have themselves been criticised,[72] and radical political slogans have concentrated more and more on differences of income between mature and underdeveloped countries rather than on differences within mature countries themselves.

It may well be that in a world setting the five twentieth-century factors discussed in this article will be considered less important than other factors – the total size of the national income in different countries, for example, and the share of that income necessary for industrial (as or when distinct from social) investment, or even, on a different plane, the nature of family structure. Is not the making of the industrial welfare state in part at least the concomitant of the decline of the large, extended welfare family? How far has the pressure of women (or just the presence of women voters) in industrial societies encouraged the formulation of welfare objectives? The historian does well to leave such large questions to be answered rather than to suggest that all or even the most important part of the truth is already known.

NOTES

1 ILO, International Labour Conference, 34th Session, *Objectives and Minimum Standards of Social Security* (1950), pp. 3-4. See also 'Survey of Post-War Trends in Social Security', in *International Labour Review*, June, July, August, September, 1949.

2 ILO, *Approaches to Social Security* (1942), p. i; *Objectives and Advanced Standards of Social Security* (1952); D. Thomson, A. Briggs and E. Meyer, *Patterns of Peacemaking* (1945), p. 340, Chapter VII, Appendix II.

3 R. M. Titmuss, *Problems of Social Policy* (1950), p. 506.

4 C. L. Mowat, *The Charity Organization Society, 1869-1913* (1961), p. 75.

5 A. V. Dicey, *Law and Public Opinion in England during the Nineteenth Century* (1914 edn), p. i.

6 Titmuss, *op. cit.*, pp. 509-10.

7 Cmnd. 6550, secs. 8, 33. See also Cmnd. 6404 and A. Briggs, 'The Social Services', in *The British Economy*, 1945-50 (ed. G. D. N. Worswick and P. Ady, 1952), pp. 365-80.

8 T. H. Marshall, *Citizenship and Social Class* (1949), pp. 47, 48.

9 J. Bentham, *Works* (ed. J. Bowring, 1843), vol. III, p. 35. Cp. J. M. Keynes' view of the agenda of the state, in *The End of Laissez Faire* (1926).

10 S. Webb, in *Fabian Essays* (1889, 1948 edn), pp. 43, 46.

11 H. Bland, ibid., p. 198.

12 J. R. McCulloch, *Treatise on the Succession to Property vacant by Death* (1848), p. 156.

13 The passage comes from his Oxford lectures of 1847-8. It is quoted in L. Robbins, *The Theory of Economic Policy* (1953), p. 45. See also for a modern comment on the history of the term *laissez-faire*, D. H. McGregor, *Economic Thought and Policy* (1949), Chapter III.

14   G. Wallas, *Human Nature in Politics* (1908, 1929 edn), p. 13. There is a fascinating, if controversial account of the relationship between Poor Law and market, in K. Polanyi, *Origins of Our Time* (1946).

15   *The Fleet Papers* (1842), p. 58; (1841), p. 39; *Leeds Intelligencer*, 10 August 1833.

16   *Deutsche Allgemeine Zeitung*, 6 July 1843; C. Driver, *Tory Radical* (1946).

17   The phrase is taken from his *Stones of Venice* (1851) (*Works*, ed. Cook and Wedderburn, vol. XI, p. 263). The term 'living wage' was first used by the English Co-operator, Lloyd James, in the *Beehive*, July 1874. The phrase 'fair day's wages for a fair day's work' was older.

18   H. S. Foxwell, *The Claims of Labour* (1886), p. 249.

19   Quoted in S. E. Finer, *The Life and Times of Sir Edwin Chadwick* (1952), p. 477.

20   N. Senior, *Journals Kept in France and Italy* (1843), pp. 150-2. In this journal Senior compared England with Switzerland. The 'pure democracies' of small Swiss cantons, he claimed, resisted the spell of 'the political economy of the poor' because all their adult males 'venerated their clergy, their men of birth and of wealth and their institutions'. He did not see that 'deference' was as much a feature of nineteenth-century England. Estimates of the likely effect of the extension of suffrage on popular demands for a new political economy were influenced by estimates of the power of 'deference'. See W. Bagehot, *The English Constitution* (1872 edn).

21   'Much of that tact which dreads the ballot is a dread of the loss of aristocratical influence which prevails by gold, and of the gain of the influence which prevails by popularity' (Letter of 14 October 1852, quoted in Finer, *op. cit.*, p. 478.)

22   For details, now see D. Roberts, *Victorian Origins of the British Welfare State* (1960), esp. pp. 152-244.

23   McGregor, *op. cit.*, p. 54.

24   J. B. Brebner, '*Laissez-faire* and State Intervention in Nineteenth-century Britain', in supplement VIII (1948) to the *Journal of Economic History*. For the dangers of explaining processes of change in terms of Dicey's 'abstractions', see also O. MacDonagh, 'The Nineteenth-century Revolution in Government: a Re-appraisal', in the *Historical Journal* (1958).

25   Bland, *op. cit.*, pp. 195, p. 200.

26   ibid., p. 200.

27   Quoted in the *New Reasoner*, no. 4, 1948, 'A Note on the Welfare State'.

28   See C. Tsuzuki, *H. M. Hyndman and British Socialism* (1961), pp. 56, 148.

29   *The Fleet Papers* (1842), p. 290.

30   Yet Beatrice Webb herself said of her Poor Law scheme in 1907: 'The whole theory of the mutual obligation between the individual and the State ... is taken straight out of the nobler aspect of the medieval manor'. (*Our Partnership* (1948), p. 385.)

31 H. L. Beales, 'The Making of Social Policy' (*L. T. Hobhouse Memorial
    Trust Lecture* (1946), p. 5). The mercantilist parallel usually refers not
    only to welfare policy but to population policy (which, through such
    devices as family allowances, has welfare implications) and to pro-
    tection (which also has labour implications).

32 A. Métin, *Le Socialisme sans doctrines* (1901). See also A. Siegfried,
    Democracy in New Zealand (1906).

33 Métin, *op. cit.*, p. 229; J. B. Condliffe, *New Zealand in the Making*
    (1930), pp. 164-5.

34 W. K. Hancock, *Australia* (1930), p. 61. For general reflections on the
    role of the state in Australia, see S. Encel, 'The Concept of the State in
    Australian Politics', in the *Australian Journal of Politics and History*,
    May 1960.

35 See A. Wilson and G. S. Mackay, *Old Age Pensions, An Historical and
    Critical Study* (1941), Chapters II, III, IV. See also R. M. Titmuss, *Essays
    on 'The Welfare State'* (1958), pp. 18-19.

36 C. L. Mowat, 'The Approach to the Welfare State in Great Britain',
    in the *American Historical Review*, vol. LXXV (1952). It has also been
    called 'an extended form of outdoor relief'. See B. Abel-Smith, 'Social
    Security', in M. Ginsberg (ed.), *Law and Opinion in England in the
    Twentieth Century* (1959), pp. 352 ff.

37 W. Pember Reeves, *State Experiments in Australia and New Zealand*
    (1902), vol. II, p. 244. For recent appraisals, see W. B. Sutch, *The Quest
    for Security in New Zealand* (1942); R. Mendelsohn, *Social Security in
    the British Commonwealth* (1954).

38 J. A. Hobson, *The Evolution of Modern Capitalism* (1902), p. 321.

39 A. Milner, Introduction to A. Toynbee, *Lectures on the Industrial
    Revolution* (1923 edn), p. xxv. Toynbee anticipated the Fabians in these
    lectures, delivered to working men in the early 1880s, by contrasting the
    age of capitalist anarchy with the age of regulation which had preceded
    it. For movements in Liberal political economy at this time, see T. W.
    Hutchison, *A Review of Economic Doctrines, 1870-1929* (1953),
    Chapter I.

40 T. H. Green, *Lectures on the Principles of Political Obligation* (1895
    edn), pp. 206-9.

41 R. B. Haldane, *Autobiography* (1929), pp. 212-14.

42 See, in particular, L. T. Hobhouse, *Elements of Social Justice* (1922);
    The Labour Movement (1893); *Democracy and Reaction* (1904);
    Liberalism (1911); 'The Philosophical Theory of Property', in *Property,
    its Duties and Rights* (ed. C. Gore, 1915). For the significance of his
    work, see J. A. Hobson and M. Ginsberg, *The Life and Work of L. T.
    Hobhouse* (1931).

43 J. A. Hobson, *The Crisis of Liberalism* (1909), p. 3. For Hobson, see
    H. N. Brailsford, 'The Life and Work of J. A. Hobson' (*L. T. Hobhouse
    Memorial Trust Lecture*, 1948).

44 R. B. McCallum, 'The Liberal Outlook', in M. Ginsberg (ed.), *Law
    and Opinion in England in the Twentieth Century*, p. 75.

45 W. H. Dawson, *Bismarck and State Socialism* (1890), p. ix.

46 S. B. Fay, 'Bismarck's Welfare State', in *Current History*, vol. XVIII (1950).

47 'A British Bismarck', Professor Driver has written, 'would have commanded all his uncritical devotion, but Wellington was no Bismarck' (Driver, *op. cit.*, p. 189).

48 J. A. Schumpeter, *History of Economic Analysis* (1954), p. 765.

49 The pre-history of this approach leads back to Sismondi who has important links with Mill and the English Utilitarians. He is a seminal figure in the critique of industrialism and the demand for welfare legislation.

50 A. Wagner, *Rede über die soziale Frage* (1872), pp. 8-9. G. Von Schmoller, *Über einige Grundfragen des Rechts und der Volkswirtschaft* (1875), p. 92.

51 For the background of these attempts, see M. Ginsberg, 'The Growth of Social Responsibility', in *Law and Opinion in England in the Twentieth Century*, pp. 3-26.

52 See G. Mayer, *Bismarck und Lassalle* (1927).

53 Dawson, *op. cit.*, p. 35. This remark was made in 1884. Five years earlier, the Emperor, referring to the anti-socialist law of 1878, had said, 'a remedy cannot alone be sought in the repression of socialistic excesses; there must be simultaneously the positive advancement of the welfare of the working classes'. (Quoted ibid., p. 110.)

54 J. H. Clapham, *An Economic History of Modern Britain*, vol. III (1938), p. 445.

55 R. M. Titmuss, 'Health', in Ginsberg (ed.), *Law and Opinion in England in the Twentieth Century*, p. 308. Cp. p. 313: 'The fundamental issue of 1911 was not ... between individualism and collectivism, between contract and status; but between different forms of collectivism, different degrees of freedom; open or concealed power.'

56 C. Booth, *Life and Labour of the People in London*, 17 vols (1892-1903); B. S. Rowntree, *Poverty: A Study of Town Life* (1901).

57 B. Webb, *My Apprenticeship* (1926), p. 239.

58 For Booth, see T. S. and M. B. Simey, *Charles Booth, Social Scientist* (1960); for Rowntree, see A. Briggs, *Seebohm Rowntree* (1961). See also B. S. Rowntree and G. R. Lavers, *Poverty and the Welfare State* (1951).

59 'In intensity of feeling', Booth wrote, 'and not in statistics, lies the power to move the world. But by statistics must this power be guided if it would move the world aright'. (*Life and Labour, Final Volume, Notes on Social Influences and Conclusion* (1903), p. 178.)

60 See, *inter alia*, C. L. Mowat, *The Charity Organisation Society;* K. de Schweinitz, *England's Road to Social Security* (1943); C. W. Pitkin, *Social Politics and Modern Democracies*, 2 vols (1931), vol. II being concerned with France; R. H. Bremner, *From the Depths; The Discovery of Poverty in the United States* (1956).

61 See M. Abrams, *Social Surveys and Social Action* (1951); P. V. Young, *Scientific Social Surveys and Research* (1950); D. C. Caradog Jones, *Social Surveys* (1955).

62 The British controversy is well described in U. Cormack, 'The Welfare

State', *Loch Memorial Lecture* (1953). For Sweden, see The Royal Social Board, *Social Work and Legislation in Sweden* (1938).

63 Mendelsohn, *op. cit.*, Chapter III: J.C. Brown, *Public Relief, 1929-39* (1940); E.A. Williams, *Federal Aid for Relief* (1939); P.H. Douglas, *Social Security in the United States* (1939 edn).

64 Quoted in W.K. Hancock, *Survey of British Commonwealth Affairs*, vol. II (1940), p. 275.

65 ILO, *Social Security in New Zealand* (1949), p. 111.

66 See A. Briggs, 'The Social Background', in H. Clegg and A. Flanders (eds), *Industrial Relations in Great Britain* (1955); L. Urwick and E.F.L. Brech, *The Human Factor in Management, 1795-1943* (1944); E.D. Proud, *Welfare Work, Employers' Experiments for Improving Working Conditions in Factories* (1916); E.T. Kelly (ed.), *Welfare Work in Industry* (1925); P.E.P., 'The Human Factor in Industry', *Planning* (March 1948).

67 PEP, 'Free Trade and Security', *Planning* (July 1957); 'A Comparative Analysis of the Cost of Social Security', in *International Labour Review* (1953).

68 E.M. Burns, *Social Security and Public Policy* (1956), p. 274.

69 For the nature of the nineteenth-century pattern, see J.M. Baernreither, *English Associations of Working Men* (1893). For industrial relations, see Clegg and Flanders, *op. cit.*

70 R.M. Titmuss, *Essays on the Welfare State*, pp. 21-2.

71 ibid., p. 19.

72 See A. Peacock, 'The Welfare Society', *Unservile State Papers* (1960); R.M. Titmuss, 'The Irresponsible Society', *Fabian Tracts* (1960); J. Saville, 'The Welfare State', in *The New Reasoner*, no. 3 (1957).

III

LOOKING BACKWARDS

I am the heir of all the ages in the foremost files of time.

Tennyson

In order to estimate its [the nineteenth century's] full importance and grandeur ... we must compare it not with any preceding century, or even with the last millennium, but with the whole historical period – perhaps even with the whole period that has elapsed since the stone age.

A.R.Wallace

These sequels of which the historian himself may not be consciously aware are of all types and levels of specificity. They are not only actions and events – they are also thoughts and sentiments. They form part of the endless reciprocity between past and present – between the historian and his subject matter – whose full complexity the idealist metaphor of 're-enactment' is powerless to convey.

H.Stuart Hughes

10   Saxons, Normans and Victorians

I

When Queen Victoria died in 1901, the *Annual Register* remarked that the feeling of forlornness which swept the country had no parallel since the death of King Alfred. The men of the new century were driven to seek a Saxon parallel. So too were men at the beginning of the Queen's reign. A William IV plate had the King's head on it and the inscription 'the first radical monarch since Alfred'. Clearly in 1837, as in 1901, you could find in England a popular view of the Saxons which had little to do with the facts of history. Nobody knew how 'England' – whatever that was – felt at the death of Alfred; as for William IV and Alfred, whether or not Alfred could be fairly described as a Radical, William IV certainly could not.

Our popular attitudes to history rest on myths, not on facts; and the early and late Victorians, for all their increasing material sophistication, were as dependent on myths as any other generations. Alfred was a Victorian hero, whose biography was written by Thomas Hughes, the author of *Tom Brown's Schooldays*. He was depicted as an inspiring leader who had created a society based not on a cash nexus but on mutual responsibility. For those Victorians who cared little about mutual responsibility, he could be treated equally enthusiastically as a hero of freedom, as in Charles Kingsley's *Hereward the Wake – Last of the English* (1866); and he could figure, too, in the Positivist calendar of 1892, *The New Calendar of Great Men*, as the first of 558 heroes 'from Alfred to Washington'.

Somewhat surprisingly, at first sight, Thomas Carlyle, who had been the most active and certainly the most articulate of all the nineteenth-century hero-worshippers, had a strong anti-Saxon bias, treating all Saxons comprehensively as drunkards 'lumbering about in pot-bellied equanimity'. For him, William the Conqueror was the hero, the man who decreed order where there had been no order. Carlyle always preferred order to freedom. He pictures William saying to his men in 1066 in authentic Carlylean style, 'Noble fighters, this is the land we have gained; be I Lord in it . . . and be ye Loyal Men around me in it; and we will stand by one another as soldiers round a captain, for again we shall have need of one another.' We are back to mutual responsibility again, this time in Norman dress. The moral was plain

215

to Carlyle. The Victorian captains of industry, in imitation of 'the Cliffords, Fitzadelms and Chivalry Fighters' should become noble knights, placing the welfare of their men and the good of society above any selfish desire for wealth and success. Then their workers would become noble workers, serving their captains with patience and loyalty, and so, peace would reign in every office, shop, and factory.[1]

Carlyle's *Past and Present* (1843) shows how the early Victorians used the past for purposes of dramatic contrast to highlight what they thought were the failings of the present. Saxons or Normans could be portrayed with long, fair hair or with bows and arrows, but they were endowed with Victorian motives and values. Nor for the popular reader was there any need to choose finally between Saxons and Normans, whatever the strength of initial prejudices might be. Both Saxons and Normans had contributed to the making of England, the England which had reached a position of world dominance in the nineteenth century. In both cases, indeed, their stock was Teutonic; and as E. A. Freeman, an academic historian, pointed out near the 800th anniversary of the Norman Conquest, 'if we allow ourselves to use, as people constantly do, the words "Saxon" or "Anglo-Saxon" as chronological terms, we altogether wipe out the unbroken life of our nation ... People talk of the "Saxon period" and the "Norman period" as if they followed one another like periods of geology or like Hesiod's races of men.'[2] William accepted much that had gone before, and in time it was possible for Normans to look back to the 'laws of Edward the Confessor', even to canonise him. 'In a few generations we led captive our conquerors.'[3]

There was a comforting sense of historical continuity in such an interpretation, which Freeman himself thought of as a national epic.[4] It is important to note, however, that though this version of history became very congenial to many Victorians, particularly historians, it never completely destroyed popular pro-Saxon prejudice. A very popular history book, Mrs Markham's *History of England*, had a catechism at the end of each chapter of narrative; which in the case of the chapter on 'England from Egbert to Harold' read as follows:

> *George:* I cannot help being sorry that we shall have no more of the Saxon kings. I do not feel as if I should like the Normans at all ...
> *His mother:* You are a little mistaken in supposing you have quite done with the Saxons. Your papa and I are Saxons.
> *Mary:* You a Saxon, mamma! Why I thought you were an Englishwoman.
> *Her mother:* So I am; but, as the Saxons continued in the country after the Conquest, and were much more numerous than the Norman settlers, we are still almost all of us chiefly of Saxon descent; and our language, and many of our habits and customs, sufficiently declare our origin.[5]

The radical historian Goldwin Smith, predecessor of J. W. Stubbs and E. A. Freeman as Regius Professor of Modern History at Oxford, settled firmly in his still readable *History of the United Kingdom* on the Saxon side.

> Philosophic historians call the Norman Conquest a blessing in disguise. Disguised the blessing certainly was to those whose blood dyed the hill of Senlac, or whose lands were taken from them and given to a stranger. Disguised it was to the perishing thousands of the ravaged north. Disguised it was to the whole of the people, enslaved to foreign masters, and for the time down-trodden and despised. But was it in any sense a blessing? Why was England in need of the Norman? ... The independent self-development of a nation purely Teutonic, not in blood only – (the Normans were that) – but in character and institutions, was lost to humanity ... Civilization generally was thrown back by the havoc. ... although so completely did the Norman element at last blend with the English, that to doubt the beneficence of the Norman Conquest seems like a disparagement of ourselves.[6]

II

To understand the pro-Saxon bias in popular writing and above all in Radical writing, it is necessary to go back for centuries through English history to trace the development of what has been called 'the theory of the Norman yoke'.[7] According to this theory, before 1066 the Anglo-Saxons had lived as free and equal citizens and had governed themselves with the aid of representative institutions. The Norman Conquest robbed them of their liberty and imposed upon them the yoke of an alien king and of alien landlords. Yet the people had never quite forgotten their lost rights and fought from time to time to recover them. The sense of lost rights was particularly strong in the struggles of the seventeenth century when 'the Saxon model of government' was extolled, and these were struggles much studied by the Victorians. It was also strong, however, in much eighteenth-century Radical writing on both sides of the Atlantic. Thomas Jefferson, for instance, collected every scrap of evidence he could find of the history of his Saxon ancestors, who had realised, in his view, his own conceptions of political liberty; while in England a fascinating political tract of 1771, an *Historical Essay on the English Constitution*, described in bold and firm generalisations how the Norman Conquest had destroyed 'all the elective power, constitutionally placed in the people of England, and reversed the Saxon form of government which was founded on the common rights of mankind.'[8] The name of Alfred was invoked – this was a relatively new theme, taken up, as we have seen, by the Victorians – as 'a prince of the most exalted merit that ever graced the English throne'. 'If ever God Almighty did concern himself about forming a government for mankind to live happily under', the pamphlet concluded, 'it was that which was established in England by our Saxon forefathers.'[9]

It is easy to see from this brief account how the idea of the Norman yoke provided a theory of history which, true or false – and again it was largely false – served as a myth and gave emotional power to people who wished to change the existing order. Some believers in the theory were moderates, seeing in the common law a continuing Saxon dispensation: others were extremists, strongly opposed to feudalism in all its forms, including landed and aristocratic power, the system of primogeniture and the game laws. Famous medieval names were used to support the argument – not least, that of Robin Hood and Wat Tyler, around whom new myths were woven. Ned Ludd was located in Sherwood Forest: one of the most active Chartists in Bradford, a man who sold pikes, called himself Wat Tyler. Although the sense of a new industrial yoke took away some of the power behind the sense of an older historical yoke, the theory of the Norman yoke did not disappear during the years of rapid economic, social and eventually political change from the 1780s to the 1830s. Tom Paine preferred talk of abstract rights to be secured to talk of lost historical rights which had to be recovered, yet even he stated categorically that conquest and tyranny, along with lawyers and tithes, had been transplanted from Normandy to England with the Norman Conquest. 'And the country is yet disfigured with the marks.'[10] Other Radicals of the 1790s explicitly dissociated themselves, as did Henry Yorke of Sheffield, from Paine's lack of interest in the Saxon constitution and extolled 'that magnanimous government which we derived from our Saxon fathers and from the prodigious mind of the immortal Alfred. '[11]

Arguments derived both from abstract rights and from Saxon rights continued to be advanced side by side both by middle-class and by working-class reformers, and the latter were particularly prominent in the different stages of the struggle for parliamentary reform from the 1780s to the 1830s. The London Corresponding Society, a pioneer working-class Radical organisation of the 1790s, declared that 'the natural and imprescriptible right of the people to universal suffrage is founded not only in justice and true policy, but in the ancient constitution of the country'. While some of the items in its programme anticipated the social welfare language of the twentieth century, the Society emphasised that 'its object was not to change, but to restore: not to displace, but to reinstate the constitution upon its true principles and original ground.'

T. H. B. Oldfield's *The History of the Original Constitution of Parliament from the Time of the Britons to the Present Day*, published in 1797, set out to prove that in pre-Norman England there had been annual parliaments and universal householder suffrage, and the six volumes of his *History of Representation*, published in 1819, elaborated the theme. The same theme can be traced in platform speeches of the Birmingham Political Union from 1830 to 1832,[12] and in orations made at Chartist demonstrations after 1836. Of course, the historic argument could be pressed to quite absurd extremes. One of Oldfield's friends claimed that he had prepared a careful plan to end the miseries of Sierra Leone, a new African settlement founded by the Evangelicals. The plan was simple – to introduce King Alfred's frank-pledge there, a certain remedy, he maintained, for all social evils.[13]

The first real Radical attack on the theory of the Norman yoke came from Richard Carlile in 1820. Parliaments, he insisted, were not a primitive institution, but had been established in 1265 by the armed violence of Simon de Montfort. 'What is called the [Saxon] constitution of England is a mere farce and bye-word.'[14] Carlile loved to strip away what he considered to be 'illusions', social, political or religious, and he demanded revolutionary changes in society and government, if need be by nineteenth-century armed force. Ten years later, the Chartist newspaper, *Cleave's Penny Gazette* also ridiculed 'demands for the restoration of Saxon rights'.[15] Yet one of the so-called 'physical force' Chartists – Peter Bussey of Bradford, a friend of Bradford's Wat Tyler – set out the full Norman yoke theory in a speech in the West Riding long after the processes of nineteenth-century industrialisation had transformed Northern society.[16]

In general, the theory of the yoke persisted longest in relation not to the demand for parliamentary reform but in relation to attacks on the aristocracy; and in these attacks there were powerful middle-class voices as well as voices of popular Radicalism or of Chartism, like William Cobbett and Bronterre O'Brien. R. W. Emerson called the Norman founders of the peerage 'filthy thieves',[17] while *The Poor Man's Guardian* described the English aristocracy of the day as:

'A most tremendous host
Of locusts from the coast;
A beggarly, destructive breed,
Sprung from the BASTARD'S spurious seed'.[18]

Julian Harney's *Democratic Review* argued in 1849 in scarcely less lurid language that

this huge monopoly, this intolerable usurpation of the soil, had its foundation in force and fraud ... From the hour of the Norman Conquest ... the whole history of the ancestors of the present usurpers of the soil is a crusade of confiscation, plunder, rapine and devastation ... The present aristocracy are the descendants of freebooters.[19]

The opponents of primogeniture – inheritance through the eldest son – continued to attack the Normans throughout the nineteenth century – down to Lloyd George's Budget of 1909. 'The custom of primogeniture', the Oxford economic historian, Thorold Rogers, exclaimed in a speech of 1873, 'was introduced into this country by William the Norman. It is a symbol of the nation's slavery to a foreign conqueror, just as it is at the present time the means by which the owners of the great landed estates appropriate to themselves all, or nearly all, the forces of government.'[20]

III

Unlike most of the other names which I have quoted in this account of the development of the theory of the Norman yoke, Thorold Rogers was an academic historian and economist and a lecturer at Oxford University. Before turning in more detail to the academic Victorian approach to the Saxons and the Normans, it is important to stress that the serious academic study of the middle ages had not gone very far by the beginning of Victoria's reign. Documentation was poor, and it was not until 1838 – one year after Queen Victoria came to the throne – that, following the report of a Select Committee, the Public Record Office Act was passed. 'The history of England is not merely imperfect and erroneous', it had been remarked authoritatively a few years earlier, 'but a discredit to the country, for almost every new document proves the current histories false. Scarcely a statement will bear the test of truth.'[21] As access improved, so too did 'legal and literary' interest increase, and fittingly a new public search room was opened in the year of the 800th anniversary of the Conquest.

The belief that access to 'true' sources would confirm or even quicken national pride in the medieval story of England rather than divide the interpreters, often served as a justification of developing policy. Before the archives were opened up, however, Sharon Turner had pointed the way with his three-volume study, *The History of the Anglo-Saxons*, which appeared between 1799 and 1805 and which ran into several editions, the 1820 edition stating appreciatively that 'the taste for the history and remains of our great ancestors has revived and is rapidly increasing'. Turner would have nothing to do with the Norman yoke. For him, the Conquest was an act of Providence. 'It was ordained by the supreme director of events, that England should no longer remain insulated from the rest of Europe; but should for its own benefit and the improvement of mankind, become connected with the affairs of the continent.'[22]

A different note was introduced into academic discussion by John Kemble, whose monograph, *The Saxons in England* (1849), was influenced by German scholarship. Kemble's belief in the 'freedom' of the Saxon community was to be shared both by the social historian, J. R. Green, and by the great Professor Stubbs, who was later to describe Kemble as 'my pattern scholar'.[23] Yet Kemble's praise of freedom was both based on different 'evidence' from that of the critics of the Norman yoke and pointed to different conclusions. In publishing a *Codex Diplomaticus*, containing 1500 documents in chronological order from the conversion of Ethelbert to the Norman Conquest, he proudly extolled 'the stores of knowledge here laid open to the philologist, the jurist and the antiquarian', which 'will produce results far beyond the limits of this country or age'.[24]

Kemble's pride was more impressive than his editing. Yet he gave a serious historical dimension to what I have called the Saxon bias. Whereas Sir Francis Palgrave, Deputy Keeper of the Records, was still prepared to relate much that was significant in native English history to the Romans, Kemble, 'the first of British Germanists', made the most of the Teutonic, as his fellow scholars in Germany were doing. Freedom had its origins not in the Roman forum, but in the German forests. 'The Englishman has inherited the noblest portion of his being from the Anglo-Saxons', Kemble wrote in the *Saxons in England*, which was dedicated to the Queen. 'In spite of every influence, we bear a marvellous resemblance to our forefathers.'[25] J. R. Green was to take up the message.

> It is with a reverence such as is stirred by the sight of the head-waters of some mighty river that one looks back to these tiny moots, where the men of the village met to order the village life and the village industry, as their descendants, the men of a later England, meet in Parliament at Westminster, to frame laws and do justice for the great empire which has sprung from this little body of farmer-commonwealths.[26]

In the light of the mid-Victorian constellation of academic medievalists – Stubbs, Freeman and Green, to be followed by Maitland, the greatest medievalist of them all – the work of Kemble was no more than a prelude. Before turning to their work, however, it is essential to fit in two other books on Saxons and Normans, one a novel, Sir Walter Scott's *Ivanhoe*, the other a history, Augustin Thierry's *Histoire de la conquête de l'Angleterre*, appearing six years later, in 1825. Thierry was strongly influenced by Scott, 'that great master of historic divination': 'I contrasted his wonderful comprehension of the past', he wrote, 'with the petty erudition of the most celebrated historians.'[27] He was also determined to do justice to the Saxons, for reasons of sympathy as much as for reasons of fact, 'because I have a sort of partiality for the conquered'.[28]

Thierry's partiality was no stronger than Scott's partisanship, for no effort was spared in *Ivanhoe*, which first appeared in 1819, to press the claims of the Saxons and to make fools or rogues out of the Normans. Scott emphasised in his introduction to the novel that as late as Richard the Lionheart's reign there was 'a striking contrast betwixt the Saxons, by whom the soil was cultivated, and the Normans, who still reigned in it as conquerors, reluctant to mix with the vanquished'. 'Long live the Saxon princes! Long live the race of the immortal Alfred', a cry of the crowd at the tournament, might well be the motto of the book, with a genuflexion towards 'the sainted Confessor' and a polite acknowledgement, always there in Scott, of the appeal of Norman chivalry. One of the verses sung by Wamba is directly concerned with 'the Norman yoke':

> Norman saw on English oak,
> On English neck a Norman yoke;
> Norman spoon in English dish,
> And England ruled as Normans wish;
> Blithe world in England never will be more,
> Till England's rid of all the four.

Another passage in the novel makes much of the point, made so often since, about the Normans providing a word for the meat and the Saxons a word for the animal.

> Pork, I think, is good Norman-French; and so when the brute lives, and is in charge of a Saxon slave, she goes by her Saxon name; but becomes a Norman, and is called pork when she is carried to the castle-hall to feast among the nobles ... Old Alderman Ox continues to hold his Saxon epithet while he is under the charge of serfs and bondsmen – but becomes Beef, a fiery French gallant, when he arrives before the worshipful jaws that are destined to consume him. Myheer Calve, too, becomes Monsieur Veau in the like manner; he is Saxon when he requires tendance, and takes a Norman name when he becomes a matter of enjoyment.

Ivanhoe was the kind of historical novel which Scott wished to be thought of as history. He acknowledged his debt to Sharon Turner, defended himself against the 'severer antiquary', who might think that by 'intermingling fiction with truth he was polluting the well of history with modern inventions', and forcefully argued that his imputation of motive and his delineation of character could be justified on general grounds. 'The passions, the sources from which these must spring in all their modifications, are generally the same in all ranks and conditions, all countries and ages.' It was a bold claim about human psychology which the late Victorians – in the light of their knowledge both of comparative history and of evolutionary anthropology – would find difficult to sustain, but if it had not been believed unflinchingly by Scott he would have found it impossible ever to write an historical novel.[29]

After reading Scott, Thierry is at least as breathtaking, not because of his views about individuals but because of his broad generalisations about society. 'English institutions contain more of aristocracy than of liberty.' The reason was that 'everything in England dates from a conquest' – this was Thierry's remark after re-reading Hume's *History of England* (1754) with its terrible judgement on the Norman Conquest that it would be 'difficult to find in all history a revolution more destructive, or attended with a more complete subjection of the ancient inhabitants.'[30] Thierry's own book advanced the thesis that the Saxons were not completely subdued in 1066, that they made attempts to recover their liberty, that there was a kind of struggle of peoples – '*une lutte nationale*' – not unlike the struggle of classes, as it was envisaged by Marx and others in the nineteenth century. Peace only came when out of the mixture of Saxons and Normans there emerged a single nation. The date of the fusion was as late as the reign of Henry VII. 'Even then, this Tudor society, composed of new elements, nonetheless maintained the forms of the older society.'

Thierry had not studied deeply enough to make the most of his theory, which critics quickly pointed out was difficult to sustain; and although he shared the same beliefs and prejudices as the popularisers of the theory of the Norman yoke, his last paragraph, for example, shows a complete ignorance of the survival of the theory, or indeed of popular historiography.

No popular tradition persists relative to the division of England into two hostile peoples, and since the distinction of the two peoples has disappeared with the rise of a common language, no political passion clings to old forgotten facts. There are no longer Normans and Saxons except in history; and since the latter do not dominate history, the mass of English readers, little familiar with national antiquities, like to sustain the illusion of a false origin, and take the sixty thousand companions of William the Conqueror as the ancestors of all the inhabitants of England.[31]

IV

Thierry's verdict cannot stand in the context even of nineteenth-century history. His comment, however, that 'the mass of English readers are little familiar with national antiquities' has a greater ring of truth. Although most Englishmen of the nineteenth century, like most Englishmen of the twentieth, knew only one date in their country's history – 1066 – they made little attempt to celebrate 1866, the octocentenary of Hastings. Saxons and Normans moved dimly in the background of a century of unprecedented social change: they were never allowed to dominate it even 800 years after the Battle of Hastings. There were no celebrations in 1866 comparable to the Victorian celebrations of Shakespeare's tercentenary or the dramatic celebrations of the origins of nonconformity in 1661. Hampden's and Milton's anniversaries received far more public attention than the struggle between Harold and William.[32]

The Times, however, produced a leader on the subject, which owed more to Kemble than to Thierry, and which was infused with a philosophy not of conflict but of consensus. 'England would have been a very barren conquest, and could never have been more than another Normandy, had the Conqueror not won the people as well as the soil.' The people, after all, had 'always claimed self-government and equal laws'; and while for a time after 1066 'the two races lived apart', 'then the lordly Norman element began to work like a leaven in the mixed mass of this people, as it has worked ever since, and works at this day'. The Normans had rightly prevailed.

> The wandering Celt, the hard-working Saxon, the adventurous Dane, whatever the peculiar and inscrutable qualities of that English race into which all are fused, might have roamed, and laboured, and fought in vain, but for the master Norman mind, that could plan, and construct, and inspire; that never intended without doing, that seldom did without succeeding, and that never began without completing its work.

Such praise had a topical dimension which showed how willingly the Victorians could trace back aspects of their own society to the society of distant times. 'In no country in the world is the relation of master and servant so firmly established, so thoroughly developed, and conducive to such great and happy results as in this country.' And a congenial comparison was drawn with the Irish who had not 'gone through the previous training and formation which made the Norman Conquest so beneficial to this country'.[33] At least the language was confident. Yet within a decade 'masters' and 'servants' became 'employers' and 'workmen', as was recognised in an Act passed by a Conservative government in 1875;[34] and even at the time the Irish were suggesting that it was not so much lack of 'previous training and formation' which was the problem.

Part of *The Times* leader was given over to a brief description of the crucial battle itself (which made no references to Norman horses and

Saxon foot soldiers). At Hastings itself in 1866 a party of 300 people, gathered together by the Hastings and St Leonards Philosophical Society, ordered a special excursion train to take them from Hastings to Battle, and by the kind permission of a Duke wandered round the site where, in the words of a local newspaper, 'our ancestors so nobly fought and died eight centuries ago'.[35] T.H. Cole, one of the Secretaries of the Society, described what had happened in 1066 as he took the party around the site: later he published in book form an account of the proceedings and a record of the two more formal lectures – one by himself on the battle, the other by J.C. Savery on the Bayeux Tapestry.[36] The day ended with a cold collation in the very aptly named South Saxon Hotel.

Savery, not surprisingly, expressed some surprise that the Sussex Archaeological Society and other learned bodies had not shared in the interest which had been manifested in the proceedings of the day. The British Archaeological Association had actually held its national conference in Hastings in July 1866, and had refused to defer its meeting till October. The Sussex Archaeological Association, founded in 1866 – and still thriving – had fixed Eastbourne for their place of meeting that year, and would not budge on the place. The Historical Society of London had at one time proposed to join its sister association in Hastings, but 'as the time drew near, it was found that if the anniversary of the Battle was to be celebrated at all, it must be under the auspices of Hastings and St Leonards Philosophical Society alone'.

This sequence of events makes up a fascinating case study in Victorian minority communication, which any student of Victorian England must understand in the same way that any student of twentieth-century England must understand mass communication. There was a grid of local antiquarians, some concerned with archaeology, some with topography, some with architecture, some with geology, some with natural history, many with all these and other topics, and through their exchanges with each other they were concerning themselves with a far wider range of historical evidence than that to be found in the documents listed by the Public Record Office. Saxon and Norman 'remains' were not usually at the centre of their interests, but in Sussex, at least, they were bound to attract. Thus – despite his first two names – Mark Antony Lower, a founding father of the Sussex Archaeological Society, dedicated his *Chronicles of Pevensey* (1846) to the Victorian freemen of that town with 'the earnest hope' that it would 'at no distant day be restored to its pristine importance and prosperity'. The Society came into being after Norman remains had been discovered at Lewes when the railway line was being built.

The Sussex Archaeological Society, like the Hastings and St Leonards Philosophical Society, was an example of Victorian amateur activity, and there was often a gulf between their members and academic historians. Freeman depended on a private income before he became a Professor at Oxford, and he doubtless irritated many antiquaries by what they must have felt was his excessive professional pedantry, not least in relation to names. He always refused, for example, to call the Battle of Hastings the Battle of Hastings and insisted on the term, Battle of Senlac. He did refer to Lower, and he was more conscious of anniversaries and centenaries than some of his amateur counterparts were. He had actually planned to complete his *magnum opus* during the octocentenary year of the Conquest, but he found, in his own words, 'that to make the main subject really intelligible from my point of view, it was necessary to treat the preliminary history at much greater length than I had originally thought of'.[37] He did not reach the battle itself until volume III, p. 452. 'The central stage of our journey is now reached', he wrote eloquently at the beginning of volume III, published in 1869.

> We are now on the threshold of the great year, of that year whose effects on all later English, on all later European, history can never be wiped out. No one year in later English history can for a moment compare in lasting importance with the year which, with some small exaggeration, we may call the year of the Norman Conquest.[38]

Freeman had been looking forward to 1866, and visited the site of the battle five times, once in the company of Green, pioneer of social history who, somewhat surprisingly given his brilliant attack on 'drum and trumpet history', was described by Freeman as a man 'with a much keener eye than I have for topography, especially for military topography'.[39] Yet 1866 came and went, with more Englishmen interested, at least for the time being, in contemporary history than in medieval history. This was the year of an English financial crisis, of unemployment, and of cattle plague, of a great burst of reform agitation, of the transatlantic cable. A few people whom one might have expected to talk of 1066 did not do so. Stubbs, who did not believe much in the value of contemporary history, and objected to the study at school of 'those points which are connected most closely with the questions and controversies of today',[40] wrote a letter to Freeman on 15 October 1866, which included no reference to Hastings.[41] Later, although he read Freeman's proofs, Stubbs was to tell Mrs J.R. Green, herself no mean historian, that 'the English Conquest is not a favourite subject of mine, as your good husband knew'.[42]

V

The appointment of Stubbs to the Oxford Chair was a landmark in the history of history, far more important in relation to interpretations of the past than anything else that happened in 1866. Two years younger than Freeman and twelve years younger than Green, he was to survive them both: indeed, he lived on until 1901, the year, too, of Queen Victoria's death.

His *Constitutional History* (1873-8) was compared soon after his death with Edward Gibbon's *Decline and Fall of the Roman Empire* – for its scale and breadth as well as its insight[43] – and more recently, with better judgement, it has been compared with Charles Darwin's *Origin of Species* – for its compelling combination of intricate detail and brilliantly simplifying generalisation.[44] It was read as an 'authority' long after Freeman and Green had ceased to be read.

There were marked differences between the three men in their temperament and outlook, not least in relation to politics and religion, major Victorian preoccupations. Freeman was a Liberal, who believed that 'our ancient history is the possession of the liberal':[45] Stubbs was a Tory High Churchman, Bishop as well as Professor: Green was a friend and supporter of Radicals. Yet they corresponded regularly with each other, had a high regard for each other's gifts (and frequently commented on them), and felt that their lives inter-crossed. They were so close, indeed, that Thorold Rogers coined the naughty verse:

> So, loading flattery from their several tubs,
> Stubbs butters Freeman, Freeman butters Stubbs.[46]

Green, who never held a Chair and who was very much a junior partner in the trio, nonetheless suggested the formation of the Oxford Historical Society and the inauguration of the *English Historical Review* in 1886, a landmark date in the development of professional history.

With Stubbs we approach Saxons and Normans in broad sweep, surveying not a day but centuries, not a battle but the gradual development of institutions. Medieval history was given a new perspective. 'The history of institutions', he wrote in the well-known preface to the *Constitutional History*,

cannot be mastered, can scarcely be approached without an effort. It affords little of the romantic incident – [go back to *Ivanhoe*, although Stubbs enjoyed Carlyle] – or of the picturesque grouping which constitute the charm of history in general, and holds out small temptation to the mind that requires to be tempted to the study of truth. But it has a deep value and an abiding interest to those who have the courage to work upon it. It presents in every branch, a regularly developed series of causes and consequences, and abounds in examples of that continuity of life the realisation of which is necessary to give the reader a personal hold on the past and a right judgement of the present. For the roots of the present lie deep in the past, and nothing in the past is dead to the man who would learn how the present came to be what it is.[47]

As far as the Norman impact on English history was concerned, Stubbs took the view that the Norman monarchy was essential to the creation of modern government and that after it 'the nation' was brought 'at once and permanently within the circle of European interests'. Although there had been in some real sense, a popular Anglo-Saxon background to free English institutions, even a constitution which the king was required to respect,[48] 1066 marked the real beginning of English history as we understand it and of English institutions as the Victorians knew them. Before 1066 the history of this island had been 'uneventful': after 1066 it sprang to life. It is not too difficult to pass from this view to the sublime simplification of *1066 and All That* – 'The Norman Conquest was a Good Thing, as from this time onwards England stopped being conquered and thus was able to become top nation.'[49]

Generations of medieval historians have been brought up on Stubbs, and his influence was always strong not only both in Cambridge and in his own Oxford, where he gave his name to its most erudite and critical historical society, but in a new nineteenth-century university like Manchester, where the great Tout was a former pupil.[50] In recent years, however, a number of writers on medieval history have dwelt not on Stubbs's strength, but on his limitations, and have even been willing to look back to Freeman instead. Such was the standpoint of H.F. Richardson and G.O. Sayles in their volume *The Governance of Medieval England from the Conquest to Magna Carta*, published in 1963, which after briefly discussing 'William Stubbs: The Man and the Historian' goes on to challenge the view that a reading of Stubbs is a necessary preliminary to any study of medieval English history, 'a kind of prophylactic even', a sovereign antidote against the tendency which young historians have (so it is alleged) to proceed from one novelty to another, from the latest periodical to the latest *Festschrift* and to become in the process up-to-date without being well grounded.'[51] While admitting Stubbs's erudition and his industry, they accused him of 'insufficient critical discernment' and of 'little capacity for thinking clearly about the nature of historical truth and its attainment'. Moreover, they went on, all too often he 'failed to view medieval men and medieval institutions operating in a medieval setting'. In the words of the French historian Petit-Dutaillis, who produced a widely-used history, *Studies Supplementary to Stubbs's Constitutional History*, 'he projected into the past the image of the constitutional monarchy which he saw working under his own eyes, and to which he attributed the greatness of his country'.[52] By contrast, Freeman was a historian 'disparaged too much by those who have not read his works but only the criticisms of them'.[53]

Not all twentieth-century scholars have been content with this judgement. It would be a great mistake, however, if in any dialogue between the nineteenth and twentieth centuries, Stubbs were thought to be more 'Victorian' than Freeman. As professional historians both were as culture-bound as their twentieth-century successors.[54] The facts of twentieth-century life have been as important as changes of scholarship in reshaping perspectives, as in Geoffrey Barraclough's conclusion that the Norman Conquest was an unmitigated disaster, a social holocaust which rapidly destroyed an old culture as irrevocably as the Spanish discoveries wiped out American-Indian civilisation.[55]

VI

As history has become more professionalised as a subject, the differences between historians have by no means been necessarily ironed out. Indeed, in the late Victorian transition to professional history, an element of distinctive rancour entered into historical disputes, which was as noticeable as the early popular rancour in relation to arguments about the Norman yoke. It was not political rancour, although Paul Vinogradoff in his *Villeinage in England* described waning of enthusiasm for Saxon democracy as a consequence of disillusionment with Liberal democracy.[56] The rancour is most obvious in relation to disputes surrounding Freeman, who himself said of Froude that 'if history means truth, fairness ... faithfully reporting what contemporary sources record, and drawing reasonable inferences from these statements, then Mr Froude is no historian.'[57] It soon was Freeman's own turn to be criticised, however, first very pertinently by J.R. Green, then very impertinently by J.H. Round. Both bouts of criticism tell us something not only about Victorian habits and styles of controversy but about Victorian approaches to the Saxons and the Normans.

According to Green, who reviewed Freeman in the *Saturday Review*, one of the most biting of Victorian periodicals, Freeman was deficient in moral and intellectual sympathy. 'He passes silently by religion, intellect, society. He admires the people gathered in its Witan but he never takes us to the thegn's hall or to the peasant's hut. Of the actual life, manners, tastes of our forefathers the book tells us nothing. It is essentially a work of historic reaction.'[58] Green had far more originality than Freeman, yet Freeman admired him so much – despite verdicts of this kind – that he always made it his duty, in his own words, 'to blow Johnny Green's trumpet'. The two men certainly knew each other well enough and respected each other in private and in public. 'I dare say you would stare', Green wrote to Freeman of his *Short History of the English People*, 'to see seven pages devoted to the Wars of the Roses and fifteen to Colet, Erasmus and More. The more I think over our story as a whole, the more its political history seems to spring out of and to be moulded into form by the social and religious history you like to chaff me about.'[59] There were clearly important historiographical issues at stake in this interchange, and not simply differences of temperament. And when Green finally produced his *Conquest of England* – a much less impressive study than Freeman's – it was very different in tone and texture from Freeman's even when he accepted Freeman's conclusions. 'The difference between Green and Freeman,' wrote Creighton after reading the two works, 'is enormous. Freeman tries to make you understand each detail by isolating it and surrounding it with nineteenth-century settings. He iterates and reiterates, but you don't see it. In the *Making* and the *Conquest* by Green the whole thing moves together.'[60]

By the end of the nineteenth-century, professional history depended on critical debate in articles, books and reviews in learned journals, and not simply on the impact of inspiring lectures or on the influence of inspiring tutors. The second Victorian attack on Freeman lacked all the friendliness of Green's criticism, but in retrospect it is equally illuminating. J.H. Round, a pupil of Stubbs, for whom he always expressed admiration bordering on adulation, subjected Freeman to relentless denigration. Starting with the Battle of Hastings itself – and Round began by ridiculing Freeman for calling it the Battle of Senlac – he accused Freeman of failing where he should have been strongest, for it was, after all, 'in his battle pieces where our author was always at his best'. Round's approach is as interesting as the content of what he had to say. After taking on not only Freeman but his supporters, he ends dramatically, 'Truth cannot be silenced, facts cannot be obscured. I appeal, sure of my ground, to the verdict of historical scholars, awaiting, with confidence and calm, the inevitable triumph of the truth.'[61] These words were written in 1893. History had come a long way since Sharon Turner.

At the heart of Round's criticism, however, was a criticism of Freeman's politics. Unlike Stubbs, who was a Tory, and supported the Austrians against the Italians, the Russians against the Poles, and hoped that Freeman would have learned from his study of Switzerland about 'the evil of republican institutions', Freeman was a liberal, a

Victorian liberal, who, like Gladstone, set out to identify nationalism and free, representative government. For Round, these were the sympathies which led him astray. When he talked about the Saxons and the Normans, he was thinking about the Victorians, and the nineteenth-century Germans, Italians and Poles. 'We know of whom the writer [Freeman] was thinking,' Round suggests, when in volume II of the Conquest, he refers to 'the mighty voice, the speaking look and gesture of that old man, eloquent, [who] could again sway assemblies of Englishmen at his will', or when he notes how we can 'revere the great minister, the unrivalled parliamentary leader, the man who could sway councils and assemblies at his will.'[62] It was not Alfred, but William Ewart Gladstone. Freeman's praise of Godwin, which incidentally Green did not share – sprang, in Round's opinion, from his natural sympathy with 'unscrupulous agitators', 'orators in Hyde Park'. No wonder, according to Round, that he got the whole moral of the Norman Conquest wrong. 'A democrat first, an historian afterwards, History was for him ... ever "past politics". If he worshipped Harold with a blind enthusiasm, it was chiefly because he was a *novus homo* (a new man) "who reigned purely by the will of the people". To him the voice of "a sovereign people" was "the most spirit-stirring of earthly sounds"; but it availed about as much to check the Norman Conquest as the fetish of an African savage, or the yells of Asiatic hordes.'[63]

Attacks of this kind – and it was an unfair attack, for there is no evidence that Freeman ever worshipped Harold – tells us at least as much about the attacker as his victim. Round, indeed, had his own political stance on 1066. 'The Battle of Hastings has its moral and its moral is for us. An almost anarchical excess of liberty, the want of a strong centralised system, the absorption in party strife, the belief that politics are statesmanship, and that oratory will save a people – these are the dangers of which it warns us.' Needless to say, for Round these were really not eleventh-century dangers but nineteenth-century dangers: there were, indeed, echoes of Carlyle in what proudly purported to be history as truth. Round eventually hammered home the attack on Freeman by himself leaving eleventh-century territory altogether. 'To the late Regius Professor, if there was one thing more hateful than "castles", more hateful even than hereditary rule, it was a standing army. When the Franco-German war had made us look to our harness, he set himself at once, with superb blindness, to sneer at what he called "the panic", to suggest the application of democracy to the army, and to express his characteristic aversion to the thought of "an officer and a gentleman". How could such a writer teach the lesson of the Norman Conquest?'[64]

A new strand emerged in late Victorian writing about Saxons and

Normans as the British Empire grew both in material strength and in emotional significance. As early as the 1860s, W. Trapnell Deverell thought that the Norman Conquest had been a 'great boon' to England because it welded together a race 'whose manifest destiny it is, under one form or another, to subjugate and civilise the habitable globe'.[65] Even the almost dead theory of the Norman yoke could be given a new twist. In a book of 1879 the conquered Saxons are equated with 'mere Afghans and Zulus, who by the divine right of triumphant scoundrelism, calling itself superior civilisation, had to put their necks beneath the yoke.'[66]

This was far from Round, yet Round's reaction to Freeman was representative of something more than his own opinions. Historians cannot avoid reading into the past the preoccupations of the present. In a period not of empire building but of the disintegration of empire, a twentieth-century historian of England writing from Toronto starts his interesting book *The Habit of Authority* with the sentence 'England begins her modern history as a colony'.[67] He is not all that far from Thierry when he suggests that our national habit of authority was Norman in origin. There is a curious sense, indeed, in which the patterns of historians are as complex as the patterns of history itself.

NOTES

1 T. Carlyle, *Past and Present* (1843), Book III, Chapter X. The reference to the Saxons is taken from his *Frederick the Great*, vol. I (1858), p. 415. For the Positivists, see F. Harrison, *Autobiographic Memoirs*, vol. II (1911). For Victorian hero-worship generally, see W. Houghton, *The Victorian Frame of Mind* (1957), Chapter 12.

2 E. A. Freeman, *The History of the Norman Conquest of England, its Causes and its Results*, vol. I (1867), p. 545. Twenty-one years earlier, Freeman had won the Chancellor's Prize as an undergraduate for an essay on 'The Effect 'of the Conquest of England by the Normans'.

3 ibid., vol. I, p. 2.

4 Note the verdict on it in J. W. Burrow's important monograph, *A Liberal Descent* (1981), p. 158: 'it is sometimes easier to think of it as a patriotic oratorio, with music by Stanford or Sullivan, with banked mass choirs ... and the Whiggish sound of a great Amen.'

5 Elizabeth Penrose [Mrs Markham], *History of England* (1823), vol. I, pp. 69-70.

6 Goldwin Smith, *The United Kingdom, a Political History*, vol. I (1899), pp. 21-3.

7 See Christopher Hill, 'The Norman Yoke', in J. Saville (ed.), *Democracy and the Labour Movement* (1954), pp. 11-16. I am deeply indebted in what follows to this pioneer essay.

8 According to this anonymous *Historical Essay on the English Constitution*, the Saxon constitution had been introduced about 450 AD. For

attitudes towards the 'old constitution', see J.G.A. Pocock, *The Ancient Constitution and the Feudal Law* (1957).

9   Thomas Hughes's *Alfred the Great* (1881) mentioned the literature on Alfred from Spelman to Pauli, but added that his book was offered 'not to historical students, but to ordinary English readers'. He quoted Carlyle, and drew many parallels between Alfred's age and the Victorian age. The pseudonym 'Alfred' continued to be used by many Victorian writers on reform.

10 T. Paine, *Declaration of the Rights of Man* (1791).

11 *The Trial of Henry Yorke for a Conspiracy*, quoted in Hill, *op. cit.*, p. 49.

12 For Birmingham, see *The Report of the Council to the Political Union of the Town of Birmingham* (1830), with its stress 'on restoring and confirming the ancient and inalienable constitutional laws', and above, vol. I, pp. 180 ff. See A. Aspinall, *The Early English Trade Unions* (1949), p. 62, for the views of Bolton weavers who were asking, 'Is it not time to drag the British Constitution from its lurking hole and to expose it in its original and naked purity to show each individual the laws of his forefathers?'

13 Quoted in L.G. Johnson, *The Social Evolution of Industrial Britain* (1959), p. 7.

14 R. Carlile, *The Republican*, vol. II, pp. 198-9, 25 February 1820.

15 Letter in *Cleave's Penny Gazette*, 6 November 1841. The same point was made by Joseph Parkes in Birmingham in 1830: 'Mr Hallam had truly said, "God forbid that our rights to a just and free Government should be tried by a jury of Antiquarians."' Henry Hallam's *Whig Constitutional History* (1827) reveals no enthusiasm for 'Saxon freedom'. Magna Carta was the beginning of English history as it was also for Macaulay. See also A. Palliser, *Magna Carta, The Heritage of Liberty* (1971).

16 *Bradford Observer*, 23 April 1839.

17 R.W. Emerson, *Works* (1882), vol. III, p. 50.

18 *The Poor Man's Guardian*, no. 55, 1832.

19 *The Democratic Review*, July 1849.

20 Thorold Rogers, reported in *Report of the Public Meeting held at the Exeter Hall, London*, 18 March 1873.

21 A comment of 1830, quoted in G.P. Gooch, *History and Historians of the Nineteenth Century* (1952), p. 267.

22 Sharon Turner, *The History of the Anglo-Saxons*, vol. I, p. 418.

23 Letter of 8 December 1859, printed in W.H. Hutton (ed.), *Letters of William Stubbs, Bishop of Oxford* (1904), p. 77.

24 Quoted in Gooch, *op. cit.*, p. 271. For German influences on Kemble, see R.A. Wiley (ed.), *John Mitchell Kemble and Jacob Grimm, A Correspondence, 1832-1852* (1971).

25 Quoted in Gooch, *op. cit.*, p. 272. Palgrave published *The History of Normandy and England* in 1851.

26 J.R. Green, *A Short History of the English People* (1874), p. 4. For Palgrave, see P.B.M. Glaas, *Continuity and Anachronism* (1978). For

German influences, see C. E. McLelland, *The German Historians and England* (1971).

27 Quoted in Gooch, *op. cit.*, pp. 163-4.

28 The 'theory of primitive conquest' was not invented by Thierry, and he was doubtless influenced by Benjamin Constant's *De l'esprit de conquête et d'usurpation* (1813). Moreover, for three years Thierry had been the secretary of St Simon, the early socialist. Guizot, who greatly admired Thierry, took over the theory in his essay *Du Gouvernement de la France* (1820); and in his *Histoire de la civilisation en Europe* (1828) he paid a warm tribute to Thierry, as did the historian Michelet. De Tocqueville was more balanced. He thought with 'horror of the inconceivable sufferings of people' during and after 1066, but 'admired' William. See his 'Reflections on English History', printed in J.P. Mayer (ed.), *Journeys to England and Ireland* (1957), pp. 21 ff.

29 The introduction to *Ivanhoe*, along with a 'Dedicatory Epistle to the Rev. Dr. Dryasdust, F.A.S.', explicitly set out most of Scott's presuppositions. 'The scantiness of materials is indeed a formidable difficulty; but no one knows better than Dr. Dryasdust, that to those deeply read in antiquity, hints concerning the private life of our ancestors lie scattered through the pages of our various historians, bearing indeed, a slender proportion to the other matters of which they treat, but still, when collected together, sufficient to throw considerable light upon the *vie privée* of our forefathers.' Scott went on to refer to his debt to 'Dr. Henry, Mr. Strutt, and above all Mr. Sharon Turner'.

30 For Hume, see Duncan Forbes, *Hume's Philosophical Politics* (1975).

31 A. Thierry, *Histoire de la conquête d'Angleterre* (1825), Conclusion. Book XI had begun with Richard I, the period in which *Ivanhoe* is set.

32 Many Victorians believed that there were links between Saxons and Puritans. See, for example, the *Bradford Observer*, 27 December 1849: 'The Commonwealth is a bright era in English history, a gleam of sunshine all the brighter for the darkness and chaos on both sides of it. Cromwell was the incarnate genius of genuine Saxon liberty ... a spirit which though long repressed ... is invincible and immortal.'

33 *The Times*, 26 October 1866.

34 See A. Briggs, 'Social Background', in A. Flanders and H. A. Clegg (eds), *The System of Industrial Relations in Great Britain* (1954), p. 16.

35 Report in *The Hastings and St Leonards Chronicle*, 17 October 1866.

36 T. H. Cole, *The Antiquities of Hastings and the Battlefield* (1867).

37 E. A. Freeman, *op. cit.*, Preface to vol. I (1867).

38 ibid., vol. III (1875 edn) pp. 3-4.

39 ibid., vol. III, p. 757.

40 W. Stubbs, *Seventeen Letters on Medieval and Modern History* (1887), p. 53.

41 Quoted in Hutton (ed.), *op. cit.*, pp. 110-11.

42 Letter of 29 March 1887, printed ibid., p. 275.

43 Hutton, *op. cit.*, pp. 137-8.

44 Burrow, *op. cit.*, p. 129, p. 145. 'Complexity', Stubbs wrote, 'is a sign of growth ... That which springs up, as our whole system has done, on the

principle of adapting present means to present ends, may be complex
and inconvenient and empiric, but it is natural, spontaneous, and a
crucial test of substantial freedom.' (*Lectures on Early English History*
(1906), p. 326.)

45 E. A. Freeman, *The Growth of the English Constitution* (1870 edn), p. x.
46 Quoted in A. Haultain (ed.), *Reminiscences by Goldwin Smith* (1910),
    p. 277.
47 W. Stubbs, Preface to the *Constitutional History*, vol. I (1874).
48 ibid., vol. I, p. 269.
49 W. C. Sellar and R. Y. Yeatman, *1066 and All That* (1930), p. 17.
50 For the tradition, see F. M. Powicke, *Modern Historians and the Study
    of History* (1949), Chapter II, 'The Manchester History School'. See
    also Helen Cam, 'Stubbs, Seventy Years After', in the *Cambridge
    Historical Journal*, vol. IX (1948).
51 Preface to H. G. Richardson and G. O. Sayles, *The Governance of
    Mediaeval England from the Conquest to Magna Carta* (1963), pp. v-vi,
    referring to Sir Goronwy Edwards's *William Stubbs* (1952), p. 20.
52 Richardson and Sayles, *op. cit.*, p. 6, quoting C. Petit-Dutaillis, *Studies
    Supplementary to Stubbs's Constitutional History* (1908), p. 307.
53 G. O. Sayles, *The Medieval Foundations of England* (1966 edn), p. 277.
54 D. J. A. Matthew, *The Norman Conquest* (1966), p. 289.
55 G. Barraclough, in *The Observer*, March 1966.
56 P. Vinogradoff, *Villeinage in England* (1892), p. 31. For Maitland's
    interesting reply, see J. Burrow, 'Village Community', in N. McKen-
    drick (ed.), *Historical Perspectives, Studies in English Thought and
    Society in Honour of J. H. Plumb* (1974). 'To English readers',
    Maitland wrote, 'this attempt to connect the development of historical
    study with the course of politics ... leads you into what will be thought
    paradoxes – e.g. it so happens that our leading village communists,
    Stubbs and Maine, are men of the most conservative type, while
    Seebohm, who is said to mark conservative reaction, is a thorough
    liberal. I am not speaking of votes at the poll but of radical and essential
    elements of mind.'
57 Quoted in *Some Modern Historians of England, Essays in Honour of
    R. L. Schuyler* (1951), p. 49.
58 His review is conveniently reprinted in J. R. Green, *Historical Studies*
    (1903).
59 Quoted in Gooch, *op. cit.*, pp. 330-1.
60 ibid., p. 334.
61 J. H. Round, 'Mr. Freeman and the Battle of Hastings', in *Feudal
    England* (1909), p. 394. Round himself described Hastings as 'Waterloo
    without the Prussians.'
62 ibid., p. 397.
63 ibid., p. 395.
64 ibid., p. 397.
65 W. Trapnell Deverell, *The Norman Conquest* (n.d.).
66 H. Evans, *Our Old Nobility* (1879 edn), p. 252.
67 A. P. Thomson, *The Habit of Authority* (1966), p. 18.

11 G.M. Trevelyan: The Uses of Social History

Future historiographers seeking to trace what happened to 'the Whig interpretation of history' in the twentieth century will turn at once to the writings of George Macaulay Trevelyan (1876-1965). Meanwhile, of course, a doubtless dwindling band of general readers, who know little or nothing about historiography, will turn to him for instruction and delight.

'The idea of a Whig interpretation of English history is simple in outline, complex in detail.'[1] There is certainly as much variety in the interpretation as there is in Whiggery itself. Whatever the particular interpretation, however, it always incorporates what Herbert Butterfield, a younger Cambridge colleague of Trevelyan, called in his brilliant essay on the subject in 1931 both 'a certain organisation of historical knowledge' and 'a tradition passed on from one generation of historians to the next'.[2] For 'Whig historians' English history has a distinctive shape, and the present is not only a part of it but the governing influence on how the interpretation of the past is organised. As for the tradition, it can at its purest be a family tradition as Whiggery itself was – a matter of kinship and upbringing.

G.M. Trevelyan followed in the wake of his distinguished great-uncle Lord Macaulay, with his father, Sir George Otto Trevelyan, who edited Macaulay's *Life and Letters*, as the intermediary. His grandfather, also Sir Charles Trevelyan, was an influential Whig, a civil servant who traced back the Whig tradition as far as he possibly could when he described himself as 'belonging to the class of reformed Cornish Celts who by long habits of intercourse with the Anglo-Saxons have learned at last to be practical men'.[3]

Macaulay, born in 1800, had written the five volumes of his *History of England* in the hope that they would live long after him: he had 'the year 2000, and even the year 3000, often in mind'.[4] He also sought the largest and broadest possible reading public in his own time. G.M. Trevelyan followed the same plan. His historical output might be 'the fruit of leisure, of freedom, of independence',[5] but the idea of appealing to a large public is at least as important a clue to the nature of his 'Whiggery', and it was already an ingredient in his first youthful enthusiasms. 'If I can do anything for democracy,' he told his brother

Charles in 1893, 'it must be through literature. Now the point is that literary people are not, most of them, democratic, and it is more than probable that unless I keep the fire kindled within me, I shall forget my "motif" and become a mere "littérateur"!'[6]

History rather than poetry was to become the kind of literature to which his name was to be attached (after he had failed as an undergraduate at Cambridge to win the Prize Poem but had gone on to secure a first in the History Tripos). And although his task, he now felt, was 'to write *heavy books*, history and the like', he was still deeply conscious of the need to appeal to an audience. The 'heaviness' was relative. G.P. Gooch, his academic senior by two years, was an active contemporary influence upon him, and the major historic influence was that of Carlyle, whom he believed should be studied not as a 'model historian' but because of 'his imagination and narrative qualities'. 'While he lacks what modern historical method has acquired, he possesses in the fullest degree what it has lost.'[7]

At this early stage in his life, Trevelyan's interests lay already as much in European as in English history, a point that is often ignored by writers on the Whig tradition; and he was to write in his *Autobiography* that when Trinity held Acton and Gooch within its walls, they contained the two Englishmen 'who knew most about modern European history and its sources'.[8] 'Under Acton's leadership,' Trevelyan was also to write, 'we learned to hold our heads high.'[9] 'The Jubilee is well,' Trevelyan told his family in 1897, 'but one flies for the refuge of contrast to the French Revolution, to see that man can on occasion be discontent as well as content, that there is the everlasting Nay, as well as the everlasting Yea'.[10]

Trevelyan's first book dealt with discontent. Yet it dealt with discontent not in France, but in England – the Peasants' Revolt of 1381. His Fellowship study which was published in 1899, when he was only just twenty-three, with the title 'England in the Age of Wycliffe', has been described as 'Whig history at its best, emphasising the struggle for personal freedom against established tyrannies, viewing the past through the glasses of a self-confident liberal faith.'[11] Trevelyan himself told his brother soon after writing it that he always read Ruskin while he was writing to prevent himself from 'falling into Macaulayese'.[12] His book was criticised at the time, as it has been since, for simplifying the issues, getting 'the lights too high and shades too deep' and, above all, for judging past people and events by nineteenth-century standards; and K.B. McFarlane deliberately did not include it in the guide for further reading in his *John Wycliffe and the Beginnings of English Nonconformity* (1952). Instead McFarlane contented himself with only two references to Trevelyan in his text, one of which read tartly, 'Regrets that some Lollards "lacked the spirit of martyrdom" (the prose is Dr Trevelyan's) come ill from those who have never been called upon to die for an unpopular opinion.'[13]

Nonetheless, Trevelyan showed what even McFarlane might have considered independence of spirit in leaving Cambridge in 1903 for a larger world, where he could freely participate in politics and write history far from 'the critical atmosphere of Cambridge scholarship'.[14] And his *England under the Stuarts*,[15] published a year later and received coolly by professional historians, as most of his books were to be, was a highly popular account (in an established Methuen series) which was to go through more than twenty reprints. It sharpened the contrast between England and the Continent, claiming that 'at a time when the Continent was falling a prey to despots, the English under the Stuarts achieved their emancipation from monarchical tyranny by the act of the national will'. The seventeenth century, not the nineteenth, was the cradle of Whiggery, and Trevelyan felt at home there. Indeed, the *Spectator* presciently singled out his chapter on social history as the best in the book, not knowing that Trevelyan's mother had read aloud to him the third 'social history' chapter of Macaulay's *History* when he was a small boy.

Once again, it was because of privileged family ties that Trevelyan felt an obligation to look outwards towards a working-class audience; and when he lectured before the First World War to the students of the Working Men's College in London – a regular activity which he enjoyed, although it began self-consciously as a 'service' to others – he chose as his first subject 'Social England in the time of the French Revolution and Napoleon'. When he started work on Garibaldi, he addressed an audience of several hundred 'nonconformist working men' on the subject at Whitefield's Tabernacle, the best audience, he said, that he had ever addressed.[16]

Trevelyan's 'Garibaldi books',[17] some of the most popular he wrote, also had a source of family inspiration. It was a chance wedding present that turned him from England to Italy. After he married the daughter of the well-known Victorian novelist, Mrs Humphry Ward, in the year *England under the Stuarts* appeared, he travelled happily through Italy (and Central America) with his wife, who shared his interests, looking at places and at people in his quest to understand not only a man, but a movement. The man had been a hero of the mid-Victorian working classes in London, and his visit in 1864 had been a triumph, while the movement had caught the imagination of almost all England's Liberal politicians.[18] And before volume I of the Garibaldi trilogy appeared, a new Liberal government had been returned to power in 1906 – after long years of Conservative rule – with a huge majority – and was carrying out reforms which were designed to appeal to the mass electorate. It was in the year of Lloyd George's controversial budget of

1909, which led to a constitutional crisis, that Trevelyan wrote in the preface to the second volume of the Garibaldi trilogy, 'To my mind the events of 1860 should serve as an encouragement to all high endeavour amongst us of a later age, who ... are in some danger of losing faith in ideals.'

Trevelyan's interpretation of Italian history has been challenged as much as his interpretations of the fourteenth and seventeenth centuries in English history, although in this case it took decades to challenge it effectively,[19] and in old age Trevelyan himself is said to have admitted that the trilogy was 'reeking with bias.'[20] Yet by then two world wars and the rise and fall of Italian Fascism had intervened. In the first of them Trevelyan had seen Italy in a different context, when he served as the Commandant of the British Red Cross Ambulance Unit there and worked with the Italian army on the Isonzo and Piave fronts. His daughter Mary Moorman, who has written his biography – something he never wanted anyone to do – covers this period particularly well with the help of his letters. Yet while the love of Italy shines through all of them, as it does in so much English writing about that country, it is the side comment in them, particularly that on Russia, which is of the greatest interest.

Trevelyan welcomed the Russian Revolution of March 1917 with as much enthusiasm as English Liberals had welcomed the French Revolution of 1789, but almost at once he concluded that the Russians of 1917 were neither like the French revolutionaries of 1789 nor the English revolutionaries of 1688 (the supporters of what Macaulay had called 'a conserving revolution'). 'I wish the Russians were Whigs,' Trevelyan wrote to his mother in England, 'but as they aren't, one must hope for the best to happen in some other odd, new democratic way.' The Bolshevik Revolution of 1917 destroyed his hope. Unless the American Senate accepted American membership of a new League of Nations, he argued gloomily, 'there will be Bolshevism and war all over Europe for a generation to come.'[21]

During the difficult post-war years – when America was not a member of the League of Nations and when Europe was in turmoil – Trevelyan turned his attention back to English history. Already before 1914 he had written a *Life of John Bright* (1913), his first incursion into nineteenth-century history. Now he went further back in the century and produced his *Lord Grey of the Reform Bill*, large parts of which were set in his own county of Northumberland. It was a congenial subject. 'I was born and bred to write about Grey and the Reform Bill,' he claimed;[22] and he returned in the preface to the same general theme that he had underlined in *England under the Stuarts*. Grey's 'paramount influence' as a 'liberal-minded aristocrat' revealed the differences between 'our island' and Germany, France and Austria.

At the 'crucial moment of the transition' from 'stagnation and all too rigid conservatism' to 'orderly democratic progress', Grey had 'averted civil war and saved the State from entering on the vicious circle of revolution and reaction.'

Such strong conviction, the starting point of the book, not its conclusion, saved Trevelyan from the kind of detailed analysis of the early nineteenth century which was to be attempted a generation later by other more research-minded historians. Indeed, at the time, there were reviewers who once again criticised *Grey* on the grounds that it was 'conceived in the unmeasured violence of a political antagonist.'[23] Yet it is significant that there was to be a gap of a whole generation before historians appeared who, after research, were capable of offering an adequate alternative version to that of Trevelyan. Moreover, there was an even bigger gap still before the idea of 'the making of a working class', itself an idea based on conviction and open to controversy, came to dominate the historiography of the early nineteenth century.

The success of Trevelyan's bigger book of 1922, *British History in the Nineteenth Century*, cannot be explained simply in terms of its style which made for readability. Its author's 'bias' was obviously congenial to large numbers of readers who liked his approach to history, 'liberal but purely English', and who shared his conviction that the main theme of English history was 'ordered progress'.[24] Other countries had turned to 'military despotism'. England had helped to overturn such despotism in the Great War which had ended with the setting up of a League of Nations.[25] There was much in common between Trevelyan's Whig 'bias' and that of Stanley Baldwin, the Conservative leader, himself an old Trinity man, who was to give his name to the age – and who was to appoint Trevelyan as Regius Professor of Modern History at Cambridge in 1927. Both believed in conciliation and in consensus, in the values of the countryside rather than those of the city and, above all, in the need to relate present distinctive national advantages to past achievements. For Trevelyan the English were of 'history's blood royal'. For Baldwin 'the preservation of the individuality of the Englishman' was essential to 'the preservation of the type of the race.'[26] And when Baldwin died in 1947, it was Trevelyan who said of him in a speech in Trinity College Hall that he was 'the most human and lovable of all the Prime Ministers', 'an Englishman ... [who] in a world of voluble hates, plotted to make men like, or at least tolerate, one another.'[27]

Their common philosophy was eloquently expressed in the speech of George V to both Houses of Parliament in 1935 on the occasion of his Silver Jubilee a speech based on a Trevelyan text. 'Beneath these rafters of medieval oak, the silent witness of historic tragedies and pageants,' the King told his Parliament, 'we celebrate the present under the spell of the past. It is to me a source of pride and thankfulness that the perfect harmony of our Parliamentary system with our Constitutional Monarchy has survived the shocks that have in recent years destroyed other empires and other liberties'. And then came a supremely Whig passage. 'The complex forms and balanced spirit of our Constitution were not the discovery of a single era, still less of a single Party or of a single person. They are the slow accretion of centuries, the outcome of patience, tradition and experience, constantly finding channels old and new for the impulse towards liberty, justice and social improvment inherent in our people down the years.'[28]

Both men fitted the new Labour Party into their picture of English history without difficulty. For Baldwin it was necessary to welcome it as a natural party capable of holding power.[29] For Trevelyan, shocked by the rise of Fascism in Italy, 'it was as natural for the Italian socialist to terrorise his fellow citizens as for the English socialist to walk to the polling booth. History can best tell you why.'[30] By a strange coincidence, he gave the Romanes Lecture in Oxford on 'The Two Party System in English History', a lecture which made much of continuities, on the very day the General Strike of 1926 was called off.

Setting out to provide the kind of history which he believed everyone should know, Trevelyan had produced his textbook *Britain in the Nineteenth Century*, a work designed 'to give the sense of continuous growth, to show how economic led to social, and social to political change, how the political events reacted on the economic and social, and how new thoughts and new ideals accompanied or directed the whole complicated process.'[31] It was an ambitious venture, far more successful in meeting this difficult specification in its early chapters on the period before 1832 than in its later ones. This was to be a continuing problem for Trevelyan, despite his willingness to incorporate the twentieth-century English Conservative Party and the new Labour Party into the Whig tradition. There seemed to be a point in time he implied, at which the Whig interpretation had broken down – or at least where it had become tenuous – the point, indeed, of his own childhood; and the break was as much linked with Ireland as with England. 'If you are writing about the past,' he had asked his parents anxiously, 'is it not artistically unfortunate to fall out of love with the present?'[32]

Trevelyan's friends believed that it was the First World War which had moved him 'to the right'. 'Is it the war that has changed him?' Lawrence Hammond asked Barbara, answering his own question 'I suppose so.'[33] There was a difference here between Trevelyan and Macaulay, who brought the Whig interpretation into the heart of his own times. But then, of course, there was an underlying difference between the England of Trevelyan and the England of Macaulay. As a young man Trevelyan deliberately did not write on current affairs; in middle age there was as much to disturb as to inspire him; in old age he was to become even more ill at ease in a country which, to his alarm, was being turned into a kind of place he could no longer recognise. Yet he saw Cambridge as a timeless place of refuge. Harold Nicolson talks in his *Diary* of dining at Trinity College in 1941, and of how as he mused on the mahogany and the silver, the madeira and port, and told Trevelyan 'It is much the same,' Trevelyan replied simply 'Civilisation is always recognisable.'[34]

In 1924 Trevelyan, still without formal university links, was invited to the United States by Harvard University to deliver the Lowell Lectures and chose as his subject the whole history of England. Inevitably, a book followed, the *History of England*. It was a far more ambitious book than *England in the Nineteenth Century*. Trevelyan set out, indeed, to present a modern version of J.R. Green's *Short History of the English People* which had appeared two generations before in 1874 and which stopped in 1815. The idea of such a book came from his publisher, Robert Longman (Macaulay had been a Longman author too), and it proved a brilliant publishing success. By the time Trevelyan wrote his autobiography in 1949, it had sold over 200,000 copies, and by 1973 when a new illustrated edition was produced, there had been no fewer than twenty-four reprints.

The qualities of Trevelyan's *History* are immediately apparent – largeness of view, freshness of expression, compression of judgement, fluency of narrative, and above all, evocative power in descriptions of events and of places as much as of people. The combination was and remains unique. The book as a whole is very much a work of its time, but its qualities have ensured that it has outlived its time. It serves now, as Plumb has written, not only as history but as 'the material of history', for it reveals how 'liberal humanists' of Trevelyan's generation, living in a world of change, 'considered their past', 'from whence they derived their tradition' and the criteria by which 'they would like themselves judged.'[35]

Reviewers were no more unanimous about the *History*, however, than they had been about Trevelyan's earlier books, and the *English Historical Review* did not deign to notice it at all. 'Many of its epigrams,' wrote the reviewer in the *American Historical Review*, 'are not strictly true.'[36] What American, he asked, could accept the passage in Trevelyan's introduction where he stated, 'Britain alone of the great national States ... elaborated during the sixteenth, seventeenth and eighteenth centuries a system by which a debating club of elected persons could successfully govern an Empire in peace and war'?

Surely, the British lost America in the eighteenth century. Moreover, in passages like this, whether true or 'not strictly true', Trevelyan took an enormous amount for granted, he claimed, and was allusive when he should have been analytical. Above all, he was too 'nationalist', and his nationalism savoured more of the late nineteenth-century and First World War variety than of the nationalism of the mid-nineteenth century years. This was a hard verdict which Trevelyan would have resented as unfair. Nor would he have been happy either about the complaint that throughout the book there was too little effective comparison of British politics, government and administration with those of other countries. When Trevelyan looked towards 'another ship', the reviewer stated, 'to consider the characteristic institutions of another country, then, like Nelson, one of his heroes, he put his telescope to his blind eye'.

Some British reviewers – like critics since – have complained that the *History* was selective in relation to British history itself. Indeed, what it left out was as considerable as what it put in. The leisure, the freedom and the independence which Trevelyan had enjoyed determined not only his angle of vision but his choice of themes and the amount of space he devoted to them. 'Broad as it is,' G.M. Young pointed out, 'Dr Trevelyan's landscape is no more than a sector of the whole.' (He did not add specifically that out of 703 pages only 88 were devoted to Young's own favourite period, that after 1815.) 'As one thinks over the book,' wrote the *New Statesman* reviewer, whose tone was enthusiastic, 'one feels a little as if one had been staying at a well-filled country house, meeting a large number of extremely interesting people, all of whom had been on their good behaviour and none more so than the host.'[37] The epilogue, Trevelyan himself admitted, had been imposed on him by his publisher: 'I don't understand the age we live in,' he wrote to his brother, 'and what I do understand I don't like.'[38] There was notable ambivalence of purpose, therefore, in the design. The last sentence of the book seemed clear enough. 'Of the future the historian can see no more than others. He can only point like a showman to the things of the past, with their manifold and mysterious message.' Yet was there anything 'manifold and mysterious' in his simple and didactic declaration that 'in answer to the instincts and temperament of her people' England 'evolved in the course of centuries a system which reconciled three things that other nations have often found incompatible – executive efficiency, popular control and personal freedom'? The ambiguity was enhanced by vague rhetorical references to 'a splendid future' and to 'new and larger means of destiny.'

Between the publication of the *History* and the publication of his *English Social History* in 1942, very much in the same tradition,

Trevelyan, now Professor Trevelyan, Fellow of Trinity College, Cambridge, wrote three volumes of a Queen Anne trilogy, and Herbert Butterfield, from not very distant Peterhouse, wrote his *Whig Interpretation of History*.[39] Butterfield did not once mention Trevelyan by name or refer to the Inaugural Lecture in which Trevelyan had stated that 'the poetry of history does not consist of imagination roaming at large, but of imagination pursuing the fact and fastening upon it.' More interestingly, perhaps, Butterfield did not mention Macaulay either, nor note the fact that Trevelyan had settled on the reign of Queen Anne because that was the point where Macaulay's history ended. The element of art in this decision had little to do with Whiggery, but it placed 'an artificial straightjacket of unity upon the years of Anne's reign which in reality existed only in the pages of his history.'[40]

Trevelyan's *Anne* trilogy was read for delight more than for information, and it has, too, obvious weaknesses for the professional historian. Moreover, it was compared inevitably at the time with Winston Churchill's four volume biography of his ancestor *Marlborough: His Life and Times*, the first volume of which appeared in 1933. Trevelyan was not granted access to the papers at Blenheim Palace because they were being used by Churchill, who, like him, had been a schoolboy at Harrow in the same decade.[41] They were very different people – as different as Baldwin and Churchill – and their philosophies of history and of life were very different too – but they shared the same interpretation of Marlborough, such a very different interpretation from that of Macaulay that John Hale has called Trevelyan's three volumes 'a brilliant reparation for Macaulay's savage caricature.'[42]

Churchill was drawn back to Blenheim by 'family piety', a quality Trevelyan fully appreciated, but Plumb has questioned whether in the case of Trevelyan, who this time had no family traditions in mind, the right place and period had been chosen. Anne's reign, he has suggested, was less fitting as a scene of action for him to describe than the Italy of Garibaldi or the England of the Stuarts. 'The worldliness and cynicism of men seeking power at all costs, twisting and debauching institutions to get it, is not a world in which Trevelyan moves with instinctive ease.'[43] Trevelyan himself was concerned lest he might be providing too much 'drum and trumpet history' of the kind J.R. Green did not like and, as one reviewer put it, he seemed bored with domestic politics. Yet he always warmed to his task when he turned from politics to society. 'What men that little rustic England could breed! A nation of five and a half millions that had Wren for its architect, Newton for its scientist, Locke for its philosopher, Bentley for its scholar, Pope for its poet, Addison for its essayist, Bolingbroke for its orator, Swift for its pamphleteer, and Marlborough to win its battles, had the recipe for genius.'

Given the selection of such diverse names and the relationships between them, such a list provokes historiographical criticism of a different kind from that presented by Butterfield in his *Whig Interpretation*. There was, indeed, more than a touch of ambiguity in Butterfield's own approach to Whig history. Whiggery, he came to see, provided a mental map and, if it were discarded, the country might get lost. In his later study, *The Englishman and His History*, published in 1944 two years after the first appearance of Trevelyan's *Social History*, he praised 'the Englishman's alliance with his history' and drew a curious distinction between Whigs and Whig historians, rejoicing throughout in 'an interpretation of the past which has grown up with us, has grown up with the history itself, and has helped to make the history.' The Whig interpretation was not something invented by 'wilful historians' but was 'part of the landscape of English life, like our country lanes, or our November mists or our historic inns ... The Whig interpretation came at exactly the crucial moment and, whatever it may have done to our history, it had a wonderful effect on English politics.'[44]

Certainly Trevelyan's *Social History* appeared at the crucial moment when, in Butterfield's phrase, 'England resumed contact with her traditions and threw out ropes to the preceding generations, as though in time of danger it was a good thing not to lose touch with the rest of the convoy'.[45] The *History* had been planned before the War, and when Robert Longman first suggested the subject, Trevelyan was at first hesitant about the idea of 'isolating' social history from the political narrative. 'What is social history?' he is reported to have asked his publisher. And the history suffered when he had to truncate it because of the War, leaving out Roman, Anglo-Saxon and Norman times. The omission of the Norman Conquest was particularly serious. It recurs again and again in later history as a major theme, carrying with it 'the myth of the Norman yoke' and a persisting 'habit of authority' in English life and thought. As it is, we start with Chaucer and what Trevelyan calls 'the modern mingling with the medieval'.

Parodoxically it was because of the curious conditions of the so-called 'People's War' that *Social History* became a success, and paradoxically too it was only his critics among the professional historians who accused it of doing just what he had been afraid of – that is, leaving the politics out. First published in the United States in 1942, where it had small sales, it had to be held back in Britain – because of the paper shortage – until the momentous summer of 1944, when the fortunes of war had turned and Britain and Allied troops had returned in force to the European mainland. The end of the war was in sight. Trevelyan's readers turned to its pages for inspiration as much as for consolation or interpretation, and most copies of it were sold after the war. In 1944, only 15,000 copies of *English Social History* could be produced because of the paper shortage, and they were all sold out before the day of publication. Another 20,000 were printed in February 1945 and 60,000 in July, by which latter date the European War had ended. They were followed by new imprints of 50,000 in January 1946 and 80,000 in May 1046, again very quickly sold out. By 1949, when Longmans published Trevelyan's *Autobiography*, nearly 400,000 copies had been sold. The first volume of a four-volume illustrated edition appeared in that year. There had been no similar historical best-seller since Macaulay, and even his remarkable work sold only 140,000 copies in one generation.

The parallels stood out, as did the continuities. There was much in Trevelyan's approach which recalled Macaulay's own introduction with its dismissal of 'important events' and its stress on the importance of uncovering materials 'sanctioned in no treaties and recorded in no archives'. Trevelyan agreed, too, with Macaulay's reflection that 'the upper current of society presents no certain criterion by which we can judge of the direction in which the undercurrent flows.' For him, the theme of social history remained the 'continuous stream of life', and when he came to the industrial revolution – outside Macaulay's time frame – Trevelyan saw it characteristically as 'the river of life itself in the lower part of its course.' It was not, like the Black Death, 'a fortuitous obstruction fallen across the river of life and temporarily diverting it.'

There was another parallel, too. When Robert Longman sent Trevelyan a royalties cheque for £14,589.11s.4d. in May 1946, he reminded him of the famous £20,000 cheque sent to Macaulay by the firm in December 1855. (This covered the royalties for Macaulay's Volumes III and IV.) Robert Longman, great nephew of the William Longman, who had commissioned Macaulay, feared that the famous cheque had disappeared in the London Blitz. Its recovery seemed a favourable omen.

On the very day that Robert Longman had written to Trevelyan in July 1944 telling him of the likely English publication date of *Social History*, the Longmans offices had been 'blasted' by enemy action. The old Paternoster Row premises had already been destroyed in December 1940, a month when the Longmans catalogue of nearly 6000 titles was abruptly reduced to twelve. 'Here I sit in Cambridge in perfect safety,' Trevelyan replied in 1944, 'while you in London are bearing the weight of the Second Battle of Britain in the last stages of the victorious war.' Yet Trevelyan, like Longman, related the violence of the immediate context to a long tradition of cultivated cooperation between the two families. 'I have been connected with your firm,' he told Longman, 'for forty-five years and have published fifteen out of my twenty books with you. My Father and Great-Uncle published with you ever since the 1820s [when the firm of Longman was already a century old]. Never once has there been any misunderstanding between the members of my Family and the members of your Firm.'

Trevelyan did not see social history as unifying history. When Mark Longman gave a dinner for him in November 1955 to celebrate *Studies in Social History, A Tribute to Trevelyan*, edited by Plumb, Trevelyan pointed to another danger – that if social history were to seek to claim too much for itself other kinds of history might suffer. 'Constitutional, legal, ecclesiastical and religious history, though affected by the growth of classes, each has a life of its own and moves actually in its own orbit to a degree that some recent historians have not been willing to recognise.' The statement sounds like a rebuke to the Left, particularly since it includes the phrase 'though affected by the growth of classes'. But it was addressed to a wider audience. Trevelyan disliked too much probing into the kind of social phenomena and relationships which sociologists set out to study. He was more interested in narrating and describing than in theorising or explaining. As an American social theorist, Everett Hagen, has written, 'each historical development [in *English Social History*] is seen to flow so logically from the preceding one that to superimpose added theory seems unnecessary depreciation.'[46]

The word 'flow' recurs again in this assessment, but it is necessary to relate it to the other phrase Trevelyan used in an early discussion with Robert Longman – 'the social side'. More recent generations of social historians have rejected the idea that there is a 'social side' to history – 'everyday things', for example, or 'the conditions of labour and leisure'. They have rather treated social history as the history of society. Meanwhile, historians of all varieties have come to share Professor Hugh Trevor-Roper's view that he 'cannot conceive of good history without a sociological dimension.'[47]

By 1955, Trevelyan discerned a 'serious interest' in social history – 'social history is particularly popular now' – but he was thinking less of professional historians than of general readers. This appeal also has grown greatly since 1955. A Social History Society was founded in 1976, following in the wake of highly successful Labour and Urban History Societies. The media have made much of social history in such adventurous series as *The Long March of Everyman*. Oral history has been transformed since the invention of the tape recorder and visual history since the improvement of the camera and the invention of the photo-copying machine. The history of every local social institution, from town hall to football club, receives devoted attention, particularly at the time of jubilees and centenaries, and the idea of the 'history workshop' ('history from below') has brought in lots of readers – and amateur writers – who might not even have heard of Trevelyan, let alone read him. Many of them are doers also, digging, operating early industrial machinery, exploring old railway tracks and canals. If they were to bother to read him, they would appreciate his strong visual sense and the fact that he strongly approved of doing as well as reading. One of the voluntary societies to which he gave his invaluable support was the Youth Hostels Association.

These are the perspectives of today. In 1944 itself, when *English Social History* first appeared in this country, there was a wider interest in history than perhaps even Trevelyan, who knew of it, recognised. Yet within that context it carries with it surprises. Above all, the Second World War itself scarcely figured in it, so that we are reminded from time to time of Trevelyan's comment on the Napoleonic Wars that 'the war was in the newspapers but it scarcely entered the lives of the enjoying classes'. There were few 'enjoying classes' during the Second World War, but paradoxically Trevelyan's refusal to integrate what was happening topically into his history may well have been a factor in its success. It took people out of the war and out of the austerity which followed it. Plumb, a pupil of Trevelyan, was told by a friend that on his military service in the Suez Canal Zone he had seen it being read by soldiers who had left school at fourteen and who had probably never held a hardback book in their hands since the day they left.

There were, of course, ample elements of adventure in *English Social History* as well as escape. Agincourt and Flodden were described, and the yeomen of England were praised as 'the nation's shield and buckler'. There was one reference, too, to the perils of losing national self-sufficiency, perils which were almost as plain in 1949 as they had been in 1942. There was also one sentence which began 'unless we become a Totalitarian State and forget our Englishry'. In general, however, Trevelyan wanted the past to speak for the poetry which it expressed and not for the propaganda which it might generate. Nor would he make any concessions to those people who felt that history might be a guide to the future. 'What will happen to England in peace and war,' he wrote on his last page, 'the historian is no better able to guess than anyone else.' At an earlier point in his book, he had remarked, for once rather ponderously, that 'truly the ways of men's history are strange and the fate of nations is inscrutable'.

It is the absence of a kind of wartime propaganda which makes the book last, although this is not to say that it is not impregnated with strong judgements of value. Leaving the war on one side, and the destruction of history which went with it, Trevelyan was alarmed that

'England was bidding fair to become one huge unplanned suburb'. Leaving on one side war propaganda, he complained of the 'mass vulgarity' which had been brought into existence by 'industrial change', 'the advent of the new journalism', 'the decay of the country-side' and 'the mechanisation of life'. 'The modern conditions of great city life and mechanised occupation had destroyed poetry and imaginative literature'. History was all that was left. 'The Twentieth Century has been kept in perpetual movement and unrest by the headlong progress of inventions, which hurry mankind on, along roads that no one has chosen, a helpless fugitive with no abiding place.' The sense of direction in Whig history had at last been lost.

We are a considerable distance away from Macaulay. And again personal experience came into the reckoning as well as historical meditation. When Trevelyan received his cheque for £14,589.11s.4d. he immediately invested £12,000 in Tax Reserve Certificates. What would Macaulay have had to say about that? Trevelyan himself had noted in Chapter V that 'an obstinate refusal to pay taxes had been a characteristic of the English in Tudor England.' It is necessary to add, however, that out of the large sum he donated £3000 to 'lead off' a National Trust Appeal Fund. He had been interested in the National Trust for twenty years, and he was prepared to put his own money into the preservation of buildings and landscape. He wrote eloquently about beauty and decay; and when he talked of the danger of England becoming a 'huge unplanned suburb', he was identifying what seemed to him to be one of the most alarming features of his age. Of the great houses which he had known as a boy, Welcombe, his mother's house near Stratford-on-Avon (and how well he writes about Stratford in *English Social History*), survived as a railway hotel, and another, Wallington, in northern border country, was actually given to the National Trust.

Just because Trevelyan loved the country and feared or disliked city, town or suburb, his last footnote in *English Social History* is of exceptional interest. The fighter pilots of 1940, Churchill's 'few', to whom the many owed so much, were the products, Trevelyan admitted, not of 'rural simplicity' but of urban sophistication. They were products too not of traditional schools but of new primary and secondary schools. Given some of the comments which he had made earlier in the book, this footnote had the air of a subversive afterthought. In writing of the seventeenth century, for example, he had stressed that 'the ordinary Englishman [a treacherous term] was not yet a townee [a dead word now?] wholly divorced from nature ... [and] unwilling to abandon the advantages of a high standard of living at home for a life of hardship and incessant toil in an unknown land'. Far back in Chapter I, he had introduced with a touch of apprehension 'our city-bred folk', and in Chapter XV he had generalised confidently that 'the vitality of the village slowly declined as the city in a hundred ways sucked away its blood and business'. There is no doubt that he saw the rise of 'urban ways of thought and action' as increasingly destructive over a long period of time. Yet he had to admit in his last footnote that it was such 'ways' which had served England in its hour of greatest need.

There are difficult problems of English social history buried away here – the attitudes of different classes towards each other and to the nation; the sources of patriotism; the varieties of communication. Many of Trevelyan's readers, like the soldiers in the Canal Zone who thrilled to *English Social History*, were 'townees' who had seen even less of country houses or haystacks than they had seen of hardback books. Many of them, moreover, had been forced, however unwillingly, 'to abandon the advantages of a high standard of living at home for a life of hardship [if not, in the Army, incessant toil] in an unknown land.' If pressed, however, – and he seldom was – Trevelyan might have suggested that such experience did not completely invalidate his thesis. He argued in literary not in sociological terms. Although he thought that the twentieth century was unlikely to produce great creative literature capable of appealing to the whole public, he also thought that history with its inherent poetry might. Indeed, in his view, it could satisfy a craving for poetry which might have been satisfied more directly in previous centuries by other forms of art.

The poetry of history was the music of time, and it was that music which appealed to people who might have spurned novels or sonnets. 'The poetry of history,' he had always proclaimed, 'lies in the quasi-miraculous fact that once upon this earth, on this familiar spot of ground, walked other men and women, as actual as we are today, thinking their own thoughts, swayed by their own passions, but now all gone, one generation vanishing after another, but now all gone, gone as utterly as we ourselves will shortly be gone, like ghosts at cock-crow.' Plumb was nearer to the truth about the spell of Trevelyan as a historian – not only of his *English Social History* – when he wrote in 1951 that for Trevelyan 'each historical fact is implicit with our doom.'

NOTES

1   J.W. Burrow, *A Liberal Descent* (1981), p. 2.
2   H. Butterfield, *The Whig Interpretation of History* (1931), p. 10.
3   Quoted in Cecil Woodham Smith, *The Great Hunger* (1962), p. 69.
4   See M.A. Thomson, *Macaulay* (Historical Association Pamphlet) (1959), p. 25.

5 See G.M. Young, 'At the Bar of History', in *Last Essays* (1950), p. 33.

6 Quoted in M. Moorman, *George Macaulay Trevelyan* (1980), p. 30.

7 G.M. Trevelyan, *Clio, a Muse* (1913), p. 11.

8 G.M. Trevelyan, *An Autobiography and Other Essays* (1949), p. 18. For a tribute to Gooch by Trevelyan, see F.E. Hirsch, 'George Peabody Gooch', in the *Journal of Modern History*, vol. 16 (1954), and for Gooch on Trevelyan, see G.P. Gooch, *Historical Surveys and Portraits* (1966), pp. 254-8.

9 G.M. Trevelyan, *The Present Position of History* (1927). See also F. Eyck, *G. P. Gooch* (1982), Chapter 3, 'Lord Acton'.

10 Quoted in J.M. Hernon, 'The Last Whig Historian and Consensus History: George Macaulay Trevelyan'. For Yea and Nay, see Thomas Carlyle, *Sartor Resartus* (1838).

11 H.R. Winkler, 'George Macaulay Trevelyan', in S.W. Halperin (ed.), *Some 20th Century Historians* (1961), p. 38.

12 Letter of 4 July 1900, cited in Hernon, *loc. cit.*, p. 101.

13 K.B. McFarlane, *John Wycliffe* (1953), p. 153. See also for a contemporary judgement on Trevelyan that of J. Tait in the *English Historical Review*, vol. XV (1900).

14 *An Autobiography*, p. 21.

15 *England under the Stuarts* (1957 edn), p. 428.

16 Moorman, *op. cit.*, p. 105.

17 *Garibaldi's Defence of the Roman Republic* (1907); *Garibaldi and the Thousand* (1910); *Garibaldi and the Making of Italy* (1911).

18 James Bryce wrote to E.A. Freeman, the historian, of the Garibaldi visit, 'the reception was the most wonderful outburst of popular enthusiasm ever seen in London' (quoted in C. Harvie, *The Lights of Liberalism* (1976), p. 103).

19 See D. Mack Smith, *Cavour and Garibaldi in 1860* (1954); *Garibaldi* (1957); and *Italy, 1860-1960* (1959). Trevelyan's final Italian study *Manin and the Venetian Revolution of 1989* (1923) was rightly criticised from the start. As J.H. Plumb, who edited the *Festschrift* volume *Studies in Social History* for Trevelyan in 1955, put it, Venetian society, 'as far gone in decay as it was developed in sophistication, was not a world for the great simplicities of Trevelyan's heart and mind' (*G.M. Trevelyan* (1951), p. 21).

20 See G. Kitson Clark, 'G.M. Trevelyan as a Historian', in the *Durham University Journal* (1972).

21 See Moorman, *op. cit.*, p. 161.

22 Moorman, *op. cit.*, p. 123.

23 See, for example, the review by C.E. Fryer in the *American Historical Review*, vol. 26 (1921).

24 Moorman, *op. cit.*, p. 165.

25 See his Bishop Creighton lecture delivered at London University, *The War and the European Revolution in Relation to History* (1920).

26 G.M. Trevelyan, Creighton Lecture, pp. 12-13; S. Baldwin, 'England', Speech at a Dinner of 1924, reprinted in *On England and Other Addresses* (1926), p. 5.

27 Quoted in H. Montgomery Hyde, *Baldwin, the Unexpected Prime Minister* (1973), p. 565.

28 *Hansard, Parliamentary Debates*, House of Lords, vol. 96 (1934-5), cols 896-8.

29 See G.M. Young, *Stanley Baldwin* (1952), pp. 70, 77.

30 G.M. Trevelyan, *The Historical Causes of the Present State of Affairs in Italy* (1923), p. 15.

31 G.M. Trevelyan, *Britain in the Nineteenth Century* (1924), p. vii.

32 Quoted in Hernon, *loc cit.*, p. 72.

33 Quoted in P. Clarke, *Liberals and Social Democrats* (1978), p. 207.

34 H. Nicolson, *Diaries and Letters, 1939-1945* (ed. N. Nicolson, 1967), p. 140.

35 Plumb, *loc. cit.*

36 *American Historical Review* (1927), pp. 571-2.

37 *New Statesman*, 24 June 1926.

38 G.M. Trevelyan, *England under Queen Anne: Blenheim* (1930); *Ramillies and the Union with Scotland* (1932); *The Peace and the Protestant Succession* (1934).

40 Winkler, *loc. cit.*, p. 48.

41 For Churchill's work on *Marlborough* and the occasional correspondence with Trevelyan, see M. Gilbert, *Winston S. Churchill*, vol. V (1976), pp. 319 ff.

42 J. Hale, *The Evolution of British Historiography* (1964), p. 70.

43 Plumb, *op. cit.*, pp. 28-30. Cp. the review of *Blenheim*, by Sir Charles Petrie, the 'Tory historian', in the *Saturday Review*, vol. CL (1930), p. 410.

44 H. Butterfield, *The Englishman and His History* (1944), pp. 4, 2, 7.

45 *ibid.*, p. v.

46 E. Hagen, *On The Theory of Social Change* (1962).

47 See H. Trevor-Roper, *Historical Essays* (1957).

12   G.M. Young: The Age of a Portrait

'To view an individual or a society primarily as a problem', R.H. Tawney once wrote, 'is to make certain of misconception.'[1] One historian who never did was G.M. Young, born at Charlton in Kent in 1882, two years after Tawney. Young did not publish a book until 1932. Nor did he ever study or teach history in a university. Yet there is no twentieth-century English historian who has illuminated the history of England in the previous century more brilliantly than he. 'I am one of the few men', he wrote after the end of the Second World War, 'who can not only write but think Victorian.'[2]

His study of Victorian England, published in 1934, took the form not of an analysis of problems but of a portrait of an age, and although it has often appeared since then within the frame of hard covers, it was originally, like most of his work, an essay rather than a book. The essay was his ideal form, and many of the paragraphs in the *Portrait* have their origins in essays produced separately. His longest book, the authorised biography of Stanley Baldwin, published after frustrating delays in 1952, was not generally regarded as a success. Baldwin was shy about asking him to write it,[3] and Young was reluctant to accept the invitation. Like everything else Young wrote, it is not lacking in insight, yet the insight is essentially that of an essayist rather than a biographer.

Insight for Young was very much a matter of *seeing*. Indeed, at the very end of *Portrait of an Age* he suggested that perhaps some day we will all acquire what 'as a race we have never possessed – the historian's eye'. 'Is it worth acquiring?' he went on to ask, however, and not surprisingly gave the answer that it is. His first reason was general. It was worth acquiring as 'any serious and liberal habit of mind' is bound to be worth acquiring in 'our age which the increase of routine and specialism on the one side, the extension of leisure and amusement on the other, is likely to make less liberal and less serious'. Young offered a more profound second answer also. 'We live in an age which can afford to forgo no study by which disaster can be averted or eluded.'

These words were written before the Second World War, before the beginnings of appeasement, before television, before the growth of 'a techno-bureaucracy', all of which came to interest and to concern him.

Indeed, the words were the prelude to Young's final generalisations about the Victorian age. 'As I see it', he concluded,

> the tradition of the nineteenth century was to disengage the disinterested intelligence ... and to set it operating over the whole range of human life and circumstance. In England we see this spirit issuing from, and often at war with, a society most stoutly tenacious of old ways and forms, and yet most deeply immersed in its new business of acquisition.[4]

There are so many and so varied insights throughout the *Portrait* that it can be read with profit time and time again at different stages of one's life – and one's study of the period – and new points in it or new aspects of it are perennially to be discovered. Like all brilliant portraits, it is more than a record: it is a highly personal interpretation. Its taut sentences, its almost omnipresent metaphor, and its web of allusion may make it difficult to read for the first time – although they never deterred me – and its selectivity, while never idiosyncratic, means that much which we may consider to be important about the 'Victorian age' is left out of it. Its generalisations, like the final conclusion, can be disputed. Yet it is a portrait which will last.

Moreover, it is not only for its insights that it should be discovered and rediscovered, nor for the 'information' which it contains, much of it difficult to discover elsewhere, some of it wrong.[5] The *Portrait* has five outstanding features, each of which can best be appreciated when Young's other writings are taken into account, for there he not only discussed periods very different from the 'Victorian age', the approach to which influenced what he had to say about the Victorians, but, very occasionally, he generalised about his methods of study and interpretation. These other writings were often ephemeral – Young enjoyed writing for newspapers as well as for periodicals – and what he thought of his own age influenced what he wrote about the 'Victorian age' as much as what he thought of previous ages.[6]

Young regarded the years after Victoria's death as a 'flash Edwardian epilogue' with 'a decline of purpose and strength', and he was even less satisfied with the 1920s and 1930s. 'To a mature and civilized man', he explained, 'no faith was possible by 1936 except for faith in the argument itself.'[7] During the Second World War, he feared that the nineteenth century 'curve' might have been broken at last. 'The area of well-informed discussion was contracting and those who are best qualified by education or experience to occupy it are gradually losing the weight they ought to carry in a well-balanced constitution.'[8] He approached the nineteenth century, therefore, from which he himself had emerged, with critical respect, and because so much could no longer be taken for granted during the 1930s, 1940s and 1950s he did not take the Victorians for granted either. Neither their achievements nor the way most people were then interpreting it was in his view straightforward.

The first extraordinary feature of the *Portrait* was that it was neither a Whig portrait nor a fashionable Radical caricature. Young has told us that he was already a Tory when he saw Queen Victoria driving through the streets of London when he was only ten years old. He was strongly opposed, he added, to Gladstone's second Home Rule Bill of 1893. His Toryism persisted, surviving – or perhaps even being strengthened by – the writing of the volume on Baldwin. When he died in 1959, that particular Baldwinite Toryism was dying too, if it had not already died: it was shaken by the beginnings of 'the age of affluence' which Young disliked as much as William Morris would have done,[9] and by a decline in the ideal of public service; and it was fitting, given his strong sense of 'decade' and 'generation', that he did not move into the 1960s.

Young would have hated Thatcherite contempt for 'consensus' as much as 'Bennism'. We do not turn to the *Portrait* either for praise of 'material progress' or for elegiac Whig meditation on its 'spiritual' limitations.[10] What we do find there, however, is a recovery of the variety of Victorian voices, the point counter point, with some of the voices sweet and others strident, and with some looking backwards and some forwards. No one was better able than Young to identify the tangled motivations lying behind Victorian fascination with the past – contrast, escape, ambiguity. He understood *why* George Eliot, 'the moralist of the Victorian revolution', felt a 'little Toryism on the sly'. He insisted, too, that it was a late eighteenth- and early nineteenth-century paradox that 'the Middle Ages in England ceased to interest the educated intelligence just about the time when they began to lay hold on the educated fancy'.[11]

Perhaps Young did not emphasise enough the limits to the free play of the 'disinterested mind' in Victorian England, although he very gently drew attention to them – for example, in a parenthesis in the key quotation 'to release it from the entanglements of party and sect – *one might also add, of sex*' (my italics). He believed, indeed, that the biggest changes between the nineteenth and twentieth centuries could be found there and in a development of a new approach to psychology. 'I doubt very much', he wrote in one early essay,

> whether there can be any continuity between a civilization based on automatic child-bearing and a civilization based on regulated child-bearing. The detachment of sex from its primeval framework of social union and domestic authority, has in my own time produced consequences

so observable that I can set no end to the consequences it may still produce.[12]

Young's interest in psychology, individual and social, is not clearly revealed in the *Portrait*. He had worked in Vienna after 1919 to administer a special relief fund granted by the British Treasury, and he was aware of the significance of Freud's work before Freud established 'a whole climate of opinion'.[13] He noted the change in his important essay 'Continuity', where he compared the reaction to Freud with the excitement that attended the arrival of the new learning of the Renaissance, observing that in his view the impact of the 'new psychology' might be more striking in the longer run than the impact of the 'new physics'. Yet there is little in the *Portrait* which points to the unconscious or its exploration. Neither Havelock Ellis nor Samuel Butler is mentioned, and it is the deliberately 'self-conscious' element in the culture of the late nineteenth century which he singled out, not the relationship between open and hidden forces influencing social and political behaviour as much as attitudes.[14] The nearest we get to a deeper analysis is an oblique and very non-Whiggish statement that in the struggles in which the Victorians were engaged, there was no victory, only victories as something was won and held against ignorance or convention or prejudice or greed.[15]

The adjective 'cultural' points to the second outstanding feature of the *Portrait*. Young was not the kind of social historian who deals fully and often convincingly with structures[16] and then goes on to deal, usually less convincingly, with dynamics. There are no 'models' behind this particular *Portrait*, only very real people; no 'trends', only light and shade. If Young has to be placed, it is as a cultural historian who deals fully and usually convincingly with processes, and occasionally, always less convincingly, goes on to separate out structures.

Young began his work on the *Portrait*, he tells us, by trying to copy Macaulay, supreme Victorian historian in reputation if not in achievement, but very wisely he cast into the flames a first draft which had 'rapidly degenerated into a flat imitation' of Macaulay's famous third chapter on the state of society.[17] He went on next to reconsider all his arts and techniques; and characteristically asking himself another leading question 'what is history about?', he framed an answer very different from that of the Whig Macaulay or for that matter from that given later by the very non-Whig twentieth-century historian, E. H. Carr.[18] 'The real central theme of history', Young came to consider – and it determined all his future writing, however ephemeral – was

not what happened, but what people felt about it when it was happening:

in Philip Sidney's phrase [and he deliberately looked before the nineteenth century], 'the affects, the whisperings, the motions of the people'; in Maitland's 'men's common thought of common things'; in mine, 'the conversation of the people who counted.' Who were they? What were the assumptions behind their talk and what came of it all?[19]

Young's way of putting his answer should not be accepted uncritically. Nor should the memorable advice to other historians which he gave later – 'Read, read, read, till you hear the people talking.' The approach lays too much emphasis on talk – not enough on action or on the events which characterise it. The articulate, for all Young's critique of the inarticulateness of the English, is endowed with supreme merit – at least as evidence. Only six years separated the first publication of *Portrait of an Age* in 1934 from Aldous Huxley's *Point Counter Point*, a brilliant novel of talk, with which it has far more in common than with Macaulay, even if many of the characters in the *Portrait* are more agreeable.[20] One of the characters in *Point Counter Point*, the Indian, Sita Ram, makes a point and asks a question which Young should have made and answered – 'Sometimes one reads a whole book without finding a single phrase one can remember or quote. What's the good of such a book, I ask you?'

Young was right (in my opinion) to imply that the historian should always start his research by immersing himself in the materials of the period he was wishing to explore rather than start with preconceived ideas about it. He was right also to suggest, although never explicitly, that the language of a period – its syntax and imagery as well as its vocabulary – needs to be understood before terminology derived from a later period – or from subsequent sociological discourse – is applied to it. What should happen next, however, he never bothered to say, although he appears to have had notions of his own about the relationship between social and intellectual history. 'We have no other word than "idea"', he wrote, 'which includes the thought, the picture, and the feeling'.[21]

The social historian baulks at his phrase 'the conversations of the people who counted'. Why stop there? Who counted, and why? Tom Jones felt when he first met Young that he was 'a distinctly able but also "superior" person', adding, 'I realised acutely that I had not been to Oxford.'[22] The 'superiority' survived Young's working closely with Arthur Henderson as his wartime Private Secretary;[23] and while he was not unaware of the fact that, to use more recent jargon, there is 'history from below', which is reflected in the conversation of the people who do not count, he doubtless felt (rightly) that Henderson was a man who did.

Much oral history has recently concentrated on 'history from below', as Mass Observation did during the 1930s, and it illuminates aspects of past periods which might otherwise have been hidden from view.[24] Young, separated by birth and upbringing from many of the people who might have widened his scope, would have been able by talking to them, more truly to test the Victorian precept which he quoted as a motto to the *Portrait*, 'Servants talk about People: Gentlefolk discuss Things'. He could write of Sir Walter Scott how his 'search for historic truth' led him to the sheepfold as well as to the battlefield, the cottage as well as the court,[25] and he could appreciate how Mass Observation enabled strata to be explored which were hitherto unexplored.[26] Young was neither Scott nor Tom Harrisson, however, and curious though he might be about all kinds of conversation, his preference was restricted. 'Talk as much as you can to educated women older than yourself; and listen, when you have a chance, to men whose profession requires them to use common words exactly – officers, civil servants and lawyers – talking about common things.'[27]

His standpoint, as Kitson Clark pointed out, was that of 'the highly educated, moderately liberal, professional middle class', a most important class, which came to maturity during the Victorian years and was responsible 'for much of the progress' of those years, but one which could not always communicate easily with the rest.[28] Its 'powers of recruitment and absorption were great', of course, but it never was more than a very small section of the nation; 'and if Young had drawn his portrait from the point of view of another group its perspective, its values, its selection of the objects portrayed would not have been the same'.[29]

This is not simply a matter of historiography, much studied in Kitson Clark's Cambridge, but of sociology; and Kitson Clark himself, a northerner by birth and, like Young, a Tory (although of a different species), knew this when he added that if Young had

> taken his stand with one section or other of the working class it is possible that harsh economic pressures and such institutions as Trade Unions would have bulked larger. If he had seen England from the point of view of the military, or of the squires, or of some group of businessmen, or of some religious body, the view of England would in each case have been different. For there are innumerable points of view from which a community can be surveyed, and in each case what is seen and what is not seen, and the light and shade in which they are seen, will differ with the standpoint of the viewer.[30]

Fair though this verdict is, it is near to a truism. We know that Young *was* a civil servant until the mid-1920s and that long after that date he continued to serve on committees.[31] We know, too, although

Kitson Clark did not mention it, how much weight Young attached to the conversation of lawyers: he spoke of their natural interest in 'the human spectacle' ever unrolling before their eyes and of their minds 'trained to disengage the relevant from the incidental, and the essential from the local: to weigh testimonies, to balance probabilities, to estimate the force of motives among all sorts and conditions of men'.[32] Not surprisingly, therefore, he set out to discover order in other people's conversations, not simply to report them – to select, to sieve, to relate – falling back on Maitland's conception of law as 'fundamentally a system of common thought about common things'.[33]

Young's way of looking at his own historiographical position was very different from – and less familiar than – that described by Kitson Clark. Near the end of the *Portrait* he approached historiography not through sociology but through art, quoting Constable's dictum that 'painting is a science of which painters are the experimenters'. It was not a coincidence that he was a Trustee of the National Portrait Gallery from 1937 to 1956:

> That there is a painter's eye, an attitude or disposition recognisable as such in Giotto and Gauguin, no one will question, yet Giotto and Gauguin confronted with the same object will make different pictures, of which no one can say that one is truer than the other: and to impose an Interpretation of History on history is, to my mind, to fall into the error, or to commit the presumption, of saying that all Virgins must look like Piero's, or that, if we were sufficiently enlightened, we should see all chairs as van Gogh saw them.[34]

Young had a strong visual sense[35] – 'everyone of us lives in a landscape of his own'[36] – and the *Portrait* draws, to an unusual extent among either intellectual or social histories of the nineteenth century, on the history of art (though not on the history of music). Young also drew exceptionally heavily on literature – and this fourth feature of the *Portrait*, not mentioned by Kitson Clark – is surely what gives it its main distinctiveness – a dependence at nearly every point on a rich and intimate knowledge of Victorian (and earlier) poetry and prose. Young was certainly not typical of the professional middle classes in this respect, however wide their reading interests were.[37] Byron is introduced in the very first sentence, two lines of Gerald Manley Hopkins are quoted in the last. For once, Young chose the wrong quotation to introduce his essay when he took a passage from Pindar – 'Great deeds are always the subject of many tales; but to embroider a few themes in a long story, that is something for wise men's hearing.' There is no embroidery in the *Portrait*: literature does not embellish, it qualifies, confirms, establishes. It was to Scott he looked for the beginnings of a real sense of history.[38]

A good example of Young's method comes at the end of section XVII, almost half way through the thirty-one sections, each a work of art in itself, into which the essay is divided. It deals with the concept of 'process', so congenial to Young. Three poems are referred to, with no elaboration, to help us 'follow the secular intellect seeking its way to such an apprehension of Being as a Process as might hereafter reconcile the spiritual demands of humanity with the rapt and cosmic indifference of Evolution'. The very long and complex sentence, of which this is the ending, starts with 'Evangelical, the Arnoldite and the Tractarian teaching' and reaches evolution via Hegel, Plato, and 'a faith more primitive than the Creeds of the Bible'. The three poems chosen are Tennyson's *In Memoriam* (1850), Meredith's *The Woods of Westermain* (1883) and the choruses of Hardy's *The Dynasts* (1903). The well-informed Kitson Clark note, which describes A.N. Whitehead's *Process and Reality* (1929) as the best philosophical discussion of the concept of 'process', does not do justice to Young's mode of treatment of 'the Immanent Will and its designs'. Young begs many questions, of course, in his last reference to the 'rapt and cosmic indifference of Evolution'. That is what he wished to do: his approach had more in common with A. O. Lovejoy in his *Great Chain of Being* (1936) than with Whitehead.

Historians who are suspicious of English literature as historical 'evidence' may well leave Young unread, dismissing such passages as 'intellectual history' with 'real experience' left out. They would be wiser, however, to be critical rather than indifferent, for although there are many places where Young seems to be confusing what writers said with the way their readers felt – and there is room for real criticism here – he is always concerned, if not with direct experience, at least with the way it was perceived. He takes full account, too, as he did in his definition of 'idea', of feeling as well as of thinking, always seeking to identify the subtleties of change, always bringing politics into his intellectual history as Trevelyan tried to keep it out of his social history. Thus, we read in section XXVIII, a particularly illuminating section, that 'Under its irridescent froth, the aesthetic movement, like the Fourth Party in Parliament, was an earnest challenge to that grey respectability which was thinning indeed but had not quite lifted.' Thus, far earlier in section IX, *en passant*, we are given a very different quotation from an extremely obscure text of a nonconformist pamphlet by J.M. Brown (1853) – 'There have been at work among us three great social agencies – the London City Mission; the novels of Mr Dickens; the cholera.'

All these are supremely English sources. Yet the fifth feature of the

Portrait is that in dealing with England it never leaves Europe out. As his friend W. D. Handcock has written, 'Young was a convinced European and advocate of the importance of teaching European history':[39] he was anxious to trace 'the European mind' to 'the doorstep, the bar, the common room, maybe the queue'.[40] He never suggested that the 'Victorian' was distinctively English – what for him was distinctively English was 'a curiously inarticulate mind, very clumsy and uncertain in its utterance' – and he could identify Victorian passages in Gogol.[41] He could also trace, perhaps too confidently, the influence of French naturalism on late nineteenth-century London tastes, and argue more generally that 'the Victorian age, as we call it, is the insular phase of movement common to the whole of Western Europe and its offshoots beyond the seas'.[42]

There is a wealth of close, textual European reference, including political reference, in the *Portrait*. The differences (and similarities) between what was obviously 'Victorian' in Britain and in the Commonwealth interested Young less. There was, indeed, a political dimension to his Europeanness, for he believed that Europeans could only talk intelligently to each other in the present if they had knowledge of the past: in this context, 'the historic view was not an indulgence of the human fancy, but a dominant and imperative necessity'.[43] Young had less to say about talking between the English-speaking peoples, except to insist that Basic English could not provide an adequate medium for communication there or elsewhere.[44]

On many of the subjects touched on by Young, monographs have now been written, some of them doubtless stimulated by his often cryptic allusions. What he said, therefore, is now subject to the tests of professional scrutiny – of students of English Literature, of which he was suspicious, as well as of History – and may be assessed differently from the way it was assessed in 1934. We have to remember – and it is the fourth main feature of the book – that the portrait is now an old one. When Young began to paint it, less than twenty-one years had elapsed since the death of Queen Victoria. Now half a century separates the portrait from us. 'The great age is not so far behind us', he was able to note, 'that we must needs have lost all its savour and its vigour.' Now we talk in a loose way, of which he would have thoroughly disapproved, of Victorian values. The picture he painted was, as he knew, 'a very different picture from the one at the time commonly accepted by popular opinion and set out by popular writers', and he hoped that its effect would be to 'induce some readers to reconsider their ideas and reorientate their attitudes: ideas and attitudes generated by an emotional antipathy to the Victorian age rather than by any insight into its historical significance'. Now we know that emotional affinity can lead astray as much as emotional antipathy.

II

In the warfare between generations, open or covert, the kind of warfare Young understood better than most historians, children in the 1930s were in revolt against their parents without necessarily feeling much sympathy with their grandparents; and as the years went by it was the grandparents rather than the parents who won. *Portrait of an Age* stands out as a landmark in the reinterpretation of Victorian England. It was preceded, as he tells us, by an essay of 1932, 'Victorian History', 'a manifesto or perhaps an outline for others to fill in', an essay which immediately made its way into a volume of *Selected Modern Essays* in The World's Classics series, published by the Oxford University Press. It was provoked by what he rightly considered 'a preposterous misreading of the age' and was followed – also under the auspices of the Oxford University Press [45] – by a longer essay on the period from 1831 to 1865 (Palmerston's death), which was designed to serve as the final summary chapter for the Oxford University Press volumes on *Early Victorian England* which he had been asked to edit.

These volumes in the same series as the volumes on *Shakespeare's England* and *Johnson's England* are of uneven quality, and it was Young's own essay, then stopping at 'the years of division', later extended in 1936 to cover the whole Victorian period, which stood out. And although the enterprise was characteristically Oxonian – as was Young himself, who was later to spend the last years of his life from 1948 onwards as a Fellow of All Souls – the historian to whom he turned most for inspiration was very much a Cambridge historian, F. W. Maitland (1850-1906). In an evocative essay about Maitland – with an omnipresent autobiographical dimension, sometimes overstressed – Young describes the evening when he took down *Domesday Book and Beyond*; and 'read, and read, till the owl in the fir tree began audibly to wonder why the lamp was still burning; the little breezes that stray down the dene from Wansdyke turned chilly; and the dawn came'.[46] In this case, the setting was not Oxford but Wiltshire (where Young spent much of his life) at Oare between Malmesbury and Pewsey. He felt a sense of historical continuity there – even greater than in either Oxford or Cambridge – a continuity which stretched back beyond the West Saxon kingdom to the prehistoric past, a continuity, indeed, which linked history with natural history, landscape with landscape of the mind.[47]

Maitland, who was just as aware of historical continuities, is now remembered mainly for his comments on the nineteenth century, although many of these are shot through with insight. It was characteristic of Young first to note, however, that Maitland was nine

years old when Macaulay died, and second to compare him with
Auguste Comte. Maitland, for him, was a 'warning voice' – warning
against 'historic systems' [48] – as well as an inspiring voice, bringing law
as much as politics or literature into the picture, law interpreted, as
Young interpreted history, as 'the things and the thoughts, the actual
doings, for example, of a villein or a trade unionist, and the reflections
thereon of Bracton or the judges in the Taff Vale case, reacting on
each other, and modifying each other into a pattern of such shifting
intricacy that the most comprehensive vision will not take in the whole
pattern'. For Young, Maitland was the perfect example of Francis
Bacon's *intellectus purus et aequus*, 'never distracted by study of
particulars and never lost in contemplation of the entirety'.

The reinterpretation of Victorian England owed little, however, to
historians like Maitland, although Cambridge, through Kitson Clark,
a transformed historian after the Second World War, had an important part to play. So, too, in a different environment, that of the
London School of Economics, and with a different philosophy, did
H. L. Beales, doyen of English social history. But it was not historians
necessarily who led the way. Some of the reinterpreters, notably John
Betjeman, used their eyes, as Young always demanded, and saw
buildings in a new way before they so saw people. Other reinterpreters
were inspired by the written word, notably Humphry House, who
spanned divides as wide as the nineteenth and twentieth centuries
when he moved from Cambridge to teach English Literature at
Oxford in 1948. [49] The contribution of the different revisionists is
discussed in the introduction to my *Victorian People* (1955), itself an
expression of the change in attitudes and an influence upon it, not least
because it focuses on the neglected mid-Victorian years. [50] Yet it would
be a mistake to underestimate the effect of twentieth-century history
(as distinct from historiography) or the interpretations of the nineteenth century. The Second World War, in particular, shaped both
the content and the imagery of Basil Willey's remark that 'in our own
unpleasant century we are mostly displaced persons, and many feel
tempted to take flight into the nineteenth as into a promised land, and
settle there like illegal immigrants for the rest of their lives.' [51]

Young was more aware of such curves in interpretation than most
historians, just as he was more aware of generational changes and he
would doubtless have recognised recent signs that amid the rhetoric
the Victorians may be on their way out again. He was always prepared
on occasion, as Willey was, in his remarks on the Victorian revival, to
relate twentieth-century imagery to Victorian experience, as when he
asked what else 'the Romantic Revolution was but an unofficial
strike?' [52] His essay on 'Continuity' offers his most general comments
on the patterns of the past. 'Culture', he wrote there,

is not a state, but a process; a body of assumptions, judgements, tastes, and habits, constantly changing, constantly reformulating themselves, but also constantly swerving back to gather up something which the grandfathers had dropped and the sons left lying beside the course. Indeed, it is by these movements, these epicycles of swerve and recovery, that the tradition is not only preserved but enriched.[53]

III

This passage is interesting not only in its awareness but in the tag which Young attached to it. 'This is a theme so abundant, and to me at least so alluring', he went on, 'that I must firmly resist the temptation to expatiate.' Why did he so resist? Was it because of the word limit imposed by the essay form itself? Was it because he was afraid of his own theorising as much as that of other people? Was it because he did not want, through lack of diligence or discipline or some other cause, to probe deeper?

The impulse behind Young's reflections on history seems to me to have been autobiographical rather than philosophical.[54] His broadcasts reveal more of it than his essays, for it was in these, notably in a broadcast on the year of Edward VII's coronation, 1902,[55] that he meditated on his own experience. He was twenty years old then, 'thoroughly enjoying that interval when one's first examination is over and the finals are too far off to think about' – 'a very good time for talking at large about everything'. He began with the books he was reading – Thomas Hardy's *Tess*,[56] Meredith's *Richard Feverel*,[57] H. G. Wells's *Love and Mr Lewisham*, Shaw's *Three Plays for Puritans*, and William James's *Varieties of Religious Experience*,[58] and went on to stress the slower pace of life: 'even the scientific achievement of the Victorian age had left the outer fabric of life very much as it always had been'. 'We looked forward', he added, 'to leading, with some improvements, the sort of lives our fathers had lived.' Young's was no rebel voice. 'It was an attractive life', he recalled, 'I think we might say the most attractive that European Civilization had ever fashioned for itself.' 'The general set of our talk was liberal in politics with an old-fashioned clinging to some sort of Tory democracy. But there were ardent spirits among us for whom this was not good enough, who were looking about for something more authoritative, more logical and above all more efficient.' Poverty, not physical insecurity, was the main problem. In a characteristic verdict, Young compared the England of 1953 with that of 1902, and found 'the frank good humour and good breeding one can count upon today' in refreshing contrast to 'the sulky servility of hopeless poverty' in 1902. 'We may not be the great power we were, but we are still a very great people.' Fortunately, Young did not have to re-examine this verdict in the bleak 1970s and 1980s, when he would have found ample evidence of a very different kind.

Young had looked briefly at the social scene at the time of the coronation of 1937, when, despite all the social problems then, he discerned 'a habit of common happiness'. 'I have never returned from abroad', he wrote, 'without feeling this happiness rising up to welcome me, seeing it in the friendliness of English eyes, hearing it in the quietness of English voices.'[59] He was then in his forties. Young always paid meticulous attention to the age of historical characters; and the absence of the chronological table with which he ended his *Portrait* was a curious omission in Kitson Clark's annotated edition. Young identified the age of thirty-five as the 'peak year' of his characters, including a column of *floruits* alongside the births and deaths. 1937 was Young's *floruit* – a little later, as he conceded was always possible, than the norm, which in any case changed from period to period. More curiously still, Sir George Clark in his biographical memoir, which introduces this edition, does not give the year of Young's death, 1959, better worth recalling as the centenary year of the great Victorian *annus mirabilis*[60] than for any twentieth-century features.

One feature of Young's life needs to be fitted in, however, before his general reflections on history are identified. His first book (1932) was neither on Macaulay nor on Maitland, but on Edward Gibbon[61] and his second was on Charles I and Cromwell. Long before that, he had submitted a specially commended, but not prize-winning, entry for the Arnold Prize Essay, not on public health nor on civil service reform but on the road system of medieval England.[62] Young was one of the last modern historians to take it for granted that the classical world provided a proper framework for comparison and contrast. Yet he always sought to relate the nineteenth century to other centuries too: he liked to move freely through time – backwards and forwards. One of the most sensitive and laudatory pieces in *Last Essays* is that on John Aubrey, 'the man who noticed', a central personage in a transformation of English society earlier than that of the nineteenth century; it had originally appeared as a review of Anthony Powell's *John Aubrey and his Friends* (1948). Young must have appreciated the first novels in Powell's 'music of time' sequence, for they rely, as Young did in his histories, on snatches of conversation and patterns in which 'accident' always had its place but was never an entirely complete explanation of what happened.

Young's own account of 'the music of time' was best set out in his essay on 'Continuity', which insists throughout on the key importance to him of the idea of 'generation', and goes on to emphasise 'the synthesising' role of history. Young had written in a much earlier essay, 'The Victorian Noon-Time',[63] of the artificiality of measuring by centuries and had introduced, without using the term 'generation', a young, new, mid-nineteenth-century generation who figured prominently in the *Portrait*. 'What sixteen to twenty-four is talking about', he argued, 'twenty-four to sixty-four will usually write or do.'[64] In 'Continuity' he expanded and refined. 'Measurement by centuries and decades is obviously mechanical and crude, and so we fall back on the generation.' Of course, 'the sequence of the generations is a continuous stream', but for once a 'theorem' (if not a model) was useful.

> Whenever I am thinking of a character, in public life it may be, or in literature, I always ask 'What was happening in the world when he was twenty?' If I am thinking of a year, the question is 'Who were in their forties then?' To the twenties I go for the shaping of ideas not fully disclosed: to the forties for the handling of things already established. And the same analysis seems to keep before our minds the further truth that, in the nature of things, mankind is divided into transmitters and receivers and a middle group facing both ways at once: and very often, trying to shake off the domination of the immediate past, and to impose itself on the immediate future. From which it might seem to follow that the continuity of a culture depends on the interest which this group takes in what has gone before and what is still to come.[65]

Young, who left out childhood altogether,[66] a serious omission, particularly for a psychologically-minded historian, admitted that things were not 'quite so simple as that'. Attachment to a past generation was renewed when the battle between parents and children was accompanied by a *rapprochement* between children and grandparents.[67]

> In the history of culture there seems to be something at work like the diplomatic law of the next-but-one allied against the one-in-between: Scotland and France against England, England and Austria against France: the Renaissance evoking Antiquity: the Nineteenth Century calling to the Middle Ages: Maynard Keynes appealing to Malthus for help in the economic troubles of our own time: and Wells casting back to the Encyclopaedists of eighteenth-century France.[68]

There was no such 'theorem' in Whig historiography. Nor any counterpart to Young's later theorem that 'all mutations of culture start with a deviation from some acknowledged norm'.[69] The norm was established, he believed, by 'the pressure of society bent, unconsciously and instinctively, on maintaining or asserting the way of life which it feels to be satisfactory'. By society, he meant 'nothing abstract or remote, but simply those conversational judgments, for approval or disapproval, to which the individual is subjected'. 'The judgments of parents, nurses, governesses, pastors and masters of all degrees, are, on the whole, the voice of society in equilibrium and bent on maintaining its equilibrium. The judgments of the younger generation are, on the whole, the voice of society dissident and exploratory. Such is the provision that Nature has made for the stability and progress of our human tribes.' 'All of which, no doubt', Young concluded characteristically, 'will need much qualification and many observations before it could be offered as an exact analysis. But for our purposes it may serve.' [70]

As for deviations from the norm, these could be initiated either by 'uneasiness' or 'resentment' [71], and they could take trivial or serious form. 'Revolt or revolution is only an instance on the grand scale of what is going on always and everywhere on a lesser scale ... The deviation may carry us into "the tumult of public revolution" ... or it may do no more than substitute a soft hat for a hard one ... just as one earthquake may do no more than rattle the teacups and another lay a city in ruins.' [72] Something is missing from Young's analysis here – a more systematic study both of 'structures' and of human motivations, a willingness to grapple with a term he does not use, 'discontinuity', above all, perhaps, an economic analysis. He would have enjoyed interpreting the 1960s, for all their 'discontinuity', but he would have been less engaged in the grim world of 1984 when the economics can never be left out.

NOTES

1   R.H. Tawney, 'Social History and Literature', in R. Hinden (ed.), *The Radical Tradition* (1964).
2   *Today and Yesterday* (1948), p. 3.
3   For Baldwin's shyness – 'it seems a tremendous thing to ask' – see T. Jones, *A Diary with Letters* (1954), p. 527. For Young's reluctance, see the useful biographical memoir by Sir George Clark, in the annotated edition of *Portrait of an Age* (ed. G. Kitson Clark, 1977), p. 6. Clark says simply of the book, 'it was not well received and it does not rank as a standard work'.
4   *Portrait of an Age*, sec. XXXI.
5   George Kitson Clark made far too much of 'information' in his annotated edition of 1977, the last book of his life and one on which he devoted a good deal of his own and much of other people's time trying to track down both Young's sources and his mistakes. 'Many of

Young's quotations proved to be inaccurate', Kitson Clark noted, 'some of his facts were mistaken or at least misdated, some of his judgements were clearly perfunctory, for they were not supported by any reasonable interpretation of the documents he cited in their favour.' (Annotated edition, p. 13.) Not uncharacteristically, Kitson Clark treated Young's essay as if it were a very superior undergraduate essay. In consequence, valuable though the annotated edition is to the scholar, it misses the real appeal of the *Portrait*. For Young on Kitson Clark, see his review of his short life of *Peel*, reprinted in W.K. Handcock (ed.), *Victorian Essays* (1962), pp.73-9. 'In Mr Kitson Clark's book I seem to feel a certain straining after impartiality which at times relieves itself in an ungainly skittishness .... He is only dull when he tries to be bright' and, more pertinently, 'Mr Clark does not quite succeed in building his views into a portrait.

6   For an example of his journalism, see 'Victorian Centenary', in *The Times*, 11 May 1937. The previous ages which interested him most included the early classical world and the seventeenth century. The Oxford University Press foolishly turned down the volume of essays which he published after *The Portrait* (Jones, *op. cit.*, p. 378). Cape took it up.

7   *Portrait of an Age*, sec. XXXI.

8   See his introduction to *Last Essays* (1950), p. 15 and his essay 'Continuity', in *Last Essays*, p.63, for the end of five assumptions on which Victorian society and culture were based.

9   His essay on Morris, 'Topsy', based on a review of May Morris's *Artist, Writer, Socialist* (1936), is reprinted in *Daylight and Champaign*. It acknowledges forcefully that Morris's 'Socialism was a trial synthesis of all his purposes, and without it his character would have been unfinished, his life incomplete'.

10   See above, p.242. Yet Harold Nicolson said of reading Young that he derived 'great pleasure from the slow sadness of his style'.

11   *Last Essays*, p. 22.

12   'The New Cortegiano', in *Daylight and Champaign*, p. 150.

13   Sec. XXVIII. Cp. H. Stuart Hughes, *Consciousness and Society* (1959).

14   To the Victorian conception of mind as 'a more and more perfectly adjusted mechanism', he wrote (*Last Essays*, p. 59) there had succeeded 'the conception, as the picture, of mind as an iceberg, the greater part out of sight, and carried by deep currents only to be tracked and calculated by whole new instruments'.

15   Sec. XXII.

16   Yet see his essay on 'Scott and the Historians', where he praises Scott for presenting the medieval world 'not as a pageant but as a social structure where all are linked together by the same customary law'.

17   For Young on Macaulay, see his essay reprinted in *Victorian Essays*, pp. 35-45.

18   See E.A. Carr, *What is History?* (1961).

19   *Portrait of an Age*, Introduction to 1952 edn. For the origins of these quotations in their precise form, see Kitson Clark, *op. cit.*, p. 194.

20   In an aside in 'The New Cortegiano' (*Daylight and Champaign*, p. 152), Young refers to one of Mr Aldous Huxley's 'more disagreeable characters, that is to say, one of his characters'. An earlier novel which for Young fell into the sure category of 'talk novels' was H.G. Wells's *New Machiavelli* (1911). Curiously he does not refer in the *Portrait* to W.H. Mallock.

21   Introduction to *Last Essays*, p. 12.

22   Jones, *op. cit.*, p. 378. Cp. Young's own introduction to *Last Essays*, p. 11, where he writes of the centrality for him, at least in the earlier years, of the old 'Attic' triangle, Oxford, Cambridge and Westminster.

23   He accompanied Henderson to Russia on his 1917 visit.

24   'The most ordinary environment is rich in surprises', we read in the first Mass Observation pamphlet of 1937. See S. Laing, 'Presenting "Things as They Are": John Sommerfield's May Day at Mass Observation', in F. Gloversmith (ed.), *Class, Culture and Social Change, A New View of the 1930s* (1980), pp. 142-160.

25   'Scott and the Historians', p. 33.

26   *Today and Yesterday*, p. 123.

27   Quoted by his friend, W.D. Handcock in the introduction to his edition of Young's *Victorian Essays* (1962), pp. 8-9.

28   For some of the difficulties of Edwardian communication, see the perceptive article by Ross McKibbin, 'Social Class, and Social Observation in Edwardian England', in *Transactions of the Royal Historical Society* (1978). Cp. Young's comment on Mass Observation that he confronted its results 'in such a state of bewildered despair as I might have felt a hundred years ago when the great administrators of that age first discovered the physical state of the nation'. He confessed 'the perennial difficulty of understanding other men's minds'.

29   Kitson Clark, Introduction to the annotated edition of *The Portrait*, p. 11.

30   ibid.

31   He was also a Trustee of the British Museum and a member of the Historic Monuments Commission.

32   *Last Essays*, p. 29.

33   *Daylight and Champaign*, p. 290.

34   *Portrait of an Age*, sec. XXXI.

35   See his essay 'Eyes and No Ears', in *Last Essays*, pp. 130-5, which contains, *inter alia*, an interesting critique of Ruskin; and 'Domus Optima', ibid., pp. 136-61, which deals with the 'architectural sense' of the landed interest.

36   Introduction to *Last Essays* (1950), p. 9.

37   See R.D. Altick, *The Common Reader* (1957).

38   See his important essay 'Scott and the Historians', in *Last Essays*, pp. 17-40.

39   Handcock, *op. cit.* In his introduction to *Last Essays*, Young wrote in 1950 that he shared 'the common belief that some form of European union is desirable, and, unless it is prevented by some violent impact from the East, is indeed inevitable'.

40 Introduction to *Last Essays*, p. 11.
41 See his essay 'Tempus Actum', reprinted in *Victorian Essays*, pp. 158-62, where he rightly points out that 'much that we call Victorianism is a picture at second-hand, a satirical portrait drawn by the Victorians themselves'. Yet he concedes (or adds) that 'the word does undoubtedly mean something, but what it means has to be built up by going behind the criticism, the invective and the caricature, and examining the originals'.
42 'The Liberal Mind in Victorian England', in *Last Essays*, p. 206. Cp. *The Portrait*, section IV, where 'the Victorian age' is described as 'only the island counterpart of a secular movement as significant as the turn from the Greek middle ages in the time of Socrates'.
43 Introduction to the 2nd edition of the *Portrait* (1953).
44 See his essay 'Basic English', reprinted in *Last Essays* (1950), pp. 78-95, which contains the interesting proposition that 'the advance of the noun at the expense of the verb is a sign of linguistic decay.... Verbs, as Aristotle said, are in time. Nouns are out of time.'
45 Young never mentioned once Lytton Strachey's *Eminent Victorians* (1918).
46 'Maitland', in *Victorian Essays*, pp. 173-7.
47 See, for example, his essay on 'The Origin of the West Saxon Kingdom', in *Last Essays*, pp. 112-30, in which he meditates on the significance of the village of Charford and the surrounding landscape. Cobbett figures in it as 'the eternal Saxon yeoman'.
48 Young had in mind his essay on the 'Body Politic', reprinted in F.W. Maitland, *Selected Essays* (1957). Young hoped that Cambridge undergraduates would not be content with the selected essays, but would read as much of Maitland as they could, and he cracked jokes about the Syndics of the Cambridge University Press. 'After all, Syndics are not like other publishers. They can always cover their losses by bringing out a Prayer Book in red, white and blue, or a new Bible.'
49 See his important collection of essays and broadcasts in *All in Due Time* (1955). I had the privilege of organising an Oxford seminar with House, designed for graduates both in History and English Literature.
50 These always appealed to Young, who thought of the 1850s as the decade during which a wise man would choose to be young (*Portrait*, sec. XI), and of the 1860s as a very special time, e.g. in his essay on 'Government' (*Last Essays*, p. 176), where he refers with considerable exaggeration to 'an almost dreamlike security of well-being' in the closing decades of Palmerston's long life. W.L. Burn's *The Age of Equipoise* (1964), which followed my *Victorian People*, was in the same line, though Burn acknowledged neither source in his valuable book. It was, after all, Young who referred in the *Portrait*, sec. XIV, to a 'brief moment of equipoise'. Subsequently, there has been scope for some 'revisionism' here.
51 B. Willey, *Nineteenth-Century Studies* (1949), p. 234.
52 'Continuity', in *Last Essays*, p. 57.
53 *Last Essays*, p. 53.

54 His view that the failure of the early and mid-Victorians to provide a
    national system of education was the great Victorian 'omission' was
    influenced by the fact that his first post in the civil service was with the
    Board of Education under the stirring leadership of Sir Robert Morant.
55 Third Programme Broadcast, 31 May 1953, produced by Ronald Lewin.
56 For Young's continuing delight in Hardy and his view that he was 'the
    last great poet who will ever write in the concert music of England', see
    his essay on Hardy in *Last Essays*, pp. 258-82.
57 Though this work had been published forty years before, it was not
    until Young was half way through it that he realised that it was not 'a
    tale of contemporary life'.
58 'Religion was a matter of deep and wide concern. The educated class, as
    we may call it, was still a churchgoing class.'
59 Epilogue to *Daylight and Champaign*, p. 305.
60 This was the year of Darwin's *Origin of Species*, Mill's *Essay on Liberty*,
    Samuel Smiles's *Self Help*, and Fitzgerald's *Omar Khayyam*.
61 He admired Gibbon's 'far-reaching irony', then he left out all mention
    of this book in his *Who's Who* entry.
62 He made gentle fun in *Daylight and Champaign* of the reaction of a
    friend to whom he had remarked that Maitland was the greatest of
    English historians and who replied sceptically, 'But he writes about law
    in King Stephen's time.'
63 *Daylight and Champaign*, pp. 167-80.
64 He referred there, too, to Dr Ghosh's *Annals of English Literature,
    1475-1920*, which gave him the framework he was to supply in the
    chronological tables at the back of the *Portrait*.
65 *Last Essays*, pp. 49-50.
66 Yet see *Portrait*, sec. I.
67 Uncles came into the picture also. 'I once heard it suggested that the
    typical Victorian saying was "You must remember he is your uncle".'
    ('Tempus Actum', in *Daylight and Champaign*, p. 261.)
68 *Last Essays*, pp. 50-1.
69 ibid., p. 55.
70 ibid., p. 56.
71 The first explained in Young's view (surely too simply) 'how inevitably
    the notion of political justice in our own nineteenth century evolved
    into the notion of social justice, and that notion in turn created a whole
    system of new institutions, some of which are already beginning to
    show the cracks of time' (ibid., p. 57).
72 ibid., p. 56.

13   Gilberto Freyre and the Study of Social History

When I first read a book by Gilberto Freyre I knew that he was a great historian. I also felt an immediate affinity with him – even though the historical experience he was describing – and recreating – was so different from the historical experience with which I myself was most familiar – in my case the experience of a society the texture of which had been totally transformed by industrialisation. The sense of affinity had much to do with his capacity to communicate a sense of experience. Distance mattered here. Unless a historian is able to take as his subject matter experience felt and not always expressed rather than lists of outstanding names or sequences of events, he will never strike chords in distant readers. Readers nearer at hand may want something different.

There were two other reasons, however, for the sense of affinity. First, Freyre showed himself outstanding among historians in his capacity to decode expressed experience – through the visual as well as the verbal record of the past – and this genius could inspire decoding of other very different societies, including my own. My mansions were different from his. Indeed, not all of them were mansions. Yet he tempted me inside his own. Second, he wrote magisterially. The beauty of historical writing is one of the keys to its long-term appeal; it can also, like all beauty, be the key to immediate attraction.

My lecture on him falls into four parts – first, an attempt to place his work in perspective; second, a more detailed assessment in relation to the study of social history; third, a personal coda to what I have already said about affinity, since as the years have gone by I have begun to know rather more directly of the kind of historical experience with which Freyre has been concerned; and fourth, a note about how the work of Freyre still influences me. I am engaged at present in trying very ambitiously to write a one-volume social history of England from prehistoric times to the problematic present. I want to try to show briefly how in writing about England I have benefited from what Freyre has written about Brazil, as I have benefited immensely too from what a number of other non-British historians, notably Marc Bloch and Lucien Febvre have written. Like them – and like Freyre – I believe, above all else, that we cannot write about the past unless we live in the present. The past is not escape: it is exploration. The perspective comes later.

Let me turn first, however, to the perspective with which we can most usefully consider the arts and techniques of social history.

The impulse to write social history can be traced back at least to Giambattisto Vico and his *scienza nuova* of the early eighteenth century – a history of the main processes and landmarks in man's developing discovery of the world of nature and in his fashioning of a distinctive culture or cluster of cultures distinct from, but related to nature.

During the nineteenth century, as history developed as a professional subject, there were some historians who continued in such a tradition, treating social history as *the* unifying history; and yet there were others who treated it as one sub-history among many, a specialised field of study alongside say, diplomatic and military history on the one hand, and political and constitutional history on the other. The former, when guided by Karl Marx, saw economic history as its foundation and cultural history as its superstructure, although there were some historians, like Karl Burckhardt, who did not. The latter, in time a majority, usually brought in values as well as facts, although they narrowed the scope of social history – sometimes, indeed, trivialised it – by eliminating from it the study of many major themes. Their values came out in such statements as that of the British historian J. M. Green, in his *Short History of the English People*, that he wanted to substitute knives and forks for drums and trumpets.

During the twentieth century, such differences in approach have persisted, although the study of history as a whole and in its increasingly specialised parts has become at once more sophisticated and more narrow. The *Annales* group of historians in France has been prepared to consider in detail the history of any human activity or of the natural forces driving or restraining human activity. Marxist historians have tried to explain different rates of change and cultural outcomes in different societies, including some with similar economic bases. Yet they have both provoked sharp critiques for trying to explain too much. G. M. Trevelyan in wartime Britain wrote an immensely popular social history which deliberately treated social history as history with the politics left out. This was an important self-denying ordnance. Yet just as important were two other aspects of Trevelyan's approach which meant that he could be subject to criticism also. First, he deliberately set out to reach as wide an audience as possible, since he believed that the social history of a country should be the property of its people – that there they would find poetry rather than prose particularly well-suited to a poetry of urban life. Second, he believed that the social historian 'in some respects' could get to know more about the past than the dweller in the past himself knew about it – since in longer perspective and with more advanced knowledge he could understand those forces which conditioned, as he put it, the everyday life of the dweller in the past. Different in most respects as Trevelyan is from Braudel in France – and the *Annales* group, formed in 1929 – they would share this second belief. They would subject it, however, to a close analysis of a kind that Trevelyan eschewed.

This is not quite the last word in this brief panorama of approaches to social history. There have been reactions both against Trevelyan, whose social standpoint seemed at times too removed from the human experience of large groups of people whose life-styles were very different from his own, and against the *Annales* school which seemed to underestimate the immediacy and the accident of history and in certain respects to impose patterns on it. As the professional study of history drew in recruits from all sections of society, it was inevitable that there should be increasing interest in what came to be called 'history from below', the history of people without remembered names, some of them the casualties of history. As history became more categorised and more elaborate in its methodologies – even in its languages – it was inevitable that a few historians should seek to recapture the direct language – and through the language – the molten experience of the past.

The Masters and the Slaves, Casa Grande, first appeared in 1933, eight years earlier than G. M. Trevelyan's *Social History*. Only in 1946, however, after the Second World War, was it available in English in a handsome Knopf edition, well translated by Samuel Putman. *The Mansions and the Shanties*, not translated into English until 1963, was published in 1936, one year after the appearance of the fascinating Brazilian volume of essays commemorating the twenty-fifth anniversary of *Casa Grande*, which covered many aspects of Professor Freyre's science, philosophy and art.

This precise chronology is itself of interest to all historians, not least, I should add, to historians of historiography. The cultural approach of both *The Masters and the Slaves* and *The Mansions and the Shanties* was not fashionable among established historians on either side of the Atlantic in 1933 or 1936. History, apart from Marxist history, was orthodox, established and non-innovative. Fascinating – and much discussed – work was being carried out by anthropologists – I think, for example, of Malinowski's *Coral Gardens and their Magic*, which appeared in 1935 – but anthropology, which was to influence the writing of history profoundly during the 1960s and 1970s, was at that time scarcely considered as a neighbour of history. Nor was psychology, though for many Englishmen, this was the time when, in the English poet W. H. Auden's phrase, Freud was not just an influence but 'a whole climate of opinion'.

The one often accepted neighbour of history was literature, sphere of a companion muse. Yet the literature tended to be past literature. Few English historians turned to Marcel Proust at that time, or for that matter to Henry James. The preferred literature was not only more remote but more decorative. By contrast, Freyre, who chose to assimilate both anthropology and psychology – thereby linking history with the social sciences – saw the form of his history as James saw the form of the novel – 'a living thing, all one and continuous . . . in each of the parts there is something of each of the other parts'. The Proustian element in his work was well described by him in the Preface to the second English language edition of *The Masters and the Slaves* in 1956, with an unconscious throwback to a widened version of J. R. Green's view of social history:

> In the story of intimate history, all that political or military history has to offer in the way of striking events holds little meaning in comparison with a mode of life that is almost routine: but it is in that routine that the character of a people is most readily to be discerned. In studying the domestic life of our ancestors we feel that we are completing ourselves: it is another method of searching for the *temps perdu* ... The past awakens many stirrings and has a bearing on the life of each and every one of us; and the study of this past is more than mere research and a rummaging in the archives; it is an adventure in sensitivity.

Or, as he put it succinctly a few pages later, 'Given a true sense of time, the past ceases to be dead in contrast with the present as the only living reality.'

This was a far more sophisticated view of the history of everyday life than Green's. Like the Goncourts, Freyre was searching after an *histoire intime*.

Although Freyre openly admitted his debt to Professor Franz Boas and to Columbia University, where he submitted his Master's thesis on 'Social life in Brazil in the Middle of the Nineteenth Century' ten years before the publication of *Casa Grande*, he was critical of most earlier Brazilian historians of Brazil, preferring to chart his own paths. Indeed, I know of no other historians like him, Brazilian or non-Brazilian, in any language before 1933. He was also uniquely willing, as he pointed out in *The Mansions and the Shanties*, to use what were then little-tapped sources like newspapers and photographs and books of etiquette and above all, perhaps, recipes. He was in no sense writing a textbook for students, and he admitted his dependence not only on analysis but on intuition.

The Preface to the first edition of *The Mansions and the Shanties* includes the following key passage:

> The human being can be understood – in so far as he can be understood – in his total human aspect; and understanding involves the sacrifice of a greater or a lesser degree of objectivity. For in dealing with the human past, room must be allowed for doubt and even for mystery. The history of an institution, when undertaken or attempted in keeping with a sociological criterion which includes the psychological, inevitably carries us into zones of mystery where it would be ridiculous for us to feel satisfied with Marxist interpretations or Behaviourist or Positivist explanations, or with mere descriptions similar to those in natural history.

Such a passage scarcely needs exegesis. Yet I would draw attention to Freyre's open recognition of 'doubt' as well as 'mystery'. This opened the way for work by other historians, some of whom might offer different interpretations from his, particularly of slavery. *The Masters and the Slaves* and *The Mansions and the Shanties* did not draw a line across the historical interpretation of the past: they offered an invitation to others. One problem in 'total history' is that, like Comteian philosophy, it seeks to explain too much for too long, that by becoming definitive it becomes congealed. This was not the spirit of Freyre's books.

A second point in the passage worthy of note is the either/or bracket when Freyre chooses to place Marxist interpretations at one end of the scale and 'mere descriptions similar to those in natural history' at the other. In other words, he is suggesting that the absence of ideology will no more solve historical problems than dependence on one single ideology. In each case, 'the characteristics of a historical process', as Hans Freyer has put it, 'cannot be reduced to the precision of a concept' (though Freyre himself would have wanted to study concepts as well as facts or perceptions). 'The subordination of the coloured people', he writes, 'was not that of race but of class', and he noted as clearly as any Marxist that while some social gulfs had narrowed with the decline of the rural patriarchy, others had been accentuated. 'However little inclined we may be to historical materialism', he wrote in another place,

> we must admit the considerable influence, even though not always a preponderant one, exerted by the technique of economic production upon the structure of societies and upon the futures of their moral physiognomies. It is an influence subject to the reaction of other influences, yet powerful as no other in its ability to make aristocracies or democracies out of societies and to determine tendencies toward polygamy or monogamy, toward stratification or mobility.

Such observations are more comprehensive – and penetrating – than most of the general observations in Trevelyan's *Social History*. Both Trevelyan and Freyre share a sense of the poetry of history, of the need to fuse science and art : both find their inspiration in literature as much as in economics, in buildings and landscapes as much as in documents. Both believe in ghosts. Yet Freyre at his best reveals three advantages over his English counterpart. First, he was more sophisticated as anthropologist, sociologist and social psychologist: his insights are supported by a more searching methodology and one which has relevance for historians of societies very different from that of Brazil. Second, his sympathies are wider. He has been concerned quite deliberately with how different groups of Brazilians participated in and perceived the development of their own society and culture. This was not social history from above, or for that matter from below, but social history from all angles. As he put it in the introduction to the first edition of *The Mansions and the Shanties* – and the title itself explains his purpose as vividly as any manifesto –

> the principal object of this work is to study the processes of subordination, and, at the same time, of accommodation of one race to another, of one class to another, of the fusion of various religions and cultural traditions into a single one, which characterized the transition of Brazilian patriarchy from rural to urban.

To be able to deal equally convincingly with 'subordination' and 'accommodation' – not to speak of 'fusion' – requires genius, the genius to get inside and then to present the experience of people very different from oneself. Trevelyan, wide-ranging though his sympathies were, was far less successful.

Third, Trevelyan left out much which Freyre equally deliberately put in. For Trevelyan, social history was conveniently circumscribed, if not necessarily completely defined, as 'history with the politics left out'. Freyre had no doubt that the politics usually had to be put in. He begins *The Mansions and the Shanties* with a brief but unforgettable picture of Dom João VI as he was in 1808. He ends with the proclamation of the Republic in 1889. In a lecture he gave in 1965 at the University of Sussex in England – of which I was then Vice-Chancellor (and I shall have more to say of this particular lecture later) – he began by quoting the French formula made famous by Charles Maurras, '*Politique d'abord!*' – and without accepting it – just as he would not have accepted Trevelyan's dictum at the other end of the spectrum of attitudes – he added rightly that it is essential 'to recognise the importance of political behaviour in the world we now live in. It is a world in which politics is playing an extremely important and, in some matters, a really decisive role.'

His recognition of this factor – and his willingness to trace how it too has not so much evolved as taken different forms at different times – distinguishes him from many other social historians – English, French, German, Spanish, Portuguese – besides Trevelyan. *Histoire intime* is not just the history of everyday things.

So much, all too briefly, about the relevant historiography. In general terms, consider the spanning dates 1933 to 1963 – 1933, the critical year in the history of the inter-war world, the year of the accession to power of Roosevelt and Hitler: 1936, a year of political drama in Europe, when the main world drama seemed then to be in Europe; the intervening Second World War, which transformed the relationships between Europe and the rest of the world; 1946, a year of austerity; 1963, a year of affluence, when on both sides of the Atlantic the talk was of economic growth.

Between the publication and translation of Freyre's volumes there were decades of political – and social – transformation. He was fully aware himself of these historic bearings. Thus, he stated quite explicitly in his preface to the first English edition of *The Masters and the Slaves* that it was difficult to find any society in the world 'with tendencies more opposed to those of the German *Weltanschauung*', and equally explicitly that 'the history of patriarchal society in Brazil is inseparable from the history of the Jew in America'. National socialist conceptions of race, fashionable during the 1930s even in some quarters outside Hitler's Germany, were at the opposite pole. Nor did Freyre share the progressive optimism of Roosevelt's New Deal circle. He was more sympathetic at a far later date to the more subtle perceptions of David Riesman's *The Lonely Crowd*, which appeared in 1952. His sense of the significance of Second World War developments and the huge changes that followed it – economic and cultural – is apparent in the revision of *Brazil: An Interpretation* (1945), based on lectures given a year earlier while the war still raged, renamed *A New World in the Tropics* (1959). His tropics are not *tristes tropiques*: there is too much libido – and fun – for that. He could understand the 1960s.

For Brazil itself, which Professor Freyre did more, perhaps, than any other writer to introduce to the outside world, *The Masters and the Slaves*, as Frank Tannenbaum put it, was 'a great deal more than just a book'. It marked 'the closing of one epoch and the beginning of another' within the world context. *The Masters and the Slaves* and *The Mansions and the Shanties* were a revelation, a revelation further explained for a foreign audience in *New World in the Tropics* (1959). Freyre explained compellingly that there had been what he called 'a Brazilian solution for coming to terms with different ways of life, different cultural patterns', but he did not disguise the fact that there had been deep maladjustment as well as felicitous adjustment. His was not a Whig version of history, like Trevelyan's, where everything led up to a modern Liberal solution. He had, after all, been an exile himself after the 1930 Revolution broke out. Brazil by 1936 might be 'becoming more and more a racial democracy, characterised by an almost unique combination of diversity and unity', but there were other elements in it which might not guarantee political democracy. 'The conservative tradition in Brazil', he wrote in *The Masters and the Slaves* (p. 77), 'has always been sustained by the sadism of command, disguised as "the principle of authority" or the "defence of order". Between the opposing mysticisms, that of Order and that of Liberty, our political life has ever sought a balance.'

Order and Progress, the third volume in the series, begun with *The Masters and the Slaves*, and which like the other two can be treated as an autonomous work, is specifically concerned with this theme and is introduced appropriately with the inevitable Comteian quotation. It goes on to deal in detail with points already hinted at in the earlier two volumes. Covering as it does the half century of Brazilian history between the 1870s and Brazilian participation in the First World War, it leads the reader from a predominantly rural, agricultural, patriarchal and religious society into a more urbanised, industrialised and secularised society. In the preface to the first English edition of 1970, however, Freyre looks forward to a rather later time, to the career of President Vargas, who came into power three years before *The Masters and the Slaves* was written. Thereby Freyre's third volume provides 'a sort of introduction to present-day Brazil and particularly to its social situation'.

In it Freyre carefully notes the role both of intellectuals and of soldiers and 'the erosion of institutions once considered stable and enduring'. At the same time, as in his earlier volumes, he makes no claim to be writing 'pure history'. He is attempting rather, he says,

> to reconstruct the essential social order existing between 1870 and 1920 through its value system, reflected in material things: houses, money, furniture, vehicles, clothing, jewelry, appliances, common household objects, as well as such factors as political and social ideologies, notions of honour, patriotism, race, family and religion. The combination of these values, as accepted more or less automatically by the majority, or by various significant minorities, constitutes altogether the most valid picture of a national culture.

Two other earlier notes were struck once again. First, the sense of time remained Proustian: 'My awareness of time as a dynamically social rather than conventionally chronological phenomenon', he wrote, 'is such that the reader will find numerous references to past periods, as well as projections into more contemporary times.' Second,

> human behaviour differs from animal behaviour .... Zoologists may be
> perfectly scientific in their studies of animals, but ... social psychologists,
> anthropologists, sociologists, historians and other students of human
> behaviour deal with subjects which are so uncertain, so complex, so
> multiple in their reactions and motivations that it is practically impossible
> for an analyst of human behaviour to be totally scientific about them and,
> at the same time, remain human. Perhaps the best solution to this prime
> problem is for the analyst of human behaviour to resign himself to being, at
> best, a scientific humanist.

This is a memorable self-assessment.

Turning to the second of my own four main points in this lecture – my own detailed assessment – I would want to concentrate on four main aspects of Freyre's unique achievement. First, he has been a genuine pioneer in the writing of what Lucien Febvre called in 1949 'a new kind of history'. Febvre was referring on that occasion to Marc Bloch's *The Craft of the Historian, Apologie pour l'Histoire*. I have already referred to my own debt to Bloch and Febvre, although I started my own historical writing, as I suspect Freyre also did, without having read a line of either of them. This rider is of little importance, since 'a new kind of history' has been the work of many hands in many places, like 'new kinds of history' in previous periods. The works of R. H. Tawney and Max Weber converge, for example, yet Tawney had reached his own similar, if not identical, answers to the relationship of religion and capitalism quite independently.

By 'a new kind of history' Febvre, like Freyre, meant a history which drew on all the social sciences without being dominated by any one single conceptual framework. Yet there is a difference between the two historians in their framing of a future agenda. In his essay on 'History and Psychology', published in 1938, Febvre emphasised that 'no true historical psychology will be possible without a properly negotiated agreement between psychologists and historians. The historian will be guided by the psychologist. But the psychologist will work in close touch with the historian and will rely on him to create his conditions of work. Work will be done in co-operation. It will be teamwork.' By contrast, Freyre, who has proved himself just as sensitive to the need to relate history to psychology, puts his trust not in teamwork, but in a personal putting together of facts and images on the part of the individual historian. It is the single historian who must grasp all the issues with which he is concerned. I suspect that Freyre would not be the least interested in 'properly negotiated agreements' of the kind which Febvre advocated.

This, indeed, is the second point in my assessment. In his preface to the French edition of *The Masters and the Slaves* Febvre himself, invited by Freyre to write it, insisted upon the complexity of Freyre's pioneering study – 'à la fois une histoire et une sociologie. Un mémorial et une introspection. Un énorme pan de passé, né d'une méditation sur l'avenir.' (At the same time history and sociology, record and introspection, a sweeping panorama of the past, created out of meditation on the future.) He implied, too, as I would choose to state explicitly, how difficult it is to describe Freyre's work without using the word 'rhythm', a very different kind of word from 'negotiation'. 'Suivant son rythme propre, sa pensée dédaigne les rythmes appris. Il revient sur ces pas, reprend, ajoute ici une tache de couleur qui, dix pages plus haut, n'eut point trouvé sa place veritable.' (Following a rhythm of its own, his thinking disdains orthodox rhythms. It retraces its steps to pick up a theme once more and adds a touch of colour which ten pages earlier would have been out of place.) No teamwork could produce such an effect. It has more in common with the intimate, personal rhythms that we can trace in the writings of Richard Cobb than with the *Annales* school, of which Cobb himself is a knowledgeable critic.

Third, the many new elements which Freyre introduced into his approach to history – notably curiosity about the sex relationships of a society; fascination with racial combinations and changing attitudes towards them; and delight in the sensuous textures of lost cultures – have all come to count for a great deal more in the world since 1933 than they mattered then – or at least they have come to be considered very differently, in ways not very dissimilar from the way in which Freyre considered them then. Almost everything Freyre has said about men, women and children, the shifting norms of behaviour in their relationships, and the changing ideals set up before them concerning what their proper relationships should be, has a contemporary note about it. So, too, have his observations on colour and class, as his French translator, Roger Bastide, noted. Moreover, such observations have even more pertinence in Europe now than they had in the Europe of Hitler, given the large-scale and during the 1930s unforeseen migration from overseas of ex-colonial peoples. As for the sensuous textures of lost cultures – and such sensuous elements can survive in present cultures, often in new disguises – this has become a major theme since the 1950s not only of historians or anthropologists. The anti-puritan reactions have been universal. Within this context, what Freyre said about food habits, for example, or music, no longer seems, as it did to some of his first critics, to be straining the acknowledged limits both of historical scholarship and of polite conversation.

In Brazil itself, as Freyre himself noted in the introduction to the

English language edition of *Order and Progress*, there was far more general interest in such themes in 1970 than there had been in 1933. By 1970 Brazilians were 'proud to acknowledge' folklore, *mestiço* ethnical types and *mestiço* cultural expressions, carnivals and *cuisines* as facets of a continuing national heritage deeply rooted in a distant past. And they were not alone in this. 'The Dionysiac elements in Brazilian culture, as in other contemporary national cultures, have tended in the last thirty or forty years to become predominant, that is, to become more freely expressive.'

There is a rare sense of life in Freyre's social history. He is not just identifying problems or finding correlations – the hallmarks of much detailed contemporary historical scholarship, quantitative and non-quantitative. He is himself a creative writer – and this is the fourth feature in my assessment – a writer who is acutely sensitive to noise and smell, shape and colour, love and hate, laughter and tears, above all to echoes and to premonitions. 'At bottom', Trevelyan wrote, 'I think the appeal of history is imaginative.' This, I believe, is profoundly true of the appeal of Freyre's history inside and outside Brazil.

It is appropriate that I now reach the third point in my lecture – what I called a personal coda. My own feeling of affinity with Freyre is a personal version of the empathy which he believes historians need in their studies of other times and other people, and I felt it at once. Yet it has deepened as a result of the extension of my own direct experience. When I had the privilege of being directly involved in the founding of a new university at Sussex in 1961, I was determined that it should not be a departmentalised university on conventional British lines. I wanted to replace departments by schools of studies, where related disciplines would be studied together and where emphasis should be placed both on the common context of those disciplines and on comparative methodologies. The School of Social Studies, there-fore, of which I was first Dean, brought together economists, sociologists, psychologists, anthropologists, geographers, political scientists and lawyers, and there was a place in that School, too, for historians, since, like Freyre, I have always believed – and it is now fashionable to believe it – that without history the social sciences can be dangerously limited. Through the experience of that and other, Schools, I came to recognise more and more how universal Freyre's various insights are. Though he has never written textbooks or put his trust in pedagogues, he has been involved in, and honoured by, many universities in different parts of the world, and his approach to scholarship is directly relevant to the tasks of the contemporary university. I should add that at Sussex all students, whatever their ultimate major discipline, were expected to begin their studies in common with a 'foundation of history' course and a course on 'language and values', the former involving a detailed study, including a historiographical study, of one great book, like *The Masters and the Slaves* or *The Mansions and the Shanties*. I should add, too, that students majoring in history were not necessarily expected to study inside the School of Social Sciences. They could major if they wished in the School of English and American Studies – thereby studying literature also – or in the School of African and Asian studies, itself a novel School of that time, where they could study history in its world context along with anthropology and religion. It has always seemed to me that the gulf between the study of the social sciences and of literature is at least as wide as the gulf between the study of the natural sciences and of literature – the so-called two cultures – and that in this connection the social historian is a key figure in bridging the gulf.

There was another feature of my work at Sussex, where I became Vice-Chancellor in 1966, which brought me closer to Freyre. We started a Research Unit for the Study of Multi-Racial Societies – with a field centre in Barbados – and through the activities of this Centre, I got to know at first hand the Caribbean world. Here I directly encountered the legacy of slavery and the plantation, with English and with French, not with Portuguese, connections, and the making of small societies – in some respects remarkably diverse in their cultures, given their common economic and social base. How economy and culture, including political culture, were related to each other in contemporary terms required historical explanation. My own work as a social historian was influenced by this Caribbean experience, and once again I found Freyre a mentor and my friend Fernando Henriques a go-between.

It was natural, therefore, that the University of Sussex presented Freyre with an honorary doctorate in 1966 and natural, too, that he should honour the University by delivering the much appreciated and subsequently published lecture on 'The Racial Factor in Contemporary Politics' to which I have already referred. It was a wise as well as a learned lecture in which, while acknowledging the social, psychological and cultural basis of *un retour aux sources* among peoples previously oppressed by 'an exaggerated and, in some cases, brutally imperial, ethnocentrism', he urged that their new political leaders 'should be orienting their political action in such a way as to minimise the importance that has recently been given, and is still being given, to the purely racial factor, and to magnifying the importance that should be increasingly given to the cultural factor'. In this analysis, history for once had a closed rather than open quality. Indeed, Freyre quoted Professor von Beckeroth's opinion that 'the way back into the white man's world of 1914 and even of the late thirties is closed'.

The social history of England – and I turn in conclusion to the last of my four points, how the work of Freyre influences my own work as a historian – has been until recently very much the history of a white man's country. And although the fortunes of that country for three centuries were bound up with an empire of many colours, the English attitude to race and class was very different from that of the Portuguese. Empires have a number of common characteristics, fundamental ones at that, but they also have many differences in attitudes, styles and structures, and the influence of empire on Englishmen living at the centre far from the moving frontiers contrasts sharply with that of the Portuguese. The English empire, moreover – and note that for the moment I am deliberately leaving out the Scots and the Irish, who played a key part in the building of the British Empire – could be 'informal' as well as 'formal', an empire not of the flag but of trade and investment.

For an Englishman some of the most interesting parts of the series of three great volumes by Professor Freyre relate to the English impact on Brazil. 'Only the vigour of British capitalism in its quest for markets for its suddenly explosive production of glass, iron, wool, earthenware and coal – a production served by a truly revolutionary system of transportation – managed to blunt, in a relatively short space of time', he wrote in *The Mansions and the Shanties*, 'the Oriental influence on the life, landscape and culture of Brazil'. The origins and growth of that vigorous capitalism provide, of course, a major theme in British social history, which it is tempting to treat in terms of the simple distinction between 'pre-industrial' and 'industrial' phases. Yet as Freyre himself suggests in one or two places, British social history is rather more complicated than this. He quotes comments by English visitors to Brazil, who knew little of or did not approve of assertive British capitalism and belonged to an older landed society, like the visitor of 1856 who observed that 'the service in their house' – a Brazilian great plantation house – 'is almost the same as in the best English country houses'.

If there are no shanties in the British social history I am writing about, there are country houses of different sizes, periods and styles, each of which had its own economy and culture. And when vigorous industrial capitalism developed in Britain – and to understand its development we require a long-term analysis – it never completely captured English society. Old and new ways of life coexisted. So did old and new values – the values of the gentleman on the one hand and of the hero of self-help on the other. Money never dominated culture. Nor did the gospel of work win universal favour. Taking English social history as a whole, some of the most interesting questions relate not to the development of vigorous industrial capitalism but to the limitations on and ultimate decline of that vigour. Britain's early industrial lead internationally had turned before the end of the nineteenth century into a handicap, and industrial revolutions in other countries in the twentieth century, with a different technological, social and political base from that of Britain, have profoundly transformed the late eighteenth- and early nineteenth-century position. Meanwhile, the growth of a labour movement with a powerful trade union component – a by-product of industrialism, which was concerned only with a labour force – has further held back late twentieth-century economic growth. To write about such subjects requires the same willingness to move easily from one period of social history into another as Freyre has displayed in his great volumes.

It also requires an understanding of the relationship between local, regional and national history, including under the last of these headings the national histories of Scotland, Wales and Ireland as well as of England. In a note on method appended to *Order and Progress*, Freyre identified 'variations in patterns of living which make it impossible to consider the Brazil of the period as a single unit in a homogeneous state of development'; and although Brazil is continental in scale and Britain consists of small islands, the same kind of statement requires to be made of Britain. We have to distinguish over the centuries between south and north, west and east, and to separate out metropolitan and provincial influences. Already in two books of mine, *Victorian People* and *Victorian Cities*, I have had to grapple with such distinctions in relation to the nineteenth century. In a single-volume *Social History* it will be necessary to treat them in their medieval and early modern context. The length of British social history is as conspicuous as the smallness of British territory, and we have to recognise throughout that even England, taken by itself, like Brazil, is, in Freyre's language, 'not one monolithic society, but rather a variety of social orders joined together into a national system, a nation both singular and plural in its life and culture'. Economic history, so generally bracketed with social history, is not enough to direct studies of such topics as the history of education and the history of communications.

There never was a time when the texture of English society and culture could be described simply as 'patriarchal', and consequently questions concerning relations between the sexes, family size and structure and the rural and urban demography defy easy, generalised answers. An upsurge of interest in recent years in historical demography and in urban studies, quantitatively based but not relying exclusively on quantitative information, separates the contemporary social historian from Trevelyan – and has led, for example, to ambitious comparisons of Manchester and São Paulo as 'shock cities' of their times, cities which you had to encounter (if only on paper) if you wished to understand what was happening to the world. But this is not all that separates the contemporary social historian from Trevelyan. 'History from below' has never been quite the same since the publication in 1963 of Edward Thompson's book, *The Making of the English Working Class*. It is not necessary to share all his conclusions – or even all his approaches – to warm to his appeal to 'rescue the poor stockinger, the Luddite cropper, the "obsolete" handloom weaver, the "utopian" artisan ... from the enormous condescension of posterity'. 'Our only criterion of judgement', he claimed, 'should not be whether or not a man's actions are justified in the light of subsequent evolution. After all, we are not at the end of social evolution ourselves. In some of the lost causes of the people of the industrial revolution we may yet discover insights into social evils which we have yet to cure.'

I hope that I shall be able to take full account of such a stance in my *Social History*, but given that I am in sympathy with Freyre's ability to get inside the 'mentalities' not just of one but of very different groups, I shall seek in my social history of England to pay attention to people who held power as well as to people over whom power – or social control – was exercised. To write the social history of a country only in terms of serfs or slaves or farm labourers or industrial workers, and to leave out masters, landlords, manufacturers and professional people, like lawyers and doctors, not to speak of kings, queens, politicans and civil servants, is to pull the social fabric apart. Because the winners of history may have received too much attention in the past when compared with the losers, that does not mean that they should disappear from social history altogether. Social history is about relationships. One of the most recent monographs on English social history by a young historian, David Cannadine, *Lords and Landlords, the Aristocracy and the Towns, 1774-1967*, hits the nail on the head in its very first paragraph:

> It is arguable that the most fundamental changes to have occurred in Britain during the last two centuries concern the decline of the hereditary, aristocratic, landed élite on the one hand, and the rise of a mass, industrialized, urban society on the other. This book is concerned, not so much to examine these themes in isolation, but to see how they are inter-related. Of course, there was much more to the decline of the aristocracy than the rise of towns, and there were many other influences on urban development besides those grandees who owned the land on to which some of the industrial and leisure towns of nineteenth-century England expanded. But the links between those who owned the land and those who lived on it – collaborative in some instances, conflicting in others – form the most precise point of contact between the old pre-industrial élite on the way down, and the new, industrial mass on the way up. The paradoxes,

contradictions and ambiguities of this encounter form the subject of this book.

In my social history I shall be as much concerned with 'paradoxes, contradictions and ambiguities' as with structures and processes. Indeed, neither structures nor processes can be considered adequately unless the paradoxes, contradictions and ambiguities in them are recognised.

One English historian from whom I have learnt a great deal – G.M. Young, author of the brilliant essay, *Victorian England, Portrait of an Age* – got very near to Freyre's Proustian outlook when he said in Cambridge in 1949 that

> culture is not a state but a process; a body of assumptions, judgements, tastes and habits, constantly changing, constantly re-formulating themselves, but also constantly swerving back to gather up something which the grandfathers had dropped and the sons left lying by the course. Indeed, it is by these movements, these epicycles of swerve and recovery, that the tradition is not only preserved but enriched.

In paying my personal tribute to Freyre today I would like in conclusion to emphasise the quality of enrichment in his work. Brazilian traditions are not only preserved but enriched, and the imagination and sensibility of those of us outside Brazil are enriched in consequence.

IV
LOOKING FORWARDS

Venerable Past, you have provided all the elements of this book, for when you had the advantage of being the present, you were already big with the future.

Felix Bodin (1834)

The paradox of prevision in human affairs: prevision which is destroyed by prevision; rule of conscious awareness ... regularities ... hopes and uncertainties.

Marc Bloch (1941)

We are always sowing our future; we are always reaping our past.

Dean W.R. Inge (1922)

14   Towards 1900: The Nineteenth Century Faces the Future

As the end of the nineteenth century approached, people showed far more interest than at the end of any previous century in summing up the record of the century as a whole and in predicting what the twentieth century would be like. In particular, newspapers and periodicals, produced in far greater numbers than in 1800 and for a greatly increased literate public, vied with each other in producing balance sheets of gain and loss.

A characteristic example was a 'golden extra' issued on 31 December 1900 by the *Daily Mail*: it declared that 'the passing of the Nineteenth Century and the dawning of the Twentieth were celebrated all over the world by demonstrations of thankfulness and gratitude'. Funded only four years before by Alfred Harmsworth – later Lord Northcliffe, one of the first of the newspaper magnates – the *Mail* included as its longest article 'The Golden Century: One Hundred Years of Glorious Empire'. It began with the proud words, 'The genius of a masterful race turns instinctively to forecast more readily than to retrospect; its leaders are ever more prone to prophesy than to search for precedent.'

Yet not everything seemed golden in 1900. From Madrid in Spain, where two out of three people were still illiterate in 1900, it was reported that 'the nineteenth century has not been kind to this country, and prayers are being universally offered tonight that the twentieth century may be more felicitous', while from St Petersburg in Russia, where four out of five people were still illiterate, there came a message from *Novoye Vremya* that

one fears for the future of mankind. The most ominous sign is not the fact that the cook, servant girl and lackey want the same pleasures which not long ago were the monopoly of the rich alone, but the fact that all ... rich and idle as well as poor and industrious, seek and demand daily amusements, gaiety and excitement – demand it all as something without which life is impossible.

Even as far as Britain was concerned, the main news headlines were more discouraging than the feature articles – 'British Reverse – Raiders

291

pushing South in Cape Colony' and 'A Black Day on the Stock Exchange: Sensational Collapse'.

Canon Charles Gore, founder of the Anglican Community of the Resurrection and a man with a 'permanently troubled conscience', had remarked in Westminster Abbey that the nineteenth century closed with a 'widespread sense of disappointment and anxiety among those who care most for righteousness and truth in the world': and there was a particularly black and bitter 'salutation speech' from the nineteenth century to the twentieth by Mark Twain in a very different vein from his captivating adventures of *Tom Sawyer* (1876) and *Huckleberry Finn* (1884):

> I bring you the stately maiden named Christendom returning bedraggled and besmirched, dishonoured from pirate raids in Kiaochau, Manchuria, South Africa, and Philippines, with her soul full of meanness, her pocket full of boodle, and her mouth full of pious hypocrisies. Give her soap and towel, but hide the looking glass.

It is instructive – still a favourite nineteenth-century word, for *'l'hérésie de l'enseignement'* was not exhausted by 1900 – to compare the substance and tone of this 'salutation' with *A Highly Amusing Carnival Lay of the Old and New Century*, written at the end of the eighteenth century by the 'Romantic' author A. W. Von Schlegel and performed on 1 January 1801. The Old Century, a withered old hag, proclaimed that she was the mother of the New Century, an innocent young child. Schlegel called this 'an impudent lie' and showed the Devil wringing her neck and carrying her off to Hell. Out of the clouds the true parents of the child then appeared – Genius and Freedom. Finally a Herald entered the stage and told the audience to return in a hundred years and watch the second act of the play:

> Which well may please us even more
> Either in this our story on Earth
> Or when in Heaven we find rebirth.

The *Daily Mail's* balance sheet in 1900 struck a less melodramatic or allegorical note. Agriculture had decayed during the century, it claimed, and with it much of 'the old joyousness of country life' had departed. There was too much dependence on foreign bread. The great towns had spread 'like some cancer'. Yet there had been immense material progress and 'unbounded prosperity':

> We have girdled the oceans with our harbours and encircled the world with our cables; we have crossed the sea with our ships; we have harnassed the forces of nature, and achieved over her victories which have only ceased to be wonderful because we are so familiar with their result. Chemistry has

resolved matter into its elements, and seems to stand upon the very threshold of yet more stupendous conquests. The spectroscope has transported the analyst to the sun and stars. Photography has caught forms as they are. The phonograph has perpetuated transient sound. Steam and electricity have revolutionized the means of communiction as machinery has revolutionized production.

Big question marks still remained. 'With all these conquests', the *Daily Mail* went on, 'it can still be asked whether mankind is happier.' Still more seriously, there were special problems for the British:

We are aware that we are bitterly envied and hated by the world, and that at this very critical moment in some inscrutable manner the old fire of energy seems to be waning within us. We are entering stormy seas, and the time may be near when we shall have to fight in very truth for our life, 'neath noble stars beside a brink unknown.

Canon Gore, a Christian Socialist, was less optimistic in 1900 than some of his fellow preachers, including the Dean of St Paul's, who were dwelling on what by now seemed ancient nineteenth-century triumphs, such as the abolition of slavery, and welcoming, almost in the style of Wilberforce at the beginning of the century, signs of a decline in drunkenness. For Gore, who wanted a radical transformation of economy and society, 'the extended suffrage, from which so much had been hoped, had disappointed its advocates and its opponents alike'. Likewise, 'the spread of education had given a vast impulse to journalism and popular literature, and had produced an enormous number of persons wishing to be clerks'. It was doubtful, however, he went on, 'whether these things were promoting character'. 'There is no Carlyle to whom all men naturally turn to find some answer to their chaotic questionings ... There is no Tennyson to put into exquisite and melodious words the feelings of the educated. There is no prophet for the people.'

Obviously Gore was out of touch with much contemporary opinion. The *avant gardes* often referred, like the Victorian rebel J.A. Symonds, student of the Renaissance, to the 'nightmare of Tennyson', while no lesser person than the first new English Prime Minister of the twentieth century, A.J. Balfour, was soon to confess that he felt no 'sentiment of allegiance' to the 'intellectual dynasties' who held sway during the middle third of the nineteenth century:

Neither the thin lucidity of Mill nor the windy prophesyings of Carlyle, neither Comte nor yet Newman, were ever able to arouse in me the enthusiasm of a disciple; I turn with pleasure from the Corn Law squabbles to the great War, the Napoleonic Wars; from Thackeray and

Dickens to Scott and Miss Austen, even from Tennyson and Browning to
Keats, Coleridge, Wordsworth and Shelley.

Balance sheets produced on the last day of a busy century, even when
in the form of sermons – still one of the most important literary forms
of the nineteenth century – should be compared with balance sheets
produced with greater leisure. In the *fin de siècle* 1890s there was
much talk, following J.K. Huysmans, of all the ends of centuries
resembling each other. '*Toutes vacillent et sont troublées.*' Huysman's
portrait in his well-known novel *À Rebours* (1884) of Des Esseintes,
the aristocratic robot who lived for the rarefication of his sensibilities,
was an obvious affront to all the 'worthy' portraits in the nineteenth-
century picture gallery. Meanwhile, a recurring phrase in the European
literature was 'we are those upon whom the ends of the world are
come'. 'Fin du siècle', remarked Oscar Wilde's Dorian Gray, 'fin du
globe.'

There was a paradox in that during the 1890s such sentiments went
with an almost exaggerated emphasis on the word '*new*'. The 1890s
saw the entry on to the stage of the 'New Woman' – the university
woman, the professional woman, the sportswoman – and the *Daily
Mail*, voice of the 'new journalism', itself remarked that the end of the
century coincided with the disappearance of daytime chaperons. *Art
Nouveau* was a term in general use, like the term 'new morality'. 'New
liberalism' was preoccupied with poverty. 'The suffering may be all
but voiceless', wrote Seebohm Rowntree in his *Poverty, A Study of
Town Life*, which he began in the spring of 1899, 'and we may long
remain ignorant of its extent and severity, but when once we realize it
we see that social questions of profound importance await solution.'
The century ended, therefore, not only with 'a vague feeling of alarm',
but for him and for many others with the recognition that there was
much unfinished business. His book itself did not appear until
1901.

I

Four balance sheets prepared during the 1890s are particularly interesting. In 1894, Charles Pearson, 'Professor of Democracy' as his
biographer calls him, and formerly Minister of Education in the State
of Victoria in Australia, had written an audacious book, *National Life
and Character: A Forecast*, in which he set out to identify the main
tendencies or trends of the times. From the occasion of a visit to the
United States in 1868 he had kept a careful note of statistics, 'happenings' and legislation which seemed to indicate future trends. The age

of individualism, he thought, was ending, and the state would increasingly take over in all parts of the world the traditional roles of family and church. 'We may imagine the state crêche, and the state doctor, and the state school, supplemented, it may be, by state meals, and the child, already drilled by the state, passing out from school into the state workshop.' 'The austere tradition of Puritan family life with its strength and shortcomings has gone for ever.'

There would be a further trivialisation of culture, too, a consequence of the great nineteenth-century growth of urban populations, a subject explored more fully in many popular articles during the 1890s. Folk cultures or even local urban cultures would disappear, and everything would become more 'standardized'.

Amusements in towns are not more intellectual than they were, but less so. The lecture has been killed by the book or newspaper. It is only an apparent exception that the drama maintains itself in Paris, and that Ibsen [Pearson read Norwegian] has had a measure of esteem. The city music hall is not appreciably superior to the city tavern.

In the arts, 'criticism of taste' had become and would become more 'variable', 'as if fixed canons could not be applied with precision to living men'. In the sciences there would be more professionalisation and less inter-communication. 'Although the results of science admit of being communicated in good style, science is passing so much into the hands of experts that its familiar interpretation will cease to be needed.' Continuing advances in scientific knowledge would improve health and lengthen the duration of life, but the increased proportions of old people in society would add to the stability of the political order only at the price of 'less adventure and energy, less brightness and hope'. 'What is a society that has no purpose beyond supplying the day's needs, and amusing the day's vacuity, to do with the terrible burden of personality?'

It was an alarming question, but most of Pearson's readers were still more alarmed by what he had to say of future international relationships. The 'higher races' would soon find themselves 'elbowed and hustled and perhaps even thrust aside' by peoples whom they had assumed far too easily during the nineteenth century to be innately servile.

The day will come, and perhaps is not far distant, when the European observer will look around to see the globe girdled with a continuous zone of the black and yellow races, no longer too weak for aggression or under tutelage, but independent, or practically so, in government, monopolizing the trade of their own regions, and circumscribing the industry of the

European . . . It is idle to say, that if all this should come to pass our pride of place will not be humiliated.

'Were the whole emigration of Europe turned into Africa, it could not build up a white people there.' 'It seems certain that sooner or later China must become a formidable military power.'

Some of Pearson's readers took his remarks to constitute yet another, relatively sophisticated, warning against the dangers of the 'Yellow Peril'. Others were contemptuous. 'Grant Duff suggests', Pearson wrote, 'that the English race will certainly awake to a sense of its duties when the time comes, and will massacre as many Chinamen and Hindoos as are found superfluous.' Yet Henry Adams, sophisticated and privileged descendant of two American Presidents, admitting that he preferred 'niggers to whites' and oriental art to European, was satisfied that what Pearson said was right. He even went on to declare that he 'inclined to make the most of the tropics while the white is still tolerated there'. Theodore Roosevelt, a future President, felt that there were few grounds for such fears.

> An insurrectionary movement of blacks in any one of our Southern States is always abortive and rarely takes place at all; but any manifestation of it is apt to be accompanied by some atrocity which arouses the whites to a rage of furious anger and terror, and they put down the revolt absolutely mercilessly.

Gladstone, who was more afraid of militarism inside Europe than of racial disturbances outside it, was not disturbed for quite different reasons. 'The future is to me a blank,' he told a friend. 'I cannot at all guess what is coming.' While he believed that Pearson's book would only disappoint the 'very sanguine believers in progress', and added that he was not one of them, he also added that if asked to choose between the nineteenth century and 'the age of Homer' he would certainly choose the latter. He had no sympathy with Bismarckian social legislation, and, unlike Pearson, did not like 'the notion of the State stepping in between parent and child when it is not absolutely necessary'. Yet plutocracy seemed to him to be just as dangerous a nineteenth-century disease as socialism and it was just as likely that it would be passed on to the twentieth century. While he hated militarism', he had few forebodings about a great twentieth-century holocaust. 'Are you not afraid of our small army being attacked by their [the Germans] huge army?' an interviewer asked him in 1896. 'How are they to cross the Channel without ships?' Gladstone asked in his turn. 'They would get very wet!'

II

There was much talk about future warfare during the 1890s, even though very few prophets foresaw trenches, tanks, gas attacks and attrition; and 'militarism' figured very prominently in the second interesting attempt at a balance sheet offered at this time – that of the biologist, A.R. Wallace, in his book, *The Wonderful Century* (1898). Wallace, who had anticipated Darwin, presented a catalogue of the century's 'successes and failures', a lively if idiosyncratic list. The 'failures' included not only 'militarism, the curse of civilization', 'the demon of greed' and 'the plunder of the earth' but 'the neglect of phrenology' and 'the opposition to hypnotism and psychical research'. The 'successes' included some on the *Daily Mail*'s list – 'modes of travelling' (down to the bicycle and tricycle, but not yet the motor car);'labour-saving machinery' (which was only just beginning to influence the home); 'the conveyance of thought' (by the telegraph, the telephone and the gramophone, but not by wireless, nor, for that matter, the typewriter): 'fire and light' (including safety matches and gas mantles as well as electricity); photography; spectrum analysis; theoretical discoveries in physics (though with no inklings of relativity); new approaches to geology, a favourite nineteenth-century science, both useful and speculative, astronomy, and, needless to say, biology and physiology (singling out, in particular, the use of anaesthetics in operations and the antiseptic treatment of wounds). 'We find only five inventions of the first rank in all preceding time – the telescope, the printing-press, the mariner's compass, Arabic numerals and alphabetical writing', he concluded, 'to which we may add the steam-engine and the barometer, making seven in all, as against thirteen in our single century.'

Wallace paid tribute also to the great advances in theoretical knowledge which had been in his view a special feature of the century as science had become more specialised and as more attention had been paid, particularly in Germany, to the quest to understand the fundamental properties of matter. 'The determination of the mechanical equivalent of heat, leading to the great principle of the Conservation of Energy' seemed to him to be as major a discovery as 'the molecular theory of gases', 'the establishment of the theory of organic evolution', 'the germ theory of the zymotic diseases', 'the cell theory and the re-capitulation theory in embryology' and 'the proof of the great antiquity of man'.

Wallace, original biologist though he was, proved himself, nonetheless, no careful historian of science: he devoted little attention, therefore, to the particular contributions made by individual scientists to the advance of particular sciences – the term 'scientist' had not been used in Britain before 1840 – or to changes in scientific organisation – the creation of laboratories – with the famous laboratory set up at Giessen in 1825 by Justus von Liebig, the German chemist, providing the first great centre of research; the development of university studies based on Chairs of Science (Britain lagged far behind Germany in this connection); and the more systematic application of experimental science to industry.

Wallace was right, however, to single out thermodynamics as a central area of advance, even though the advance took place long after the invention of the steam-engine as a practical achievement. He did not note, however, how economic thinking, a major nineteenth-century preoccupation, coloured the work of James Clerk Maxwell, the brilliant Scottish physicist, who thought of the universe as 'a system of credit', with the first law of thermodynamics establishing a kind of profit-and-loss account of the heat-work cycle. Maxwell understood balance sheets. The problem of 'entropy', a term coined by Clausius in 1840, provoked little concern in 1900. It was only gradually that the great technological relevance of the laws of thermodynamics was fully appreciated. The refrigerator, the internal combustion-engine (not mentioned, as we have seen, by Wallace) and the steam turbine, invented by Parsons in 1884, were their offspring. In the meantime, J. Willard Gibbs, an American, had applied thermodynamics to chemistry and in so doing had laid the foundations of modern chemical engineering.

There were so many twists and lags in this story that it is impossible to tell it in terms of the simple linear history which was fashionable when the laws of thermodynamics were propounded. Electromagnetic theory, scarcely mentioned at all by Wallace, had also produced tangible results by the end of the century. The researches of Michael Faraday, a blacksmith's son, had established the relationship of electricity to magnetism, but it was left to Clerk Maxwell to establish mathematically the quantitative relationship between the basic units of electricity and magnetism. The electromagnetic theory of light, further advanced in Germany by Heinrich Hertz, pointed to an unprecedented break with Newtonian physics; and the search for other forms of electromagnetic radiation led to the discovery of X-rays ('X' stood for 'unknown') and radio-waves and to the twentieth-century conceptions of electron flow. Wallace recognised the importance of the discovery of X-rays by W.C. Röntgen in 1895, but he did not foretell that radio, introduced into Britain a year later by the young Guglielmo Marconi, would become a major force in twentieth-century history. Nor did Marconi or any other commentator clearly forecast that radio-telephony would become a practical possibility and that, as a consequence, a new 'medium of communication' could be brought into existence. The isolation of radium from pitchblend by Pierre Curie and his Polish-born wife Marie came too late (1898) for Wallace to comment upon, nor did Merz mention it in his massive history of scientific thought completed between 1904 and 1912.

There were many other nineteenth-century developments which produced striking results only in the twentieth century. Dmitri Ivanovich Mendeleev, fourteenth child of a Siberian teacher and a Tartar mother, formulated his famous table of the elements in 1869, but the profound significance of his work, particularly in relation to the structure of atoms, took years to be recognised. Three of the elements which he had said must exist were, in fact, discovered by the end of the century – gallium, scandium and germanium, the names of which bring out both the nationalism and the internationalism of nineteenth-century science. Helium was discovered by Sir William Ramsay in 1895. Likewise, the pioneering work in biology of Gregor Mendel in discovering the mechanism by which natural evolution worked remained virtually unknown before 1900.

The identification of bacteria by men like Robert Koch, Paul Ehrlich and Sir Ronald Rose, who isolated the mosquito as the carrier of malaria in 1897 and won one of the first Nobel prizes in 1902 (the Dutchman H.A. Lorentz, who helped to revolutionise twentieth-century physics, won another), was a nineteenth-century triumph. But it was left to the twentieth century to make the most of the initial discoveries of the 1880s and 1890s which prepared the way for chemicotherapy with its panoply of sulphonamides and antibiotics. When Pearson predicted, as so many others did, that the twentieth century would see a lengthening of the duration of life, he was thinking less in terms of drugs or medical equipment than in terms of a further improvement in environmental or public health, which the nineteenth century had done so much to regulate, although he did consider the possible future disappearance of malnutrition associated with poverty. In fact, there were to be huge improvements in health on many different fronts.

Science and technology were beginning to come together only during the last decades of the nineteenth century, making it an even more 'wonderful century' than Wallace knew, but there was much technology which developed outside the world of science. The internal combustion-engine, a discovery of the 1880s and 1890s, was known negatively in its days of 'first fine careless rapture' as the 'horseless carriage' (compare wireless) and it was destined to transform ways of life in the twentieth century. yet it resulted from work carried out not by scientists but by practical men with a flair for improvisation with either good luck or good business sense (sometimes both). So, too, did the new petroleum industry following the first oil strikes of 1857 and

1859. Marconi had none of the scientific abilities of Hertz; and the great American, Thomas Edison, who played such a prominent part in the story of the telephone, the phonograph and the cinema – not to speak of the incandescent lamp – was a self-taught 'rough-hewn, old-fashioned American individualist'.

Edison's genius lay in his ability to apply invention to the world of the consumer, the new world which was opening out as wealth increased; and the greatest of all his inventions was the world's first industrial research laboratory which he created at Menlo Park, New Jersey, in 1876. In retrospect, although it would not have been clear to most people in 1900, he belonged as much to 'an age of transition' as the uneasy Romantic writers who were still as prominent in the 1890s as the scientists. As Norbert Wiener, twentieth-century prophet of cybernetics, has suggested, Edison was a true transitional figure, arriving on the scene when the unsophisticated mechanical inventors had for the most part exhausted their role and when systematic experiment and organised research were henceforth to be undertaken by skilled and specialised men on a far bigger scale than ever before.

III

One man who in 1900 would have understood Wiener's assessment was H.G. Wells, the young Fabian novelist, who stated explicitly in 1901, having already written several novels about the shape of things to come, that it would soon be possible to embark upon 'a systematic exploration of the future'. 'I think', he went on, 'that we are inclined to under-rate our chances of certainty in the future just as I think we are inclined to be too credulous about the past.' There had, in fact, been much thinking and writing about the future in the nineteenth century, much of it concerned with the future forms of technology, some of it designed to fashion the future, not just to forecast it, some of it escapist and romantic.

The prolific and percipient Jules Verne produced a novel each year, except for one, between 1863 and his death; and although many of them were time-bound, a few offered uncanny glimpses into the space travel of the future, a subject where fiction and fact were already beginning to fuse during the last decade of the nineteenth century. Konstantin Tsiolkovsky, born in 1857, was already working on the theory of rocket propulsion and multi-stage space ships.

Edward Bellamy produced a best seller in his *Looking Backward 2000-1887* (1888), set in a Boston where the nation guaranteed 'the nurture, education and comfortable maintenance of every citizen from the cradle to the grave': his sketch, which took full account of 'new women' as well as 'new men', inspired critics as well as admirers to examine the same themes, with Mark Twain falling into the first category and scribbling in his notebook that in the America of 1985 – not 1984 – the 'age of darkness' would be back again. 'The Pope here and an Inquisition .... A fitted aristocracy and primogeniture. Europe is *republican* and full of science & invention – none allowed here.' In France, the brilliant draughtsman, lithographer, architect and satirist, Albert Robida ranged comprehensively over the institutions and the issues of the future – cities, power, medicine, war – conscious intuitively of the immense potential of science and technology.

In studying the shape of things to come, H.G. Wells had special advantages – a knowledge of science, a keen interest in current social debate, a planner's mind and a lively pen. Nor had his curiosity been tamed by a conventional upbringing and education. He found nineteenth-century bourgeois conventions inhibiting, and he wanted to appeal to the common man rather than to the *avant gardes*. His novel, *The Time Machine* (1895), looked into the world of 802701 ; his *War of the Worlds* (1898) had a Darwinian twist. The world was saved not by its ingenuity or its knowledge – the Martian invaders were as superior to the earthmen as the Europeans had been in the nineteenth-century extermination of the Tasmanians – but by 'microscopic allies', germs of disease against which 'by virtue of this natural selection of our kind we have developed resisting-power' and against which the Martians had no defences.

His *When the Sleeper Wakes* (1899), projecting only 200 years ahead, looked at the place of the common man in a world where disease had been conquered and everyone had a sufficiency of food and clothing, and where there had been universal peace for 150 years. *Anticipations* (1902) was an even more remarkable book. The 'New Republic' of the future would consist of 'all those people throughout the world whose minds were adapted to the demands of the big scale conditions of the new time – a naturally and informally educated class, an unprecedented sort of people'. Society would be managed by 'a confluent system of trust-owned business organisms, and of universities and re-organized military and naval services' discovering through their co-operation 'an essential unity of purpose, presently thinking a literature, and behaving like a state'.

Wells was extraordinarily perceptive in his assessments of certain aspects of the future – the relationship between welfare and warfare, in particular; the expansion of the revolutionisation of education, not least higher education; and transport, including air transport, still a dream in 1900. Yet his vision rested on judgements about the present and the recent past. As he was to explain in his later books, the nineteenth century for him had been an 'age of relative good fortune, an age of immense but temporary opportunity' in which men were too complacent and never stopped to consider 'the real dangers of mankind'. They were 'overtaken by power, by possessions and great new freedoms, and unable to make any civilized use of them whatever'. They thought in too small terms, and were only just able to give up concentrating on the horse at a time when the aeroplane was becoming an imminent possibility. Many of the most successful men were the least educated, and the most expensive education of the time was the least profitable. There were too many amateurs. At best, the nineteenth century had been 'a hasty, trial experiment, a gigantic experiment of the most slovenly and wasteful kind'.

Wells had very little indeed to say about how a future transformation of society would take place, except perhaps through the growing influence of its educated class; and afraid as he was of the spell of 'superstition', he would not have agreed with an earlier nineteenth-century writer, the utilitarian Goldwin Smith, when he claimed that 'the denial of the existence of God and the future state is the dethronement of conscience' and that 'society will pass, to say the least, through a dangerous interval before social science can fill the vacant throne'.

IV

When Wells published his *Anticipations*, he was thirty-five years old. Across the Atlantic, in a country which could already claim that it was far ahead on the way at least to one future, W.G. Sumner, a Yale professor and pioneer of American sociology, then aged sixty-one, produced an equally remarkable essay, not published until twenty-three years after his death, called 'The Bequests of the Nineteenth Century to the Twentieth'. The differences between the two men were not merely differences of age or nationality. Sumner's views on economics, grounded in Ricardian principles of political economy, were diametrically opposed to those of Wells. He distrusted all forms of state intervention, arguing that 'at bottom there are only two chief matters with which government has to deal – the property of men and the honor of women. These it has to defend against crime.'

Economic life left no place, Sumner believed, for 'the negligent, shiftless, inefficient, silly, and imprudent', yet it rightly rewarded millionaires as products of a Darwinian natural selection. Competition was a law of nature which 'can no more be done away with than gravitation'. Unlike Wells, Sumner also believed that human customs – 'folkways' – were so entrenched that reform proposals were usually useless. Even democracy was a 'pet superstition' of the nineteenth century: 'If you have abundance of land and few men to share it, the men will all be equal.' Europe was not in this respect fortunate.

Yet Sumner accepted the great nineteenth-century shift from a society based on status to a more mobile society based on contract with more warmth than if he had thought of it simply as a *fait accompli*.

> Whether social philosophers think it desirable or not, it is out of the question to go back to status or to the sentimental relations which once united baron and retainer, master and servant, teacher and pupil, comrade and comrade. That we have lost some grace and elegance is undeniable. [Sumner would have been most unhappy in a Hapsburg court, or even in baronial Scotland.] But it seems impossible that anyone who has studied the matter should doubt that we have gained immeasurably, and that our further gains lie in going forward, not in going backward.

Sumner put much of his trust in what he called unforgettably 'Forgotten Man', the middle-class man who made no demands upon the state. 'Let every man be sober, industrious, prudent and wise, and bring up his children to be so likewise, and poverty will be abolished in a few generations.'

These passages taken from Sumner's scattered writings provide a perspective for judging his essay on the bequests of the nineteenth century to the twentieth. First and foremost among the beneficial bequests Sumner chose the increased inheritance of economic power: 'The talent which was received from the eighteenth seems insignificant.' Sumner looked at this inheritance not in American but in world terms. 'The outlying parts of the earth are made available and stand open to the use of the next generations. ... There are unexhausted improvements all over the globe [the phrase recalls Joseph Chamberlain] which the nineteenth century undertook and paid for, the gain of which will come to the twentieth.' Second, Sumner spoke in much the same terminology of the increase in 'acquired knowledge'. 'There are acquisitions in the higher branches of pure mathematics, which are fruitless at present but which are certain to prove of inestimable value to sustain the development of the applications of electricity.' Third, given both these aspects of the inheritance, there was every reason 'for even rash optimism in regard to the material or economic welfare of mankind'. 'While numbers increase, the comfort *per capita* will increase. Popular education will pay. The life-conditions will improve. The chances for those who inherit nothing will be good provided that they are industrious, prudent and temperate.'

So far, so good – very good, indeed. Yet Sumner went on to consider the more awkward aspects of the inheritance. He foresaw international disputes in which alliances of powers, including the United

States, would be arrayed against each other. 'The probability is that a great war will result, and even that the century will be as full of war as the eighteenth century was and for the same reasons.' 'The case of China', he went on – and it was difficult to forget it in 1900 – 'is already actual, and the course of things suggests doubt and fear of the future. The possibilities of mischief and disturbance are very great, and they will so far as they occur traverse the realization of economic welfare which the economic powers and organization promise.'

It was on questions of 'organization' that Sumner had his most interesting things to say. The nineteenth century had seen a great increase in the powers of the state: 'To get the use and avoid the abuse of the state is harder than it ever was before. It is harder in the democratic republic than in any other form of the state.' Sumner thought of 'social democracy' as an abuse of democracy: he was alarmed also at the growth of 'bureaucracy', at the increase in the number of civil servants and inspectors called into the service of the state during the course of the century.

He was less alarmed, however, at the increase in the scale of business organisation and foresaw the rise of the 'multinationals'. 'The immense increase in all facilities of transportation and communication has made it not only possible but necessary to organize industry in cooperative combinations which reach over state boundaries and embrace the world.' But it was 'idle to criticize or bewail this fact'. 'If we use steam and electricity we must get space for their evolutions, and we must adjust our plans to their incidental effects.' For the first time the analyses of Sumner and Wells began to converge. 'The little independent man is forced into a place in a great organization where he may win more but will lose his independence. It is as inevitable as the introduction of machinery and the consequences of machinery.'

Sumner and Wells were right to draw attention to this change, different as were the deductions which they drew from it. Nor, of course, were they the first to do so. There was a marked trend towards industrial 'combination' and 'amalgamation' in all parts of the world during the last two decades of the nineteenth century, sometimes protectively under the influence of falling profit margins, sometimes aggressively in order for businessmen of exceptional drive to carve out new business empires. Trusts, monopolies and oligopolies pointed the way forward to a new phase in the history of capitalism, as Marx had predicted when he made the trend towards concentration a main corner-stone of his economic analysis. In Germany and the United States, countries with very different political and legal systems, there were already huge business organisations, like the Rhenish-Westphalian coal cartel (1893), controlling half the coal production of the country, and Standard Oil (1882) with international as well as national ramifications.

One of the main events of 1901 – one satirist called it the first real reorganisation of the world since God created it in 4004 BC – was the founding of the huge United States Steel Corporation. The trend towards combination was actively encouraged by the state in imperial Germany and challenged in the United States, yet in the latter country 'trusts' controlled two-fifths of the manufacturing capital of the country by 1904. America, indeed, was already set on the road towards becoming a country of giant corporations. Britain, like France, lagged behind in the story. The establishment of limited liability in Britain in 1856 had little immediate effect on well-established individual or family businesses, and trade associations and mergers developed significantly only during the last two decades of the century. There was a burst of new public company formation during the 1890s, but in technical as well as in financial terms British and French enterprise at the end of the century worked on a smaller scale than that of their biggest competitors. The biggest British steel mills were turning out only as much steel as the average Westphalian mills, and in what was thought of by the *Daily Mail*, Wallace, Wells and Sumner alike as the key industry of the future – electricity – there was no British counterpart of the German *Allgemeine Elektrizitäts Gesellschaft*, founded in 1883 and managed by the father of one of the pioneers of twentieth-century planning, Walther Rathenau.

One branch of the pedigree of twentieth-century planning must be traced back to such beginnings, not all of them obviously visible even to the most expert students of the economy in 1900. While socialism remained a gospel, the so-called socialisation of large-scale enterprise was already becoming a fact.

There were two other implications of the process which Sumner, fond as he was of millionaires, did not dwell upon. First, there was a bigger threat to 'individualism' than he implied as business organisations grew in scale and complexity, and as management, increasingly specialised management, became further separated from direct financial control. At a time when the numbers of professional people were growing in most countries – their numbers trebled in Britain between 1841 and 1881, and leapt further ahead during the 1890s – the old entrepreneurial ideal, which had so strongly influenced the making of nineteenth-century Liberalism and which had done so much to shape the socialist response, was losing its momentum and its spell. New middle classes emerged which neither owned property nor worked in trade and industry. There was less talk, therefore, of the driving force of active, individually deployed capital and of the merits of open competition. 'The day of combination is here to stay', remarked

J.D. Rockefeller, the supremely ruthless individualist, 'individualism has gone, never to return.' The same point was hammered home by the German socialist revisionists.

Increasingly business, which had been for so long on the offensive, if often a muted offensive, against older aristocratic modes of behaviour, was becoming identified either with impersonal organisation or with wealth rather than with work. The concern expressed about 'pluto-cracy' by people like Gladstone during the 1890s – and they were to be found in Germany as well as in Britain and the United States – must be studied against this background, the background of Shaw's *Socialism for Millionaires* (1901). Socialism and plutocracy, indeed, were twin bogeys for Gladstone, because he thought that one grew with the other. Sumner also saw the future in terms of their ultimate twentieth-century conflict. 'Will the state degenerate into the instrument of an attack upon property, or will it cripple wealth-making or will the wealth-making interest, threatened by the state, rise up to master it, corrupt it and use it?' 'This', he went on, 'is the alternative [and to him it was a terrifying alternative] which the twentieth century must meet. It is the antagonism of democracy and plutocracy. It is the most momentous antagonism which has ever arisen in human society because ... it is in the vitals of society.'

There was no element of Marxism in Sumner which would have enabled him to place this 'momentous antagonism' within the longer perspectives of industrialisation. Nor could he see – and this was the second of the big implications of what was happening which he missed – that there was a direct connection between the growth of trustification in the armaments industry and the 'militarism' which he deplored as much as Wallace or Wells. In 1886 Alfred Nobel, the inventor of dynamite, had established the first international trust, the Dynamite Trust Ltd: by 1900 it was the centre of an international web of interlocking armaments interests. The Chairman of the Trust realistically told his shareholders in 1899 that the continuing pros-perity of their undertaking depended on 'keeping pace with the times'. 'We have constantly striven', he went on, 'to find suitable branches of industry which can be linked with your undertaking, and have chiefly developed a large business in war material, both in the manufacture of smokeless powder and ammunition.' This was one, at least, of the routes into the twentieth century, and it is still a crowded route.

The last section of Sumner's essay shows just how far he was removed from Wells. He cared nothing for the 'common man' as distinct from the 'forgotten man' and spoke instead of 'the man-on-the-curbstone'. Yet, like Wells, he believed that his day was dawning. 'He is now in full control, and his day of glory will be the twentieth century. He is ignorant, noisy, self-sufficient, dogmatic, and impatient of opposition or remonstrance.... The newspapers bow down to him, flatter him, and treat him as the specimen type of "the people".'

'Militarism' for Sumner was explicable not in terms of the armaments industry but, as it was for J.A. Hobson, in terms of mass psychology. The man-on-the-curbstone was 'always great on patriotism. He supposes that patriotism is an affair of enthusiasm and brag and bluster.' In the twentieth century he would be increasingly discontented as well as increasingly bellicose, for 'the natural and necessary effect of the increased material comfort of the nineteenth century is to increase discontent'. Who knew what damage he could do to the fabric of society? 'The young century inherits turmoil and clamour with little knowledge or sense.' Its bequest would lead it not towards greater planning, but towards greater confusion. The newspapers would make things even worse. 'They have no time for quiet and sober reflection. They never finish anything. They never go back deeply into anything and never go back to correct mistakes.'

It is tempting to leave Sumner at that point having, as it were, rounded the circle and once again reached the *Daily Mail*. Yet he had one last point which is pivotal to any interpretation of the century. He pitted against the man-on-the-curbstone the 'expert'. 'We must look for truth and wisdom to the specialists – and the work of society is to be carried on by combining the knowledge which they all bring to the common stock.' Here Sumner was certainly leaving his own century behind and peering into the future. The essential quality of mid-nineteenth-century thought was that it was not specialist in the twentieth-century sense. Although there had been many signs of increasing specialisation, particularly in higher education, during the last two decades of the century, signs to which Pearson (like many other academics) was pointing, the great earlier nineteenth-century thinkers, following Goethe, had struggled hard to maintain a synoptic view of ideas, of problems, and of life itself.

Darwin learned from Malthus; Marx learned from Hegel and Darwin; Ruskin straddled art and economics; Comte systematised everything; Gladstone studied Homer and Adam Smith. There were innumerable cross-linkages between Biblical criticism, history, philology, geology, biology, anthropology and economics. During the bridge years between the eighteenth and nineteenth centuries Utilitarianism and Romanticism, both of which need to be considered in the broadest terms, had fused the sense of understanding, not fragmented it; and the possible mid-nineteenth-century tension between positivist and historical thinking was resolved in sweeping theories of evolution which held everything together in an age of intellectual discovery and change. The concluding passages of *The Origin of*

Species, one of the century's most controversial books, lie at the very heart of the century, in their style as in their substance:

> It is interesting to contemplate a tangled bank, clothed with many plants of many kinds, with birds singing on the bushes, with various insects flitting about, and with worms crawling through the damp earth, and to reflect that these elaborately constructed forms, so different from each other, and dependent upon each other in so complex a manner, have all been produced by laws acting around us .... From the war of nature, from famine and death, the most exalted object which we are capable of conceiving, namely the production of the higher animals, directly follows. There is grandeur in this view of life, with its several powers, having been originally breathed by the Creator into a few forms or into one; and that while this planet has gone cycling on according to the fixed law of gravity, from so simple a beginning endless forms most beautiful and most wonderful have been, and are being evolved.

Freud, for all his contribution to the making of a new climate of opinion in the twentieth century, largely after 1918, belonged to this nineteenth-century tradition of thinking and writing. So, too, in Britain did the 'neo-classical' economist Alfred Marshall, who turned to economics from ethics and who provided the foundations for a very different (but related) twentieth-century economist, J.M. Keynes, to build upon. Yet it was from the 'experts', sooner in the physical sciences than in economics, that the twentieth century was increasingly to draw its substance. As R.K. Webb has perceptively written:

> Professionalism, growing in every field, made Victorian amateurism impotent and ridiculous, and in pursuing researches more deeply [and this, too, was to bring in the state] broke up the unity in culture, invented new languages and created enormous gulfs which the amateurs could neither understand nor bridge .... More and more, men were forced by facts and events to a humility early Victorians could feel only towards God, if there, or to an apathy unknown to the preceding generation.

V

The four balance sheets drawn up at the end of the nineteenth century and the beginning of the twentieth inevitably look different in the light of what has happened since. There have been such great divides in twentieth-century experience that many people living during its most troubled years have been 'tempted', as Basil Willey put it, 'to take flight into the nineteenth as into the promised land'. Nostalgia, however, is a poor substitute for understanding, and most of the problems of a crowded nineteenth century, when there were enormous variations of experience even for members of the same generation, belonged to the same matrix as those of our own century, at least until the late 1950s and 1960s when there was an enormous break.

Few people living in the nineteenth century, even its greatest admirers, would have thought of it as a 'promised land'. They believed rather, with Victor Hugo, that they were on a journey '*à l'avenir divin et pur*'. The most optimistic of them were sure of their sense of direction: the most sensitive of them were worried even about that. They all knew, if they knew much at all, that they were taking the brunt of a unique development in human history. Some were confused, some alienated. Some tried to climb out of history: most, with Ernest Renan, maintained that 'now everything is considered as in the process of formation'. Each period, Michelet had written, had a physiognomy and character of its own. According to Burckhardt, 'History is the record of what one age finds worthy of note in another.' As we move 'towards 2000', it is illuminating to look backwards to see how men – and women – moved – on the whole with expectation – towards 1900.

15   The Historian and the Future

When the great French historian Marc Bloch was in a German prison camp in 1943, finishing off his fascinating book *The Historian's Craft*, he contemplated concluding it with a seventh section called 'The Problem of Prevision'.[1] Before he had time to complete his text, he was taken from his cell and shot in a open field near Lyons with twenty-six other members of the French Resistance.

Bloch's faith in the future remained unshaken until the very end of his life, but it is difficult to reconstruct what he would have chosen to write about the shape of that future on the basis either of his personal experience or of his historical scholarship. He was a brilliant analyst of past events, but there is very little detail in his work about tendencies, trends and forecasts relating to the twentieth century. He believed, however, that history is not 'the science of the past' – there is just 'one science of men in time' – and that 'the faculty of understanding the living' is 'the master quality of the historian'. He also called prevision 'a mental necessity', suggesting as sub-headings of his seventh section 'the ordinary errors of prevision' (selecting as variables economic fluctuations and military history); 'the paradox of prevision in human affairs' (prevision which is destroyed by prevision); the 'role of conscious awareness'; 'short-term prevision'; 'regularities'; and 'hopes and uncertainties'. It is tempting to try to fill in his outline.

Most other historians have been far more chary of identifying tendencies and trends in their own lifetimes than Bloch was, and of making forecasts, however provisional, about the future. Increasingly, indeed, they have become specialists in short periods or highly specific problem areas of history, losing, in consequence, much of their freedom as travellers in past time. Some, like A. J. P. Taylor, have looked at history quite differently. A few historians concerned with historical methodologies have turned, however, to the problem of 'predicality' (and probability) and the role of 'prediction', including what they call 'prediction in the past' and its 'uses' in professional historical scholarship.[2]

Professional historians engage in 'prediction' exercises, often without knowing it, when in their work they anticipate later sequences of events in the past and try to account for them or fill in their detail.

Often, indeed, they will sort out ranges of possible outcomes, not very different from the 'possible futures' sorted out by futurologists, except that historians, unlike futurologists, can benefit from hindsight. Thus, the American historian J. H. Hexter, one of the most refreshing methodologists, has drawn the following instance from his own detailed study of the seventeenth-century English Civil War:

> If a distinct cleavage separated war party from peace party, given the side a Member of Parliament took on one question involving war or peace, we should be able to predict his position in regard to any other question involving the same issue. For example, if a Member voted against a treaty of peace in February that would identify him as one of the war party. We should then expect that in July as well as February he would oppose a treaty ... Let us try the powers of prediction with which this hypothesis endows us on the stubborn facts that we find in the journals and in the diaries of the Civil War Parliament.

Hexter found that his predictive hypothesis did not stand. The subsequent pattern of voting did not conform. He demonstrated, therefore, that there was no 'war party' or 'peace party'.[3] Hexter was was honest as well as sophisticated in the testing of such predictive hypotheses, subjecting his own work to such analysis, putting 'causality' to the test as well as probabilities. Bloch had called history *une petite science conjecturale*; and Hexter distinguished between history with a capital H and history without it, urging 'de-escalation', coming down from capitals to lower case.[4]

This is just what three major groups of historians who have been concerned with the future as well as the past – the historians most read by our futurologists – have refused to do. The first major group were the prophets of decline, like Oswald Spengler, who have had considerable influence on a broad public. The second were the confirmed believers in 'progress', who have seen no break between past and future but merely an upward or onward linear movement. The third group – Marxists, of many shades – treat laws of historical motion, which cover both past and future, as scientific. Marx's own thought about society was historical: his unrest about the present and his vision led him to the future.

The prophets of decline have followed in the wake of what a recent Swiss writer, with Jakob Burckhardt and Friedrich Nietzsche in mind, has called the nineteenth-century 'tragic futurologies'.[5] Spengler, like Toynbee after him, thought in cyclical rather than in linear terms, and concerned himself with 'cultures', not with nation states. They both refused to start, as both Marx and many of the confirmed believers in progress did, with the economic sub-structure and the way it evolved. Some of their long-term prophecies, like those of Burckhardt and

Nietzsche before them, look perceptive. So, too, do those of the French writer Paul Valéry, who wrote briefly on themes which Spengler and Toynbee covered at great length.[6] Valéry started not with war or empire, however, but with the acceleration of rates of technical change in his own lifetime and their human and cultural consequences – a problem which also interested Bloch and his interpreter Lucien Febvre and which has interested futurologists like Peter Drucker and Herman Kahn. The relationship between economic history and cultural history seemed basic, and it has been given new point with growing interest in the theories of Kondratiev and others about 'long cycles' following an earlier debate about 'limits to growth'.[7]

'Decline theories', which often echo earlier cyclical theories of history, are in a sense replies, in a sense parallel counterparts, to earlier theories of progress. Ruins and achievements always attract different temperaments. J. B. Bury, the historian of progress, dedicated his volume to the memories of the Abbé de Saint Pierre, Condorcet, Comte, Spencer and 'other optimists' he had mentioned in his text. Two of his named writers belonged to the eighteenth-century 'Enlightenment', which produced new vistas of the future (along with one immensely influential work on ruins – Volnay's *Les Ruines* (1791)): two belonged to the nineteenth century, when the idea of progress was translated into visible material expression. Yet Bury traced ideas of progress back through Bacon and into the ancient world and gave due weight to nineteenth-century Darwinian theories of evolution and their influence on historians.[8] He made much of Sébastien Mercier, 'the father of Historical Futurity', who had published his *L'An 2440* anonymously in 1770, but he did not once mention Macaulay who usually figures so prominently in the historiography of progress.

Historiography has come to be regarded as a necessary dimension of the study of history, so that writers like Macaulay have been studied in depth and in perspective as, of course, have both Bury's confirmed believers in progress and the prophets of decline. One general theme in historiography is the debate between different historians about the same topic – and why we can never have one definitive version of the past. A second theme is why particular historians range themselves on one side or the other, or neither. A third theme is why particular methodologies are chosen. The most challenging in recent years being what has come to be called quantitative history. A fourth theme is why particular topics are chosen for debate at particular times. This leads from biography into intellectual (and political and cultural) history.

The same kind of concerns could well guide critical studies of futurology, which already has its own history. Indeed, it may be that stronger links between historians and futurologists could be estab-

lished through historiography than through history itself.[9] Futurologists have emphasised recently that they are avoiding 'fatalism' and
treating 'futures', not *the* future; we always have to look, they say, at a
range of possible futures.[10] This is not very different from the
historian's emphasis not on one past, but on many – with the sense of
the past shifting in each generation at the same time as the sense of the
future, except, again, that historians enjoy the benefit of hindsight.
Even the language is similar. Historians talk of 'landscapes' and
'watersheds': futurologists of 'scenarios'.

Futurologists include a strong quantitative-minded contingent,
dependent on the computer. They have so far been less concerned,
however, with studying the effects of the stance of the particular
futurologist on his conclusions than they have been with the influence
on forecasting of different 'vantage points'. They have been able to
distinguish sharply say between Herman Kahn and Seymour Melman,
but they have devoted little time to the way particular futurologists
'rig' scenarios. It is interesting to note, for example, that the Open
University's collection of readings, *Man-made Futures*, which insists
that 'alternative directions can and should be the subject of open
debate', ends with an index of concepts but with no index of persons.[11]

It is easier, perhaps, to deal with vantage points than with individual
futurologists. Inevitably, both the futurologist and the historian start
from the present. What they select from the accessible past or forecast
for the future is influenced directly or indirectly, therefore, by present
preoccupations. Daniel Bell made this quite explicit in his account of
the American *Towards 2000* project. His main interest, he said, was
less in predicting the future than in making explicit the structure of his
own society; for this reason, Raymond Aron claimed that *Towards
2000* was merely a way of trying to secure better planning: it was less
imaginatively stretching than history. Likewise, many historians have
emphasised, as Herbert Butterfield has done, how difficult it is to
escape from the attitudes of the present in writing about the past.
People of the past are treated as if they were people of the present, and
this is a restriction on imagination also.[12]

For those historians who are content to write narrative history –
with occasional survey passages and summaries of events and the
people who made them – links with futurology at first look unim-
portant or irrelevant, although it is often in relation to such
historians – Ranke is a good example – that historiographers have been
most illuminating when they set out to place and to interpret them.[13]
Narrative historians may be mainly concerned with events and the
order in which they took place, but they give themselves away both in
their selection and their presentation.

Since futurologists are in no position to predict precise events or, equally important, the time when 'events' will happen, their field of interests contrasts sharply at first sight with that of such narrative historians. Nor can futurologists tap the rich resources of personal biography. Through historiography, however, the apparent contrast between the operations of historians and futurologists looks less sharp. The narrative is not definitive, and historians know far less about the depths of personality and intention in their individual 'characters' than they wish. Even the most systematic 'new' social historians who treat 'chance happenings' in history as 'grit' in their analysis, are forced to admit, even if they regret, that the grit is there.

It is obvious, of course, that the more historians turn from narrative to 'problems' and 'patterns of interpretation' and that the more they show themselves prepared to examine past people and events out of their strict time sequence, the more the fields of the historian and the futurologist will converge or overlap. For many social and cultural historians the 'fact' is no longer a datum in itself; it is considered in relation to structures of similar 'facts', not necessarily chronologically close. It can be argued, indeed, that both historians and futurologists are concerned with change and resistance to change – which is achieved not by simple cause and effect, but by and through elaborate 'network' or webs of interrelated variables. The word 'network' is a key twentieth-century concept. In dealing with the processes of change, and their controversial implications, both futurologists and historians have to concern themselves with secular and cyclical changes, with the relationship between planned and unplanned changes, with varying contemporaneous rates of change, with constants, a theme which greatly interested Bloch, and not least, with contingencies.

Historiography is useful (again) in pointing to the choice both of themes and of methods. Of course, historians do not have to 'invent' contingencies. They have to get behind them. They start with specificities and go on to try to explain them. Naturally, they very frequently get caught up in the detail. Indeed, they may find the detail more significant to them, through the multiple meanings it conveys, than broad generalisations, particularly when generalisations (of the kind which appeal to many futurologists) are based on incomplete sets of data and inconclusive documentation. The futurologist has to proliferate his own detail, and the critical reader will be more sceptical about accepting it than he will in treating the detail provided by the historian.

In both cases, particularly the latter, there may be 'anachronisms'. These are particularly prominent in science fiction about the future unless the novelist 'thins out' his plots; and many science fiction novelists, particularly, perhaps, Americans, find it impossible to avoid them. Yet such writers often introduce historians into their novels – a theme in itself[14] – and a few of them have been ingenious in trying to deal with the 'individual' in the future. One man may be unpredictable, they say – Isaac Asimov can envisage a mutant – but in large numbers, people can 'be measured, examined, classified'.[15] These words of Robert Heinlein were written in 1940, a 'year of destiny' when fortunately more than one man, the man who had conquered Holland, Belgium and France, proved 'unpredictable'. The 'mass' theory, which was forecast in some of the 'tragic futurologies' of the nineteenth-century prophets of decline, is problematic, not proven.

Given that more historians are now concerned with 'problem history', including 'history from below' (that dealing in detail with people whose names have long been forgotten) and with counter-factual history, the history of *ifs*, rather than with narrative history, which deals with leaders and 'great events', it might be concluded that the *rapprochement* between the historian and the futurologist will grow stronger. Yet this is not the whole story. Prophets are treated with suspicion in an age when counting is considered more important than prophesying and no one would now think of writing a contemporary version of H. G. Wells's *Outline of History*, the future in reverse.[16]

Wells remains interesting because he wrote novels as well as articles and books about both past and future. He also gave one fascinating lecture 'The Discovery of the Future' to the Royal Institution in 1902, in which he called for a study of 'inductive history' which would be concerned with 'working out the biological, intellectual and economic consequences of the social forces unleashed by that technology'.[17] Wells allowed freer play for his fantasy than either analytical historians or committed futurologists usually allow themselves. Although he has often been dismissed as a somewhat crude spokesman of material progress, he was sensitive and subtle enough to recognise that historical evolution might itself move in reverse. It was not only late in life that he tasted despair, but even when young, he felt no confidence in man's permanent ascendancy. In a fascinating article written in *The Gentleman's Magazine* in 1891, he suggested that 'the Coming Beast must certainly be reckoned in any anticipatory calculations regarding the Coming Man'. He ranged far wider than the 'tragic futurologists' of the nineteenth century into the realm of first and last things, the realm where cosmography and eschatology meet.[18] He would have appreciated a remark of Claude Lévi-Strauss that 'the world began without man and will end without him'.[19]

If historiography is one field which could be profitably explored by historians and futurologists together, another – with Lévi-Strauss in mind and with Wells's novels as much as his histories and anticipations – is the relationship of both history and futurology to anthropology. The 'history of events' looks inadequate in the light of concern for 'structures' and 'myths', but so, too, do those versions of futurology which are concerned solely with extrapolation and probabilities. The 'otherness' of both past and future needs to be felt. So also, however, does the 'otherness' of much in our present. 'The virtue of anthropology consists in reminding us that we have to discover the rules of our own society just as we discover those of other societies.[20] Our task starts here and now. And *our* here and now are as far removed as they can be in place and time from those of the Arab historian Ibn Khaldun who was content to observe that past and future are as alike as two drops of water.

NOTES

1   M. Bloch, *The Historian's Craft* (English trans., 1954), Introduction by Lucien Febvre, p. xvi.
2   'Covering law' theories of history have treated prediction of the future and explanation of the past in terms of the same model of logic, suggesting that in both cases the analyst must deduce desired statements from a covering law that covers all the phenomena studied. See A. Grünbaum, *Philosophical Problems of Space and Time* (1963). Their critics have treated explanation of the past and the prediction of the future as different operations. See M. Scriven, 'Truisms as the Grounds for Historical Explanation', in P. Gardiner (ed.), *Theories of History* (1959).
3   See J. H. Hexter, *The History Primer* (1972), pp. 46 ff.
4   ibid., p. 59.
5   A. Reszler, 'L'Europe et le mythe du declin', in *Cadmos*, vol. 1 (1978), p. 96. Reszler starts his study of 'decline as a prospective study' with Gobineau's *Essai sur l'inégalité des races humaines*, commenting that 'history is of interest to Gobineau only in so far as its study facilitates the anticipation of the future'. (ibid., p. 94.)
6   P. Valéry, *Variété I* (1924).
7   See C. Freeman, J. A. Clark and L. L. G. Soete, *Unemployment and Technical Innovation: A Study of Long Waves and Economic Development* (1982) and C. Freeman, 'Prometheus Unbound' in *Futures* (October, 1984), a reply to N. Onuf, 'Prometheus Prostrate' in *ibid* (February, 1984).
8   J. B. Bury, *The Idea of Progress* (1932).
9   Nonetheless, Ernest Gellner has argued in *The Historian Between the Ethnologist and the Futurologist* (1973), p. 21, that 'the curious and ironic role of history' is that 'it helps to prejudge questions for which if we had to face them rationally we could simply have no determinate answers. All the premises would be too slippery.'

10 See J.H. Goldthorpe, 'Theories of Industrial Society: Reflections on the Recrudescence of Historicism and the Future of Sociology', in the *European Journal of Sociology*, vol. XII (1971).

11 N. Cross, D. Elliot and R. Roy (eds), *Man-Made Futures* (1974). For concern with values, see, in particular, K. Kumar, 'Inventing the Future in spite of Futurology' (pp. 129-33), and S. Encel, P.K. Marstrand and W. Page, *The Art of Anticipation: Values and Methods in Forecasting* (1975). For technocratic approaches to the future, see E. Jantsch, *Technological Forecasting in Perspective* (1967). See also *The Future as an Academic Discipline* (Ciba, 1975).

12 H. Butterfield, *The Whig Interpretation of History* (1931).

13 See F. Le Roy Ladurie, *The Territory of the Historian* (1979), pp. 113-14.

14 Note how A.C. Clarke introduces his historian in *Prelude to Space* (1954), and Asimov deals with psycho-history in *Foundation* (1955). Asimov has explained some of his interests in his notes on 'Social Science Fiction', in R. Bretner (ed.), *Modern Science Fiction: Its Meaning and Future* (1953), p. 181. For the use of Spengler in science fiction, see also R.D. Mullen, 'Blish, Van Bogt and the uses of Spengler', in the *Riverside Quarterly*, August 1968, pp. 172-86. Some of the most sophisticated writers of science fiction have stressed that science fiction is rarely trying to predict what will happen and it should not be judged by its predictive accuracy. Rather it examines various things which might happen, and tries to imagine their consequences if they do. See R. Schmidt, 'The Science in Science Fiction', in T.D. Clareson (ed.), *Many Futures, Many Worlds* (1976), p. 29.

15 See R.A. Heinlein, 'The Roads must Roll', in his collection *The Past Through Tomorrow* (1967). Heinlein, like Asimov, has always been interested in history and sociology. See, for the latter, *Words from the Myths* (1961).

16 See W.H. Dray, *Philosophy of History* (1964), pp. 60-6.

17 See S. Lilley, 'Can Prediction become a Science?', in B. Barber and W. Hirsch (eds), *The Sociology of Science* (1962), pp. 142-6, where he notes that Wells's lecture was printed in *Nature* and in the *Annual Report of the Smithsonian Institution*. See also W. Bell and J.A. Mav (eds), *The Sociology of the Future* (1971).

18 See the anthology of critical articles on Wells, in B. Bergonzi (ed.), *H.G. Wells: A Collection of Critical Essays* (1976) and N. and J. Mackenzie, *The Time Traveller* (1973).

19 C. Lévi-Strauss, *Tristes tropiques*, quoted in Reszler, *op. cit.*, p. 115.

20 Gellner, *op. cit.*, p. 33.

Index

Acland, H.W., 165, 170
Acton, Lord, 51, 60, 64, 237
Adams, H., 296
Addison, J., 244
Adelaide, 9
Africa, 89ff., 153, 296 (see also South Africa)
Albany, 167
Alexandria, 15, 167
Alfred, King, 215, 217, 219, 222, 231
Anne, Queen, 244
Anthropology, 62, 274, 275, 277, 281-2, 283, 307, 315
Anti-Corn Law League, 40, 43
Appleton, T., 13
Arnold, Matthew, 15, 121, 260
Arnot, Dr N., 135, 169
Arnot, R. Page, 121
Aron, R., 313
Ashley, Lord, 133, 136, 148, 149, 150, 190, 194
Asimov, I., 315
Athens, 5, 10, 15
Attwood, Mrs T., xvii
Aubrey, John, 265
Auden, W.H., 275
Austen, Jane, 72, 294
Australia, 89, 90, 92, 105, 108, 195, 294
Austria, 16ff., 103, 118, 239, 266

Babylon, 5
Bacon, Francis, 312
Bagehot, W., 192
Baker, Dr R., 169
Baldwin, Stanley, 240-1, 253
Balfour, A.J., 293
Ballaret, 90
Balzac, Honoré de, 13, 14
Bamford, Samuel, 44
Barbados, 283
Barcelona, 9

Barraclough, G., 229
Basel, 17
Basic English, 261
Bastide, R., 281
Baudelaire, Charles, 14, 15, 25
Beales, H.L., 263
Bell, Daniel, 313
Bellamy, E., 300
Benthem, J., Benthomites, 129, 130, 137, 184-5, 190, 196
Bentley, Phyllis, 72
Bentley, Richard, 244
Berlin, 4, 16, 17, 20, 22
Bermondsey, 158
Berne, 9
Bevan, A., 182, 192
Beveridge, William, 82, 186, 205
Bichet, F.X., 56
Bilston, 157, 162
Birmingham, 5, 50, 157, 170, 219
Bismarck, Otto von, 18, 198, 199, 200
Blackburn, 157
Blackley, W.L., 201
Blake, William, 6, 120
Blanchard, E.L., 11
Bland, H., 187
Blatchford, R., 124
Bloch, M., xiv, 272, 280, 287, 310, 311, 312
Blomfield, Bishop, 133, 160
Boas, F., 275
Bodin, F., 287
Bolingbroke, 244
Bolton, 138, 157
Booth, Charles, 23, 202
Bordeaux, 155, 161
Boston, 99, 106, 300
Bradford, 146, 219
Braudel, F., 274
Brazil, 4, 272ff
Bright, John, 144, 239

Bristol, 9, 146
Brontë, Charlotte, 68 ff
Brontë, Patrick, 73
Brown, J.M., 260
Browning, Robert, 294
Brussels, 9
Buccleugh, Duke of, 132
Bullett, G., 49
Burckhardt, Karl, 16, 273, 309, 311
Bury, 157
Bury, J., 312
Bussey, P., 219
Butler, Samuel, 256
Butterfield, H., 237, 244, 245, 313
Byron, Lord, 10

Cadiz, 9
Cambridge, 107, 237, 238, 240, 262, 263
Campbell, general, 75
Camus, A., 159
Cannadine, D., 286-7
Carlisle, R., 219
Carlyle, Thomas, 4, 5, 38, 82, 97, 98, 119, 147, 190, 215, 216, 231, 237, 293
Carr, E.H., 256
Cartwright, W., 74
Chadwick, Edwin, xiv, 60, 129 ff., 163, 190, 191, 198
Chamberlain, J, 170, 303
Chartism, 40, 102, 177, 201, 219
Chaucer, Geoffrey, 245
Chesterton, G. K., 50
Chevalier, L., 154 ff.
Chicago, 3, 5-6, 99, 102-3, 107
China, 304
Cholera, xvii, 57, 59, 153 ff., 260
Churchill, W.S., 244, 249
Cities, 3 ff., 249, 250
Clapham, J.H., 201
Clark, G. Kitson, 258, 265
Clark, Sir George, 265
Cobb, R., 281
Cobbett, William, 22, 46
Cobden, Richard, 40, 103
Cockshut, A.O.J., 29
Cologne, 3, 17
Colvin, S.S., 55
Communism, 39, 44, 122, 124-5
Complete Suffrage, 40
Comte, Auguste, 263, 293, 312
Condorcet, Marquis de, 312
Constable, John, 259

Constantinople, 9
Crabbe, George, 37, 45
Cracow, 9
Crane, Walter, 117
Crystal Palace, 116
Curie, P., 299

Dagognet, F., 127
Darvin, C., 307
Deverell, W. Trapnell, 232
Dicey, A.V., 52, 180, 191, 192
Dickens, Charles, 7, 11-12, 14, 24 ff., 50, 106, 127, 260, 294
Dieppe, 160
Disraeli, B., 3, 23, 50, 82, 96, 132, 147, 201
Drucker, P., 312

Edison, T., 300
Edward VII, King, 254, 263
Education, 150, 285
Edward the Confessor, 216
Egypt, 165, 166
Ehrlich, P., 299
Electricity, 41
Eliot, George, xvii, 1, 11, 49 ff., 71, 255
Eliot, T.S., 15
Elliott, Ebenezer, xvii, 36 ff.
Ellis, Havelock, 256
Emerson, R.W., 8, 219
Engels, Friedrich, 82, 121
Etienne, L., 1
Eversley, D., 156
Exeter Hall, 95, 133
Eyre, governor, 98

Fabianism, 186-8, 190, 192-3
Faraday, M., 298
Fascism, 241
Febvre, L., 272, 312
Fichte, 18
Finer, S.E., xiv
First World War, 240, 241
Fitzwilliam, Carl, 80
Flaubert, Gaston, 11
Florence, 3, 5, 9
Fox, W.J., 40
France, 3, 10 ff., 94, 101, 154, 155, 239, 261, 305, 315
Frankfurt, 3, 9, 17
Freeman, E.A., xvii, 216, 217, 221, 226, 227, 229
Free Trade, 36 ff., 102-3, 293

French Revolution, 39, 237, 239
Fréour, Dr, 161
Freud, Sigmond, 256, 275, 308
Freyer, H., 276
Freyre, Gilbert, 272ff.
Froude, J.A., 97
Frye, N., 7
Futures, futurology, 310ff.

Garribaldi, 238-9, 244
Gaskell, Elizabeth, 29, 70, 72, 86
Gauguin, P., 259
Geddes, P., xvii, 24
Gelsenkirchen, 3
George V, King, 240
Germany, 16, 153, 185, 198ff., 239, 297, 304
Gibbon, Edward, 227, 265
Gibbs, J.W., 298
Giotto, 259
Gissing, George, 30
Gladstone, Mary, 51
Gladstone, W.E., 147, 231, 255, 296, 306
Glass, D, xvii
Godwin, Earl, 231
Gogol, N., 261
Goldsmith, Oliver, 8
Gooch, G.P., 237
Gore, Charles, 292, 293
Governesses, 73, 83ff.
Graham, Sir James, 61
Grasmere, 36
Green, J.R., 221, 227, 229, 230, 244, 273, 275
Greenock, 141
Grey, Earl, 239-40
Grillparzer, F., 16, 20
Guiral, M., 157, 159
Guy, Dr W.A., 132

Hagen, E., 247
Haight, G., 49
Hale, J., 244
Halévy, E., 179
Halifax, 75, 157
Hamburg, 153, 162, 166
Hammond, B., 241
Hammond, J.L., 241
Handcock, W.D., 261
Hardy, Thomas, 260, 264
Harmsworth, A., 291

Harney, Julian, 219
Harold, King, 224, 231
Harrison, Frederic, 13
Harrisson, Tom, 258
Harrop, John, 78, 82
Hastings, 224, 225
Hauptmann, Gerhardt, 18
Haussman, Baron, 12
Hawthorne, Nathaniel, 8, 18
Hay, Rev. W., 79
Haydon, Benjamin, 22
Health of Towns Association, 132ff.
Hebbel, F., 16
Hegel, G.W.F., 16, 307
Heidelberg, 16
Heine, Heinrich, 12
Heinlein, R., 315
Henderson, Arthur, 257
Henriques, F., 283
Henry VII, King, 223
Hexter, J.H., 311
History, xiiiff., 2, 51, 64, 68, 104, 237, 243ff., 273ff., 307, 309, 310-11, 312, 313
Hoberson, Rev H., 74, 78, 81
Hobhouse, L.T., 197
Hobson, J.A., 189, 197, 307
Hofmannsthal, Hugo von, 21
Hofstadter, R., 7
Homer, 307
Hong Kong, 4
Hood, Robin, 218
Hopkins, Gerald Manley, 259
Hornsey, 148
Horsfell, William, 74
Hotels, 93-4
House, H., 28, 127, 263
Huddersfield, 75, 76, 134, 146
Hughes, H.S., 213
Hughes, Thomas, 215
Hugo, Victor, 10, 11, 12, 13, 309
Hume, J., 160
Huysmans, J.K., 294
Huxley, A., 257
Hyndman, H.M., 193

Industrial Revolution, 183
India, 153, 160, 163, 165-6
Inge, W.R., 287
International Labour Office, 179, 180, 205
Ireland, 91, 154, 224, 284, 285
Italy, 3, 91, 230, 231, 239

James, Henry, 1, 9, 11, 12, 24, 30, 51, 52, 120, 275
James, William, 264
Jefferson, Thomas, 7, 8, 217
Jerusalem, 10, 15
Johnson, Samuel, 6
Jones, Ernest, 41
Jones, Tom, 257
Joyce, James, 15
Judson, E.Z.C., 11

Kahn, H., 312, 313
Kay, Dr, 169
Keats, John, 294
Keighley, 68
Keller, Gottfried, 16, 17, 19
Kemble, J., 221, 224
Keynes, J.M., 266
Khaldun, Ibn, 316
Kingslake, A., 64
Kingsley, Charles, 56, 57, 63, 64, 215
Kingston, 89, 105
Kipling, Rudyard, 89, 105
Koch, R., 299
Kokoschka, Oskar, 21
Kraus, Karl, 20

Lake District, 36, 45, 46
Lamb, Charles, 22
Landor, W.S., 37
Lane, J., 192
Lassalle, F., 177
Lawrence, D.H., 30
League of Nations, 240
Leavis, F.R., 49
Lecky, W., 50
Leeds, 74, 75, 80, 145-6
Le Havre, 5, 160
Leipzig, 17
Leith, 158
Levin, H., 15
Levi-Strauss, C., 315
Lewes, G.H., 56, 70, 72, 73, 83
Liebig, J. von, 298
Lille, 9, 155
Lincoln, 142
Limerick, 9
Lloyd George, D., 198, 201-2, 220, 239
Locke, John, 244
Lohmann, T., 200, 201
Lollards, 237-8
London, 4, 5-6, 9, 10, 22ff., 97, 145, 160, 165

Longman, M., 247
Longman, R., 242, 245, 246
Longman, W., 246
Lorentz, H.A., 299
Lovejoy, A.D., 260
Lowell, 106-7
Lowell, J.R., 45
Lower, M.A., 225
Lubëck, 3
Luddites, 69ff., 286
Lynch, K., xvii
Lyons, xvii, 9, 157

Macaulay, T.D., 237, 238, 242, 246, 256, 263, 265, 312
Madrid, 291
Maitland, F.W., 221, 259, 262, 263, 265
Malinowski, B., 274
Mallarmé, S., 15
Mallock, W.H., 1
Malthus, T.R., 266, 307
Manchester, 3, 4, 5, 9, 45, 107, 146, 157, 285
Mann, Thomas, 19
Marconi, G., 298, 300
Markets, 3, 183, 187ff.
Markham, Mrs, 216
Marlborough, Duke of, 244-5
Marseilles, 155, 158, 159, 167
Marshall, A., 308
Marshall, T.H., 182
Martin, F.M., xvii
Marx, K., 119, 120, 121, 122, 189, 194, 273, 307, 311
Marx, L., 21
Mass Observation, 257-8
Mattison, A., 119
Maurras, C., 273
Maxwell, J.C., 298
Mayhew, Henry, 23
McCulloch, J.R., 188
McFarlane, K.B., 237
McGregor, D.H., 191
Medicine, xiv, 51ff., 127, 137ff.
Meier, P., 121
Melbourne, 9, 164
Mellor, G., 75
Melman, G., 313
Melville, Herman, 8
Mendel, G., 299
Mendeleev, D.T., 299
Mercier, G., 312

Meredith, George, 260, 264
Methodism, 46
Meyer, C.F., 16
Michelet, 309
Mill, J.S., 98, 102, 141, 187
Miller, H., 25
Miller, T., 11
Milner, A., 197
Moorman, Mary, 239
Morpeth, Lord, 137, 138, 139, 140, 142, 146, 163
Morris, May, 121
Morris, R.J., 154
Morris, William, 30, 116ff., 190, 255
Moscow, 9, 158, 163
Mumford, L., 24, 28
Munich, 16, 17
Muntz, G.F., 144

Naples, 3
Napoleon, 238
National Trust, 249
Nelson, Lord, 243
Netchkina, Mme., 160
Newcastle-on-Tyne, 135
Newman, 293
Newspapers, 4, 145-7
New York, 24
New Zealand, 89, 90, 92, 105, 106, 108, 195
Nicholas, H.F., 54
Nicholas, J., 38
Nicolson, H., 242
Nietzsche, F., 21, 311, 312
Nobel, A., 306
Normanby, Lord, 133, 146
Normans, 215ff., 245
Nottingham, 76
Nurremberg, 3
Oakeshott, M., xviii
Oastler, R., 189, 194, 195
Oldfield, T.H.B., 218, 219
Oldham, 157
Oporto, 9
Orders-in-Council, 81
Owen, Robert, 39
Oxford, 107, 165, 170, 197, 241, 262, 263

Padua, 3
Paine, T., 218
Palgrave, F., 221
Palmerston, Lord, 99, 165, 262

Parent-Duchâtelet, 11
Paris, 3, 4, 5, 10, 11, 12, 13, 25, 57, 155, 158-9, 162, 167, 295
Parsons, 298
Pater, Walter, 15
Pearson, C., 294-6
Peel, F., 68
Peel, Sir Robert, 40, 147
Pettenhafer, M. von., 156, 157, 167, 168
Petit-Dutaillis, C., 229
Philadelphia, 180
Philpotts, Bishop, 167
Pinthus, K., 22
Pittsburgh, 3, 99
Playfair, L., 135
Plumb, J.H., 242
Poetry, 1, 14-15, 16, 23, 36ff., 237, 250
Poor Law, 179, 180, 186, 188, 195, 197, 200, 203, 204, 205
Pope, Alexander, 244
Powell, Anthony, 265
Preston, 135, 139, 157, 169
Progress, 3, 6, 312
Proust, Marcel, 64, 275, 279, 287
Psychology, 21, 255-6, 274-5, 276, 277, 280
Public Health, 11, 28, 56ff., 129ff., 185, 299
Public Opinion, 127ff.
Public Record Office, 221, 225
Punch, 23, 91, 163

Raabe, Wilhelm, 19
Radcliffe, Sir Joseph, 73, 75, 76, 77, 78, 79
Railways, 6, 8, 25-6, 93
Ramsey, W., 299
Ranke, L. von., 17, 313
Rathenau, W., 305
Reeves, P., 195, 196
Religion, 39, 133, 137, 184, 189, 237-8, 260
Renan, E., 309
Reynolds, G.W.M., 11
Richardson, B.W., 130, 150
Richardson, H.F., 228
Riessman, D., 278
Rilke, R.M., 16
Rimbaud, A., 15
Rimlinger, G., 127
Robinson, G., 161

Rochdale, 157
Rockefeller, J.D., 306
Rodbertus, J.K., 199
Rogers, T., 220
Rome, 10, 13
Röntgen, W.C., 298
Roosevelt, F.D.R., 205, 278
Rothenberg, 3
Rotherham, 36
Round, J.H., 229, 230, 231, 232
Rousseau, J.J., 6
Rowntree, B.S., 201, 202, 203, 294
Ruskin, John, 30, 98, 102, 119, 120, 121, 189, 190
Russell, Lord John, 142
Russell, G.W.E., 63
Russia, 163, 230, 291
Russian Revolution, 239

Saintsburg, G., 63, 64
'Sanitary Idea' see Public Health
Saar, Ferdinand von, 20
St Petersburg, 5, 163, 291
St Pierre, Abbe de, 312
Sao Paulo, 285
Saxons, 215 ff.
Sayles, G.O., 228
Scheu, A., 118
Schlegel, A.W. von., 292
Schmolle, G. von., 199
Schorske, C., 20, 21
Schumpeter, K., 179, 201
Science, xv, 52ff., 295, 298ff., 315
Scott, Sir Walter, 11, 221, 222, 223, 258, 260
Second World War, 181, 182, 206, 245-6, 248, 253, 254, 263, 278
Self Help, 38, 185
Senior, N., 188
Shakespeare, William, 8, 39, 224
Shaw, G.B.S., 117, 264, 306
Sheffield, 36ff., 138, 218
Shelley, P.B., 294
Sherwell, Arthur, 24
Shyrock, R., 127
Sibthorpe, Colonel, 142, 143, 144
Sidorov, A.L., 160
Sierra Leone, 219
Sivrov, K.V., 160
Slaney, R.A., 131, 132
Smiks, Samuel, 38, 61, 185
Smith, A., 188, 307
Smith, Goldwin, 217, 302

Smith, H.L., 24
Smith, H.N., 7
Smith, Toulmin, 148
Snow, Dr, 158, 166, 169, 170, 182, 189
Socialism, 39, 40, 44, 117ff., 182, 187, 189, 196-7, 199, 200, 306
Sociology, 5, 182, 257, 267
South Africa, 89, 90, 99ff., 292
Southey, Robert, 36, 37, 38, 43
Southwood Smith, Dr, 130, 131, 132, 148, 149, 169
Spencer, H., 312
Spengler, O., 311
Stael, Madene de, 17
Stafford, 142, 143
Standard Oil, 305
Statistics, 1, 11, 23, 127, 131, 154, 168
Stead, W.T., 6
Steam Power, 6, 41, 297, 298
Stendhal, 14
Stephen, L., 53
Stifter, Adalbert, 16, 18, 21
Stubbs, J.W., 217, 221, 227ff.
Sturge, Joseph, 40
Stuttgart, 9
Suburbs, 26-7
Sue, Eugene, 11
Sumner, W.G., 302-7
Sunderland, 158, 161
Sussex, University of, xviii, 277, 282-3
Sweden, 203
Switzerland, 16, 94
Sydney, 9, 108
Symonds, J.A., 293

Tannenbaum, F., 279
Tawney, R.H., 49, 253, 280
Tennyson, Alfred, 108, 117, 213, 260, 293
Thackeray, W.M., 293
Thatcher, Margaret, 255
Thierry, A., 221, 222, 223
Thompson, E.P., 121, 286
Thompson, James, 8
Thompson, Paul, 121
Thompson, Perronet, 42
Thoreau, H.D., 8
Tillotson, K., 26, 73
Titmuss, R.M., 201
Tocqueville, A. de, 99, 206
Tönnies, F., 17

Tories, Toryism, 144-5, 189-90, 255
Toynbee, A., 311
Trakl, Georg, 21
Tremenheere, H.S., 23
Trevelyan, Sir Charles, 236, 237
Trevelyan, G.M., xvi, 236ff., 260, 273,
    277, 279, 282, 285, 286
Trevelyan, G.O., 236
Trevor-Roper, H.R., 247
Trollope, Anthony, xi, 88ff.
Tsiolkovsky, K., 300
Turin, 9
Turner, S., 220, 222, 230
Twain, Mark, 8, 292, 301
Tyler, Wat, 218

Unemployment, 177, 184, 198, 204, 205
United States, 3, 6, 7ff., 45, 71, 88,
    90ff., 170, 185, 203, 204, 239, 242-3,
    303-4
Urquhart, David, 142

Valéry, P., 312
Verne, Jules, 300
Vico, Giambattisto, 273
Victoria, Queen, 116, 117, 215, 220,
    255, 261
Vienna, 20, 256
Vinogradoff, P., 229
Volnay, 312

Wagner, A., 199

Wakley, T., 55, 61
Wallace, A.R., 213, 297
Warburton, H., 161
Ward, Mrs H., 238
Washington D.C., 28, 106
Watt, J., 46
Webb, B., 202, 204
Webb, R.K., 308
Webb, S., 122, 186, 192, 195
Weber, Max, 280
Welfare State, xiii, 177ff.
Wellington, 90
Wells, H.G., 30, 213, 264, 300ff., 315
Wesley, J., 133, 136
West Indies, 89, 90, 93, 94ff.
Whigs, Whiggism, 177, 236ff., 255
Wiener, N., 300
Wilberforce, William, 293
Wilde, Oscar, 294
William I, King, 215, 220
William IV, King, 215
Willey, B., 36, 263, 308
Williams, Eric, 95, 97
William, R., 30
Woolf, Virginia, 49
Wordsworth, William, 23, 36, 46, 294
Wren, Sir Christopher, 244
Wycliffe, John, 237-8

Yorke, H., 218
Young, G.M., xvi, 117, 123, 125, 243,
    253ff., 287
Youth Hostels Association, 248